THE PLANTING OF CHRISTIANITY IN AFRICA

LUTTERWORTH LIBRARY, VOL. XLIII

*This book is published under the auspices of
the Department of Missions, Selly Oak Colleges*

THE PLANTING OF CHRISTIANITY IN AFRICA

By
C. P. GROVES
Professor of Missions in the Selly Oak Colleges
Birmingham

VOLUME TWO
1840–1878

LUTTERWORTH PRESS
LONDON

PRINTED IN GREAT BRITAIN BY
LATIMER, TREND AND CO. LTD., PLYMOUTH

Have patience, patience, patience, and you will succeed.

ROBERT MOFFAT to F. S. ARNOT

Patience, patience, patience is the watchword of Africa.

W. HOLMAN BENTLEY

PREFACE

THE ATTEMPT made in this history to carry the whole story forward by stages, rather than to offer merely parallel regional records, has presented greater difficulties in the period covered by the present volume and its sequel than in the first. Whereas before 1840 the development may be envisaged, in spatial terms, as a vertical extension, after that date it becomes almost a horizontal expansion, with the remarkable fanning out of the missionary enterprise consequent upon the opening up of the continent both by exploration and by political occupation.

In the attempt to offer a conspectus of this development without sacrificing the major purpose, the period 1840–1914 has been reviewed in four main sections into which it naturally appears to fall, the nodal points being: Livingstone's transcontinental journey which first lifted the veil from Central Africa; Stanley's Congo journey, closing the period of major exploration; the approximate termination of the main activity in the political scramble; and the First World War. While these periods have, in consequence, been assigned dates as determined by these events, it has clearly not been possible (or indeed necessary) to measure out the record to fit in each case such a Procrustean bed. On the whole the chronological limits have been respected, but where some antecedent cause or some subsequent development appeared to demand it the story has been allowed to spill over beyond such rigid limits.

While for convenience of publication the history of the period 1840–1914 is issued in two volumes (Vol. II, 1840–1878; Vol. III, 1878–1914), it is nevertheless offered as depicting a continuous development throughout, with 1878 as no more than a useful nodal point in the progress of the narrative, as stated above.

In the matter of African tribal names, the modern ethnologist's use of the significant root, with an English plural suffix when required (e.g. Kwena(s) for the older Bakwain or Bakwena) has been followed, save where the African form has become so embedded in the literature as to make it still generally acceptable (e.g. Makololo, Basuto).

I am once again under deep obligation to Dr. Edwin W. Smith who has read the entire MS. and added to the interest and accuracy of the narrative from his wide and deep knowledge of African affairs as well as his extensive experience of life in South and Central Africa. By placing at my disposal relevant chapters of his *Roger Price: His Life and Times*, in advance of publication, he has enabled me to have access to the most detailed study yet made of events in which that missionary played a part.

Dr. Pierce Beaver, Director of the Missionary Research Library, New York, has generously given his expert help in relation to specific inquiries submitted to him; while Dosent O. G. Myklebust, Director of the Egede Institute for missionary research in Oslo, has safeguarded the accuracy of the references to Norwegian Missions. Without the resources of the Central Library of the Selly Oak Colleges the work would have suffered a heavy handicap; Mrs. J. M. Leonard, the Librarian, has in addition secured literature from this country and the Continent which it proved necessary to consult. Mrs. M. Stephenson, who has prepared the fair copy of the MS., has spared no pains in carrying out an exacting task. Dr. R. Dunkerley has again read the proofs with his expert eye. To all these friends I am much indebted for help always generously given. Such errors as may remain are my own responsibility.

My wife, who has shared in the work more intimately than any other, has given that constant support which has enabled me to press on with what, at times, has loomed up as an undertaking too daunting to succeed.

C. P. GROVES

SELLY OAK
December 1953

ACKNOWLEDGMENT

The map of Africa in *1878*, on pp. *190-191*, is based on Keith Johnston's Africa (*Edward Stanford, 1878*) by kind permission of George Philip and Son Ltd.

CONTENTS

II PRESSING THE ADVANTAGE
1858–1878

CHAPTER 6
PRELUDE TO PROGRESS

CHAPTER 7
DEVELOPMENTS IN THE NORTH AND WEST

CHAPTER 8
ADVANCES IN THE SOUTH AND EAST

CHAPTER 9
LIVINGSTONE'S LEGACY

MAPS

I. RECONNOITRING FOR ADVANCE
1840–1858

CHAPTER I

THE ATTEMPT IN THE WEST

THE MAP of Africa in 1840 shows at a glance how little was then known of it. It remained to the outside world a continent of coast-lines and little more. The great rivers had not, for the most part, yielded up their secrets. True, the course and delta of the Niger had been recently determined, but the Nile sources remained an unsolved puzzle, the Victoria Falls on the Zambezi were undreamed of, and the Congo was known for the merest fragment of its course—a course which, placed upon the map of Europe, would sweep from Istanbul to London. Of the great lakes of Central Africa not one was yet upon the map. The towering mountain peaks of East Africa, the loftiest in the continent, could not be marked because the cartographer was unaware of their existence. There were, indeed, mapmakers who, as Dean Swift reminds us, sought to compensate for ignorance of geographical fact by flights of artistic fancy:

> So geographers in Afric maps
> With savage pictures fill their gaps,
> And o'er unhabitable downs
> Place elephants for want of towns.[1]

Within half a generation of 1840, however, the veil began to be lifted, and by the close of the century a new map of Africa had been given to the world. The opening up of so vast a continental area in so short a time was without parallel in the annals of exploration. The effect upon the Christian enterprise was profound: societies already at work rapidly extended their operations into new fields, while organizations new to Africa entered by the score. Not only was the Christian advance into interior Africa dependent upon this opening up of the continent to the peoples of the West: the initiative itself came in large measure from men whose ultimate purpose was to plant Christianity in Africa.

Attempts to penetrate the continent were first made from the west coast and from the east. These would seem to be the natural starting-points for such an operation, yet these early efforts

---

[1] J. Swift, *On Poetry: A Rhapsody* (1733). For reproductions of such maps, see Scott Keltie, *The Partition of Africa* (1893), facing p. 46; R. V. Tooley, *Maps and Mapmakers* (1949), 97, 98–9.

failed to achieve the result at which they aimed. The successful break-through was made from the south and was carried out so unostentatiously that the first an astonished world heard of it was when the accomplished fact was reported by the man who had done it singlehanded—singlehanded, that is to say, with generous African co-operation.

These various attempts were not deliberately concerted, yet an interplay of influence may be discerned.

(1) *The Plan of 1841*

The first attempt to break into the interior on a major scale was made in the west. The River Niger, its widespreading delta at last identified, seemed to provide the obvious artery for inland traffic. Explorers from Mungo Park to Richard and John Lander had revealed its course from the mighty "Niger bend", where it swept up to the very confines of the Sahara, down to the sluggish estuaries on the fever-infested coast.[1] Not only was this new knowledge attractive to an effort here, but an entry at this point would penetrate behind the slave-trading middlemen of the coastal region to the slave-providing chiefs and peoples of the interior, and so enable the positive policy for the suppression of the trade to be applied.

The anti-slavery campaigners were faced by the fact that the legal prohibition of the traffic was not in itself proving finally effective. A new policy was demanded which, by substituting a profitable commerce in the resources of Africa, would deal the death-blow to the trade in men. Such a legitimate commerce, first conceived by Granville Sharp for the Sierra Leone Settlement, it had been from 1807 a principal object of the African Institution to promote. Little, however, had been done, for attention had been diverted to the unanticipated threat of the continuing external slave-trade.[2] The new positive policy now

---

[1] Mungo Park, ascending the River Gambia, first sighted the Niger in 1796; on a second expedition in 1805 he lost his life in the Bussa rapids. In 1821 Denham, Clapperton and Oudney set out from Tripoli for the Hausa States where they travelled, but without reaching the Niger. In 1825 Clapperton and Richard Lander went inland from Badagry, but were foiled in their attempt. The brothers Lander started from the same point in 1830, reached Bussa, and eventually completed the journey down the Niger to the sea, emerging through one of the many mouths. This solved the problem why no single estuary could be found equal to the discharge of the waters of so mighty a river.

[2] E. C. Martin, *The British West African Settlements* (1927), 108; *Report of the Committee of the African Institution* (1807), 65–71; *Fourth Report of the African Institution* (1810), 1.

4

to be advocated was the proposal to use this very development of natural resources and legitimate trade as a principal means of countering the human traffic.

Thomas Fowell Buxton, with the Emancipation Act of 1833 crowning his parliamentary labours as Wilberforce's successor, soon turned to this new task. Public opinion must be aroused to the situation and the Government be induced to adopt the positive policy as its own. With this twofold aim in view he prepared a study of the continuing slave-trade, marshalling evidence as to its alarming extent and heavy mortality. This was a full generation after the Abolition Act, and exposed a situation in which the profit incentive had proved more powerful than all the notable efforts at suppression.[1] The only remedy, then, that could hope to be finally effective would be the development of the resources of Africa on a scale sufficient to displace the slave-trade. In a word the policy was to be "the deliverance of Africa by calling forth her own resources".[2]

Buxton first prepared in 1838 a statement intended only for members of the Government and described as a "Letter to Lord Melbourne".[3] The response of Ministers was better than he had dared to hope. The facts were admitted as beyond dispute; the immediate question was what should be done. Buxton had recommended certain specific steps as auxiliary measures: a more adequate naval preventive force on the West Coast, and a series of treaties with important chiefs beyond the coast; but as the final remedy, the development of Africa's resources. "The real remedy, the true ransom for Africa", he declared, "will be found in her fertile soil," a proposition that was argued with wide reference to existing authorities. The Niger, it was claimed, offered unusual facilities for reaching the interior, and

[1] The British slave-trade had been brought to an end, but that under Spanish, Portuguese and Brazilian colours still flourished. Through the failure of the United States to agree to reciprocal right of search, the American flag was also resorted to for protection.

[2] Memorandum of April 1839.—C. Buxton, *Memoirs of Sir Thomas Fowell Buxton* (3rd 8vo. ed., 1851), 459. Buxton seems to have hit on this as a new discovery, and finding Palmerston of the same opinion, remarked: "I now find that either the observations, which I made in a conversation with Lord Palmerston some time ago, or which is much more likely to be the case, his own wit, has led him to the same conclusion as my own, viz.: that the slave-trade is to be abolished by legitimate trade."—*Ibid.*, 442, 446. But Palmerston's comment to Glenelg in the same year (1838), indicated a rather different attitude: "No doubt the extension of commerce in A rica is an object to be aimed at, but I am inclined to think that such extension will be the effect rather than the cause of the extinction of the Slave Trade."—Quoted in R. Coupland, *East Africa and Its Invaders* (1938), 288.

[3] In view of its purpose only twenty copies were printed.—C. Buxton, *Memoirs*, 446.

the island of Fernando Po was an ideal centre for the head-quarters of the enterprise.[1]

Next in importance to Fernando Po, Buxton claimed, was a settlement to be made at the junction of the Benue and the Niger, where Africans could be trained in up-to-date agricultural methods and British rule would guarantee security. "The proposal of a settlement in Africa", he admits, "necessarily recalls to mind our vast empire in India," but emphatically declares: "I entirely disclaim any disposition to erect a new empire in Africa."[2] Nevertheless, even with this disclaimer, the proposal to acquire sovereign rights over new territory however limited ran directly counter to British policy in West Africa for half a generation.[3]

At the same time Christian missions were to advance into the interior territories, for without the indispensable moral and spiritual contribution of Christianity the whole undertaking would be incomplete. "It is the Bible and the plough that must regenerate Africa," wrote Buxton in a phrase that became famous.[4] The immediate starting-point for this comprehensive programme should be, he proposed, an expedition to the Niger in sufficient force and with adequate authority to conclude treaties with the more important chiefs upon its banks, to explore the possibilities for agricultural and commercial undertakings and to make some beginning with them.[5] The whole situation was finally set forth by Buxton in a work that had

[1] *Ibid.*, 449, 451–2. For a period after 1827 the British Government had actually maintained an establishment on the island for Africans emancipated under the Slave Trade Abolition Treaties, but later withdrew as Spain was unwilling to consider a transfer of sovereignty.—T. F. Buxton, *The Slave Trade and its Remedy* (1840), 537.

[2] T. F. Buxton, *op. cit.*, 353, 453.

[3] The relation of Buxton's proposals to existing colonial policy is discussed by J. Gallagher, "Fowell Buxton and the New African Policy, 1838–1842" in *The Cambridge Historical Journal*, Vol. X, No. 1, (1950), 36–58, who comments: "On *a priori* grounds the plan would seem doomed for rejection, for it flagrantly violated the canons of British colonial policy. . . . Yet in principle the scheme was adopted." Palmerston's recent refusal to acquire so eligible a base as Mombasa in East Africa may be noted.—R. Coupland, *op. cit.*, 287–9.

[4] C. Buxton, *op. cit.*, 451; T. F. Buxton, *op. cit.*, 483. As Buxton remarks, a similar conjunction had been made by James Read thirty years before.—Cf. I, 244, *n.* 3.

[5] James MacQueen, who had foreseen the Landers' discovery, had proposed a similar plan some years before, involving both Fernando Po, and a station under the British flag at the Niger-Benue confluence.—W. L. Mathieson, *Great Britain and the Slave Trade, 1839–1865* (1929), 31. An expedition, promoted by Macgregor Laird in the interests of exploration and trade with Fernando Po as a base, made two ascents of the Niger to the Benue confluence and beyond in 1832–33. Mortality was heavy, only nine Europeans surviving out of forty-eight.—A. C. Burns, *History of Nigeria* (3rd ed., 1942), 101–2.

a wide circulation and influence, *The Slave Trade and its Remedy*.[1]

Meanwhile there had been formed in June 1839, under Buxton's leadership, the Society for the Extinction of the Slave Trade and for the Civilization of Africa. Leaders in Church and State served on its committee and Buxton wrote with much satisfaction of the first meeting, held in July: "It was a glorious meeting, quite an epitome of the state. Whig, Tory, and Radical; Dissenter, Low Church, High Church, tiptop High Church, or Oxfordism, all united . . . good men and true came to my assistance . . . and no one better than the Bishop of London."[2] A few days later a deputation from the Society was informed that the Government had decided to send an expedition of three ships to the Niger. This was gratifying news indeed. The "Comptroller of Steam Machinery", having been instructed to prepare the vessels required, reported on investigation that these would have to be specially built.[3] This meant an unfortunate delay, but in so important an undertaking it was vital that the best equipment available should be used. The building of three iron steam-vessels adapted to the work required of them was accordingly authorized.[4]

Within a week of this being reported to the House of Commons there appeared the prospectus of the Society for the Exitnction of the Slave Trade and for the Civilization of Africa.[5] It was and remains a notable document. At the outset of the

---

[1] The first part, delineating the extent and horror of the continuing slave-trade, was issued in 1839. A second edition was soon called for, and to this was added the positive programme advocated by Buxton, the combined work, issued in 1840, bearing the above title. James MacQueen had collaborated with him.—C. Buxton, *Memoirs*, 446. There has been some criticism of Buxton's exposition.—See Mathieson, *op. cit.*, 37–45. The book aroused much interest in Germany, as well as in Austria and Switzerland, and in July 1841 a German edition appeared in Berlin.— *The Friend of Africa* (1841), 13–16, 186–7, 220–2.

[2] Buxton to Trew, Secretary of the Society.—*Memoirs*, 462.

[3] Steam was still struggling into favour for ocean voyages, and was chiefly found as an auxiliary to sail. The first regular Atlantic service under steam was begun in 1840 by the forerunner of the Cunard Company. In 1841 out of 23,172 vessels of all classes belonging to the United Kingdom, only 790 were under steam.—*Ency. Brit.* (1947), XX, 544, 549.

[4] The proposals were set out in a letter from Lord John Russell to the Treasury, dated December 26, 1839, which was submitted to the House of Commons, February 8, 1840. The letter is printed in T. F. Buxton, *op. cit.*, Appendix F. The expedition was under the immediate command of the Admiralty. The estimated expenditure for capital outlay and twelve months' running expenses was £79,143. —Allen and Thomson, *A Narrative of the Expedition sent by Her Majesty's Government to the River Niger in 1841* (1848), I, 500–2.

[5] On February 14, 1840. A copy was prefixed to the 1840 edition of Buxton's book.

statement of principles it is affirmed: "It is the unanimous opinion of this Society, that the only complete cure of all these evils, is the introduction of Christianity into Africa." But the Society had no intention (its broad-based support would alone scarcely permit it) of engaging directly in missionary activity, even to the extent of opening schools. Giving unqualified support to Buxton's proposal for an expedition to the Niger, they sketch an ambitious programme of the activities they are prepared to promote in its train, when treaties have been successfully concluded and possibly certain districts secured for settlement. Their proposals are remarkably comprehensive and farsighted: a survey of the leading languages and dialects and the reduction of the more important to writing; the introduction of the printing press and the local manufacture of paper; an investigation of the climate in various localities and the introduction of medical science "to prevent or mitigate the prevalence of disease and suffering among the people of Africa"; the engineering of roads and canals for transport, and a suitable system of drainage for health; the sharing with Africans of the best knowledge available in agriculture, and the provision of approved implements and tested seeds, together with advice as to the best economic crops to produce for world markets.

This programme would not come amiss at the present day, but a century ago, with the meagre knowledge of inland Africa then prevailing, and the current experience of the slave-ridden coast, it was indeed remarkably enlightened. There were naturally critics who scented in such proposals the mad excursion of incorrigible idealists who could only be disciplined by disaster. But such was the national will to see the slave-trade effectively abolished that the proposals secured far-reaching support.

The Society's first anniversary was celebrated by a great public meeting in Exeter Hall on June 1, 1840. It was an impressive occasion. The meeting was presided over by Prince Albert, and as this was his first public engagement in the country, attendance was overflowing long before the appointed time. The distinguished platform included many peers, M.P's and bishops. Among the Members of Parliament were Sir Robert Peel and Mr. Gladstone. A young medical missionary candidate, David Livingstone, was in the audience.[1] The resolutions laid before the meeting were enthusiastically endorsed.[2]

---

[1] W. G. Blaikie, *The Life of David Livingstone* (1906 ed.), 23.
[2] A full account of the meeting, with a number of the speeches printed verbatim, appeared in *The Times*, June 2, 1840.

Thus when the three specially constructed ships, christened *Albert*, *Wilberforce*, and *Soudan*, sailed in the spring of 1841 the eyes of the nation were upon them.[1] In addition to the officers appointed by the Government, there was a team of scientists sent by the African Civilization Society. An Agricultural Society, which had been formed as an auxiliary, was specially concerned with the establishment of a model farm, and had its representative with the Expedition for this purpose.[2] The Church Missionary Society also co-operated with a view to discovering what opportunities for missionary settlement might offer in the interior; they were represented by J. F. Schön, an able linguist and one of the distinguished band of German missionaries who came to the Society from the Basel Mission Seminary, and by the African catechist, Samuel Adjai Crowther. These joined the Expedition at Sierra Leone, as did selected liberated Africans to serve as interpreters to the Niger tribes and others to work on the model farm.[3]

The Rio Nun, the branch of the Niger chosen for entry, was reached by mid-August and the ascent of the river begun. The much-dreaded delta had been safely passed by the end of the month, without a single case of malaria on board. Within a further week, however, there were cases in all three ships, and these soon multiplied.[4] There ensued a valiant struggle against heavy odds to carry out the Expedition's commission, but the odds finally proved overwhelming. Not only were the malaria victims soon completely incapacitated, but fatal cases began to occur. By September 18 it was decided to despatch the *Soudan* with ineffectives to the sea, and the question of all vessels returning was considered. Opinion was divided, but a natural reluctance to surrender while even a slender hope remained, together with the expectation of a healthier climate being reached,

[1] One special feature of their construction was an ingenious ventilation system, devised to neutralize by a chemical filter the dreaded "miasma" from swamp and marsh regarded together with other noxious gases as the cause of malaria. For a full description of the system with diagrams, see *The Friend of Africa* (1841), 43-7, 65-73.

[2] Allen and Thomson, *op. cit.*, I, 37-8. The sum of £4,000 for the model farm had been subscribed with generous Quaker support.—C. Buxton, *Memoirs*, 526-7.

[3] Allen and Thomson, *op. cit.*, I, 78-9. J. F. Schön and Samuel Crowther kept their own journals of the expedition which were afterwards published. That of Schön is particularly valuable.

[4] Entry in Journal of Dr. M'William, the chief medical officer: "*Sept. 4th.* Fever of a most malignant character broke out in the *Albert*, and almost simultaneously in the other vessels, and abated not until the whole expedition was completely paralysed."—J. O. M'William, *Medical History of the Expedition to the Niger* (1843), 73-4.

determined Captain Trotter, R.N., who commanded the Expedition, to hold on.[1] On the 19th the *Soudan* left with forty fever cases on board, but two days later the *Wilberforce* was compelled to follow her with yet more ineffectives. The *Albert* steamed pluckily on alone. But as one man after another became prostrate with malaria and the risks of getting aground increased in the now rapidly falling river, on October 3 the resolution was sadly taken to return to the coast with all speed. It was the death-blow to high hopes entertained by the promoters and the leaders of the Expedition, but there was now no other choice.[2] The *Albert* limped its way painfully to the sea, with the geologist in the engine-room (all three engineers were down with malaria) and the doctor helping to run the ship, as well as caring for patients night and day from the captain down —a sorry end to so proud an enterprise. Malaria and man had been pitted against each other and malaria had won.

On October 13, while still in the river, they were met by the *Ethiope*, a trading company's steamer under Captain Beecroft, and received the help they so desperately needed. The final vital statistics showed that among the 145 whites in the Expedition there were 130 cases of fever and forty deaths.[3] There was no disputing the verdict. The attempt to break through on the west had failed.[4]

The Expedition had failed, and the immediate impression was one of unrelieved gloom. One of the objects had been to enter into treaties with chiefs of importance on the banks of the Niger for the suppression of their part in the slave-trade in supplying cargoes for the coast traders. Two such treaties were concluded with some difficulty—it was part of royal etiquette to keep the commissioners waiting for an audience—on the understanding that the Queen, in whose name they were made, would see that ships engaged in legitimate commerce came regularly up the river. That obligation could not now be hon-

---

[1] M'William, *op. cit.*, 78–9, 81; Allen and Thomson, *op. cit.*, I, 358–60. Captain William Allen, R.N., commander of the *Wilberforce*, who had served with the Macgregor Laird expedition of 1832–34, was for immediate withdrawal of all vessels.

[2] M'William, *op. cit.*, 81–2, 94–5; Allen and Thomson, *op. cit.*, I, 359–69; II, 1–3, 110–11.

[3] M'William, *op. cit.*, 103–4, 128. The Rio Nun was now christened the "Gate of the Cemetery".—Allen and Thomson, *op. cit.*, II, 328.

[4] The expedition retired to Fernando Po, from which visits were paid to Cameroons and the islands of Principe, San Tomé and Ascension. Preparations had been made for a second attempt when, on the very eve of departure, instructions arrived from the Home Government ordering the expedition back to England. —Allen and Thomson, *op. cit.*, II, 324.

oured, and the treaties must therefore lapse.[1] One article had secured to missionaries permission to teach the Christian religion without hindrance, but this opportunity afforded by the treaties vanished with them.[2] Again, a beginning had been made with the model farm on an eligible site on the western bank of the Niger, facing the Benue confluence, where some twenty acres were speedily under cotton. This had later to be dismantled and abandoned.[3] The Agricultural Society that had promoted it had perforce to acquiesce in this decision. Professor Coupland's verdict on the total effort is severe: "The Niger Expedition of 1841 had no effect whatever on the subsequent development of Nigeria. It made no valuable new discoveries. It discredited and retarded the 'positive policy' it was meant to serve."[4] There is no denying the seriousness of the setback. The effect on Buxton was damaging; he survived the failure but three years. "He rarely spoke of the Expedition," writes his son, "—to Captain Bird Allen's death he could scarcely allude at all; but his grave demeanour, his pale worn face, the abstraction of his manner, and the intense fervour of his supplications that God would 'pity poor Africa'—these showed too well the poignancy of his feelings."[5] When about to attend the meeting called in January 1843, to dissolve the African Civilization Society, he said: "I feel as if I were going to attend the funeral of an old and dear friend."[6] Dr. Eugene Stock goes so far as to say: "The failure of the Niger Expedition as distinctly killed Fowell Buxton as the Battle of Austerlitz killed Pitt."[7]

The objections raised in advance had ranged from such indisputable perils as fever and climate to the less substantial grounds of theological presupposition.[8] The critics, each to his

[1] Allen and Thomson, *op. cit.*, I, 217–30, where the conference with Obi Osai of Abo (in Iboland) some 100 miles up the river, is reported. The text of the treaty is also given.—*Ibid.*, 253–60. A second treaty was concluded with Ocheji, the Ata of Idah, chief of the Igara, who professed Islam, another 200 miles up-stream, similar in terms to the first.—*Ibid.*, 296–302, 314–15.

[2] *Ibid.*, I, 254–5, *n.*

[3] *Ibid.*, II, 335–8, *n.*, 358–66. For an account of the start that had been made, see *The Friend of Africa* (1842), 22–4, 173–8; (1843), 6–7.

[4] R. Coupland, *Kirk on the Zambesi* (1928), 262.

[5] C. Buxton, *op. cit.*, 564.

[6] *Ibid.*, 573.

[7] Stock, *History of the Church Missionary Society* (1899), I, 455.

[8] William Simpson, a civilian clerk attached to the *Wilberforce*, in his *A Private Journal kept during the Niger Expedition* (1843), reports that some of his friends opposed his engagement on the ground that this attempt to help Africa did not accord with the word of God. The Divine order was to be :(1) restoration of the Jews to Palestine; (2) light from Jerusalem for the whole world; (3) Africans turning to God.—*Op. cit.*, 131–2.

own satisfaction, had now been proved right. Their echo was to be heard a decade later when Charles Dickens somewhat ungallantly held up the enthusiastic "philanthropists" to ridicule in the person of Mrs. Jellyby.[1]

The failure of the Expedition in its declared objectives must be conceded, but not its total failure as an effort to do good to Africa. Robert Moffat, then on furlough in England, had eagerly followed its fortunes, and would only admit that it had "in a measure failed" in the wider purpose.[2] The Committee of the Church Missionary Society, directly concerned with two of its own agents as members of the Expedition, while granting that its immediate objects were "imperfectly accomplished" proceeded to point out important facts bearing on the evangelization of Africa which had been established in the course of the Expedition, and to adjust its own policy accordingly, not by way of restricting its activities in West Africa but of expanding them.[3]

In short, there had indeed been a disaster—there was no gainsaying that—but there were compensations, and those concerned with Christian missionary affairs in West Africa had the faith to believe it.[4] To consideration of these compensations we must now turn.

(2) The Sequel

No enterprise could be heralded with such publicity and royal favour as the Niger Expedition had received without leaving notable influences in its train, whatever the immediate lack of success, for it declared to the world a cause for which people and rulers cared supremely. Even the critics had not been critics of the benevolent purpose in view, but of the method proposed for achieving it. Two men with long and intimate ex-

---

[1] *Bleak House*, chap. 4, "Telescopic Philanthropy"; cf. also chap. 14. "We hope by this time next year", said Mrs. Jellyby, "to have from a hundred and fifty to two hundred healthy families cultivating coffee and educating the natives of Borrioboola-Gha, on the left bank of the Niger." She would smile "at the limited vision that could see anything but Borrioboola-Gha". By contrast her long-suffering and much put-upon daughter exploded with, "I wish Africa was dead!" *Bleak House* was begun in November 1851, and first published serially from March 1852 to September 1853.—*D.N.B.* (1921–22), V, 931.

[2] R. Moffat, *Missionary Labours and Scenes in Southern Africa* (1842), 615.

[3] *Proceedings of the Church Missionary Society* (1842), 40–1.

[4] "What is not permissible, for a Church at any rate, is to believe that Providence is going to cease its care for the world or rob even disasters of their possible compensations, whatever the next turn in the story may be."—H. Butterfield, *Christianity and History* (1949), 107.

perience of Africa and her peoples and unusual capacity for passing judgment, claimed these influences as a great positive result of the enterprise. Robert Moffat wrote in the year of the Expedition's recall: "It has taught the world what England can do, and what she is ready to do again. It has taught the Africans that their cause is not forgotten at the foot of the British throne, and that it has pledged itself to encourage every project calculated to bring about the anticipated event, when Ethiopia will stretch forth her hands unto God."[1] David Livingstone, writing fifteen years later, endorsed the verdict: "One invaluable benefit it conferred was the dissemination of the knowledge of English love of commerce and English hatred of slavery, and it therefore was no failure."[2]

But above and beyond such general influences were specific developments in West African affairs. The object of associating J. F. Schön and Samuel Crowther with the Expedition had been to discover the possibility of extending missionary operations in the region it was hoped to open up, and to advise on suitable locations for European workers. J. F. Schön's observations were recorded in his *Journal*,[3] and his considered conclusions on future policy in a letter addressed to the Society.[4] He was already a tested missionary of eight years' experience, with proved linguistic ability; his *Journal* reveals him as a careful and accurate observer and a man of sound judgment. His recommendations determined the future policy of the Society in West Africa for some time to come. In brief, they were as follows: no suitable locations for European missionaries were to be seen on the 300 miles of the Niger navigated, though admittedly inland from the river they might possibly be found. More important than the threat of the unhealthy climate he regarded the lack of regular communications which would leave the missionaries stranded. He therefore could not advise a European mission.[5] While this was at first sight regrettable in view of the willingness, and in places eagerness, of the people to receive Christian teachers, yet it threw into clear relief the importance of a native agency. Not only was the health verdict in their favour

[1] R. Moffat, *op. cit.*, 615.

[2] D. Livingstone, *Missionary Travels and Researches in South Africa* (1857), 679. That Livingstone had followed carefully the fortunes of the expedition is evidenced by references in his letters when on his own Zambezi Expedition.—W. Monk, *Dr. Livingstone's Cambridge Lectures* (2nd ed., 1860), 356, 371.

[3] *Journals of the Rev. James Frederick Schön and Mr. Samuel Crowther who accompanied the Expedition up the Niger in 1841 in behalf of the Church Missionary Society* (1842).

[4] *Ibid.*, Appendix II, 351–70.

[5] *Ibid.*, 151, 182–3, 365–6.

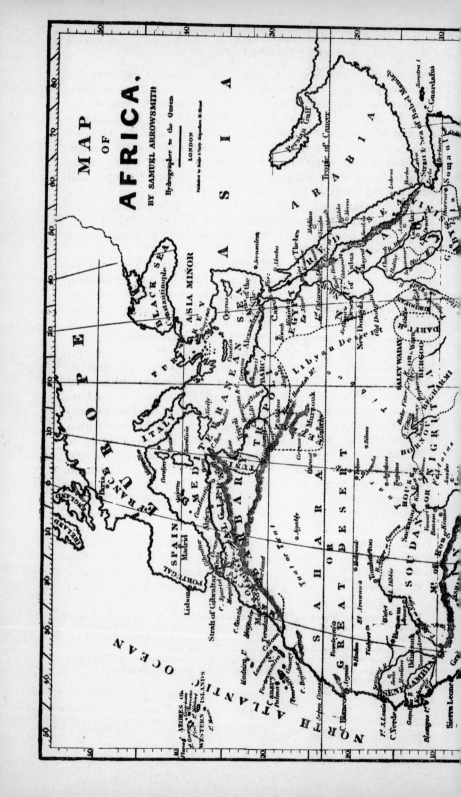

MAP
OF
AFRICA.

BY SAMUEL ARROWSMITH

Hydrographer to the Queen

LONDON

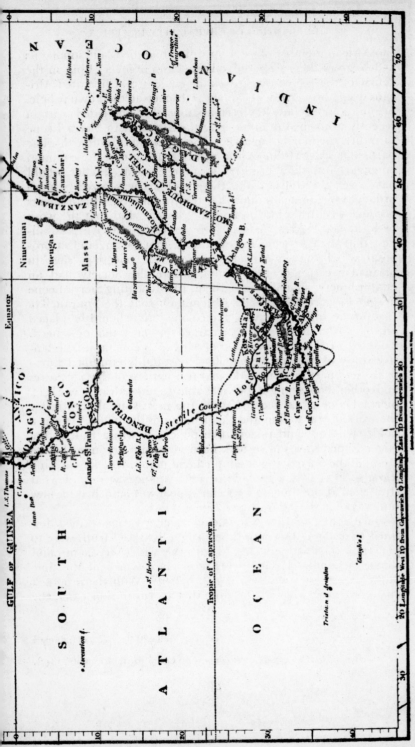

AFRICA IN 1840

(no African member of the Expedition had died, and among its 158 Negroes there were only eleven cases of fever),[1] but in the course of the Expedition it became evident that liberated Africans would be warmly welcomed as teachers to their own people. Schön pointed out how remarkably this coincided with a recently awakened desire among the liberated in Sierra Leone to return to their homelands.[2] There was in addition to these particular circumstances the obvious advantage in common language and thought-forms that an African teacher would have over a European. On these grounds was based Schön's principal recommendation: that the training of African agents become a central obligation of the Society, and that the work be located in Sierra Leone. He reviewed alternative possibilities: that such Africans in training be sent to England, a proposal which he gave cogent reasons for rejecting, save in particular cases; or that Malta, where the Society had an establishment, should receive them. In advocating Sierra Leone he put forward the practical suggestion that the Fourah Bay Institution, hitherto serving the colony only, should be placed on a broader basis and be enlarged to meet this new need. Coupled with this preparation of African agents must be intensive study of relevant vernaculars by suitably equipped Europeans set apart for this work, that translations of the Scriptures and other books might be available to the African workers. Sierra Leone again seemed to be the most suitable centre for the work of translation and the printing of the books.[3] It was a bold, well-knit, and imaginative policy. It was a fruit of the Niger Expedition and so took hard facts into account. To the credit of the Society it was adopted and plans made for carrying it out so soon as funds should permit. Finances were somewhat straitened at the time, so a special appeal was launched for new buildings for the Fourah Bay Institution.[4]

Once again, as forty years before, Sierra Leone seemed destined to become the centre from which light and truth were to penetrate the continent. It was with this wider service in mind that educational developments took place which at the time might otherwise have been hard to justify. With the proposed changes in the work of the Fourah Bay Institution came the

---

[1] M'William, *op. cit.*, 128.
[2] Schön, *Journal*, 361–2.
[3] *Ibid.*, 362–4. Samuel Crowther independently endorsed the policy of training a native agency.—*Ibid.*, 349–50.
[4] *Ibid.*, Appendix IV, 387–93; *Proceedings of the Church Missionary Society* (1842), 40–1.

necessity for a school that should be intermediate between it and the village schools. The decision was therefore taken to establish a Grammar School which would recruit from the village schools and offer "a sound religious and general education". Those suited to a vocation as Christian teachers would pass on to Fourah Bay; others would pass out, it was hoped, to leaven the social life of the community. The Grammar School was opened in 1845, and reported thirty pupils. So ambitious were they to receive a classical education that Latin and Greek were offered for advanced students.[1] During the first four years out of ninety-four pupils received eight had become schoolmasters and fifteen had passed on to Fourah Bay.[2]

The education of girls, which was often undertaken in missionary families, received separate provision when a "Female Institution" was opened at Regent in 1845, the station made famous by the ministry of W. A. B. Johnson, but was shortly removed to Freetown. A second was opened in due course. While the preparation of schoolmistresses was one object in view, there was a more comprehensive purpose: "The Committee have been induced to establish these Female Schools from the conviction that the education and training of Christian mothers is essential, on various accounts, to the establishment of any Native-Christian Church."[3]

The overriding interest was naturally in the Institution at Fourah Bay. Progress was such that the first stone of the new buildings was laid on February 5, 1845, by the Governor, William Fergusson, the first Negro to attain to the high office. In his address on the occasion he referred movingly to the fact that on the very spot where a building dedicated to the Christian service of Africans was to be built, there stood but forty years before a factory engaged in the slave-trade.[4] If this was the case with the site it was equally noteworthy that the rafters of the roof when completed were made for the most part from the masts of condemned slave ships. Truly a consecration unto the Lord.[5]

---

[1] *Proceedings of the C.M.S.* (1844), 27; (1846), 40; (1847), 28–9; (1848), *liv.*
[2] *Ibid.* (1850), lxiv. The Wesleyan Methodists had also established a Training Institution for African Teachers in Sierra Leone.—*Report of the Wesleyan Methodist Missionary Society* (1845), 68–9.
[3] *Proceedings of the C.M.S.* (1845), 35; (1847), 29; (1849), lxvi. Miss Susan Crowther, daughter of Samuel Crowther, was on the staff of one of these schools. —*Ibid.* (1850), lxvi.
[4] *Ibid.* (1845), 35; (1846), 41. On Fergusson's Warrant as Governor, see F. W. Butt-Thompson, *Sierra Leone in History and Tradition* (1926), 247.
[5] *Ibid.* (1847), 28.

Four years later the Society issued a comprehensive statement on their educational policy in Sierra Leone. The purpose of the Fourah Bay Institution was to be the preparation of suitable young men "for the Native Ministry, chiefly as Missionaries to the interior of Africa, by a regular theological training, and the study of Hebrew and Arabic". There was reiterated the view of Sierra Leone as a base from which trained workers might advance into the continent: "The chief importance of Sierra Leone, and that which the Committee have ever kept in view, is its relation to the interior of Africa. To cherish a Missionary spirit among the inhabitants of the Colony, to train up Native Missionaries for carrying the Gospel among their countrymen, are the objects. . . . For this end it is that we endeavour to enlarge and invigorate their minds by a sound literary education, and to qualify them—by the knowledge of the Arabic, and of the original languages of Scripture—for the difficulties with which they may be called to contend in their Missionary excursions among the Mahomedan tribes, and the more civilized kingdoms of the interior."[1]

The first-fruits of the policy of preparing Africans for ordination were to be seen in Samuel Crowther himself. His contribution as Schön's colleague on the Niger Expedition and his own *Journal* produced on that occasion had so impressed the Home Committee that in 1842 he was brought to England and the following year admitted to Anglican orders by the Bishop of London. On his return to Sierra Leone at the end of 1843 he received a great welcome and conducted in English his first service. But his mother tongue was not forgotten, and he soon took a service in Yoruba, probably the first to be taken in that language.[2] However, he was not long to preach in Yoruba in Sierra Leone; before the year was out he had sailed for Yoruba-

---

[1] *Proceedings of the C.M.S.* (1849), lxvi. The Fourah Bay new building had been formally opened in 1848. It was reported a year later when twenty-one students were in residence: "Mr. Koelle's examination of his Hebrew Class was a remarkable event in the history of the Mission. To hear a class of African youths, the immediate descendants of emancipated slaves, reading the Holy Scriptures of the Old Testament in the original language, and evincing their knowledge of that language by answers to minute as well as important questions on its grammatical construction, appeared to me singularly striking, and certainly was not anticipated a few years ago."—*Ibid.* (1850), lxv. In this same year the work in Sierra Leone began to be reported significantly under three heads: (1) Pastoral work in the Colony; (2) Preparatory measures for extension into the interior of Africa; (3)Missionary effort for extending Christianity into the interior.—*Ibid.*, lii.

[2] *Proceedings of the C.M.S.* (1842), 35; (1844), 28; (1845), 36; Stock, *History of the C.M.S.* (1899), I, 457-8.

land. There we follow him and his European colleagues in due course, but first it is necessary to notice what had happened in respect of Schön's second major recommendation—that concerning the study of language.[1]

J. F. Schön had himself given particular study to two languages to be met on the banks of the Niger: Ibo in the lower reaches and Hausa to the north. He carried forward the study of Hausa to such effect on the Expedition that in 1843 he was able to complete and publish a Grammar and Vocabulary of the language, while Samuel Crowther had done the same for Yoruba. The translation into Hausa of the Gospels according to St. Matthew and St. Luke and of the Acts of the Apostles was completed in the course of the next four years.[2] A great step forward was taken with the appointment of S. W. Koelle, yet another German recruit to the Society's work, who was destined to render distinguished service.

Sigismund Wilhelm Koelle came to the C.M.S. from Basel and after a period at the training institution at Islington was ordained and sailed for Sierra Leone on November 3, 1847. He was appointed as a tutor to Fourah Bay Institution and as research student of African languages. He threw himself into his linguistic work with an enthusiasm matched only by his capacity for detailed and accurate investigation. J. F. Schön had stressed the value of Sierra Leone, with its mixed population of liberated Africans, as a centre for such study. Despite the official use of English, all new arrivals who had companions with whom they could converse continued the use of their mother tongue. Schön had estimated that not less than thirty-six languages and dialects were in current use.[3] When Koelle got to work he found the number, amazing as it may seem, to be five times as great, and that he could secure reliable representatives of more than one hundred of them. It was thus that he compiled his masterpiece of philological research, the *Polyglotta Africana*, pub-

---

[1] Schön, *Journal*, 358–61. He has wise things to say about the study of a language not yet reduced to a written form.

[2] *Proceedings of the C.M.S.* (1843), 37; (1845), 36; (1847), 30. The Hausa and Yoruba Vocabularies were submitted before publication to Dr. Samuel Lee, Professor of Arabic (from 1819) and later Regius Professor of Hebrew (from 1831) at Cambridge, one of the profoundest linguists of his day. He advised the authors on general principles.—*D.N.B.*, *s.v.*

[3] Schön, *Journal*, 358. It is of interest to recall Hannah Kilham's conviction, twenty years before, of the value of such study.—See Vol. I, 286–8. That her work survived is evidenced by the reprinting of a number of her vocabularies in a handbook prepared for the Niger Expedition.—Allen and Thomson, *Narrative*, II, 461 *et seq.*

lished in London in 1854.[1] The fact that he carried through the work singlehanded gave it unusual authority in questions of linguistic affinity.[2] The Secretary of the Royal Asiatic Society, to whom Henry Venn[3] submitted the work, was "perfectly overwhelmed at the magnitude and importance" of it. Koelle was honoured in the award of the Volney prize by the Institute of France for the most outstanding linguistic publication of the year.[4]

But Koelle was more than a distinguished student of African languages. He was at heart a fully committed missionary, and language study was for him but a means to an end—the carrying of the Christian gospel to the non-Christian world. An instance of this was his great interest in Bornu bordering on Lake Chad, and his selection of the language for intensive study. He based his choice on missionary strategy for penetrating the interior of Africa. He pointed out that Crowther and others were already active in Yorubaland from Badagry to Abeokuta, and that Schön was concentrating on the study of Hausa in the hope of one day going to Hausaland. Bornu was the next stage for advance: "By these three languages, then—the Yoruba, Haussa and Bournu—we should be enabled to proceed from the coast into the very heart of Africa."[5] He adds that an alternative road of entry would be from the north. He had been informed by the traveller James Richardson that there was regular

---

[1] *Polyglotta Africana, or A Comparative Vocabulary of nearly three hundred words and phrases in more than one hundred distinct African Languages.* Koelle states: "It was usually supposed that there were in Sierra Leone the representatives of about forty different tribes; but the searching examination amongst the people, which the collection of this vocabulary demanded, discovered individuals from more than two hundred different tribes and countries."—*Op. cit.* iii.

[2] Not only was it written in a simple and uniform orthography, but also: "It was always the same ear which caught the sounds from the different natives, and the same hand which represented them. Living natives were the only source from which the information was derived: no book or Vocabulary of any sort was consulted."—*Ibid.*, iv. A brief biography of each African speaker was supplied, giving exact place of origin, number of years in Sierra Leone, and so forth, to enable his trustworthiness to be estimated. As an example of linguistic discovery, Koelle was the first to record the duodecimal systems of numeration found in the Bauchi area.—C. K. Meek, *Northern Nigeria* (1925), II, 142.

[3] Senior Secretary of the Church Missionary Society.

[4] Stock, *op. cit.*, II, 102–3. J. F. Schön received the same award twenty years later.

[5] *Proceedings of the C.M.S.* (1849), lxviii. The Kanuri tribes have dominated Bornu south-west of Lake Chad from the fourteenth century, and Kanuri is the name now used of the language.—C. K. Meek, *op. cit.*, I, 84; II, 138. Koelle published a grammar of Kanuri in 1854.—*Ency. Brit.* (1947), III, 916.

traffic between Tripoli and Bornu, and that Bornu merchants were quite willing to take an Englishman to their country. His missionary conviction again shines out: "The time will, I believe, at length come, when also in such entirely Mahomedan countries as Bournu the banner of the Cross will be unfurled; but whether the time is still distant or just at hand I cannot say." He proceeded to suggest that he might himself visit Bornu from Tripoli, as he would not venture on a translation of the Scriptures without some residence in the country.[1]

At the end of 1848 some exciting news reached Sierra Leone. Captain Forbes, R.N., reported that near Cape Mount in Liberia (some five days' sail south-east of Sierra Leone) he had lighted upon Africans with a written language and books of their own. S. W. Koelle was at once despatched to visit the area and investigate. He discovered that the art of writing was a recent invention and was limited to the Vai people. He found the inventor, a man about forty years old "of great intelligence and much religious feeling", who as a small boy had spent some weeks with an American missionary and learned from him the Roman alphabet. When he was about twenty-four, he had in a dream the first suggestion to express his own language in written characters. With a few friends he produced a syllabic script of some 200 symbols, though Koelle was of opinion that 100 would have covered all distinct syllables in the language. With the encouragement of the chief, schools were begun, but tribal war interrupted the good work, and it was not resumed. Koelle reported: "In Bandakoro (the chief town of the tribe) all grown-up people of the male sex are still able to read the country books and in all other Vei towns there are at least some who can do the same. I have myself witnessed, several times, that they use their writing for correspondence. Books, also, they seem to have had in considerable numbers, but the greatest part of them was lost in the conflagration of Dshondu. Nevertheless, I succeeded in getting some . . . their contents are of a mixed kind—family notices, journals, religion. In the religious part the

---

[1] *Proceedings* (1849), lxviii–xix. James Richardson was a Saharan traveller of note. His last expedition was a mission authorized by the British Government in 1849. He was accompanied by Drs. Barth and Overweg. He died in March, 1851. His Journal was published, as was the narrative of Henry Barth, who continued the expedition.—J. Richardson, *Narrative of a Mission to Central Africa* (1853); H. Barth, *Travels and Discoveries in Central Africa* (1857), Richardson is credited with the first publication in Kanuri, a translation of St. Matthew's Gospel, chapters 2 to 4: 5, issued in 1853.—E. M. North, *The Book of a Thousand Tongues* (1938), 189.

influence of Mahomedanism is evident."[1] In due course Koelle published a grammar of the language.[2]

With some regard to the comity of missions it at first seemed appropriate to commend this interesting people to the care of American missionaries in Liberia, when events occurred which made it unnecessary. The country called Gallinhas by the Portuguese, in the neighbourhood of Cape Mount,[3] had long been infested with slave-traders. In 1849 Captain Dunlop, R.N., concluded a treaty with the chiefs eliminating the trade. The slave-traders fled, some 1,000 to 2,000 slaves were taken to Sierra Leone and liberated, and three sons of chiefs were placed in the Grammar School. The officer then desired the Church Missionary Society to enter the area cleansed so far of the trade. The chiefs in council, consulted by a representative of the Society, consented to the proposal, when catastrophe overwhelmed them. The African who had been appointed as British Agent in the area was murdered, and on the chiefs refusing to surrender the criminals punitive action was taken which resulted in the destruction of the principal towns and the dispersal of the people.[4]

Unhappily Koelle's health compelled his withdrawal from Sierra Leone after barely a decade of service. He was transferred to the Near East where his linguistic gifts had ample scope, and in Constantinople he rendered distinguished service for over twenty years to the Christian cause in the Muslim world.[5]

Before pursuing beyond Sierra Leone the working out of the policy we have so far traced, it is necessary to cast our eyes farther afield and take note of certain contemporary happenings across the Atlantic.

[1] *Proceedings of the C.M.S.* (1850), lxvii–viii; H. H. Johnston, *Liberia* (1906), II, 1107–15. Johnston reproduces the list of symbols used in the syllabarium, both original and modern, together with specimens of Vai writing.—*Ibid.*, 1116–35. In 1920 the wife of the present writer met in Victoria, Cameroons, a member of the Vai tribe who still used the script, and provided plentiful specimens of it. F. W. H. Migeod regarded the Vai language as of sufficient interest to devote a chapter to it. —F. W. H. Migeod, *The Languages of West Africa*, II (1913), chap. XIX. A valuable study is provided by A. Klingenhaben in "The Vai Script"—*Africa*, VI (1933), 158–71.

[2] S. W. Koelle, *Outlines of a Grammar of the Vei Language* (1854),

[3] Because of the large numbers of domestic fowls found there.—Johnston, *op. cit.*, I, 49.

[4] *Proceedings of the C.M.S.* (1850), lxix; (1851), lxxxiii–viii.

[5] Stock, *op. cit.*, II, 153; III, 114–15, 122–3.

CHAPTER 2

CONTRIBUTION FROM THE CARIBBEAN

THE SUCCESS of the anti-slavery movement, in its effect on Christian missions in Africa, had on the negative side dissociated the slave-trade and slavery (for the most part) from the Christian name, while on the positive it had enlarged the opportunity for recruiting Christian Africans as a missionary native agency. We have already seen the beginning of such a policy among the liberated Africans of Sierra Leone.[1] The West Indies were also concerned.

(1) *After Emancipation*

After the Emancipation Act of 1833 had become effective, the considerable Negro population of the British West Indies became a potential source of recruitment for African service.[2] T. F. Buxton had seen the possibility of such an interest arising and wrote in 1840: "I have a great satisfaction in finding, that among the liberated Africans in our West Indian colonies, we are likely to be furnished with a number of persons in whom are united the desirable qualifications of fitness for the climate, competency to act as teachers, and willingness to enter upon the work."[3] He was greatly enheartened to learn of the initiative that was being taken in Jamaica. Early in 1839 a meeting of some 2,000 to 3,000 people was held in Kingston "for the pur-

---

[1] In addition to the direct action of Missionary Societies there was formed in London the African Native Agency Committee, whose object was to work through existing organizations. This Committee made periodic grants, for example, to the C.M.S. or the training of suitable Africans at the Grammar School in Sierra Leone and at Fourah Bay.—*Proceedings of the C.M.S.* (1844), 27; (1846), 40; (1847), 28; (1848), liii.

[2] The Act of 1833, which became operative on August 1, 1834, had allowed for an apprenticeship system in a transition period. This was finally terminated in 1838. For a detailed account see W. L. Burn, *Emancipation and Apprenticeship in the British West Indies* (1937), chap. ix.

[3] T. F. Buxton, *The Slave Trade and its Remedy*, 492; cf. 11, 524. He had said earlier in a letter to Trew: "The idea of compensation to Africa, through the means of the West Indies, is a great favourite with me."—C. Buxton, *Memoirs of Sir Thomas Fowell Buxton, Bart.*, 458. And in the same year (1839) to J. J. Gurney: "We want black persons from all conceivable situations . . . and every one ought to be a real Christian; but a good Providence has prepared these in the West Indies and at Sierra Leone."—*Ibid.*, 464.

pose of considering the best means of Christianizing Africa, by such Christian agency as we could collect in this island".[1]

It would appear, however, that the first proposal had been made by the Moravians in Jamaica as early as 1835 when they considered a plan "for training native missionaries and teachers for needy Africa".[2] The inspiring leader was Jacob Zorn who superintended the Moravian Western Province of the West Indies from 1834 to 1843. He saw the opportunities that emancipation offered, of which this was one. With Government grants first available for education in 1835, he was anxious to establish Boarding as well as Day Schools, but found this difficult. Eventually in 1840 he opened a Manual Labour & Training School, a genuine residential institution, from which much was hoped—but the hopes did not mature.[3] When, however, the Basel Mission was in search of West Indian helpers for its work on the Gold Coast, Zorn cordially co-operated.

The Basel initiative was due to Inspector Hoffmann. When he took the helm in Basel Mission affairs a new energy appeared in the conduct of its West African enterprise. In particular he sponsored the policy of establishing a settlement of Christian Negroes in the Danish territory where the Mission was at work, with a twofold purpose in view: to lift the burden of manual labour from the missionaries' shoulders (and thus, he believed, prolong their expectation of service), and at the same time to demonstrate by their way of life to the surrounding African community that Christianity was in truth effective for the black man as well as for the white.[4] For various reasons Sierra Leone did not appear to be a practicable source, so he turned to the West Indies. The Moravian authorities at home had been hesitant about the proposal, and La Trobe, their representative in London, had sent warning of the opposition of the planters to a

---

[1] T. F. Buxton, *op. cit.*, 494. Buxton's correspondent was the president of the meeting in question. Further instances of this spontaneous movement and of considerable sums raised are reported in *The Friend of Africa*, I (1841), 39, 41, 52. For West Indian interest in the Niger Expedition, *ibid.*, 205–6, 208.

[2] T. F. Buxton, *op. cit.*, 516, *n*. In the previous year William Knibb of the Baptist Mission in Jamaica had looked with hope in the same direction.—E. A. Payne, *Freedom in Jamaica* (1933), 73.

[3] J. E. Hutton, *A History of Moravian Missions* (1923), 217–19. Hutton says Zorn must be valued "not so much by what he accomplished, but by the ideals he cherished" in a period of pessimism. Five of his training school students had offered for missionary service, and he saw in these the vanguard of a missionary force in Africa.

[4] This was a more limited form of Christian witness by native agency than others intended by their use of the term.

scheme that would draw on an already shrinking labour force.[1] Nevertheless it was carried forward, and Riis, to whose fortitude and endurance the survival of the Gold Coast mission was due, sailed with two colleagues from London for Jamaica in May 1842. With considerable difficulty he succeeded in assembling a company of twenty-four emigrants from Jamaica and Antigua, among whom were six families with children. In the terms of agreement it was stated that the Mission would be responsible for the emigrants' support on the Gold Coast for the first two years. Land and houses would be assigned to them on arrival, and free time allowed for cultivation. After two years their time would be their own save that the Mission would expect their services to be available when required at reasonable recompense. At the end of five years the Society would defray their return passage to Jamaica if they wished to go and providing their moral record had been satisfactory. They sailed direct to West Africa, the voyage taking sixty-eight days.[2] Their arrival signalized the second start of the Society's work in this field. Reinforcements from Basel soon joined them.[3]

This West Indian experiment was by no means an unqualified success. Perhaps the expectations of its promoters had been pitched too high. Certainly the situation in which the West Indians were called upon to co-operate with the European missionaries was a difficult one. Mortality was still serious. At one time, despite reinforcements, there were but three missionaries surviving on the field (and this after eighteen years of occupation), and the West Indians did not escape.[4] With the starting of a new station at Aburi, on high land twenty-six miles inland from Accra, two West Indian families were associated. At first all was enthusiasm among the African population until they discovered that from this white man no brandy was to be had. They then deserted. Here the West Indians served loyally, completing the half-begun mission house, but such a situation was difficult, to say the least. Indeed, it would seem that not enough allowance had been made for the fact that Jamaica was not Sierra Leone. The slaves in Jamaica, in the nature of the case,

[1] As early as 1834 emigration of African labour from West Africa to the West Indies was encouraged by planters with the countenance of the British Government. By 1843 some 28,000 such immigrants had arrived in the British West Indies.—*The Friend of the African*, I (1844), 246; cf. 34–7, 58–9.
[2] From February 8 to April 17, 1843. An Irish brigantine had been chartered for the purpose at a cost of £600.
[3] W. Schlatter, *Geschichte der Basler Mission, 1815–1915* (1916), III, 34–6.
[4] The Home Board was at one time compelled to review its position; it was even questioned whether the curse of Ham lay upon the land.—*Ibid.*, III, 41.

soon lost their various mother-tongues, whereas the liberated Africans in Sierra Leone were free to meet and use them. Thus the older Christian families from Jamaica had English only, and language was a barrier for them as well as for the missionary when indeed it was not something more, even leading them to look down upon the Africans they had been brought to serve. This attitude of aloofness proved a real limitation of their missionary usefulness, so much so that the interested Africans looked rather to the Europeans than to them. In the matter of the manual service for which they had partly been recruited, they seem to have discharged their obligations quite satisfactorily. With the expiry of the five years of their original engagement, those who had not found themselves at home in the mission departed: a few returned to Jamaica, others settled down on the coast. Three or four families, however, held on and provided a solid core for the little Christian community. Thus at Akropong in 1851 out of a total community of thirty-one, twenty-five were West Indian. Moreover the next generation provided several loyal leaders. But the Society had regretfully to acknowledge that the ideal of "a colony of heaven"[1] was not realized by the West Indian emigrants.[2]

The Church Missionary Society did not recruit West Indians for its native agency. True, the African Native Agency Committee was concerned with preparing those of African descent, whether in Sierra Leone or the West Indies, at Church of England institutions for service in West Africa.[3] But advice had been tendered against West Indian recruitment. J. F. Schön, while urging the expansion of African agency after the Niger Expedition experience, had written: "West Indian people may in many respects be better qualified than the Liberated Africans at Sierra Leone: they have seen more of European habits; are better acquainted with agricultural labours; and have a much greater taste for European comforts, if that be considered an acquisition. But . . . the high notions which they have acquired of their own importance, have, I am afraid, rendered them, in a great measure, unfitted for Africa."[4]

---

[1] Philippians 3: 20 (Moffatt).
[2] W. Schlatter, *op. cit.*, III, 36, 40–1, 42–3.
[3] *The Friend of the African*, I (1844), 185–6. The membership of the Committee is here given. It made grants to the West Indies as well as to Sierra Leone.
[4] J. F. Schön, *Journal*, 62–3. He has still more strictures to offer, and concludes: "It may be that I have wronged the West Indian people in some things attributed to them: if that is the case it is owing to my having compared them with the Free Blacks in the American Settlements of Liberia, of the greater number of whom my statement is correct."

This view was confirmed by Archdeacon Holberton of Antigua. Writing to Mr. Trew in 1839, he expressed the view that when careful selection had been made on lines he proposed, there should follow a year's training in England, and further: "When you forward them from England, send as their superintendent, one of ourselves, a minister who shall direct their energies, bear with their weaknesses, and keep united heart and mind in the great work on which they had been sent out."[1] These were wise words and the experience of other Societies proved their truth. Four years later Archdeacon Holberton, having read Schön's *Journal*, entirely approved the selection of African agents from the ranks of the liberated in Sierra Leone, and so warmly did he and others endorse it that he sent two successive contributions of ten pounds each from his congregation towards training at Fourah Bay. His earlier misgivings had hardened into a conviction that West Indians would not prove suitable for the work.[2] Thanks to the Grammar School and the Fourah Bay Institution the resources available in Sierra Leone were such that the Church Missionary Society had no occasion to attempt the expensive experiment of West Indian recruitment.

(2) *Initiative in Jamaica*

Two missionary movements originated in Jamaica that in due course developed into major enterprises in West Africa under the parent Societies. To these, Baptist and Presbyterian respectively, we must now turn.

The Baptist Missionary Society made an outstanding contribution to the welfare of Negroes in Jamaica from the inception of its work in 1814. With emancipation there developed an interest in Africa that crystallized into an expressed desire that a mission from the Baptist Churches should be begun. On the one hand a spontaneous concern seems to have arisen, and on the other there was wise leadership from William Knibb and his colleagues who had hoped for this development. Early in 1839 T. F. Buxton received, through the Secretary of the Baptist Missionary Society, a letter from Jamaica stating that thousands of Negro Christians were moved by a deep concern: "The sub-

---

[1] T. F. Buxton, *op. cit.*, 495–7. Some were more optimistic about the immediate usefulness of West Indian recruits. Buxton wrote to Trew, also in 1839: "I send you Miller's letter from Antigua, telling me that he has already ten good Christian Blacks ready to be located on the Niger."—C. Buxton, *Memoirs*, 458.

[2] *Proceedings of the C.M.S.* (1844), 41.

ject is, a mission to the interior of Western Africa. . . . The conversion of Africa to God is the theme of their conversation and their prayers, and the object of their most ardent desires." Later in the year John Clarke of the Baptist Society in Jamaica wrote direct to Buxton that, so keen was the interest in a mission to Africa, he already had offers of personal service.[1] The genuineness of such offers is attested by the lone venture on which some individual Negroes embarked. William Knibb reported in 1839 that one Thomas Keith, an African by birth and a Christian convert, had set out with nothing more than a letter of recommendation from his minister, to be a missionary to his people. He worked his passage from Jamaica and reached the spot where he had been stolen as a boy and sold into slavery. But then the curtain falls. Nothing more was heard of him.[2] That the interest of others was grounded in a real concern is shown by the contributions freely made for a mission to Africa. Unsolicited gifts were reported as early as 1838, and when money could not be given, the contribution might take another form, as at one meeting where "one hundred of the poor labourers, having no money to give, stood up and expressed their readiness to devote the hire of one week towards carrying it forward".[3]

When the first proposal from Jamaica for a mission to Africa reached the Home Committee they felt unable to entertain it. Knibb, disappointed but not daunted, urged a beginning with a group of Jamaica Negroes to be given a short preparation in England and sent out with a missionary as superintendent. But this was not accepted. Happily Knibb was on furlough in 1840 and pressed the claim. At a meeting in Exeter Hall he pledged his own church in Jamaica for £1,000 towards the work; with indefatigable zeal he stirred the churches. The cause was won. In June 1840 the Committee resolved: "That, in compliance with the representations of our brethren in Jamaica, and following what we apprehend to be the clear indications of Providence, we determine, in reliance on the divine blessing, to commence a mission to Western Africa." It was agreed that an exploratory visit should be the first step, and for this purpose there were appointed John Clarke, an ordained missionary who

[1] T. F. Buxton, op. cit., 492–3, 497.

[2] E. A. Payne, op. cit. (1933), 73–4. Buxton received from a Jamaica correspondent a strikingly similar story: "One poor African, named James Keats, left this country a few months ago, really on a pilgrimage to his native land, that he might carry the gospel there. We are anxious to hear of him. He had reached Sierra Leone, and had, I believe, embarked in Her Majesty's ship *Rattlesnake* for the Congo river, which he intends to ascend."—T. F. Buxton, op. cit., 495.

[3] *Report of the Baptist Missionary Society* (1838), 21; (1841), 23.

had served in Jamaica since 1836, and a medical man, Dr. G. K. Prince, a one-time slaveowner, but for ten years a loyal member of the Baptist Church.[1] It seems that the Niger was in mind as a possible line of entry, and application was made for the inclusion of the party in the Niger Expedition. As, however, arrangements were already in hand for J. F. Schön and Samuel Crowther to join it with liberated Africans of their selection from Sierra Leone to act as interpreters, the request could not be complied with. Clarke and Prince therefore took ship for Fernando Po, as a natural base from which to conduct their inquiry; they arrived in January, 1841.[2]

Fernando Po had been in British occupation from 1827 to 1834 and was still a base for the British naval patrol on the West Coast. During the occupation period a court for adjudicating on captured slave-ships sat at the settlement called Port Clarence, and liberated Africans were often placed there. The population was between 800 and 900, almost entirely African, but of varied origin from Sierra Leone and the Kru Coast to the Cameroons.[3] English was the natural lingua franca. The Niger Expedition first called here in October, 1841, and Schön and Crowther found Clarke and Prince already actively engaged in ministering to the people. They had attempted contact with the shy and timid forest folk known as Bubis and estimated their number at some 15,000. Samuel Crowther reported a day-school kept by a Cape Coast man with some forty children of the settlers in attendance.[4]

Clarke and Prince were concerned with more than Fernando Po. As soon as opportunity offered they crossed to Cameroons

---

[1] *Report of the Baptist Missionary Society* (1840), 29–30; (1841), 33; F. A. Cox, *History of the Baptist Missionary Society* (1842), II, 351–5; E. A. Payne, *op. cit.*, 75–7.

[2] Schön refers to a Mr. Kingdon on the Niger Expedition, a regular member of the *Soudan's* company, who hoped to serve as a religious teacher. He had joined "with a view to make himself useful to the Natives, wherever he should find an opening. He is in connexion with the Baptists, but not sent by them as a Missionary." Schön was apparently aware of the Baptist interest in the Niger, for he says of the Niger–Benue confluence, "If the Baptist Missionaries, who are at present at Fernando Po, should ascend the Niger . . . they might occupy this place as a Missionary Station at once . . . the question of its eligibility for a Missionary Station by our own Society would soon be decided, by its admirable rule of non-interference with any Protestant Missionary Society."—Schön, *Journal*, 134–5.

[3] Allen and Thomson, *op. cit.*, II, 191; M'William, *op. cit.*, 112–13.

[4] The parents paid him from a penny to sixpence weekly, according to the improvement of the child! Many parents besought Schön to baptize their children, and at various services he baptized seventy-seven. At their own request Crowther enrolled a class of adults seeking baptism. These Schön declined to baptize, with such limited instruction and testing.—Schön and Crowther, *Journals*, 246–9, 339–44.

on the mainland, and thanks to a letter of introduction from Lieut.-Colonel Nicholls, Governor of Fernando Po to 1834, were well received. Their commission discharged, they sailed for home. They had spent fourteen months in Africa. At Clarence they had ministered to a congregation of two to three hundred; seventy inquirers had been enrolled, five had been baptized. Bible classes with fifty members and a school of seventy scholars had been started. Contributions had amounted to £55, of which £18, at the instance of the missionaries, had been collected for the African Civilization Society; the balance had been given unasked for the Baptist Missionary Society. Fruitful contacts had also been made with mainland chiefs. They thus had a good report to give. But some adventure still lay before them, and their intention to sail to England direct was thwarted. They embarked at Clarence on February 3, 1842. Then one disaster followed another, and they finally made land in British Guiana on April 11. The opportunity to report first in Jamaica was naturally taken, and the churches responded with enthusiasm. When Clarke and Prince sailed for England they had with them two West Indian recruits, Joseph Merrick and Alexander Fuller. Meanwhile the Home Committee had decided that Fernando Po was an eligible first station, and had sent Thomas Sturgeon as a reinforcement. "It seems on all accounts desirable", they recorded, "to make that island the first of a series of stations which, it is hoped, may ultimately reach into the interior."[1]

The main decision having been taken, there was immediate action to put it into effect. Prince, Merrick and their wives with Fuller sailed together to Fernando Po, arriving in September 1843. Clarke with Alfred Saker and his wife left England in July 1843 for the West Indies in the *Chilmark*, a sailing ship of only 179 tons. Two months later they reached Jamaica where a company of men, women and children, thirty-nine in number, joined the party. Some were going as evangelists and teachers, others as settlers. The Jamaica churches had promised to support the Home Committee in a mission to Africa, and once again proved as good as their word. The Society had provided the vessel; Jamaica met the outfit cost of the emigrants to the tune of £500; this was additional to an equivalent sum they had been sending yearly for the African Mission. An eleven weeks' voyage brought the party to Fer-

[1] *Report of the B.M.S.* (1841), 34; (1842), 29–30; F. A. Cox, *op. cit.*, II, 357–78; E. A. Payne, *op. cit.*, 77.

nando Po in February 1844. Then the testing time began. As with the Basel Mission experience so now, the stern conditions of life in the new land brought disillusion. John Clarke reported five months after landing: "I think most of our Jamaica friends will turn out well, but they need at present constant watching, directing, instructing. . . . They are in a new situation altogether . . . we shall not expect too much at first." These words contained a warning. Then malaria began to take its toll.[1] Personal relations suffered a decline. Political change came as a shock: in 1846 Spain re-occupied the island.[2] Port Clarence became Santa Isabel. Spanish priests arrived and the Baptist missionaries received notice to quit. Circumstances supervened, however, under which they were permitted to continue, though within a restricted field, until 1858 in which year they had no option but to withdraw.[3] By that time there was a small but established work on the mainland in Cameroons.

These political and other circumstances led to the return of a number of the Jamaicans to the West Indies in 1847, in which year Clarke himself returned to Jamaica where he continued to serve the churches for a generation.[4] John Clarke was a language student of some note and was the first to publish records of the speech of the indigenous Bubis. He seems also to have had some idea of the relationship and extent of the Bantu

[1] H. H. Johnston has pointed out that the rank vegetation around the settlements provided an ideal breeding-ground for the insect vector, while infected Africans from the mainland supplied the parasites, so that "the fevers of Fernando Po—from 1780 to (say) 1900—were more frequent and more fatal than those of Old Calabar or the Cameroons estuary."—H. H. Johnston, *George Grenfell and the Congo* (1908), I, 23.

[2] Fernando Po was transferred by Portugal to Spain in 1777 but was abandoned in 1782, malaria being one reason. The British occupation in 1827, to which Spain had consented, was terminated in 1834 because Spain had refused to consider a transfer of sovereignty.—*Ibid.*, I, 20; T. F. Buxton, *op. cit.*, 537.

[3] *Report of the B.M.S.* (1846), 37; (1847), 29–30; (1859), 6–8; E. A. Payne, *op. cit.*, 80–1; E. B. Underhill, *Alfred Saker, A Biography* (1884), 81–3; H. H. Johnston, *op. cit.*, I, 22–3. Johnston has reviewed the unsatisfactory compensation arrangements for expropriated land and buildings. Casualties were severe: Sturgeon died in 1846, Fuller in 1847, and Merrick in 1849.—*Centenary Volume of the Baptist Missionary Society* (1892), 321.

[4] According to the Committee minutes of the B.M.S. a letter was received from Clarke on July 8, 1846 intimating that there were native teachers anxious to return to Jamaica; a year later it was recorded that on July 15, 1847 "ten assistant missionaries" returned to Jamaica on the boat of the United Presbyterian Mission in Calabar which was accustomed to call at Fernando Po. On August 5, 1847 a letter was received from Clarke announcing his own arrival in Jamaica. He survived to give twenty-eight years' further service in that island, making thirty-eight in all, in addition to the years spent in Fernando Po. He died in 1879 at the age of seventy-seven. I am indebted to the Rev. A. S. Clement, Editorial Secretary of the B.M.S., for the above information from the minutes of the Society.

languages, and even anticipated, on a small scale, S. W. Koelle's *Polyglotta Africana*.[1]

Joseph Merrick reached Fernando Po in September 1843 and soon crossed to the estuary of the Cameroons River on the mainland opposite. Here the Duala people had settled two centuries or so before. According to tribal tradition their ancestor, Mbeli, had two sons, Koli and Duala. From Koli came the Isubu people of the Bimbia peninsula; Duala's posterity kept his as the tribal name. John Clarke and Dr. Prince had visited the two Duala chiefs, "King Bell" and "King Akwa", in 1841. Merrick now went to each and in March 1844 reported he had purchased two pieces of land on the Cameroons River for mission stations. It was not until 1845, however, that missionaries settled on the mainland. Merrick and his wife then went to Bimbia, and Alfred and Mrs. Saker to the Duala people.[2] Merrick thenceforward made the Isubu people his care, and pursued a study of their language, which was a dialect distinct from Duala. He made the first Biblical translations into it, and these were printed on the mission press at Bimbia: St. Matthew's Gospel (1846), Genesis (1847), Selections from St. John's Gospel (1848).[3] The following year he died, worn out by his many labours which had included journeys into the immediate interior. His was devoted service and a worthy contribution from the West Indies.

Alfred Saker, who also passed to the mainland in 1845, went to the Duala shore. He had accompanied Clarke in the *Chilmark*, and spent a year in Fernando Po. He had been trained as an engineer, and while he was engaged at the Devonport

---

[1] H. H. Johnston, *op. cit.*, I, 19*n*. Johnston suggests that Clarke's *Specimens of Dialects: Short Vocabularies of about Two Hundred African Languages* (1849), which he secured from liberated Africans, may have given Koelle the same idea. That is possible, but Hannah Kilham and J. F. Schön in Sierra Leone had used the method still earlier on a limited scale. For the Bubi language and Clarke's studies in it, see H. H. Johnston, *A Comparative Study of the Bantu and Semi-Bantu Languages* I (1919), 813; II (1922), 159–61; F. W. H. Migeod, *Languages of West Africa*, I (1911), 189. In August 1848 Clarke informed the B.M.S. Committee that a new edition of his *Introduction to the Fernandian Tongue* was ready for publication.

[2] *Report of the B.M.S.* (1844), 45; (1845), 30–1; (1846), 35; F. A. Cox, *op. cit.*, II, 359–62. The name Cameroons, derived from the Portuguese *Camaroes* (=prawns), is due to the Portuguese discoverers finding prawns abundant in the estuary. "Bell" is an anglicized corruption of Mbeli.—H. H. Johnston, *George Grenfell and the Congo*, I, 27, 30.

[3] E. M. North, *The Book of a Thousand Tongues* (1938), 175; *Report of the B.M.S.* (1849), 18–19; (1850), 27; (1852), 52; H. H. Johnston, *op. cit.*, I, 27, *n.*; *A Comparative Study of the Bantu and Semi-Bantu Languages*, I, 811; II, 146; C.M. Doke, *Bantu: Modern Grammatical, Phonetical and Lexicographical Studies* (1945), 3; R. Kilgour, *The Bible throughout the World* (1939), 84.

Dockyard Clarke and Prince had visited the town as a deputation on behalf of the West African mission, when Saker and his wife became recruits. They proved well matched to their task. Saker established his station in Akwa's territory and named it Bethel. He had not long to wait to find how stony was the ground. Akwa soon died, when an orgy of quarrelling and rioting broke out. Even the mission house was attacked with violence and its contents rifled. But his devoted service and that of his wife were still to continue for many years. We meet them again; meanwhile it is sufficient to record his study of the Duala language and the beginning of translation. St. Matthew's Gospel was printed at Bethel at the "Devonport Press" (1848), the first-fruits of a work he was destined to complete—the translation of the Scriptures.[1]

If the West Indian settlers did not for the most part find acceptable the new home they had expected in Fernando Po, there were nevertheless families who remained and gave more than one generation of service, as well as later individual arrivals. The work in Cameroons was indebted to them, and when political events once again compelled withdrawal, there were those who served the Society in its developing Congo field. Indeed, the last of these, who gave thirty-five years' service on the Congo, survived until 1932.[2]

The notable mission of the Scottish Presbyterians on the Cross River also had its origin in Jamaica at this time. The Scottish Missionary Society (by which name the Edinburgh Society of 1796 was now known) had begun work in Jamaica in 1824. When the United Secession Church undertook its own Mission in 1835, Jamaica became its field of operations. The agents of the two bodies formed a joint Presbytery in Jamaica until the dissolution of the Scottish Society in 1847, in which year also a further Scottish union (of the United Secession Church with the Relief Synod) issued in the United Presbyterian Church.

It was this joint Presbytery that first had before it in 1839 the question of a mission to Africa, a prime cause being the spon-

---

[1] E. B. Underhill, *Alfred Saker, A Biography* (1884), *passim*; E. M. North, *op. cit.*, 106; H. H. Johnston, *op. cit.*, I, 811; II, 146; *Report of the B.M.S.* (1852), 52; (1853), 49–50; (1858), 61; R. Kilgour, *op. cit.*, 84.

[2] E. A. Payne, *op. cit.*, 81–4. An interesting interview with Dr. Prince on the outcome of the West Indian experiment, giving reasons for his disappointment, was reported by the American Board in 1847 when they were themselves reviewing the possibility of such recruitment.—*The Missionary Herald* (A.B.C.F.M.), (1847), 254.

taneous interest of the people. As one of the missionaries reported: "Our emancipated people, finding their condition so much improved by freedom, and appreciating their Christian privileges, began to commiserate their brethren in Africa. . . . All our congregations held meetings for consultation and prayer about the subject, and also began to form a separate fund for the benefit of Africa, which in the course of little more than a year amounted to six hundred pounds. In these efforts they were stimulated by the Baptist congregations, especially that of Mr. Knibb."[1] By 1840 information on many points was still so slender that the Presbytery deferred its decision till 1841. Meanwhile Hope Masterton Waddell of the Scottish Society had received a copy of Buxton's *The African Slave Trade and its Remedy*. At the Presbytery of 1841, when two days were spent in prayer and deliberation, Waddell introduced the subject, reading extracts from Buxton's book.[2] As the climax of the second day's deliberations eight of the missionaries offered themselves if needed for the proposed mission, and the general purpose was expressed in six resolutions, of which the first asserted the time as opportune and the last called on their supporting Societies to undertake the Mission.[3] But the Home Boards were not encouraging, to say the least. The fate of the Niger Expedition was now public knowledge; was it not premature, not to say presumptuous, of the Jamaica Synod to make so bold in a situation where larger plans than theirs could ever be had suffered such spectacular collapse? Indeed, H. M. Waddell recorded that a letter from the Secretary of his own Society "was enough to frighten us, by its long array of previous failures." But the Jamaica Presbytery was not frightened. At its meeting in 1842 it recorded "that the desire of members to aid in introducing the gospel into Central Africa is unabated . . . and that they entertain the same sense of their duty in relation to it as at the first". In the same year two of the Jamaica missionaries on health leave, George Blyth and Peter Anderson, met in Liverpool sea captains with personal knowledge of Old Calabar who encouraged them to look in that direction for a possible mission centre. Thereupon Blyth and Anderson went so far as to transmit by Captain Turner, one of the number, a letter to the chiefs

---

[1] G. Blyth, *Reminiscences of Missionary Life* (1851), 178.
[2] On the first day a dozen copies of the book were fetched post-haste from Kingston where a consignment had just arrived, for the instruction of the various congregations.
[3] J. M'Kerrow, *History of the Foreign Missions of the Secession and United Presbyterian Church* (1867), 368–9, where the Presbytery's resolutions are given in full.

with the proposal of a mission.[1] He reported immediately on arrival its delivery and favourable reception, but it was later in 1843 when he was able to send the result of a consultation among the chiefs on the subject: "The king and chiefs say they are desirous of your coming amongst them, and are full of the scheme, hoping to have their children taught in English learning." This letter was attested by eight chiefs. Further, an eligible site for the mission had been chosen and was to be guaranteed for its use without interruption.[2] Blyth and Waddell thereupon acknowledged the message, accepting the chiefs' invitation. They also corresponded with Captain Beecroft, Governor of Fernando Po at the time and a man of influence with the Calabar chiefs to whom he warmly commended the Scottish missionaries. When Beecroft's report of the expectant chiefs reached Jamaica, it was decided that action was necessary. A special meeting of the Presbytery was called in September 1844 at which it was resolved to form a new missionary society to carry out their purpose. H. M. Waddell was asked to lead the new mission, and the consent of the Scottish Missionary Society to two years' leave of absence was obtained. Colleagues from Jamaica were to join him in Scotland. The original idea to take some West Indian families as settlers with agricultural experience was not pursued.[3] The Waddells left Jamaica early in January 1845. After shipwreck and detention, first in Grand Cayman and then in New Orleans with adventures commensurate with the opportunity for them in those regions, they landed at last in Liverpool. Waddell was relieved of the formidable undertaking of organizing a new Society as the United Secession Church had now consented to adopt the proposed mission.[4] But the claims of public advocacy still lay on Waddell and were so effectively discharged that within a year £4,000 had been secured from members of various denominations. Mr. Jamieson, the ever-generous Liverpool merchant, placed the

[1] G. Blyth, op. cit., 179–80.

[2] The chiefs declined to sell the site outright, and this was in accordance with African views of land tenure. Land is one of the primary elements for subsistence and not a marketable commodity. The community remains the owner, acting through the chief, and an occupancy right is all that can be granted. But in this the holder is recognized as having good title and can rest secure. His occupancy right is hereditary, but the land itself cannot be alienated. The site granted in this instance was to be in occupation of the mission in perpetuity.

[3] When West Indian colonists were at first in mind, an annual rent was required by the Calabar chiefs, but when this plan was given up, a free grant of the land was made.—J. M'Kerrow, op. cit., 371.

[4] J. M'Kerrow, op. cit., 372. Waddell's original appeal to the Christian public is printed in The Friend of the Africans, III (1846), 15–16; cf. 73–4.

Warree, a brigantine of 150 tons, at the disposal of the mission with an annual grant of £100 towards running expenses. On January 6, 1846, the pioneer party sailed from Liverpool. It consisted of seven persons: Mr. and Mrs. Waddell and their son, Mr. and Mrs. Edgerley, Andrew Chisholm and Edward Miller. The Edgerleys were seconded, as were the Waddells, from the Jamaica Mission; Chisholm and Miller were the West Indians in the party. In three months they reached Santa Isabel in Fernando Po, and on April 10, 1846, anchored in the Calabar River. At last the Calabar Mission had begun.[1]

The Efik people of Calabar[2] are a branch of the Ibibio tribe which lies to the west of the Cross River. The Efik section seems to have split off and migrated early in the seventeenth century, and by the end of the eighteenth to have been settled in four towns on the Calabar River, an eastern tributary of the Cross: Creek Town, Duke Town, Henshaw Town and Old Town, to give the names by which they were known to Europeans.[3] They lay some forty to fifty miles from the sea. From the seventeenth century the slave-trade was active and European traders regularly visited the river. Trade jealousy among the towns led to conflict, and early in the nineteenth century Duke Town, the most favourably placed for trade, seized the hegemony of the group.

The Wesleyan Conference of 1778 had before it a proposal to send missionaries to this area. It originated with the introduction to Methodist circles of "two young princes from Calabar in Guinea". They had been carried off as slaves and sold in America. After some seven years they took the advice of an English captain and ran away. He thereupon brought them to England, about 1775, where they were declared free. They came into contact with Methodists in Bristol and were given Christian instruction; one was baptized. They returned to Calabar and

---

[1] H. M. Waddell, *Twenty-nine Years in the West Indies and Central Africa* (1863), 206–23, 228–40; J. M'Kerrow, *op. cit.*, 368–74; H. Goldie and J. T. Dean, *Calabar and its Mission* (1901), 69–78. The commission to the work and credentials of H. M. Waddell are supplied in Appendix III of his book.

[2] It is suggested that the name Calabar comes from the New Calabar River, so called from the Kalabari living there. The name came to be applied to the Cross River estuary which was then called Old Calabar River to distinguish it from the Kalabari River, which in its turn was called New. A contributing factor may have been the Portuguese use of "Calabaros" for people by the Rio del Rey which empties itself by the Cross River estuary.—P. A. Talbot, *Southern Nigeria* (1926), I, 183–4; H. M. Waddell, *op. cit.*, 309. Du Plessis offers an alternative explanation.— *The Evangelisation of Pagan Africa* (1930), 151. "Old Calabar" was officially superseded by "Calabar" in 1904.

[3] The political background is summarized by H. M. Waddell, *op. cit.*, 309–15.

asked for missionaries to be sent. Two German brothers, Syndrum by name, members of the Methodist Society at Bristol, went out in response, but soon died. The opening was not followed up by the Conference.[1]

In 1842 Commander Raymond, R.N., negotiated with the chiefs of Calabar a treaty proposed the previous year for the abolition of the slave-trade. At the same time the two chiefs of Duke Town and Creek Town respectively asked for missionaries to instruct their people, with a view to developing legitimate trade. This request was passed on to the Society for the Propagation of the Gospel. The Society was prepared to seek for a missionary if the Government would undertake his support, but no appointment was made.[2]

When Clarke and Prince were on their exploratory visit in 1841 for the Baptist Society they are said to have undertaken to open a station in Calabar. Dr. Prince visited the place in 1843 and was well received. In 1845 a station was claimed in Duke Town but no permanent worker was appointed.[3] Waddell was not unaware of this situation. He had written to Captain Beecroft in 1844: "It is not our wish to disturb any other body of Christians who may be engaged in similar labours. We would rather co-operate with them; and . . . would respect their arrangements for the benefit of the natives." Further, he arranged with the Baptist Society's secretary before sailing that if he found Calabar occupied by them, he would go elsewhere. On reaching Fernando Po, he learned that Calabar was unoccupied, though Clarke and Sturgeon were of different views on the matter. In the upshot Sturgeon proposed a joint occupation, but the matter was settled by the chief whose decision was sought. Waddell and his pioneer company were to remain.[4]

Eyo Honesty II of Creek Town who gave this decision was a

---

[1] L. Tyerman, *The Life and Times of the Rev. John Wesley, M.A.* (1890), III, 271–3. A Miss Johnson of Bristol, who had been the special instructor of the young Africans, left a legacy of £500 to promote a mission to Calabar. To one young minister in Dundee who offered his services John Wesley wrote: "You have nothing to do at present in Africa. Convert the heathen in Scotland." It may be that an echo of these events is to be found in what John Adams wrote of the Calabar people as he knew them in 1789: "Many of the natives write English: an art first acquired by some of the traders' sons, who had visited England, and which they have had the sagacity to retain up to the present period. They have established schools and school-masters, for the purpose of instructing in this art the youths belonging to families of consequence."—Quoted in P. A. Talbot, *op. cit.*, I, 190.

[2] P. A. Talbot, *op. cit.*, I, 193; C. F. Pascoe, *Two Hundred Years of the S.P.G.* (1901), I, 260.

[3] *Report of the Baptist Missionary Society* (1844), 45; (1846), 34, 35–6.

[4] H. M. Waddell, *op. cit.*, 229, 240, 241, 242–3, 245–6.

chief of character. He had succeeded to the chieftainship in 1825. He could speak and read English through having served as cabin boy on an English vessel. About 1834 he had seized the opportunity to restore Creek Town's independence of Duke Town. He was interested in legitimate trade; when in 1842 Commander Raymond, R.N., had negotiated the treaty referred to above, it was Eyo with Eyamba of Duke Town who had asked for missionaries to instruct them in the production of export crops such as coffee and cotton, and in the preparation of sugar.[1] It was but natural therefore that the mission should be welcomed for the material benefits it was expected to confer rather than for its religious message. Eyo, however, proved a loyal friend. He himself acted as interpreter at the Sunday services. Waddell found that belief in a Supreme Being could be taken for granted: "Every man knows that God lives," Eyo told him, "and that he made all things."[2] In presenting the Christian message Waddell found that the idea of salvation first became significant for his hearers in relation to the prevailing dread of witchcraft, the shadow over Africa as it has been so aptly termed.[3] Human life was lightly valued, and the missionaries were greatly shocked at the easy taking of it on the death of a chief or other person of standing to provide a retinue for him in the world of shades. They denounced the practice and continued their protests until some reform was secured. But it was an uphill fight. Meanwhile of the three towns in which work had been begun it was at Creek Town under Eyo's rule that the mission began to take root. A school started by Andrew Chisholm made good progress, and Sunday congregations were large, thanks to the chief's personal interest and example.[4] Eyo already had certain standards that led him to be more appreciative than Eyamba and others were of the missionaries' purpose. He was a total abstainer from conviction,[5] he warmly approved of the education of his people, and was so enlightened as to despise the use of charms.[6] He was the first to be prepared

---

[1] P. A. Talbot, *op. cit.*, I, 191, 193.

[2] H. M. Waddell, *op. cit.*, 275. "Some of the commandments took his attention much, and his mode of interpreting them attracted mine." His comments are recorded.—*Ibid.*, 275–7; cf. 492–5.

[3] *Ibid.*, 278–80.

[4] Three years later Chisholm retired from the mission to reside in Fernando Po. —*Ibid.*, 509.

[5] "It is not fit for a man who has to settle palavers in the town", he said, "to spoil his head with rum."—*Ibid.*, 250.

[6] His own charm for the white trader, he said, was to have plenty of puncheons of palm oil ready for sale!—*Ibid.*, 277.

to discourage certain customs contrary to the dictates of humanity which were still approved among his neighbours.[1]

After six months' intensive work with his colleagues Waddell sailed for Jamaica to report progress and recruit workers. He was reappointed by the Presbytery as leader of the mission so encouragingly begun, and given the helpers he sought, both from the ranks of the European missionaries and the West Indian churches. Notable among the former was Hugh Goldie, destined to become a recognized authority on the Efik language. The West Indian helpers were to serve for a trial period, to be renewed if desirable. Waddell commented on this arrangement: "We had already seen that such an agency could not be implicitly relied on at the outset. The missionary service, like every other, needs training in its practical working, as well as mental preparation; classes need experience as well as individuals; and our coloured West India churches were in that respect very deficient . . . we must not expect from the raw recruits of our Jamaica mission churches the conduct of veterans."[2] In 1849 William Anderson and his wife, who had already served nine years in Jamaica, came to Calabar and rendered notable service, Mrs. Anderson giving thirty-three years and William Anderson forty to the Calabar Mission.[3] When in the following year Waddell commenced to explore higher up the Cross River, he discovered there was uneasiness among the Calabar chiefs; the fear was a personal one, that they would lose their lucrative status as middlemen in the palm oil trade if once the river was opened up. But with courteous reassurances explorations were continued and in due course up-river stations occupied.[4] The fact of the European traders being resident on their vessels at Calabar while securing their cargoes would have been a source of strength to the mission had they been practising Christians. On questions of humanity they did indeed support

[1] Waddell said of Creek Town by contrast with Duke Town: "Our intercourse with the king and chiefs of that town evidenced their superiority, in good sense, good manners, and good feelings, to those of its competitor lower down the river." —*Ibid.*, 275; cf. 428–31, 433. This is not to go so far as to say that Eyo's was *anima naturaliter Christiana*. He never became a confessor, but in disagreements with the missionaries he seems at least to have been without the prejudice that inhibits a frank discussion of the points at issue. When converts began to appear there were times of tension and his very strength of character expressed itself in the assertion of his chieftainship and his refusal to tolerate any suggestion, as he saw it, of *imperium in imperio*.

[2] *Ibid.*, 301–2.

[3] W. Marwick, *William and Louisa Anderson* (1897), *passim*.

[4] H. M. Waddell, *op. cit.*, 456, 595–6.

the missionaries' efforts at reform, but as Waddell expressed it, questions of religion and morals divided them.[1]

In 1858 H. M. Waddell found it necessary to retire from the mission. S. Edgerley, who accompanied Waddell in 1846, had died at his post in the previous year. Waddell had faithfully carried out the commission first entrusted to him in Jamaica more than twelve years before. He left a well-established work, with two regularly constituted churches in Duke Town and Creek Town respectively, together with various up-river stations. In September of that year the Presbytery of Biafra was formed as the local ecclesiastical authority, with William Anderson as the first moderator. In December 1858 a local era came to an end with the death of Eyo Honesty II of Creek Town.[2]

The link between the Jamaica churches and the Calabar Mission was still in being two generations later. It was not as settlers but as teachers that West Indians served the mission, and served effectively.[3]

(3) *Mission from Barbados*

There remains an Anglican contribution from the West to record, later in time by half a generation than the preceding earlier ventures. When in 1851 the Society for the Propagation of the Gospel celebrated its third jubilee, it invited the co-operation of the West Indian Church. The Bishop of Barbados replied: "The chief commemoration of the Jubilee which I propose in my own diocese and venture to suggest also to the other West Indian Bishops is to commence an African Mission."[4] The idea was taken up and a distinct organization for the purpose was decided upon, the West Indian Church Association.[5] An

---

[1] *Ibid.*, 486–92, where discussions with the traders are set down. Various circumstances from time to time continued to inflame their hostility to the Mission; cf. 578–86, 609–11.

[2] Goldie and Dean, *op. cit.*, 192–6.

[3] When the Phelps-Stokes Education Commission visited West Africa in 1920 they found two outstanding educational institutions under the Scottish Mission: the Hope Waddell Training Institution with 400 pupils, and Duke Town Day School with 1,300. On the staff of the former were three Jamaican teachers. Duke Town School was under a Jamaican principal with three Jamaican colleagues and sixty African teachers; high praise was given to it: "The Education Commission has not observed a better institution of the same type anywhere in Africa."— T. Jesse Jones, *Education in Africa* (1922), 164, 166–7.

[4] C. F. Pascoe, *Two Hundred Years of the S.P.G.* (1901), I, 260.

[5] It laboured under a cumbrous title, designed to express its origin, purpose, affiliation and support: The West Indian Church Association for the Furtherance of the Gospel in Western Africa, in connexion with the Society for the Propagation of the Gospel in Foreign Parts, as Trustees of Codrington College.—*Ibid.*, I, 261.

outbreak of cholera caused a serious interruption, and a leader for the mission was difficult to find. Finally in 1855 H. J. Leacock, an English clergyman born in Barbados, gallantly responded. "The Church calls, and someone must answer. But few years' service are now before me," he wrote, saying he might thereby save others with heavier commitments. J. H. A. Duport, a West Indian Negro, went with him. Care was taken not to enter an area already occupied, and in the end the suggestion of a trader was acted upon: that they should locate the new mission on the Rio Pongas, some 130 miles north of Sierra Leone. On December 12, 1855, they arrived at Tintima on that river.

Their introduction to Chief Ali was an official one. Lieut. Buck, R.N., commanding H.M.S. *Myrmidon,* had offered to convey them, and on arrival he commended the missionaries to the chief. The latter was diplomatically agreeable to the proposal, but his behaviour when the naval officers had departed led Leacock to write a few days later: "Considering his mode of life, having twenty-one women who are called his wives, and his principles, which can be accommodated to Heathenism, Mahommedanism, or any other *ism,* I can conceive no other reason for his support of Christianity than the retaining of a pension awarded by the British Government for himself abandoning the Slave Trade, and endeavouring to check it in others."[1]

Leacock had received from the Sierra Leone trader who had advised the location of the mission at Rio Pongas a letter of introduction to a chief, Richard Wilkinson of Fallangia. This produced an invitation which Leacock accepted, with surprising results. He was warmly welcomed by the old chief and then: "He seemed greatly agitated, and, a few moments after, rising from his chair, broke forth with that incomparable song of praise, the 'Te Deum Laudamus'; repeating it with great solemnity and accuracy"—surely a reception without parallel for a pioneer! This clearly required some explanation. The Church Missionary Society had begun a mission on the Rio Pongas in 1808. In 1812 Leopold Bütscher, one of the founders of the mission, brought a Negro boy to England who was instructed and baptized. His tutor was no other than Thomas Scott, to whom William Carey confessed his deepest debt.[2] On his return the boy was unsatisfactory, and when the mission

---

[1] *The Mission Field* (1856), 49–51, 55.
[2] And also first Secretary of the Church Missionary Society, and author of a well-known *Commentary.*

closed down soon after he was lost sight of.[1] For some twenty years he lapsed from his Christian faith, but in 1835 a serious illness led to repentance: "From that time", he said to Leacock, for the boy was baptized as Richard Wilkinson, "I resolved that 'I and my house would serve the Lord'; and I earnestly prayed that God would send a Missionary to this Pongas country whom I might see before I died. . . . You are, Sir, an answer to my prayers for twenty years."[2]

With so sincere and heart-warming a welcome, Leacock and Duport at once transferred to Fallangia where the chief had assigned them an attractive site of some two and a half acres.[3] A picture of Leacock's children had delighted him; not long after, while reading in St. Matthew's Gospel, he said he had discovered why the missionary had come (10: 37–8). Rarely is the missionary motive so appreciated. If Leacock received such encouragement near at hand it was also offered from afar. A clergyman had passed on to his congregation of slaves in the State of Tennessee an account of the Rio Pongas Mission, by which they were so affected that they collected among themselves seven dollars to be used for clothing for the children in the school.[4] It is not likely that Leacock ever received the clergyman's letter to him, for he died in Freetown on August 20, 1856. His name remains as that of the worthy pioneer of the West Indian mission.

As the work on the Rio Pongas had been confided to the care of the Bishop of Sierra Leone, he now took the step in October 1856 of ordaining J. H. A. Duport who had proved himself an able and faithful missionary. During Duport's ten weeks' absence in connexion with his ordination, the chief himself took charge of the religious activities. On Duport's return the first baptisms on the mission took place: twenty-seven on December 7, 1856 and thirty-two on January 11, 1857. These fifty-nine persons—a daughter of the paramount chief of the Pongas

[1] The reason for the abandonment was the destruction of the mission premises by fire—an act instigated by slave-traders, so that the missionaries had to retire to Sierra Leone. It was hoped that a British treaty with the chiefs for the extinction of the slave-trade might open the way for return. This hope remained unrealized.— *Proceedings of the Church Missionary Society* (1851), lxxxii–iii.

[2] *The Mission Field* (1856), 57–9; (1857), 174; (1858), 138; Stock, *op. cit.*, I, 162.

[3] On the usual African tenure as an occupancy right: "He says . . . this land is given to the West India Church Association, for the use and accommodation of its Missionaries, as long as the Mission exists amongst them; and that when it is removed it shall revert to him and his heirs."—*The Mission Field* (1856), 60. A site of fifty acres for a church and other buildings was later granted on the same terms.— C. F. Pascoe, *op. cit.*, I, 264 *n.* 1.

[4] *The Mission Field* (1856), 224–5.

among them—now constituted an infant church in a troubled borderland of pagan and Muslim.[1] Not that the Muslim Mandingoes seem to have actively sought Susu converts, but they were commercially interested in providing amulets of their own making—leather cases containing Arabic words from the Koran —at four or five dollars a time. Their opposition sprang from a familiar motive.[2] The pagans also were not inactive but their efforts to frustrate the building of the church were foiled; on November 15, 1857 St. James's Church, Fallangia, was opened for public worship.[3]

A colleague for Duport was soon on the way—a young West Indian Negro from the Bahamas, named Higgs, commended by Archdeacon Trew. Higgs's African experience was tragically short. He arrived at Fallangia on May 16, 1857 and died on June 21.[4] Meanwhile an African schoolmaster—David H. Cyprian—had arrived from Sierra Leone, and taken charge of a school of fifty-two scholars.

Teaching and services had at first been in English as this seemed to be acceptable. But it was soon discovered that English as understood was not equal to this demand, and Susu interpreters were therefore used. Duport then directed attention to Susu as the medium that must be employed, and with the chief's assistance had by 1858 produced a translation of the Prayer Book together with a Catechism and a Susu primer. Meanwhile Bishop Bowen of Sierra Leone, himself an able language student, urged the necessity of the vernacular: "To be efficient, the Missionaries at the Pongas should acquire the Soosoo language. The Fullah and the Arabic would be also very useful."[5]

Thus the work became established, and more missionaries were recruited for it, among whom the West Indian members were not unworthy. Seven Negro clergymen besides Duport served in the mission before the end of the century, four of whom had been trained at Codrington College, Barbados.[6]

---

[1] *Ibid.* (1856), 247–8, 269; (1857), 63–4, 65.
[2] *Ibid.* (1856), 230; cf. Acts 19: 23–6.
[3] *Ibid.* (1857), 124–5; (1858), 37–8.
[4] *Ibid.* (1857), 22, 173–4, 199. J. M. Trew had served as Secretary of the African Civilization Society in Buxton's day. He became Archdeacon in the Bahamas in 1843.—Buxton, *Memoirs*, 584. Higgs's death was due to exposure in an open boat for five days in transit from Freetown to Fallangia in the worst period of the tornado season.
[5] *The Mission Field* (1856), 185, 229, 270; (1857), 125–6; (1858), 36, 156–7, 223.
[6] C. F. Pascoe, *op. cit.*, II, 891. Richard Wilkinson survived until 1861, ever a loyal friend. On the side of trade, the positive policy proved so successful that in 1864 a French merchant declared he got more produce from Fallangia than from any six towns in the country.—*Ibid.*, I, 265.

In the light of these varied enterprises the return contribution from the West Indies to the evangelization of Africa can perhaps be fairly assessed. That there should have been any contribution possible at all is in itself a tribute to the generosity of spirit of the so recently emancipated Negroes. Had their first and only concern been for themselves they could scarcely have been blamed. Without a traditional social structure and language of their own to link them with their past, denied the status of marriage but encouraged to breed their kind, torn at their masters' convenience from those to whom they were bound by ties of natural affection, it would not have been surprising had the springs of generosity dried up. But the evidence to the contrary is plain to read.

Moreover, it seems to have been overlooked that the mere fact of African descent did not necessarily qualify for successful settlement. There had often enough been adaptation to a new physical and social environment, and allowance was not made for this. In confirmation is the fact that those whose work was sustained were the evangelists and teachers recruited on terms comparable to those of the European missionaries, as were the teachers of the Scottish Presbyterian Mission in Calabar, returning on regular leave to Jamaica.

If the West Indian contribution did not always take the form or reach the level others had anticipated, yet the simple fact of its existence is a notable event in the Christian story.

CHAPTER 3

HOPE RESTORED

COMMENDABLE AS the efforts originating in the Caribbean had proved to be, yet at the moment they left the problem of a break into the interior unsolved. They every one entered coastal regions as was perhaps inevitable, and regions where the white trader—until quite recently as slave-trader—had for long been a familiar figure. They did not reach the interior tribes at this period. There was, however, one adventure—and the term is merited—which was truly co-operative between black and white, that penetrated behind the traders' coastline and held out renewed hope of advance to the regions beyond. It began from Sierra Leone.

(1) *Outreach from Sierra Leone*

In pursuing the missionary strategy of advance from Sierra Leone as a base into interior Africa there were in theory two possibilities open: to go direct from Sierra Leone by land to the regions of the Upper Niger, or to proceed by sea along the Guinea Coast and break in at some favourable point. It was the second that in practice proved possible, but at one time the first seemed likely to happen. In Zachary Macaulay's day the Sierra Leone Company had despatched a goodwill expedition to Teembo in Fula territory some 250 miles north-east of Sierra Leone, with encouraging results, but it had not proved possible to follow it up.[1] In 1841 the Colonial Government decided to renew relations, which it was understood the Fula king desired. W. C. Thomson of the Temne mission in Sierra Leone was seconded at the request of the Governor to conduct the embassy, the Society seeing in this the possibility of a missionary road into the interior.[2] Thomson set out in December 1841, and successfully reached Teembo after various frustrations not unknown in African travel. Friendly relations were established with chiefs *en route* as well as in the Fula kingdom, and a welcome promised for schools and missionaries. A number of chiefs, indeed, were said to be prepared to send their sons to

---

[1] See Vol. I, 210 and *n.* 1.
[2] *Proceedings of the C.M.S.* (1842), 40. The expedition was promoted jointly by local merchants and the Colonial Government.

school in Sierra Leone. While at Teembo Thomson received an invitation from the king of the Bambara, an important tribe on the upper Niger, to visit Segou, his capital, half-way to Timbuktu.[1] The Home Committee saw in this a possible "door of entrance into the hitherto inaccessible interior of Africa".[2] Unhappily it could not be entered. Civil disturbance in the Fula kingdom led to a change of ruler and fresh obstacles arose under which Thomson's health finally gave way, and he died at the post of duty in November 1843.[3] The promise of this opening, together with the hopes entertained of the Niger Expedition of 1841, at one time appeared to offer a so-called pincer movement, with the river as the highway of approach. But the picture faded out and the interior remained remote as ever.

Then an opportunity for an advance came through African initiative. It was not unnatural that a heart-stirring for return to their homelands should survive among the liberated in Sierra Leone. This was stimulated for the Yoruba-speaking element by some of their number who in 1838 served on a trading ship that reached Lagos which they recognized as the slave-port from which they had been shipped. They managed to make their way inland to Abeokuta, their home town. Such was the vigour of purpose and capacity for achievement of these able people that a passenger service for "emigrants", as the returning Yorubas came to be called, was soon in active operation. The fare was twelve dollars (some £2 12s.) per person, passengers to find their own provisions. Some sailed to Lagos and passed up the River Ogun; others to Badagry to the west, thence trekking overland several days' march to Abeokuta. Rough handling at Lagos, which was a slaving centre, led to concentration on Badagry as the port of arrival. It is estimated that within three years more than five hundred people had returned to Abeokuta in this way. A number among them missed keenly the spiritual ministrations they had enjoyed in Sierra Leone, and sent urgent requests for Christian leaders to join them. Indeed, it was said that many more would have left Sierra Leone but for the spiritual isolation in which they would find themselves. This situation soon became an important concern of the leading

[1] The Bambara were a people of the Western Sudan who had remained little affected by Islam; cf. Vol. I, 103, 104 n.; C. G. Seligman, *Races of Africa* (1930), 60–2. Mungo Park had his first sight of the Niger at Segou in July 1796, and described the city. He estimated the population at 30,000.—Mungo Park, *Travels in the Interior Districts of Africa* (1799), 194–6.

[2] *Proceedings of the C.M.S.* (1843), 42.

[3] *Ibid.* (1844), 34.

Missionary Societies at work in the Colony, the Anglican and the Wesleyan. They took action almost simultaneously.[1]

The Wesleyan missionaries in Sierra Leone reported to the Home Committee this emigration of numbers of their people, and Dr. Beecham, the Secretary, proposed that Thomas Birch Freeman should be deputed to visit both Badagry and Abeokuta, with the prospect of Badagry becoming a mission station of the Society. Freeman, whose two visits to Kumasi had revealed him as an able pioneer, accordingly set out and reached Badagry in September 1842. With his customary regard for African etiquette, he first sent a message forward to the chief of Abeokuta, Shodeke, who not only replied assuring him of a welcome, but sent an escort with a mount for Freeman. They reached Abeokuta early in December.

Freeman found himself in an African city of some 45,000 population (so he estimated), built among rocks that made it a stronghold. Indeed, this situation had given the place its name (Abeokuta=Under the Stone). It had only been established for a dozen years. The extensive Yoruba kingdom was already in decay by the beginning of the century, and by the second decade internecine strife among the Yoruba clans intensified the process. This fatal disunion exposed them to the aggressive Fulani from the north who overran much of the country, imposing their rule and practising Islam. From these disturbances came many unhappy victims to feed the slave-trade. That section of the Yorubas known as Egbas had been based on Ibadan as their principal centre, but through the pressure of events, in particular of a civil war, withdrew in a body to the south-west and eventually established themselves in Abeokuta under Shodeke who is said to have been indicated by the diviners as the head of the new colony. He proved an unusually able and far-sighted ruler of this city of refuge. In a manner reminiscent of his great contemporary, Moshesh of the Basuto, he welcomed Egba refugees from all parts of the country, deserting slaves, and other groups into the new settlement, in which their principal family distinctions as far as practicable were still observed. Shodeke wielded the paramount authority from the foundation of the present Abeokuta, about 1830, to his death in 1844.[2]

It was from this chief that Freeman and his companion De

---

[1] *Wesleyan Missionary Notices* (1841), 609–11; (1842), 66–8; *Proceedings of the C.M.S.* (1843), 42–3; F. D. Walker, *Thomas Birch Freeman* (1929), 146–8.

[2] Johnson, *The History of the Yorubas* (1921), 225–6; A. C. Burns, *History of Nigeria* (3rd ed., 1942), 35–6.

Graft received a truly warm-hearted welcome. Freeman held several religious services, and on one occasion on Shodeke's initiative the Muslims, the pagan priests and the Christian missionary had respectively to state their case before the chief. Freeman won from him the verdict that the Christian religion was plainly the true one. After ten days Freeman and his companion returned to Badagry to find Henry Townsend of the Church Missionary Society recently arrived on the same quest as their own. The next day was December 25, and they united in the conduct of the Christmas services—a happy augury of Christian co-operation that later events were to confirm.[1]

William de Graft was then established in Badagry as the Wesleyan pastor responsible for Methodist emigrants both there and in Abeokuta. Freeman had become aware during this visit of a sinister shadow over life in Badagry—the ever-present fear of a surprise attack by the powerful king of Dahomey, to which kingdom Badagry had been subject two generations earlier. Moreover there was fear in Abeokuta of aggression from the same quarter. The fury of the Amazons of Dahomey was no idle tale. With the courage which characterized the man, Freeman determined to pay a visit to the Dahomian monarch, in the hope that personal relations might be established which would prove a safeguard to the Christian work now begun in Badagry and Abeokuta. As he purposed so he performed, and from January to April 1843, was on the soil of Dahomey. In the first momentous interview, which was a state occasion, Freeman clearly created a favourable impression, as he had done before at Kumasi. A number of private interviews ensued during which he came to discover that the king, despot though he was, had the qualities of an able ruler. Testimony that his talks with the king were not unfruitful was provided three years later by John Duncan who found that restrictions had lately been imposed in the matter of human sacrifice and the death penalty reserved to the royal prerogative. These changes he attributed to advice tendered by Freeman, "who is much in favour with his Majesty". But in respect of Badagry and Abeokuta being secured from aggression Freeman did not succeed.[2]

It was to be a dozen years before the Wesleyan Society com-

---

[1] *Wesleyan Missionary Notices* (1843), 372–85 (text of Freeman's Journal); F. D. Walker, *op. cit.*, 157–9.

[2] *Wesleyan Missionary Notices* (1843), 385–400 (Freeman's Journal); F. D. Walker, *op. cit.*, 160–79; J. Duncan, *Travels in Western Africa in 1845 and 1846* (2nd ed., 1847), I, 258–9. Duncan, a member of the First Life Guards, became an explorer of note. He had served with the Niger Expedition of 1841 as master-at-arms.

menced operations in the king's country, with a mission at Whydah. On a personal visit in 1854 Freeman secured the royal consent for an African agent to be stationed there with status for the missionary equivalent to that accorded the Portuguese and others.[1]

The Church Missionary Society was intimately concerned in the Yoruba emigration from Sierra Leone, and Henry Townsend, then a missionary in the Colony, was appointed to survey the land. He was afforded a free passage in the trading-vessel *Wilberforce* by its African owner, and landed at Badagry on December 19, 1842. Ten days later he left for Abeokuta, arriving on January 4, 1843 when he received a cordial welcome from Shodeke. The chief asked him to write in his name to the Governor of Sierra Leone, expressing his gratitude for what the British had done for his people, and stating his own determination to suppress slave-trading wherever his authority was effective. He also said he would welcome white men, both missionaries and merchants, to his country.

Townsend's favourable report determined the Society to establish the Yoruba Mission, with Abeokuta as its first station. Meanwhile Townsend, who had served as schoolmaster in Sierra Leone, was ordained by the Bishop of London, and together with Samuel Crowther and C. A. Gollmer appointed to the new enterprise. Gollmer was yet another of the able band of German missionaries trained at Basel. He had received Anglican ordination in 1841 and sailed for Sierra Leone in the same year. In December 1844 Townsend, Crowther and Gollmer with their wives and four African teachers left Freetown on their momentous mission—the first effective outreach from the base at Sierra Leone, so long and patiently developed, to a field a thousand miles away and a hundred miles inland. Looked at on a map of Africa to-day the penetration appears slight, but at that period, in relation to a slavery-infected coast and to the intermittent ferment of internal wars, it was indeed a heroic adventure.[2] The Society's estimate of its importance is worthy of notice: "The Committee regard this hiving-off of the Liberated Africans from Sierra Leone to the countries whence they have been 'carried away captive' as full of promise for Africa. They regard it, also, as proving the important bearing of the Colony

---

[1] *Report of the Wesleyan Methodist Missionary Society* (1855), 60–1; *Wesleyan Missionary Notices* (1855), 168–70.
[2] *Proceedings of the C.M.S.* (1844), 35–6, 39; C. H. V. Gollmer, *C. A. Gollmer* (1889), 3–14.

of Sierra Leone on the evangelization and civilization of that desolated and deeply injured country. The formation in the interior of Africa, of communities of Natives from Sierra Leone—already benefited more or less by Christian instruction and education—sensible of the advantages which they have thus acquired—carried forward in the paths of truth and righteousness by competent Native Teachers, themselves superintended and directed by a European Missionary—presents a prospect of good to Africa of deep interest and animating anticipation."[1]

(2) *Establishment in Yorubaland*

The mission party arrived at Badagry in January 1845, but did not reach Abeokuta until August 1846. Within eight days of landing they had learned that the friendly Shodeke was dead, and hot on the heels of this came the news that the king of Dahomey had seized the Egbas' fortified post on the road to Badagry and thus closed communications with the interior. Happily an African teacher of character and ability, Andrew Wilhelm of Sierra Leone, had been left in Abeokuta to represent the Society. When eventually the advance was made Townsend and Crowther went forward and Gollmer remained in charge at Badagry. Here the Wesleyan Society already had its representative, settled there by Freeman, and had decided as early as 1844 to transfer to Abeokuta Samuel Annear, a European missionary in Sierra Leone personally known to many of the emigrants. Actually he succeeded De Graft at Badagry and paid a visit only to Abeokuta before the road was closed. Wesleyan entry was thus deferred until 1848 when an African teacher was placed there. The more vigorous and sustained work in the Egba city was therefore that of the Church Missionary Society under the joint leadership of Townsend and Crowther.[2]

When conditions had quietened down after the high enthusiasm of their first welcome, the situation in which the missionary party found themselves was seen to be anything but easy. It was indeed dangerous in many ways for much of the

[1] *Proceedings of the C.M.S.* (1844), 40. This estimate from the pen of Henry Venn witnesses to his statesman-like vision. It is interesting to note that at a later date the missionaries at Sierra Leone were of one mind in judging liberated Africans to be the most receptive of Christian teaching in the community, and the second generation among them to be "a salt among our people—the leaven of our churches".—*Proceedings of the C.M.S.* (1848), lxii.

[2] *Report of the Wesleyan Methodist Missionary Society* (1844), 80–3; (1845), 78; (1846), 94–5; (1848), 96–103. In 1856 the African Agent, Edward Bickersteth of Sierra Leone, reported a Wesleyan membership at Abeokuta of 174.—*Ibid.* (1856), 70–2.

succeeding decade, a situation in which great courage and much wisdom were demanded and, happily for the Christian cause, were possessed by the devoted pioneers. Chiefs and people were by no means all of one mind on critical questions and cross-currents of opinion demanded careful navigation, for here was no British political control, as in Sierra Leone, but a fully African authority in command. The solid success of the missionaries' achievement will be best appreciated against an analysis of this situation.

There were definite assets to the enterprise. Perhaps the most significant of these was the firm trust in the goodwill of Britain generated by the return flow of the liberated Yorubas from Sierra Leone. Their return, as if from the dead, and their testimony to British concern for their welfare were hard facts not to be gainsaid. When relations who had never hoped to meet again were restored to one another the deepest emotions were aroused, not only among those immediately concerned, but also in the sensitive community. The experience of Samuel Crowther and his mother and sisters in their reunion after twenty-five years was typical of many more.[1] The exceptional opportunity such a situation offered for presenting the Christian gospel was expressed by Townsend: "God has given us means of gaining access to the hearts of this people, such as were never possessed by any Missionaries before; if we are only alive to the opportunities presented to us of making known the CAUSE of British humanity—Christianity."[2]

Associated with this confidence in British goodwill was the endorsement of the mission by naval commanders who were respected as the active agents in liberation. There was an atti-

---

[1] J. Page, *The Black Bishop* (1908), 95–6.

[2] *Proceedings of the C.M.S.* (1847), 41. A couple of examples will illustrate the disinterested care, shown in the highest quarters, which secured wide publicity among Africans. The son of an Abeokuta chief had been sent to the Grammar School at Sierra Leone. One day he heard by accident that his brother was in the West India Regiment there. The brother had been kidnapped after his own departure, sold to the Portuguese, captured by a cruiser and liberated. The terms of release from the regiment were a payment of £12 and the sanction of the Commander-in-Chief, the Duke of Wellington. African friends subscribed the sum and the commanding officer transmitted the application; "by the very next mail an order was sent out to give the young recruit his discharge without payment, if the Church Missionary Society would agree to receive him into the Grammar School and afterward to send him home to his father."—*Ibid.* (1850), lxvii.

In the war with Dahomey of 1851 a Christian convert had been taken prisoner, sold into slavery and carried to Cuba. Action initiated by Lord Clarendon, the Foreign Secretary, through the British Consul at Havana, eventually secured his release and restoration to his family and friends, to the utter amazement of the African community.—*Ibid.* (1858), 54–5.

tude of genuine regard in the British squadron for the missionaries and their work. Officers and men alike, in their detestation
of the slave-trade and concern for African welfare, shared with
them a certain community of purpose, and regarded their own
work as clearing the ground of evil that the positive contribution of the Christian mission might be made. When circumstances arose leading to treaty-making by the Commodore with
local rulers, security for the work of the missionaries was included. How close the understanding could be is seen in the
case of Dr. Irving, R.N., who on his own initiative was seconded
by the Admiralty to serve the Yoruba Mission. He was appointed public relations officer, as well as medical supervisor,
and took up his duties with enthusiasm. His service to the
mission, however, was short-lived.[1]

A favourable feature internally was the recognition by the
Abeokuta elders of religious liberty. Persecution there was of
Christian converts, and often enough it was severe, but this was
at the domestic level. Moreover, the decision of the elders, when
appeal was lodged with them, gave effective protection. Thus
Crowther recorded a case where a man was arraigned for refusing to worship the god Ifa: "The elders, however, decided
he was at liberty to do as he pleased about his religion."[2] Then
there was often enough the desire of a chief for the prestige
brought by the residence of a white man in his town. This
might lead to admission and permission to teach when there
was little sympathy with the missionary's purpose. Thus at
Ijaye, a Yoruba town of some 40,000 population which Townsend first visited in 1852, the chief invited a missionary to enter,
but would only intervene if the white man himself was threatened with molestation.[3] But there were chiefs of liberal outlook
also to be found who did appreciate the missionary purpose and
whose welcome was sincere. When Crowther visited Ketu, a
town of some 20,000 to the west of Abeokuta, he found a chief
opposed to slavery who would not permit a slave-market in his

[1] *Proceedings of the C.M.S.* (1854), 38–40; (1855), 42. He had served nine years in
the naval squadron on the coast, but had given little more than a year of mission
service when he died. He had been accredited to his new post by both the Foreign
Secretary and the First Lord of the Admiralty, commending him to consuls and
naval commanders.

[2] *Proceedings of the C.M.S.* (1848), lxv; cf. *Ibid.* (1855), 47–8; (1856), 45–6. Later,
at Ibadan (e.g.) where the authority of the chiefs was not so decided, domestic
persecution was less subject to restraint.—*Ibid.* (1856), 47–8.

[3] *Ibid.* (1855), 54–5; (1857), 47. This motive of prestige was double-edged, for
when the missionary contemplated extension to new areas the reluctance of the
chief to share his own advantage might prove an awkward obstacle.

domain. He told Crowther he would welcome and protect forty missionaries if they would come![1]

If these were some of the assets—and wasting assets to some extent, as the early glow of gratitude passed away and the Christian demand began to prove somewhat irksome—what of the disabilities? These were serious. First and foremost came the resentment and active opposition of the slave-traders, including slave-trading chiefs on the coast and in Abeokuta itself. They pursued a high strategy: to crush the infant mission by a combined threat to Badagry from Lagos on the east and from Porto Novo on the west (both active slave-trading centres), thus isolating and eventually eliminating the Christian movement at Abeokuta. In the total situation the attempt was ill-conceived and doomed to failure, but not before it had caused deep anxiety.[2]

The hostility of those devoted to their pagan faith was an obstacle to be expected. It naturally found expression as converts began to appear, with consequences in the family (the extended family of African society) and affecting the priesthood, which provoked attack. The pantheon of the Yoruba peoples included a Supreme Being, Olorun, with a large number of subordinate deities or *orishas*. Two of these figure particularly in the missionaries' reports: Ifa, the great oracle of the Yoruba country, and Shango, the god of lightning.[3] On the domestic side the disruption caused by a nonconforming member, coupled with fear of the consequences of such neglect, stirred up considerable opposition. The priesthood was confessedly moved by professional self-interest but was not on that account necessarily insincere. Indeed, Townsend reported: "The great oracle that is to them as a Bible, has been consulted again and again about us, and has, I am told, never been induced to utter a word against us." On the contrary, it had said that the white people must be permitted to teach.[4]

[1] *Proceedings of the C.M.S.* (1853), 50.

[2] *Ibid.* (1851), xciii–iv; (1852), 46. In 1851 Consul Beecroft intervened with good effect, strengthening the hands of the well-disposed chiefs and enheartening the Christian workers.

[3] For some account of these, see: O. Johnson, *History of the Yorubas* (1921), 32–6; S. S. Farrow, *Faith, Fancies and Fetich* (1926), 35–41, 47–51; G. Parrinder, *West African Religion* (1949), 41–3, 152–6; *Religion in an African City* (1953), 17–21, 31–6. Ifa is sometimes referred to as the god of palm-nuts, as these later replaced the pebbles said to have been used at first in divination.

[4] In a letter of August 27, 1850.—*Proceedings of C.M.S.* (1851), c–ci. After saying that it was the undisguised work of the priests to stir up and carry on the persecution, Townsend comments: "It is in the power of the priest to falsify, but he does not, although unquestionably it would be to his interest to do so." An ingenious argument was later put forward that the white men should recognize Ifa since it had approved of them; was it not therefore true?

In the political field the external relations of Abeokuta were uneasy. Dahomey on the west was a declared enemy, and open war was not long delayed. To the south the situation at Lagos, as a leading export centre of the slave-trade, reacted on affairs in the interior and intimately concerned the fate of Badagry. The constant alarms and occasional actual explosions were severe handicaps to the Christian undertaking. Both situations, continually simmering, eventually boiled over with threat of immediate danger but promise of eventual advantage.

Throughout the early years there was the burden, not peculiar to the Yoruba Mission, of maintaining an effective staff, despite the inroads of malaria in particular. The rate of invaliding was high and mortality was severe. Thus in 1853 seven European recruits joined the mission. Within the year three had died, including a doctor, and a fourth been invalided.[1] Happily for the work there was a nucleus of stalwarts who were spared to give many years of continuous service—Townsend, Gollmer and the Hinderers are outstanding names—together with the invaluable Samuel Crowther and others from Sierra Leone.

Some reference must be made to the ordeal of war as it affected the work. With the passing of 1850 stirring events were afoot. A state of war had long existed between Gezo of Dahomey and the Egbas of Abeokuta.[2] It was an inflammatory episode of it that had delayed the missionary entry. Gezo's intention to launch a full-scale attack upon Abeokuta becoming known, Consul Beecroft and Commander Forbes, R.N., jointly visited Dahomey to counsel restraint but in vain. The Commodore thereupon warned Gezo that he would be held responsible for British subjects, whether European or African, and at the same time he sent naval protection to Badagry and an offer to the missionaries in Abeokuta, either to remove them or to supply them with arms. They acknowledged his kind concern but declined both offers. At last in March 1851 the blow fell. The aggressors had been robbed of the advantage of surprise, but advanced in massed formations with all the confidence inspired by their past victories and the renown of their chief, Gezo, the "Leopard" of Dahomey. The missionaries reported the numbers of "well-trained warriors, male and female, at from 11,000 to 16,000, well armed with muskets". They were, however, re-

---

[1] *Proceedings of the C.M.S.* (1854), 34. The first European death on the field was that of J. C. Müller in 1850, who had already served in Sierra Leone. In the early years the Europeans were seasoned workers from Sierra Leone; the mortality rate rose with recruits appointed to Yorubaland direct.

[2] O. Johnson, *op. cit.*, 296–7.

pelled with heavy loss—3,000 casualties, the missionaries estimated, against some 200 to 300 on the Egba side. A thousand prisoners were taken, and here the missionaries intervened and secured an exchange with Dahomey. "This disposal of the prisoners", it was claimed, "was in itself a signal triumph of Christian principles, as hitherto they had always been regarded as the private property and slaves of those who happened to be their captors." Further, the victory was ascribed by all to the presence of the Christians with them, and the help of the Christians' God. All persecution came to an end, and the leading chiefs sent their children to the schools. Whatever the eventual embarrassment of interpreting military victory as a mark of divine favour, the immediate opportunity was a real one.[1]

Soon after these events Samuel Crowther was called to England for consultation. On his arrival in London in August 1851 he was received by Palmerston at his home as the spokesman of the liberated Africans then resident in Abeokuta, estimated at some 3,000, in whose welfare the Foreign Secretary expressed the lively interest of the British Government.[2]

The enemy on the west had been routed but the peril of war was not past. Lagos was a nest of slave-traders, whose hostility to the mission was implacable. Kosoko, a nephew of Akitoye the ruling chief who had been legally installed, had usurped the chieftainship in 1845 and driven his uncle into exile. Kosoko was devoted to the slave-trade and in consequence resented the presence of the British, whether naval forces restraining the trade or missionaries weaning the chiefs in Abeokuta from participating in it.[3] Akitoye, the lawful ruler, was resident in Badagry and was still recognized by the Abeokuta chiefs. After the failure of the Dahomian aggression which Kosoko had abetted, he became more menacing towards Badagry. The attempt of his agents to seize its people for the slave-market led to the destruction of the place by fire, save for some trading stores and the premises of both the Church and Wesleyan Societies.[4] Akitoye petitioned the naval commander for support and a

---

[1] Proceedings of the C.M.S. (1851), xcv–vi; (1852), 47–8, 50; O. Johnson, op. cit., 313–16; A. C. Burns, History of Nigeria, 125.

[2] Proceedings of the C.M.S. (1852), 45–6, where Palmerston's letter of 18.12.51 to Crowther on his departure is printed.

[3] As evidence of the restraining effect of the naval patrol, it is interesting to note that when, with the onset of the Crimean War in 1854, the naval forces on the coast were reduced, a revival of the trade immediately took place.—Proceedings of the C.M.S. (1858), 43–4.

[4] Proceedings of the C.M.S. (1852), 50–1.

message from Abeokuta proposed that Queen Victoria should take possession of Lagos in order to bring the country peace.[1] The next phase was Consul Beecroft's attempt, acting on instructions from Palmerston, to conclude an agreement with Kosoko for the abolition of the slave-trade. A first visit proved fruitless. A second, under escort with flag of truce, drew the fire of Kosoko's well-equipped garrison. The die had been cast. The succeeding naval operations were difficult and not pursued without loss. By the end of December 1851 Kosoko had fled, and Akitoye returned to the vacant throne.[2] The victory was momentous. At a single stroke a great export centre of the slave-trade was shut down, Dahomey was deprived of its most powerful ally and Abeokuta given a security it had not before enjoyed. The Commodore immediately negotiated a treaty with the reinstated Akitoye and the chiefs of Lagos in which the missionaries and their work were explicitly safeguarded. The eighth article of the treaty read in part: "Complete protection shall be afforded to Missionaries or Ministers of the Gospel, of whatever nation or country, following their vocation of spreading the knowledge and doctrines of Christianity, and extending the benefits of civilization . . . nor shall any subject of the King and Chiefs of Lagos who may embrace the Christian faith be, on that account, or on account of the teaching or exercise thereof, molested or troubled in any manner whatsoever."[3]

Lagos, the natural base for advance into the Yoruba country —water transport by the River Ogun linked it up with Abeokuta, for example—had hitherto been denied to the missionaries. The naval officers now urged their immediate entry. Akitoye was still a pagan, but Muslim influence was active in Lagos and the king's adoption of that faith seemed a possible

---

[1] A. C. Burns, *op. cit.*, 125–9, where both letters are given in full. Some three years earlier, in 1848, the Abeokuta chiefs had petitioned Queen Victoria to open for them the road to Lagos for lawful commerce. The Queen's reply by Lord Chichester, the President of the C.M.S., contained the well-known reference to England's greatness and Christianity, and was accompanied by two Bibles in English and Arabic respectively.—Stock, *The History of the Church Missionary Society* (1899), II, 104–5, where the two letters are quoted.

[2] A. C. Burns, *op. cit.*, 129–33. In addition to firearms Kosoko's armament included over fifty canon well placed for defence.

[3] A. C. Burns, *op. cit.*, Appendix C, where the full text of the treaty is given. Other articles prohibited the slave-trade and explicitly forbade human sacrifice "on account of religious or other ceremonies", and also the killing of prisoners of war. In communicating this information to the missionaries Commodore H. W. Bruce concluded: "I am not without hope that the measures I have carried out may be the means, under God's blessing, of contributing in some degree to the success of the most important undertaking which devolves upon you."—*Proceedings of the C.M.S.* (1852), 51–2.

development. Badagry as a base had now lost its usefulness and had always proved stony soil. It was therefore an early decision of the Church Missionary Society to remove its staff to Lagos and initiate a mission there. C. A. Gollmer, who was its leader, and his wife soon had their courage tested to the full. In 1853 Kosoko, with some 1,500 armed men, staged a fierce attack upon the place; he was foiled by parties landed from the men-of-war, but not before alarm and confusion had overspread the town. Gollmer received a personal letter from the Commodore for the "perfect devotion" and "no small degree of moral courage" he had exhibited. A few weeks later Akitoye died and was succeeded by his son Dosumu. Kosoko was still at large and life in Lagos was subject to constant alarms. It was 1861 before the inevitable step of annexation was taken as indispensable to the complete suppression of the slave-trade.[1]

Such, then, were some of the conditions under which the Yoruba Mission passed its first decade. Yet the work went forward, though with greater encouragement in the interior than in such sophisticated coast centres as Badagry and Lagos.[2] The first Christian baptisms in Abeokuta took place on Sunday, February 6, 1848 before a congregation of some 250 people. Two men and three women, of whom Samuel Crowther's aged mother was one, were received into the fellowship of the Christian Church. One of the men was first brought to desire Christian instruction by Andrew Wilhelm, the African catechist who laboured alone while the missionaries were detained in Badagry. This man, Bankole (i.e. the builder of a house or family), was therefore the first to embrace the faith in Abeokuta. Christian names were bestowed, the African names becoming surnames.[3] Thereafter a steady stream of inquirers came under instruction in Yorubaland until the fifty-two communicant members of 1847 (including Sierra Leone repatriates) had become 827 ten years later. Towards the end of the decade Townsend wrote frankly of their quality: "I believe our converts sincerely give up all worship of false gods. It is seldom we detect anyone

[1] A. C. Burns, op. cit., 134–38; Proceedings of the C.M.S. (1854), 36–7. The Home Government expressed its reluctance "to extend the number of British Dependencies on the African coast", but found no other course open in pursuit of its declared policy to wipe out the slave-trade.

[2] When Crowther was removed from Abeokuta to Lagos he found the people there "by the infusion of nominal Christians, more degraded and profane, and more hardened against the gospel of Christ, than the native inhabitants of the interior towns".—Proceedings of the C.M.S. (1856), 42.

[3] Proceedings of the C.M.S. (1849), lxxii–iv. Samuel Crowther appropriately chose "Hannah" for his mother.

in idolatry, except under great fear of man; but Christian morals are more frequently violated. But, sad to say, in several instances of immorality that have called for dismissal from the Church, Sierra Leone people have had a hand in teaching them to think lightly of their sin, before or after the fact."[1]

An event of commanding importance on the pastoral as well as the organizational side of the life of the Church was the appointment in 1852 of a Bishop of Sierra Leone. This in itself was evidence of the development of the Society's work at this point, but the diocese was not limited to the Colony, for the Yoruba Mission in view of its origin naturally fell within the bishop's jurisdiction.[2] O. E. Vidal, who was consecrated the first bishop, was a gifted linguist but had never served overseas.[3] In Sierra Leone he held confirmations for some 3,000 already admitted communicants, and in due course proceeded to Lagos and Abeokuta for the same purpose, when some 500 to 600 converts received the rite. It was on this visit in 1854 that the first two Africans to be ordained in Yorubaland were admitted to deacon's orders. But it was the bishop's last service to his diocese. He died at sea on the return voyage to Sierra Leone.[4] His successor, J. W. Weeks, had already given twenty years to the Colony as lay evangelist and clergyman and had retired from the field in 1844. In 1855 he was consecrated and, like his predecessor, after confirmations and ordinations in Sierra Leone, sailed for Lagos and Abeokuta. Here three Africans were admitted to holy orders and important disciplinary regulations adopted.[5] On his return in March 1857 he, too, was taken ill at sea, and only reached Sierra Leone to die.[6] A heavy price was

[1] *Proceedings of the C.M.S.* (1854), 40–1.

[2] *Ibid.* (1853), 24–5. Associated with this step were others in Sierra Leone in the direction of self-government and self-support. In 1854 (e.g.) the elementary schools were transferred to local management, with a diminishing grant looking to complete self-support in five years.—*Ibid.* (1855), 36–7. In 1856 the first African ordinands, six in number, who had been wholly trained within the Colony, were ordained by the Bishop, thus marking in the fullest sense the beginning of an indigenous ministry.—*Ibid*, (1857), 21–2.

[3] He had studied Tamil to correspond with converts in South India, had prepared a Malay grammar for the Borneo Mission (later under the S.P.G.), had helped Crowther with his Yoruba publications, and corresponded with J. L. Krapf about the languages of East Africa.—Stock, *History of the Church Missionary Society* (1898), II, 121.

[4] *Ibid.*, II, 122; *Proceedings of the C.M.S.* (1855), 28–9, 42–3, 45–6.

[5] These concerned domestic slavery and polygamy. No Christian was to buy or sell a slave, and those owned before conversion were to have facilities for buying their freedom and meanwhile to receive Christian instruction. A polygamist might become a catechumen but should not be baptized, though the wives of polygamists might be admitted.—*Proceedings of the C.M.S.* (1858), 46.

[6] Stock, *op. cit.*, II, 122–3; *Proceedings of the C.M.S.* (1857), 32.

being paid for episcopal direction of the far-flung diocese. Third
in the succession came John Bowen, who had served in the Near
East and was equipped with a knowledge of Arabic. The fact
that the appointment was marked as one of danger did not
deter him: "Were I offered a bishopric in England, I might feel
at liberty to decline it; one in Sierra Leone I must accept." He
was consecrated in September 1857. Within two years he also
had died, but not before he had rendered episcopal service to
the Yoruba Mission, and even reached the Delta of the Niger.[1]

The policy of the Yoruba Mission was a comprehensive one.
Evangelism was a first priority, but not to the exclusion of welfare projects designed to improve the life of the people by
stimulating a healthy external trade and sharing with them
improved methods and techniques. Even during the first period
of waiting at Badagry, Samuel Crowther sought to encourage
agriculture. He successfully had forest land cleared and cultivated, introduced the plough, and instituted prizes for the best
farms. A steel corn-mill with which T. F. Buxton had provided
him proved so popular that he had to ration its public use.[2]

At Abeokuta the missionaries used their influence to encourage trade in the products of the country, and once Lagos was
taken and the River Ogun opened to lawful commerce, traffic
began to flow.[3] A few years later Samuel Crowther received
striking testimony to the success of the policy. He was visiting
the Ijebu clan of the Yorubas:[4] "Their head chiefs could not
help confessing to me, that they, aged persons, never remembered any time of the slave-trade that so much wealth was
brought to their country as has been since the commencement
of the palm-oil trade the last four years; that they were perfectly satisfied with legitimate trade, and with the proceedings
of the British Government."[5] But the Mission was not content
with the success of the palm-oil trade. They wished to enlarge
the resources of the country, and they encouraged the growing

---

[1] Stock, *op. cit.*, II, 123; *Proceedings of the C.M.S.* (1858), 34–5; *Memorials of John Bowen, LL.D., Late Bishop of Sierra Leone* (1862), 587–99.

[2] *The Friend of the Africans*, III (1845), 7, 9–10; *Proceedings of the C.M.S.* (1847), 36–7.

[3] C. A. Gollmer reported from Lagos, January 3, 1855: "Two years ago there was not a puncheon of palm-oil from Abbeokuta sold at Lagos. The last flotilla brought upwards of 300 puncheons . . . also beniseed, ivory, gum and spice . . . and seven bales of clean cotton sent by Mr. Crowther to England."—*Proceedings of the C.M.S.* (1855), 46.

[4] The Yoruba people, numbering to-day some four million, were divided into a number of clans, of which the most important were the Oyos, Egbas, Ifes and Ijebus.

[5] *Proceedings of the C.M.S.* (1857), 38.

of cotton and its preparation for export. The Egba chiefs began to turn their attention to this, and were assisted in their handling of the crop by an industrial institution established by the mission. Here the pupils were instructed in the cleaning and packing of cotton and in the repair of machinery. The capital cost of this centre was met from private sources.[1] Thus the positive policy advocated by T. F. Buxton was being implemented at last. It had been a slower and more painful process than was envisaged in terms of the Niger Expedition, but it was in a measure a definite realization of that earlier hope, and a realization of it in a densely populated region that had supplied the last great slave emporium of the coast. It was natural that the education policy of the mission should be influenced by these considerations. When a central training institution was established in 1856, agriculture, carpentry and printing were included in the curriculum.[2]

Meanwhile Abeokuta had become the centre of a series of stations as town after town in Yorubaland was entered. Henry Venn, whose interest in West Africa was exceptionally keen,[3] wrote in 1852 of the opportunity Yorubaland presented: "It is a vast field now unfolding before us, and we would have the Christian Church awake to the new responsibilities imposed upon it by the almost boundless facilities presented by the Yoruba Mission. It is no sparse or scanty population that occupies the region skirted by the Bight of Benin. Populous towns, not inferior in size to Abbeokuta itself . . . almost remind us of the crowds that have congregated in the valley of the lower Ganges. . . . If you travel a day and a half to the north-eastward you arrive at Ibadan, with a population reported at 60,000. Two days more would bring you to Ogbomosho, an old town which has never been captured, numbering at least 45,000 inhabitants. A journey of two days northward from the same centre conducts to Ijaye, a town said to contain 40,000 souls; while

---

[1] Thomas Clegg of Manchester, whose concern was to make legitimate trade more profitable to Africans themselves than the slave-trade, was the principal donor. He soon reported receiving 150,000 lb. of clean cotton which sold well, and also the supply of some 150 cotton gins to the African planters. The African superintendent of the Institution had been trained for the work in England.—*Proceedings of the C.M.S.* (1858), 58. In 1859, Crowther reported the arrival of four Manchester merchants in Abeokuta, prepared to buy as much cotton as the African farmers could produce.—S. Crowther, *The Gospel on the Banks of the Niger* (1859), 444. Henry Venn was the active promoter of the policy. Cf. Stock, *op. cit.*, II, 109–10.

[2] *Proceedings of the C.M.S.* (1857), 40–1. A dozen years later General Armstrong, the founder of the famous Hampton Institute, Virginia, was the pioneer of a similar policy for the American Negro.—F. G. Peabody, *Education for Life* (1918), *passim.*

[3] "His heart was there in a peculiar sense," says Stock, *op. cit.*, II, 100.

three days' journey in the same direction reaches Isehin, whose 70,000 inhabitants have hitherto successfully withstood the assaults of slave-dealing chiefs. . . . A point further to the west lies Igboho . . . a smaller town in that direction, Ketu . . . is estimated at 20,000. To the north-east again lies Ilorin . . . said to contain from 60,000 to 70,000 souls. . . . At the same distance, but more eastward, is the large and famous town of Ife, from whence all the idols in this part of the country are said to emanate. . . . Again, south-eastward of Abbeokuta . . . runs the territory of the Ijebus, whose numbers are said to amount to 160,000."[1] Small wonder that the heart of the missionary statesman was thrilled with an opportunity so unparalleled in West African experience. Venn was indefatigable in his efforts to secure for the work as full a measure of support as his influence could command. The result was a steady advance that can only be chronicled here in barest outline. In 1851 Ibadan had been visited by David Hinderer, thanks to the good offices of the Abeokuta chiefs. In 1853 the work began when David and Anna Hinderer settled in Ibadan where they were to give seventeen years' memorable service.[2] Following on Hinderer's visit to Ibadan in 1851 came an invitation from the Oni of Ife that missionaries might come to teach him "the new way of happiness". It was flattering, to say the least, to receive such an invitation from the acknowledged religious head of the Yoruba nation, but we do not read of an early entry.[3] Ijaye was next occupied; in 1853, the year of the Hinderers' settlement in Ibadan, A. C. Mann, a Württemberger, also from Basel, began the work there.[4] Of more than ordinary importance was Oyo, the political headquarters of the Yoruba people, whose ruler, the Alafin, retained the prestige if now only vested with a semblance of the power once enjoyed by his predecessors. Townsend, on a notable tour in 1853, first visited Oyo and met the king of all the Yorubas, but it was not until 1856 that a teacher was placed there.[5] Oyo was an outpost but not a terminus; it

---

[1] *Proceedings of the C.M.S.* (1852), 57–8.

[2] *Proceedings of the C.M.S.* (1852), 56; (1854), 47; *Seventeen Years in the Yoruba Country: Memorials of Anna Hinderer* (1872), *passim*. David Hinderer was another of the Basel men who so ably served the Society.

[3] *Proceedings of the C.M.S.* (1852), 56–7. "There can be little doubt that Ife was the first settlement of the Yorubas in their present country. Ife remains to this day the spiritual headquarters of the race."—Burns, *op. cit.*, 32.

[4] *Proceedings of the C.M.S.* (1853), 48; (1854), 49.

[5] *Proceedings of the C.M.S.* (1854), 46; (1857), 45. On the former power of the Alafin of Oyo, and his later fallen fortunes, see Burns, *op. cit.*, 33–7. It is even suggested that at one time his authority extended from Accra to Benin.

was the policy to advance as far as resources and opportunity might permit. In pursuance of this A. C. Mann undertook a journey to the north-east of Oyo in 1855. He first visited Ogbomosho where he secured a site for the mission, and then pushed on to the frontier of Hausaland at Ilorin, only some sixty miles from the River Niger itself. The rulers were Muslim and the Christian missionary for the first time on his travels was received as an inferior.[1] He was received, it is true, with all courtesy—when it was known he had lost his horse in a river, another was at once sent out to him—but when granted an audience the experience was somewhat intimidating: "At the first view of the new scene I felt something like fear coming upon me. I saw I had entered upon a new field; the keen eyes of the alufas plainly telling me of their contempt of the heathen from whom I came, as well as of the annasaãra, among whom they counted me; then the cries of the crowd in praise of God and Mahommed, taken from the first and third Sura of the Koran; others contemptuously crying—'Annasaãram', i.e. 'Nazarenes'." The Emir, however, was friendly and granted several interviews. He asked questions about England and Constantinople, and even accepted the gift of an Arabic Bible. The permission requested for a missionary to reside in Ilorin was not given, on the ground of personal risk, but there would be no objection to occasional visits of even two to three months' duration.[2] The position of the emirate, abutting on Yorubaland, laid it open to such influences as these from the south which were in the nature of the case denied to the more remote.[3] Mann recorded in his journal that he met at Ilorin various people from the north: people of Timbuktu who reminded him of Mandingoes met in Sierra Leone;[4] a messenger from Sokoto, sent with a demand from the suzerain for 200 slaves; traders from Tunis who spoke of the peoples of Mediterranean lands.[5]

News travels fast and far in Africa, and the solid achievement of the Christian pioneers in Abeokuta, with the deep satisfac-

[1] Ilorin had been added to the Fulani empire some thirty-five years before.—C. K. Meek, *Northern Nigeria* (1925), I, 101. It was therefore tributary to the Sultan of Sokoto.—See Vol. I, p. 307.

[2] *Proceedings of the C.M.S.* (1856), 51–2.

[3] Cf. M. Perham, *Native Administration in Nigeria* (1937), 142.

[4] "They told me last rainy season a white man stayed in their town. This 'last' would be the year 1854, as they had spent several months on the journey down."—*Proceedings of the C.M.S.* (1856), 52. This must have been the distinguished traveller Henry Barth, who was in Timbuktu from September 7, 1853, to April 19, 1854.—H. Barth, *Travels and Discoveries in North and Central Africa* (1857), chaps. 65–73.

[5] "They mentioned the names of Frenci, Napolitani, Inglisi, and Malta, distinctly."—*Proceedings of the C.M.S.* (1856), 52.

tion at the presence of the missionaries experienced by chiefs and people, had eased the way for these extensions of the work. The nature of the reputation the missionaries had won can best be given in the words of the Alake and his chiefs. In 1855 when Townsend and Gollmer were on furlough a petition was drawn up by Lagos traders to prevent their return. This drew a counterblast from the Alake of Abeokuta. In the course of a remarkable and lengthy letter, he said: "Now, although I myself am still a heathen, yet I am not blind to facts. The first is, that the present state of Abeokuta is not what it was ten years ago, for instead of war there is peace. The second is, that Christianity is a really powerful religion, for its effects upon the minds of my people are so well marked that we all admire it. And thirdly, that the Oyibos [missionaries], although a small and weak body, observing them outwardly, yet they are stronger than any of my mighty men in the country. One instance of this will suffice. In the case of the Adu war . . . who were those that pitched their tents of conciliation in a most dangerous spot, between the camps of two savage and hostile people? They were the two missionaries, Messrs. Townsend and Crowther. In a few days after, to my great astonishment, these Oyibos actually brought the warriors home.[1] . . . One last point . . . the liberty we now enjoy. Within six years back the roads to Ijaye, Ibadan, Ketu, and Jebu were very dangerous; a caravan of fifty could not pass them with safety. Kidnappers made these roads their homes, and the chiefs and rulers of these several towns countenanced the actions of these men-stealers. But observe the contrast. At present, a single female could travel three days' journey without any fear of danger, for where there is no danger there is also no cause for fear. Little boys and girls can go eight, nine, ten miles beyond the walls of Abeokuta safely, no one daring to touch them. Is this not really a cause of much thanks to you for sending us such men? . . . It is their peace we now enjoy. The absence of these missionaries, therefore, from us has made us chilly. We pray you to send them us again, and many others like them."[2] At the end of this same year a compact was entered into by the chiefs of the great Yoruba towns to give up the prac-

[1] An account of this notable success of the missionaries as peacemakers, where others had tried their hand and failed, will be found in *Proceedings of the C.M.S.* (1854), 43-4.
[2] *Proceedings of the C.M.S.* (1856), 41-2; Gollmer, *Charles Andrew Gollmer*, 111-15, where the full text is given. The letter was dictated in Yoruba and translated by one of the Sierra Leone teachers for transmission to London, unbeknown to the one European missionary left at Abeokuta.

tice of kidnapping one another's people and encourage friendly relations among themselves. There was immediate evidence of their goodwill in the return by Ibadan to Abeokuta of prisoners taken by a party who had set out before the agreement was reached. As Henry Venn remarked, the possibility of the compact was "chiefly owing to the presence of the Missionaries and to their influence over the minds of the leading chiefs".[1]

Deeply gratifying as the progress of the Yoruba Mission had been—*Sunrise within the Tropics* was Miss Tucker's title for the account of its early years[2]—it was but one phase of a larger enterprise: that of reaching interior Africa with the Christian message. This was never lost sight of, either by the directors at the home base or by workers in the front line. But before pursuing this development note must be taken of the coming of American partners beyond the boundaries of Liberia.

(3) *Enterprise from North America*

The interest of Christian circles in the United States in the efforts to enter the interior of Africa from the west was at first somewhat diffused. Their own missionary activities in this region had so far been confined to the American Negro colonies in Liberia—in 1847 these colonies were declared independent and granted a constitution—together with the neighbouring African tribes in the coastal belt. But an interest in wider fields now began to crystallize in new undertakings. T. F. Buxton, in expressing the hope that the missionary advance in the west would be a fully representative one, had welcomed the suggestion of American help in the enterprise.[3] In particular there were three ventures in this period which fall to be noticed here. They were independent of one another and widely different in the particular occasions that called them forth.

The first relates to Mendeland, adjoining the Colony of Sierra Leone as it then was. In July 1839 a slave cargo from the West

[1] *Proceedings of the C.M.S.* (1856), 40–1. The compact was real enough when it was made, but the goodwill on which it rested was not equal to the strain of economic ambition. The Ibadans desired a direct trade-route to Lagos and this the Egbas denied them. Within a decade there was war.—C. A. Burns, *op. cit.*, 142–3.

[2] *Abbeokuta; or Sunrise within the Tropics: an outline of the origin and progress of the Yoruba Mission*, by Miss Tucker (1853).

[3] He quotes from the published letter of an American correspondent to the effect that the people of the States were prepared to share in the welfare activities that were afoot, and that a party might even "follow the course of the newly-opened Niger". This was written, of course, before the Expedition of 1841 with its daunting outcome.—*The Slave Trade and its Remedy*, 515–16 n.

Coast reached Cuba, where two Spanish traders purchased it and transferred the slaves to the schooner *Amistad*. A report on the ensuing voyage, that they were to be eaten on landing, stirred the slaves to revolt under an able chief, one of their number. They secreted weapons and secured possession of the vessel, killing captain and crew in doing so, but sparing the Spaniards. These, pretending to navigate the ship towards Sierra Leone as the Africans demanded, actually brought it to the New England coast where it was seized by a U.S. naval patrol. The forty Africans aboard were reported by the Spaniards, and were thereupon committed to prison at New Haven, and charged with murderous conspiracy on the high seas. News that they had mutinied to recover their liberty soon spread, and generous-hearted men formed a committee and received subscriptions to defend the accused Africans. Thanks to the interest of Professor Gibbs of Yale, an able Mende interpreter was secured.[1] In the U.S. District Court of Connecticut the Africans won their case, but the Spaniards forthwith lodged an appeal to the United States Supreme Court in Washington. Here the Africans were ably defended, their leading counsel being none other than John Quincy Adams.[2] The verdict of the lower court was upheld, and the Africans were finally declared free men and discharged. During the considerable interval between the trials (the Supreme Court decision was given in 1841), the men had been under Christian instruction. As a result, they asked to be sent home to Mendeland with their teachers. The *Amistad* Committee had funds available, and it was decided to start a mission. In November 1841 the returning Africans and the outgoing missionaries—James Steele and William Raymond and his wife, both ordained men—were bidden God-speed in the old Broadway Tabernacle, the New York equivalent of London's Exeter Hall. The party reached Sierra Leone on January 15, 1842. The upper Mende country which they had hoped to reach proving inaccessible, they settled some 100 miles south-east of Freetown at Kor-Mende, east of Sherbro Island. As certain of the repatriated Africans hailed from Sherbro, a site of some 400 acres was secured at Bonthe on that island, and a second station opened.

---

[1] Professor Gibbs used the following ingenious method: he laid down coins before the Africans and counted them, and got them to do the same. Thus armed with the Mende numerals, he visited vessels in New York harbour, and on a British warship found a Negro delighted to hear his mother-tongue, if only from one who had learned to "lisp in numbers".

[2] President of the United States, 1825–29.

The hope that the *Amistad* Africans might form a little Christian colony was not realized: they slipped into the surrounding African society as was but natural, though as individuals continuing in happy association with the missionaries.[1]

In 1844 Steele returned to the States, and the following year Raymond died at his post. The mission was now leaderless save for Thomas Bunyan, a Mende who had served as interpreter and teacher and who now assumed responsibility pending the arrival of American colleagues. Meanwhile the *Amistad* Committee had become merged in the Union Missionary Society formed at Hartford, Connecticut. This Society joined with two others on September 3, 1846 to constitute the American Missionary Association, under whose auspices the Mende Mission now came.[2] In 1848 two missionaries sailed under the Association: a Mr. Carter who survived but one week after landing, and George Thompson, under whose leadership steady development took place. For two years he was single-handed. In 1851 Thompson sought African helpers from the Church Missionary Society in Sierra Leone, and from those who responded to the appeal there were selected three schoolmasters, a pastoral worker and an interpreter who, with their families, joined the Mende Mission; two sawyers soon followed. The American missionaries were deeply grateful for so practical a demonstration of Christian co-operation.[3]

In 1855 Mendeland was entered by a second American mission: the Society of the United Brethren in Christ.[4] Three missionaries formed the pioneer party, of whom D. K. Flickinger, the founder of the mission, alone remained after the first few months, his two companions having returned to the States. The proposal to open a station at Mokelli, some forty-five miles in-

[1] A. T. Pierson in *Missionary Review of the World*, XXI (1908), 185; T. J. Alldridge, *A Transformed Colony* (1910), 258–61.

[2] The other two organizations were the Committee for West India Missions, whose interest lay in Jamaica, and the Western Evangelical Missionary Society, concerned with Amerindians. These and the Union Society are said to have been formed in protest against the comparative silence of the older societies with regard to slavery.—*The Encyclopaedia of Missions* (2nd ed., 1904), 37.

[3] *Proceedings of the C.M.S.* (1851), lxxxvi. At about the same time the question arose of a mission at Bendu in the Sherbro country. The American missionaries had sought entry, but the chief already had links with the C.M.S., he and his family having been educated in the Society's schools. If his request to C.M.S. for a missionary—it would be a new undertaking—could not be contemplated, it was proposed to recommend him to receive the Americans.—*Ibid.* (1851), lxxxvii.

[4] Constituted in 1853 as the "Home, Frontier, and Foreign Missionary Society of the United Brethren in Christ", and in 1905 as a Foreign Missionary Society.

land on the Jong River, proving impracticable, a settlement was eventually made at Shengeh, about half-way between Bonthe and Freetown. Progress was slow for the first fifteen years. Encouraging development in the Sherbro country followed, and in 1883 the American Missionary Association handed over its four stations to the United Brethren.[1]

The second venture to be recorded was made by the oldest of the American Societies: The American Board of Commissioners for Foreign Missions. The Board were not new to West Africa, for they had pioneered in Liberia at Cape Palmas in 1834, but had not found there the opportunity they had anticipated. Accordingly, in 1842, John Leighton Wilson and Benjamin Griswold set out on an exploratory tour to search for the site of a new station. "We have our eye on two points," wrote Wilson before leaving, "Cape Lahou and the river Gaboon." They gave their verdict for Gabon. They found the river a fine waterway, some fourteen miles wide at the estuary and navigable for thirty. Trade was active, vessels from Bristol, Liverpool and London visiting it, with some from America. The people in the immediate vicinity were pronounced a good type, and as for future plans, "No obstacles will be thrown in our way", wrote Wilson, "by the maritime tribes, in penetrating as far into the interior as we choose." The local chiefs welcomed the proposal of a mission. The decision was accordingly taken to transfer the work from Cape Palmas.[2] The stations there were accordingly handed over to the Protestant Episcopal Mission.[3]

The immediate people among whom they were to work were the Mpongwe, a tribe settled in Gabon, belonging to the western Bantu. Wilson had a high idea of their capacity, and regarded them as well-fitted to be Christian pioneers in Lower Guinea. But he also had his strategic eye on a more roving group of the interior—the virile Pangwe, also Bantu-speaking, whom he regarded, not unjustifiably, as coming from the neighbourhood

---

[1] T. J. Alldridge, *op. cit.*, 261; D. K. Flickinger, *Our Missionary Work from 1853 to 1889* (1889), 44–5, 134–6.

[2] *The Missionary Herald* (A.B.C.F.M.) (1842), 381; 497–8; (1843), 156–7, 231. The north side of the river was visited mainly by English vessels, with a few French and American, and hence "the inhabitants regard themselves as somewhat identified with the English and with English commerce". French, Portuguese and Spanish vessels were to be found more on the south side; here slave factories were still active.—*Ibid.* (1843), 404. The river was named Rio de Gabāo by the Portuguese from its fancied likeness to a cabin.

[3] *Ibid.* (1844), 2.

of East Africa.[1] The prospect of working among such peoples after the frustrations at Cape Palmas proved exciting.[2]

But a cloud soon descended on the bright prospect the early reports envisaged. In February 1843 the Prince de Joinville with a small French squadron visited the Gabon river and sought to purchase land on the south side, but failed. Later a French commander tried to do so on the north side, and one chief was said to have consented. This was some two miles from the mission premises. A year later, in March 1844, the French secured from "King Glass", in whose territory the mission was located, his signature to a document purporting to cede his country to Louis Philippe. The signature, the missionaries contended, was extorted by fraud. The chief himself was aghast, and his people in active protest, at what was claimed. But the French pressure was relentless. Appeal to Paris had no result, for the Minister of Marine confirmed the action of his officers. A hope that Britain might intervene also faded out. Events mounted to a crisis in July 1845 with the firing of the warship's guns upon the town, not excluding the mission premises (a thirty-two pound shot landed in the church), and the retreat of the inhabitants to the surrounding forest. Much property was destroyed or looted. With the tricolour at last waving over the land, the commander was content, and there was no further interference. The people gradually returned and normal life was resumed though under a heavy feeling of constraint.[3]

In the face of these events the future of the mission seemed uncertain. The missionaries were in doubt as to whether the French motive was desire for a naval base or a political control to facilitate the entry of Roman Catholic missions. In the latter case the Protestant future might be in jeopardy as contemporary events in Fernando Po under the recently imposed Spanish régime showed all too clearly. Meanwhile the Commodore of the United States squadron, visiting the Gabon, left with the missionaries a letter for the French Admiral which re-established friendly relations.

These critical events raised the whole question of mission

[1] C. G. Seligman says of the Pangwe and others, collectively known as the Fang, that they "appear to have originated somewhere west of the Congo-Nile divide and to have raided across Africa to the west coast".—*Races of Africa*, 211.

[2] *The Missionary Herald* (1843), 229–40.

[3] *The Missionary Herald* (1843), 404, 440; (1844), 349–52, 381; (1845), 394; (1846), 25–31. In 1847 the French commodore visited Calabar but failed to persuade king Eyo to fly the tricolour so that he might salute him. News of the happenings on the Gabon had preceded the visit.—H. M. Waddell, *Twenty-nine Years in the West Indies and Central Africa*, 350–2.

policy. Wilson urged that, with the Gabon now a French province, another station beyond the jurisdiction of the French should be commenced, so that in the event of expulsion a continuing work could be maintained. He proposed either Cape Lopez, sixty miles south of the Gabon, or Cape Saint Catharine's 100 miles farther to the south, or both. The same language would be spoken so that existing translations could be employed. But a fresh accession of American staff would be required. At this point the Board considered the advisability of enlisting either American or West Indian Negroes, in the latter connexion reviewing the experience of the Basel, Baptist, and Scottish Presbyterian Societies. The evidence was regarded as on the whole unfavourable, and the Board concluded: "The idea, therefore, of dispensing with the agency of Europeans and Americans in evangelizing Africa ought not at present to be entertained."[1]

Wilson urged these immediate proposals that he felt to be expedient. But he also lifted his eyes to far horizons. He suggested the opening of a station among the Swahili of East Africa by Zanzibar, and proceeded: "Now if a station should be established there, and the one at Gaboon be continued, it would be perfectly reasonable to expect that a line of missions might be extended from one of these points to the other, in less than twenty years, and thus lay open one of the most interesting and extensive fields of missionary enterprise that can be found on the continent."[2] What sublime optimism, we are tempted to comment in the light of later events! But there were still more optimists to follow. The Board itself regarded the local mission as a step to penetrate a closed continent, and in 1849 inquired whether additional African missions should not be attempted for this purpose.[3] But meanwhile much needed reinforcements for the Gabon were not forthcoming. In 1853 John Leighton Wilson retired from the field. He had rendered notable service as the pioneer, and had by his pen been the outstanding advocate of the mission in the home churches.[4]

The annual report for 1857—the sixteenth year of the mission —showed three main stations established: one on the Gabon

---

[1] *The Missionary Herald* (1846), 210–11; (1847), 253–5.
[2] *Ibid.* (1847), 260. In justice to Wilson, it should be stated that he prefaces his proposal with a consideration of linguistic evidence, and of actual African movement from east to west, suggesting that the road was open.
[3] *The Missionary Herald* (1849), 343–4.
[4] *Ibid.* (1854), 3. He became a Secretary of the Board of Missions of the Presbyterian Church.

river among the Mpongwe people; a second some thirty miles inland among the Bakele; and the third, begun in 1854, some ninety miles inland, with a mixed population of Bakele, Shekani and Pangwe, and regarded as the advance post to the Pangwe country. Boys' and girls' schools had been maintained almost from the start at the first station. But missionary reward in the form of conversions was meagre.[1]

The third American venture takes us back to Yorubaland. In 1845 Southern Baptists seceded from the Baptist General Convention of North America and formed the Southern Baptist Convention. The Foreign Mission Board of the newly formed Convention decided on a mission to the Sudan and on February 22, 1849 Thomas J. Bowen of Georgia was accepted as the first missionary. There were appointed as his colleagues Hervey Goodale of Massachusetts and Robert F. Hill, a Negro of Virginia. The idea was to move inland from Badagry. The party, however, was soon reduced. They left the States on December 17, 1849 and reached Monrovia on the following 8th of February. Hill was detached from the party in Liberia, Goodale did not survive to the end of the year. Bowen was left as sole pioneer. For some years his was a lone adventure.[2]

In August 1850 Bowen landed at Badagry which he described as "the vile old town". His objective was "Bohoo" or Igboho, some 200 miles due north of Lagos, and he anticipated that about three weeks' travel from Badagry into the interior would bring him to his destination: "One of my first cares on entering Badagry, was to inquire the way to Bohoo, for this was the place to which I had started, and no other town in Africa would satisfy my desires." He was told that the road had long been closed by Yoruba wars, and that Abeokuta was the only interior town he could hope to reach. He therefore set out for Abeokuta, not as a second best but as a stage on the way. Once again he was frustrated. He was detained at Abeokuta for a year and a half before the chiefs would authorize his advance.[3] During this time he resided in Townsend's mission quarters. Various attempts to move on, including a visit to Iketu, some

---

[1] *Ibid.* (1858), 201–2.

[2] T. J. Bowen, *Adventures and Missionary Labors in several countries in the interior of Africa, from 1849 to 1856* (1857), 25–6, 27, 79; S. G. Pinnock, *The Romance of Missions in Nigeria* (1918), 99, 169.

[3] T. J. Bowen, *op. cit.*, 92, 99–100, 125–31, 145–50. This enforced delay led to his being in Abeokuta during the Dahomian attack, of which he has left an eye-witness account.—*Ibid.*, 116–20.

sixty miles west, proved unavailing. During this time he acquired a good knowledge of the Yoruba language, quickly realizing the significance of its tones. In a manner reminiscent of Robert Moffat's withdrawal, he used to spend several days at a time with people on their farms, a dozen miles outside the city.[1] In February 1852 he set out northwards on his exploratory tour, but the chief of Ijaye desired his presence, and had arranged that further towns on his route should restrain his advance. In the upshot he yielded to this pressure, but with a deep sense of frustration.[2] However, the welcome of the chief was sincere, and a site for the mission was assigned. Thus Bowen's exploratory wanderings came to an end in a town of some 40,000 people where he was assured of his opportunity as Christian missionary. At this stage he decided to return to the States to report progress, replenish his funds, and secure recruits.[3]

After a year he returned with two colleagues, J. S. Dennard of Georgia and J. L. Lacy of Virginia, and their wives, Bowen also taking out his bride. They landed at Lagos on August 28, 1853. The party was soon disrupted. They reached Abeokuta where malaria laid them low. The Lacy's were invalided home forthwith; Mrs. Dennard died in January 1854 and J. S. Dennard six months later. The Bowens were the sole survivors within a year of their arrival.[4]

Bowen and his wife proceeded to Ijaye to begin at last the Baptist Yoruba Mission. They found A. C. Mann of the Church Missionary Society already in residence,[5] but the sphere was wide enough to accommodate both missions. Indeed, so faithfully did both serve their people in the distress of war that they have left treasured memories at Ijaye: "The names of the Rev. Adolphus Mann, C.M.S., and Mr. J. T. Bowen, American Baptists," writes the African historian of the Yoruba people, "can never be forgotten by any Ijaye born."[6] In September 1854 the Bowens welcomed a colleague in W. H. Clarke of Georgia who was to give five years' service. This enabled them in the autumn of 1855 to move fifty miles to the north-east to Ogbomosho where a second station was opened. Meanwhile

---

[1] *Ibid.*, 135–6.
[2] "My ardent and too precious hopes were blighted, and the disappointment preyed so much on my feelings, in spite of my better reason, that I fell into a dysentery, which came near endangering my life."—*Ibid.*, 171–2.
[3] *Ibid.*, 175–6.
[4] *Ibid.*, 179–80; S. G. Pinnock, *op. cit.*, 100.
[5] See above, p. 61.
[6] S. Johnson, *History of the Yorubas*, 345.

J. M. Harden, a Negro missionary from Liberia, had begun work for the Mission in Lagos.[1] But the objective still lay beyond in the Sudan, and for this purpose Ilorin, under the rule of the Muslim Fulani, would have to be occupied. Would this be possible? In April 1855 Bowen visited the town, and in the following July Clarke did the same, the latter including the original lodestar Igboho in an extensive tour. Bowen has left on record an account of his reception at Ilorin. Without seeking official permission to enter, which he felt sure would be refused, he passed through the gates with composure and calmly asked for a drink of water. "Why didn't you send a messenger to let the king know you were coming?" the old captain of the gate asked him. "Because I am a messenger myself," came the reply. The king was informed, and he was given permission to enter but kept in custody for a time. He discovered that during this interval the king, his chief men and the Muslim alufas were met in council with their Korans before them to determine what action they should take. In due course he was granted a public audience by the king, who was himself screened from the public gaze. Yoruba, which Bowen knew well, and Hausa, which he in a measure understood, were the languages used. He was first asked a series of questions about himself, among them the name of his king. "God is our king," he replied, and said the king appeared impressed for he commented, "God is enough." When asked if he knew Muhammad he answered yes, and that he had two Korans. "Do you serve Moses?" they asked him. "No; Moses wrote the truth, but he was my fellow-servant, not my master. We deny allegiance to all creatures, even to angels." Their glances and smiles of approbation, says Bowen, made it clear that he had produced the effect intended. When asked why he had come, he spoke of the Christian gospel and they listened with courteous attention. A private audience with the king followed later. He was interrogated again as to his purpose, and what he preached. The king expressed his fear that Islam and the gospel would not mix: "If any man should believe here in Ilorin, what would he do?" "If any one should believe, I would baptize him in the river Assa, and thenceforth, if he were really a believer, he would lead a new and holy life." The king, lost for a time in thought, was heard to mutter in Hausa: "There are Muslims, there are heathen, there are Nasara (Christians)." But permission to reside was not then granted. Bowen confesses he scarcely expected it.[2]

---

[1] T. J. Bowen, *op. cit.*, 182–3, 185.   [2] *Ibid.*, 185, 191–9.

Six months later he paid a second visit. It would seem that A. C. Mann's contact had been made in the interval, but the German's aloofness had not been as acceptable as the American's ease of manner.[1] At all events, in the meantime opinion had hardened, and Bowen was informed that he might live in Ilorin only on condition that he did not preach. "But let me preach to the heathen," persisted the missionary. "It won't do," replied the king, and terminated the interview. But before his final departure Bowen was invited to pay occasional visits: "We parted in friendship and evidently with mutual sorrow."[2]

Reinforcements had meanwhile arrived for Ijaye and Ogbomosho. But Bowen's adventurous and self-giving service had not been without cost: failing health compelled his retirement from the field early in 1856. With his withdrawal the pioneer era of the mission was closed. Work was opened in Abeokuta in 1857 and in Oyo the following year, but Bowen had already blazed the trail. His personal fearlessness in the pursuit of his calling and his resource and persistence in the execution of his plans commended him as a real man to African rulers. His name has been worthily treasured as that of a courageous leader and a faithful missionary.

(4) *The Niger Once More*

"In the hope", wrote Henry Venn in 1856, "that the river Niger may be again visited by an expedition under the authority of Her Majesty's Government, or that, in some other way, that most important line of communication with the interior may be rendered available for the progress of the gospel, Mr. Crowther has been directed by the Committee to collect materials for the Ibo language."[3] At the same time, in expectation of the new advance, J. F. Schön was commissioned to revise and prepare

---

[1] Nasamu under whom Bowen had been in custody "had various complaints to make against other white men who had been there since my visit . . . that they were stern and unsocial, etc."—*Ibid.*, 202.

[2] *Ibid.*, 202–4.

[3] *Proceedings of the C.M.S.* (1856), 50. Ibos among the liberated Africans in Sierra Leone had petitioned Bishop Vidal on his arrival that they, like the Yorubas, might return to their native land and have a Christian Mission established among their people. The Rev. Edward Jones (a Negro clergyman, ordained in the United States, who had been Principal of Fourah Bay Institution since 1841, and under whom Europeans had been happy to serve) was deputed with three Ibo companions to survey the situation and report. From Fernando Po they visited the Cross River and found the Scottish Presbyterians established in Old Calabar. They found no ready means of ascending the Niger.—*Ibid.* (1853), 50–1; (1854), 33–4. For an account of the visit, see *The Church Missionary Intelligencer* (1853), 33–4.

for the press his translation of parts of the New Testament into Hausa—echoes of the Expedition of 1841. David Hinderer had originally been appointed to the Yoruba Mission to give particular attention to Hausa, and to be prepared to move into Hausaland as soon as an opportunity should offer by an overland route, with the Niger itself as the objective. However, the country proved inaccessible owing to internal disturbance, and as for Christian teaching, the self-complacent Muslim Hausas would have none of it. So the plan collapsed.[1]

There remained access by the river itself. The fate of the 1841 Expedition had left the dark river almost inviolate for a dozen years, but in 1854 the British Government tried again, in conjunction with Macgregor Laird.[2] The *Pleiad* of 260 tons under Dr. Baikie with a ship's company of a dozen Europeans and fifty-four Africans ascended to the Benue confluence and proceeded up that tributary for 250 miles beyond any previous point reached, and all this without a single fatality from malaria or other cause. This success led Macgregor Laird to propose annual expeditions.[3]

Samuel Crowther had been released to accompany the *Pleiad*, and his published *Journal* provides a valuable record of the expedition. He was greatly encouraged by the evidence of missionary opportunity, and reported to the Society: "The reception we met with all along from the kings and chiefs of the countries was beyond expectation. I believe the time has fully come when Christianity must be introduced on the banks of the Niger: the people are willing to receive any who may be sent among them."[4] When therefore a further Government expedition was projected for 1857, which it was intended to support in following years, the invitation to the Society to share in it was cordially accepted and two representatives—Samuel Crowther of the Yoruba Mission and J. C. Taylor, an Ibo ordained in Sierra Leone—were appointed. At the same time the decision was taken to begin a Niger Mission, and to empower Crowther and Taylor to take immediate steps to establish it.[5]

---

[1] *Proceedings of the C.M.S.* (1851), ci–ii; (1852), 54.

[2] "Almost inviolate", for in 1845 Consul Beecroft made an attempt, but with considerable loss of life. Macgregor Laird was an enterprising London merchant who had commanded the first expedition to ascend the Niger (1832–33), when the loss of life—forty out of forty-nine Europeans—was truly intimidating.

[3] S. Crowther, *Journal of an Expedition to the Niger and Tshadda Rivers* (1855), vii, ix–xi, 195.

[4] *Proceedings of the C.M.S.* (1855), 56. Cf. Crowther, *Journal* (1855), 19–20, 34, 158–9, 168, 180, 181–2, 191–2, 207, where specific opportunities are noted.

[5] *Proceedings of the C.M.S.* (1857), 49–50.

Dr. Baikie of the 1854 expedition was again in command.[1] Lieut. John Glover, R.N., later to become a distinguished Governor of Lagos, was appointed by the Admiralty to undertake river survey and was second in command. Glover was a sincerely religious man, and he and Crowther had a genuine appreciation of one another. A steamer was specially constructed for the enterprise and in token of its beneficent purpose for Africa was christened the *Dayspring*.[2] The objects were similar to those of 1841: the concluding of treaties with chiefs for the promotion of trade, the exploring of openings for missionary work, and the survey and charting of the Niger itself. The *Dayspring* left Liverpool on May 7, 1857 for Fernando Po, where Crowther and Taylor joined her. These both kept journals of their experiences, and Lieut. John Glover also kept his, starting with the first day at sea.[3] On June 29 they sailed from Fernando Po for the Delta, that vast triangle of interlacing waters almost 120 miles in depth. This took the *Dayspring* some twelve days to traverse, but they emerged into the main river without a casualty. By July 25 they reached Onitsha, where the first permanent station of the Church Missionary Society on the banks of the Niger was to be established. Here J. C. Taylor was left to begin the work, and remained twenty months.[4] By mid-August the *Dayspring* was at the confluence. In addition to Onitsha, Crowther now had mission sites assigned at three places: Abo just north of the Delta, Idda north of Onitsha, and Gbebe at the confluence. He had the promise of the sites, but for the moment could only give the promise of a teacher in return. The journey continued to Rabba in the kingdom of Nupe where the Muslim Fulani now ruled. A dynastic quarrel in Nupe had led to a request to the Fulani for help, who gave it

---

[1] Hence this became known as "the Baikie Expedition". William Balfour Baikie, M.D., was a naturalist by profession. He is commemorated by an effigy in St. Magnus Cathedral at Kirkwall, his birthplace, as "Explorer of the Niger and Tchadda." He continued his exploration with Lokoja as base, and when returning on leave died at Sierra Leone in 1864.

[2] The *Dayspring* was a small vessel of only 77 gross tonnage, with engines of 30 h.p. Her draught, 5 feet 8 inches, admirably suited her to river work.

[3] The C.M.S. published Crowther's and Taylor's Journals under the title, *The Gospel on the Banks of the Niger: Journals and Notices of the Native Missionaries accompanying the Niger Expedition of 1857–1859* (1859). Glover's Journal has been edited, with much illuminating comment from personal experience in the region concerned, by A. C. G. Hastings in *The Voyage of the Dayspring, Being the Journal of the late Sir John Hawley Glover, R.N., G.C.M.G., together with some account of the Expedition up the Niger River in 1857* (1926).

[4] His experiences during that time, with much information on life in Onitsha, are recorded in *The Gospel on the Banks of the Niger*, 241–383. The population of Onitsha was estimated at that time to be some 13,000.—*Ibid.*, 426.

and then decided to stay. Later conflict led to the destruction of Rabba the capital, so that at the time of the visit of the *Dayspring* the ruling Emir resided at Bida, inland from the river. Glover and Crowther together paid him a visit, declared their purposes, and were well received.[1] Crowther entered in his Journal: "I introduced myself to him as a mallam sent by the great mallams from the white man's country, to see the state of the heathen population, and to know the mind of the rulers, whether we might teach the people the religion of the Anasara [i.e. Nazarenes], and at the same time introduce trade among them. To this he at once gave a full consent, saying that it was all one, we might teach them, and that he would give us a place for a station at Rabba."[2]

On September 22 they reached Rabba and on October 7 weighed anchor to continue their journey. It was their last day on board. While navigating a narrow passage by the so-called Ju-Ju rock at Jebba there was disaster. The engines of the little ship were not powerful enough to stem the strength of the current, and she was swept on to a rock. She was badly holed and soon settled with only masts and funnel showing. It was a total wreck. With the fall of the river a few articles were salvaged, but the loss of stores and personal effects was heavy. Happily there was no loss of life. A camp was soon improvised ashore and the party waited hopefully in expectation of the relief ship *Sunbeam*, the arrival of which was part of the original plan. But the *Sunbeam* had been detained and only reached them a year later, in October 1858.[3]

Before the end of the year they had a welcome visitor in the person of W. H. Clarke of the American Baptist Mission at Ogbomosho, who brought with him an unexpected supply of

---

[1] Crowther, *Journal*, 81–93; Hastings, *op. cit.*, 94–104.

[2] Crowther, *op. cit.*, 86. Crowther says that two Muslim African members of the expedition who were with them were questioned about their treatment by the Anasara, and their favourable report created a good impression at the court.

[3] The "Ju-Ju rock" was so called as the abode of the god Ketsa, and local opinion ascribed to the god the wreck of the *Dayspring*. Relics of the engines were later placed in Ketsa's shrine, where engineers building the railway bridge at Jebba found them in 1916. It turned out that the colour red was anathema to Ketsa; none who passed his rock on the river dare wear it, and the display of red on board the *Dayspring* was said to account for the god's anger. Later Glover's red tunic gave the priests offence, but he declined to doff it, saying: "If he did so he must change his red face also, which they said was impossible for him to do"!— Crowther, *op. cit.*, 115–16, 216. Although in Nupe territory and only patronized by Nupe-speaking worshippers, the god's ritual had to be conducted in Yoruba. As the Yorubas at one time occupied the country, this would seem to be a case where invaders for their greater security propitiated the earlier god of the land.—*Ibid.*, 117–18. Cf. 2 Kings 17: 24–9.

sugar, tea and coffee. This was their first contact with the outside world since their entry of the river five months before. They now learned for the first time of the Indian mutiny.[1]

The period of enforced waiting was used by the leaders of the expedition to good purpose. Glover had lost in the wreck a great part of his original survey papers, but nothing daunted he continued assiduously to map the channels. For this purpose he ascended the ninety miles to Bussa just south of which, at the Bubari rapids, Mungo Park met his tragic end in 1805.[2] Crowther, too, was anything but unemployed. The pages of his Journal for this period display the importance of Rabba as a centre through which caravans between Kano and Ilorin were constantly passing, and contain many observations of interest on both the Muslim and the pagan population.[3] On the eligibility of Rabba for the Niger Mission he says: "As a Missionary station, it would be a connecting link between Yoruba and Haussa, and a stride into a Mohammedan country, under a direct Mohammedan government."[4] He secured a site for the mission and began to build. In due course visitors from passing caravans would assemble to have talks on religious subjects and hear readings from the New Testament in Hausa: "If we can do nothing more for the present at Rabba than spread the truth of the Gospel among the thousands of the interior, in this way, ought we not to be thankful?"[5]

When the *Sunbeam* finally arrived and took off the waiting party, Crowther disembarked at Onitsha where he remained for a period, making the return journey of 300 miles or so to Rabba by canoe.[6] He then returned to Lagos by the overland route, visiting the king of Ilorin on the way, and seeking to set

[1] Mail which had been sent to Lagos soon after the accident by the overland route via Ilorin had been detained at the latter place. The rulers at Ilorin acknowledged this but said the mail must be accompanied by a member of the expedition or it would be regarded as a charm sent secretly by them to damage the Yorubas. Accordingly D. J. May of the expedition was despatched for the purpose. It was from him that Clarke had heard of the expedition's predicament.—Crowther, *op. cit.*, 112, 120–1, 135–6.

[2] Hastings, *op. cit.*, 113–83. Glover was thus the first white man to travel the 700 miles of the river up from the Delta to Bussa. Hastings offers an attractive theory as to how the Mungo Park disaster may have happened, based on a careful survey of the rapids. He suggests that the excited shouting of Africans on the banks may have been warnings rather than war cries.—*Ibid.*, 177–81.

[3] Crowther, *op. cit.*, 104–239.

[4] *Ibid.*, 210.

[5] *Ibid.*, 440.

[6] *Ibid.*, 385–420. The journey took him from December 2, 1858 to February 2, 1859 of which nineteen were working days. He had had to hire in succession eighteen canoes since transport through different tribal territories was a difficult and delicate affair.

persuasively before him and his nobles and mallams the truth of the gospel. His facility in references to the Koran as well as the Bible deeply impressed them, and they acknowledged with gratitude the wealth of information on political, commercial and geographical matters he was happy to share with them: "I left the court with kind expressions of God's peace and blessing to be with me." Crowther had every opportunity, against the background of his experience in Nupe, for a sound estimate of the situation at Ilorin, and he stated it in these terms: "Through our influence as Christian teachers, Abbeokuta is becoming a marked place for prosperity in this part of the country; though our religion is not asked for, yet the inseparable advantages, peace and prosperous trade, which follow in its train, are most eagerly sought; and they will not object to the introduction of our religion for the sake of its worldly advantages, which they mostly look for."[1]

At last the Niger Mission had been begun, notably among the Ibo people at Onitsha, but it was to be two years before another visit could be paid. Moreover the site at Rabba, that seemed so full of promise, lapsed, and that outpost in Muslim Nupe had to be written off. The jealousy of the Muslim mallams rather than the unwillingness of the secular rulers Dr. Stock would judge to have been the cause—the vested religious interest once again a prime obstacle.[2] Meanwhile the Home Committee had not been inactive: already in 1859 five Europeans—three English and two German—had been sent out to the Niger Mission; but Sierra Leone and Abeokuta claimed three of them, and the two who reached the Delta got no further. Malaria smote them: one was invalided, the other died at Lagos.[3] The promise of the Niger Mission remained: how to secure its realization was the problem. It was to Samuel Crowther, who was already meriting the title of the apostle of the Niger, that the Society eventually turned.

Thus nearly twenty years from the great Niger Expedition of 1841 hope was restored—hope restored, yet still deferred.

[1] Crowther, *op. cit.*, 441–43. Crowther repeatedly stressed the necessity of a positive approach to the Muslim: never to open with attack, but to present the truths of the gospel. Cf. *Ibid.*, 237–8.
[2] Stock, *History of the Church Missionary Society*, II, 452.
[3] *Ibid.*, II, 453.

CHAPTER 4

PROBING ON THE EAST

DURING THE period of valiant effort on the western side of Africa that we have been traversing, there was also some activity on the east. In comparison it was slight in extent and disheartening in the immediate issue, yet full of significance for the future. The heroism of the leading figures was no whit inferior to that of their comrades on the Guinea Coast. Moreover, the overriding objective was the same: to penetrate beyond the coastal strip into interior Africa.[1]

Two main regions were here involved. There were first those lands in the north-east which had been reached by the early Church and which still seemed a possible vantage ground for advance; and then, the unexplored regions to the south, of which little was known beyond the coastal strip. Islam was to be found in both regions side by side with Christian survivals in the first and with an untamed paganism in the second. Once again we find the Church Missionary Society in the van, with German missionaries trained at Basel as its most distinguished representatives, while Roman Catholic orders enter the field with their customary devotion.

(1) *Activity in Lands of the Early Church—Egypt and Nubia*

In Egypt the initiative had been taken by the Church Missionary Society in 1825 in pursuance of the policy of seeking to revive the ancient Christian Churches of the Near East. There was no attempt to proselytize but rather the desire to infuse leaders of the Coptic Church with deeper spiritual understanding and concern. An entry into Abyssinia for the same purpose was hoped for. Of the five Basel men commissioned to Egypt in 1825—Gobat, Kugler, Lieder, Müller and Krusé—J. R. T. Lieder was to render the longest service, labouring for a full generation, and at times doing so single-handed. He died at Cairo in 1865. Samuel Gobat—to become Bishop of Jerusalem in 1846—was expected to proceed eventually, with Christian Kugler, to Abyssinia, a commission they were first able to fulfil in 1830. There Kugler died within the year.

---

[1] The impression all made on their contemporaries was reflected in current literature; thus, Anthony Trollope in *The Warden* (1855): "He was animated by as strong a sense of a holy cause as that which gives courage to a missionary in Africa."

In carrying out the Society's policy in Egypt two main activities were pursued: the circulation of the Scriptures and Christian tracts, and the development of Christian education. The New Testament and portions had long been available in Arabic through the British and Foreign Bible Society, and the Malta Press of the Church Missionary Society produced other Christian literature. Further, in 1829 an edition of the Coptic Gospels, prepared by the Coptic Patriarch, had been issued, with the Arabic version in parallel columns.[1] Lieder and his fellow missionaries undertook extensive itineration for the distribution of the Scriptures and Christian tracts, seeking contact with Coptic Christians rather than with Muslims. They travelled throughout the Delta and even ascended the Nile into the ancient Nubia. The distribution was considerable. For the years 1843 and 1844, for example, Lieder reported a total issue of over 9,000 copies: "Many have gone into Upper and Lower Egypt, by people who have asked for them; and not a few have found their way to the Coptic convents in the Desert."[2] Lieder was more than a distributor. He was competent in Coptic and Arabic, and superintended the translation into Arabic of the Homilies of Chrysostom and of certain works by Macarius "whose authority is much respected by the Coptic Church; but from whose principles that Church has grievously declined".[3]

The weightier emphasis, however, was given to educational effort. Day schools, including one on the Lancasterian model, had been begun in Cairo, and by 1840 these boasted over 200 scholars of both sexes. The Minister of Public Instruction who visited them was "surprised to see Christians of different denominations, Jews and Mahomedans, brought under one and the same rule of Christian instruction, and living together in harmony, as if they were all of one faith". Five years later the number was over 300 of whom some 260 were Copts. This was largely due to the fact that the Coptic Patriarch had given his countenance to the schools. By 1850, some economy having become necessary, the boys' day school was discontinued, alternative schools being available, but that for girls was maintained as the only one of its kind in Cairo.[4]

[1] W. Canton, *History of the British and Foreign Bible Society*, II (1904), 26.

[2] *Proceedings of the C.M.S.* (1845), 46. Of the total of 5,044 for the year 1844, 115 copies of the Scriptures and 1,587 Malta Press publications were distributed in the schools, while 367 and 2,975 copies respectively were taken by the public as gift or by purchase.

[3] *Ibid.* (1845), 48. There would seem to be no evidence to identify Macarius among the several early Christian writers of this name.

[4] *Ibid.* (1840), 45; (1845), 47, 48; (1850), lxxix–lxxx.

The distinctive service, however, which the Society attempted to render to the Coptic Church was the establishment of an institution for the training of young men designated to their ministry. In 1842, therefore, the boys' boarding school was converted into a theological seminary with accommodation for fifteen or more students. The type of candidate forthcoming, however, was disappointing. As they were illiterate even in their own language, a groundwork of literacy had first to be laid before the specific theological studies could be commenced. The experience of half a dozen years led to the conclusion that the institution was not serving its purpose: it was clear that only an inferior type of candidate was being recommended to it, and that the few who responded to the Christian instruction offered would have no scope within the existing Coptic organization to express a vital faith. The decision was therefore taken in 1850 to close the Seminary. One of Lieder's pupils in it, at least, rose to high office as *abuna* of the Church in Abyssinia.[1]

In 1855 the Society's establishment in Egypt was strengthened by the appointment of S. W. Koelle who had been invalided from the West Coast. In his view of the situation he spoke with no uncertain sound: "That the gospel is needed in Egypt, as much as anywhere else, of this I am deeply convinced. So long as I was in Egypt I could never get rid of the painful impression that I was in a country of dead men: spiritual death seems to reign all around one. The great majority of the population are held in spiritual bondage by petrified Mahommedanism; and the Copts confess a kind of Christianity, which has degenerated into a mere external mechanism." He noted the happy relations of friendship which Lieder had succeeded in establishing with the Coptic Patriarch and several bishops, but concluded that the Society must adopt a more vigorous missionary policy if it sought to secure any real change in the situation.[2]

With Lieder's death in 1865 Cairo was no longer occupied. There followed an interval of twenty years before the work was resumed in 1882, and then not as coadjutor of the Coptic Church but as a mission to Muslims.

Contemporary with these events was a revival of Roman

---

[1] *Ibid.* (1843), 47; (1845), 47–8; (1847), 46–7; (1848), lxxiii; (1850), lxxix; (1858), 78.

[2] *Ibid.* (1856), 64–5. Koelle also offered a keen appraisal of Islam as he found it in Egypt, characterizing the *literati* as fiercely anti-Christian, and the peasantry as sunk in ignorance. He had also discovered liberal-minded Muslims, but these found it easier to conform than to become reformers. On account of the failure of his health in Egypt, Koelle was transferred to the Palestine Mission in 1856.

Catholic missionary activity in the country. The vicariate of Egypt was erected in 1839 with the first cataract at Aswan as its southern boundary. In 1844 priests of St. Vincent de Paul and Sisters of Mercy respectively set up their establishments in Alexandria, and two years later Sisters of the order of the Bon-Pasteur d'Angers settled in Cairo where a boarding-school, a home of refuge and an orphanage were founded, which met with considerable success.[1] It was, however, to the south of Aswan that the notable pioneer Roman Catholic mission of the period belonged.

In 1846 the vicariate apostolic of the Sudan or Central Africa (officially designated by the alternative titles) was erected by decree of Pope Gregory XVI. It was given generous boundaries, comprising the whole of the Anglo-Egyptian Sudan together with the Chad province of French Equatorial Africa and the Nile province of the Uganda Protectorate as they were later known.[2] It was specifically a "mission to Central Africa" with the combined objectives of conversion of Africans to the faith, the service of Christian traders in the Sudan, and the countering of the slave-trade. It was established and maintained at considerable cost in human life and devoted service, and reached its centenary.

The pioneer party represented varied national backgrounds: Maximilian Ryllo, S.J. (Pole), Annetto Casolani (Maltese), Emmanuel Pedemonte, S.J. (who had served as an officer under Napoleon), Ignaz Knoblehar (Slovene) and Angelo Vinco (Italian). Ryllo, who had seen missionary service in Syria and had Arabic at command, was appointed leader.[3] After useful official contacts in Egypt, during which they received letters of commendation to officials in Egyptian territory south of Aswan, they ascended the Nile towards the end of 1847. Arrived at the boundary of their assigned sphere, they decided to celebrate mass in honour of so significant an occasion: the return to ancient Nubia to claim again a territory once loyal to the faith. They did so with due ceremony one morning at sunrise, in the ruins of the temple of Isis converted to Christian use in the sixth century, on the once-famed isle of Philae. Curiosity drew

[1] *Annales de la Propagation de la Foi*, XXVIII (1856), 345–6 (Report by Fr. Perpetuo Guasco, the first vicar apostolic). An account of the imposing establishment in Cairo is given in *Proceedings of the C.M.S.* (1847), 48.

[2] *Cath. Ency.*, XIV, 325.

[3] Casolani, as the first proposer of the mission, was elected vicar apostolic of the new vicariate, but preferred to serve under Ryllo, with his missionary experience, who was pro-vicar. Knoblehar is found alternatively, in its Germanized form, as Knoblicher and Knoblecher.

local inhabitants to the spot, and Ryllo says they afterwards exclaimed: "Our fathers were once Christian; then they were happy people, they built stone churches and stone houses; but as for us, ill-fated that we are, we live in huts of mud and wattle."[1] Memory of the Christianity of Nubia, that survived for wellnigh a thousand years, had not yet entirely faded away.

By December 1847 the expedition was at Dongola, in the neighbourhood of the Third Cataract, capital of the ancient Makurra. On February 11, 1848 they entered Khartoum where the Blue and White Niles converge. They were now in the ancient Alwa. As Khartoum seemed the most suitable centre for development and further advance, they made it their headquarters. Ryllo, however, was soon a victim of malaria and dysentery, and died on June 17, 1848. His office of pro-vicar was transferred to Knoblehar. Casolani was invalided, and as the mission was in financial straits, Vinco returned to Europe in search of support. But the year 1848 in Europe, with its widespread liberal movements issuing in revolution, was no year for liberal support of Roman Catholic enterprise. The Propaganda indeed became so seriously affected that it authorized the abandonment of the Central Africa mission if need be. But the devotion of the missionaries, cultivating their own local food supplies, together with the stout leadership of Knoblehar, tided them over the crisis. In Khartoum itself a stone church and school were erected. Pupils for the latter were partly recruited from local Coptic and other families and partly secured from the slave market.[2] John Petherick, pioneer European trader at Khartoum, visited the mission in 1850 and commended its attractiveness.[3]

With the return of Vinco from Europe, Knoblehar determined to explore the territory to the south, in search of centres for extension. With Vinco and Pedemonte he set out from Khartoum in November 1849 and was away four months. Khalid Pasha (Governor-General for the region of the Upper Nile, 1846–50) had consented to their accompanying the annual Turkish trading expedition. Their farthest south was Rejaf, 1,000 miles by the river from Khartoum. They came into con-

---

[1] *Annales*, XX (1848), 450–1.

[2] Daniele Comboni, a later leader of the mission, wrote in 1867 in a historical survey in French of the vicariate: "In 1848 the missionaries purchased in the slave market many youths who looked very intelligent. . . . They started to teach them. . . ."—Quoted in *Sudan Notes and Records*, XXVII (1946), 102.

[3] J. Petherick, *Egypt, the Sudan and Central Africa* (1861), 131–2. Petherick entered following the cessation of the Government monopoly in trade in 1849. He was later appointed British Consul for the Sudan.

tact with the pagan tribes of the Upper Nile known as Nilotes, principally the Shilluk, the Dinka, the Nuer and the Bari.[1] It could be no more than a prospecting tour, with the handicap of their Turkish hosts, but the resolution to attempt a mission had been taken. Resources for such an enterprise had first to be secured. This took Knoblehar to Europe.

Here he contended for the mission. In Vienna a society to organize support was set up,[2] and the interest of the Emperor Francis Joseph secured. Indeed, the Emperor took the mission under his protection, with the result that it was granted the status of Roman Catholic missions in the Ottoman Empire, and an Austrian consulate was opened at Khartoum in its interest.[3] This gratifying support was scarcely secured when papal action threatened to jeopardize it. A combination of causes had led to a decree abolishing the vicariate of Central Africa: through Knoblehar's personal intervention with Pope Pius IX the decree was rescinded.

Knoblehar now returned to the Sudan with welcome reinforcements: five of his Slovene fellow-countrymen, together with lay mechanics. During Knoblehar's absence Vinco had returned to the Bari country and set about starting a mission early in 1851. Two years later, in January 1853, he died of fever, just surviving to welcome Knoblehar with three Slovene companions. His was the first life given among the Bari for the Sudan mission. It was but the first; within a year to the day Dovjak had died, and his companion Trabant two months later. Knoblehar arrived from Khartoum only to find their graves. He had just left two such graves at Khartoum itself, four of his five Slovene recruits of 1851 buried within four months. The Bari mission at Gondokoro was for the time being in suspense.

Meanwhile work went on apace in Khartoum where a trade school was begun. In 1854 eight recruits arrived, two of whom were posted to the Bari mission.[4] Two years later further reinforcements came, but the sickle of death was now busy. Knoblehar himself was worn out and reached Naples only to die in

[1] The Nilotes are the group of hamiticized Negro tribes inhabiting the Nile valley from some 200 miles south of Khartoum to Lake Kioga. A summary account is supplied by C. G. Seligman, *Races of Africa*, 172–80.

[2] *Der Marien-Verein Zur Bedförderung der katholischen Mission in Central-Afrika.*

[3] *Cath. Ency.*, XIV, 325; *Annales*, XLIII (1871), 113; *Sudan Notes and Records*, XXVII, 104.

[4] In 1855 J. L. Krapf of the Church Missionary Society visited the Khartoum mission and recorded his impressions.—*Travels, Researches and Missionary Labours in Eastern Africa* (1860), 476–8.

April 1858. He was but thirty-eight years of age. From 1851, when the Vienna Society was founded, to 1858 there had been twenty-two deaths, not to speak of missionaries invalided. The Sudan mission was proving costly in more than funds. Once again a proposal to abandon the mission was withdrawn.

Meanwhile the Seminary of Verona for Africa had been seeking a sphere in the Sudan.[1] At the end of 1853 two Italian missionaries, A. Castagnaro and G. Beltrame, had arrived at Khartoum with that object. The former died, a victim of dysentery, within a few weeks. Beltrame had proceeded up the Nile and been assigned, by Knoblehar as pro-vicar, a mission to the Dinka. He secured six helpers from Verona, among whom was Daniele Comboni, later to rise to leadership. Further reinforcements arrived in 1858 and 1859, but losses were so heavy that the surviving missionaries were withdrawn in 1860 to the "acclimatization centre" at Shellal by the First Cataract. In 1861 the Franciscan Order came to the rescue at the call of the Propaganda.[2]

It was a bitterly disappointing outcome to half a generation's devoted service and a lavish contribution in human life. But the missionaries were now known to the Dinka and Bari in particular and were trusted by them. In critical situations they had seen the missionaries act as their friends, and goodwill had been established that stood as credit for the future. Furthermore, good linguistic work had been done that was a permanent asset. Knoblehar had made minor translations into Bari. A. Ueberbacher, a recruit of 1854, had been assigned to the Bari mission and devoted himself to the language; the result was seen in translations from the New Testament and in original compositions. Professor J. C. Mitterützner of Brixen made a notable contribution by preparing grammar and dictionary in both Dinka and Bari.[3]

(2) Activity in Lands of the Early Church—Abyssinia

Abyssinia was a land still held dear by the Roman Church, from the days of the Jesuit debacle under Mendez in the seventeenth century and the subsequent devoted but futile effort of

[1] Schmidlin, *Catholic Mission History*, 570.
[2] *Annales*, XLIII (1871), 114–20; E. Tomiolo in *Sudan Notes and Records*, XXVII (1946), 99–114. Tomiolo belongs to the Verona Fathers.
[3] *Die Dinka-Sprache in Central Afrika* (Brixen, 1866); *Die Sprache der Bari* (Brixen, 1867).—*Sudan Notes and Records*, XXVII, 109.

French Capuchins at re-entry. A renewal of the attempt to win the country for the Roman tradition was made at this time. In 1839 Italian Lazarists heralded the enterprise, while in 1846 Italian Capuchins followed with the Gallas as their objective.[1] They both entered at a time of political unrest which was in itself embarrassing to any such missionary endeavour and the climax to which was to prove fatal for the time being to their efforts.[2] With the shadow only of the old monarchy surviving, power was divided among three men: Ras Ali, ruler of Amhara though of Galla descent, inheriting Portuguese-built Gondar as capital but preferring Debra Tabor; Ubié, as viceroy of Tigré to the north nominally vassal of Ras Ali, with Adigrat super-seding the earlier capital, Adowa; and Sahela Selassie of Shoa to the south-east, with Ankober as capital and declining to recognize the overlordship of Ras Ali. Each of these rulers had been brought into some touch with the outside world. The British Government of Bombay was interested in commercial opportunities as far as the Somali Coast, and as Ankober was at the western terminus of a caravan route of importance steps were taken to despatch a mission of friendship. In 1841, under the command of Major W. Cornwallis Harris, it reached the capital, created a highly favourable impression, and accom-plished its purpose in securing a treaty.[3] Meanwhile it was French policy to enter into similar relations with Ubié of Tigré. Ras Ali likewise came into the picture through the adventurous visit of two Englishmen, Walter Plowden and John Bell, in 1843. When they made a second visit in 1848 Plowden returned as British Consul. Both men were destined to play a leading part in later events.[4]

With Shoa lying more remote from her northern neighbours, it was between Ras Ali and Ubié, or so they thought, that the bid for power was to be made. But by one of the most dramatic turns of history both they and the Shoan ruler were soon to be submerged. An officer of Ras Ali's, Kassa by name, of humble origin yet with not only martial but imperial ambitions, was destined to supersede them. An immutable destiny he believed

---

[1] Schmidlin, *op. cit.*, 587.

[2] Wallis Budge notes as an era of anarchy in Abyssinian affairs the period from 1800 to the rise to power of Theodore II in 1855, during which kings were such in name only, governors and chieftains did as they pleased, and the soldiery ran amok.—E. A. Wallis Budge, *A History of Ethiopia* (1928), II, 483-4.

[3] *Ibid.*, II, 491; D. Mathew, *Ethiopia* (1947), 163-70. Harris left his record of the mission in *The Highlands of Ethiopia* (1844). Prediction of a lunar eclipse greatly enhanced the mission's reputation.

[4] Budge, *op. cit.*, II, 491-2; Mathew, *op. cit.*, 180-2.

it to be. By 1852 Kassa sat in Ras Ali's seat; by 1855 both the Tigréan and Shoan rulers had capitulated and he was crowned emperor of Ethiopia as Theodore II. The *abuna* Salama, who had at one time "toyed with Ubié's pretensions", performed the ceremony—the last of its kind at Gondar.[1]

Justin de Jacobis who led the Lazarist enterprise landed at Massawa in 1839 and reached Adowa in Tigré on November 1. Here he and his two companions, Montuosi and Sapito, took counsel together. They observed due caution so as not to precipitate hostility, and on the rare occasions when mass was celebrated did so behind closed doors, as if in the catacombs, for fear of the "heretics". In the first instance it was decided to disperse: de Jacobis to be at Adowa, and Montuosi at Gondar in Amhara.[2] Their commendation of their mission was so far satisfactory, in Tigré at least, that Ubié countenanced de Jacobis and the latter was able within a couple of years to conduct a party of Abyssinians to Rome, there to disclose to them the power and the glory of the Roman Church. The twenty-three pilgrims returned deeply impressed, and duly related to others the wonders they had seen. For Ubié there were brought, as from one sovereign to another, gifts from the Pope and the King of Naples. Ubié's gratification was intense, and as de Jacobis expressed it, his heart was torn between admiration and friendship.[3] Ubié's cordial welcome gave de Jacobis confidence that he need not remain, as it were, in continual attendance, but could securely proceed to develop his plans.[4] One of his cherished projects was to gather Abyssinian Catholics together as they appeared, and constitute separate mission colonies on the model of the famous "reductions" of the Jesuits in Paraguay, but this he was not able to put into effect.[5] What he did do, however, without delay was to secure a site near Massawa for a college for young Abyssinians.[6] Another feature of his policy related to the monasteries of the country. He described their historic function on the frontiers of Abyssinia as at once that of a rampart to contain the pressure of the external paganism, and of a lighthouse to scatter beams of Christian light to these same pagan neighbours. It was this twofold mission of the monas-

[1] Budge, *op. cit.*, II, 483–6, 489; Mathew, *op. cit.*, 182–3.
[2] *Annales*, XIII (1841), 505–6.
[3] *Ibid.*, XV (1843), 66, 71; XVI (1844), 12; XVII (1845), 276.
[4] *Ibid.*, XVII (1845), 277.
[5] *Ibid.*, 276–7. For a very full account of the Reductions of Paraguay, see *Cath. Ency.*, XII, 688–700.
[6] *Annales*, XVII (1845), 277–8.

teries, as he perceived it, that led him to seek their conquest for the Roman Church.[1]

The actual achievement of the Lazarist mission is not easy to assess. The French explorer, Antoine d'Abbadie, wrote of the varied reception it was given.[2] The missionaries won converts to the Catholic faith, and there were Abyssinians in training for the priesthood. By 1853 the Catholic community is reported as 5,000 in number.[3] Their successes were largely in Tigré in the plain of Adigrat, and stretching northwards into the modern Eritrea.[4] One factor in winning the sympathetic assent of the Abyssinians is said to have been the devotion of de Jacobis to the cult of the Virgin Mary which, by contrast to the strictures of Protestant missionaries, commended him to a people themselves devoted to the veneration of the Virgin.[5] Whatever the skill and persuasiveness with which the religious appeal was presented, the political situation was unpropitious. Despite vacillations in his attitude, Ubié seems to have been regarded by de Jacobis as the rising star of hope for the Roman cause. Apart from the miscalculation of Ubié's political future, which any contemporary might have made—that he was so soon to be a falling star could scarcely have been foreseen—there was the failure, it would appear, to appreciate Ubié's motives of self-interest. So informed a student of Abyssinian affairs as Wallis Budge has described him as "a master of duplicity".[6] There is little enough to suggest that the crafty and ambitious Ubié was at heart even a Christian, let alone a Catholic believer. But when the wheel of fortune turned, more Roman missionaries than the Lazarists were involved.

In 1846 Gregory XVI divided Ethiopia into two vicariates apostolic: that of Abyssinia, which was entrusted to the Lazarists, with de Jacobis to be the first vicar apostolic (an elevation he at first declined);[7] and that of Galla, which was allotted to

---

[1] *Ibid.*, XXI (1849), 328. In pursuance of this policy visits were paid to monasteries of repute and friendly relations established. De Jacobis gives an account of three such visits.—*Ibid.*, 329–37. He was also impressed by the fact that education was the prerogative of the monasteries.—*Ibid.*, 337–8.

[2] In a letter of October 19, 1843: "En Tigré les Missionnaires sont reçus avec indifférence, à Gondar avec défiance, au Gojam oú ils n'étaient pas encore allés l'an dernier, on les interrogerait avec curiosité. . . ."—*Annales*, XVII (1845), 284.

[3] K. S. Latourette, *A History of the Expansion of Christianity*, VI, 32.

[4] D. Mathew, *op. cit.*, 155, 187.

[5] *Ibid.*, 156.

[6] *A History of Ethiopia*, II, 485. "He owed much to the native clergy and monks, . . . but this did not prevent him from giving substantial aid to Romish priests, when he thought they could further his plans."

[7] *Annales*, XXIII (1851), 443.

the Italian Capuchins, having as vicar apostolic Guglielmo
Massaja. He was a man of ability and distinction, who had been
tutor to King Humbert and had attained his majority as a
member of the Franciscan Order. He was to give thirty-five
years' service in stirring and troubled times.[1]

Massaja with three companions landed at Massawa in
October 1846.[2] There was a difficult terrain to traverse to reach
the appointed field, and there were intermittent hostilities between rival rulers to make harder the advance. But the decisive
blow came from another quarter: Massaja was denounced to
the *abuna* as a rival prelate, and persecution of him and his
party became the order of the day. The *abuna* Salama, who was
reputed of humble origin, had been trained for a period under
Lieder in Cairo, and was naturally predisposed to maintain his
Protestant connexions.[3] Furthermore, it was traditional that
there should be one *abuna* in Abyssinia. On both points, therefore, Salama found Massaja's presence in the country highly
objectionable, and exerted all his influence to chase him out. He
succeeded. Roman reports, indeed, said that there was a plot
to take Massaja's life, and that this was communicated to de
Jacobis who at once, without disclosing his reason, had the
persecuted party brought to safety in the mountains. A sentence
of excommunication against them was issued. This compulsory
retirement took place in May 1847.[4] After a series of threatening
adventures, they reached a haven of safety at the settlement of
de Jacobis.[5]

Meanwhile some missionaries of the party had penetrated to
the Galla frontier and Massaja was restive to join them. He
decided to attempt to reach Ubié, who was reputed to be prevented from turning Catholic only by political considerations,
and to find out for himself his attitude to the Roman mission.
Sacrificing his handsome red beard and disguised as a merchant
he succeeded in his enterprise, and was assured by Ubié of his
personal friendship.[6] He proceeded to Gondar but his situation
grew distinctly awkward, so he next made the military camp of
Ras Ali his objective. Here he was received in audience on

---

[1] *Cath. Ency.*, I, 77; VI, 348. He left his memoirs in Italian (Rome, 1885-93). He
was created a Cardinal by Leo XIII on his retirement from the vicariate.

[2] *Annales*, XXIII (1851), 435.

[3] *Ibid.*, 437; *Proceedings of the C.M.S.* (1842), 51-2. He was supplied with copies o
the Scriptures and Malta Press publications by the C.M.S.

[4] *Annales*, XXIII (1851), 437-41. At the *abuna's* request, Ubié had provided the
soldiery that pursued the flying missionaries.

[5] *Ibid.*, 445-7.

[6] *Ibid.*, 445-7.

arrival, but could make no headway with the Ras. However, he met John Bell who proved a friend in need—"Protestant though he was".[1] After more than a month spent in futile conferences with the Ras, all hope of securing his interest had vanished, and the missionaries departed. Once again hairbreadth escapes awaited them, but on March 7, 1850 they saw once more the gleaming waters of the Red Sea.[2]

Massaja now transmitted his views on the situation. He regarded the heretical persuasion of the Abyssinian Christians as only one of the obstacles to progress; the outstanding threat to success he found to be Islam. Further, he recognized that Ras Ali, who was titular monarch of the country, and the *abuna* Salama were in effective alliance for the extinction of the Roman mission. Were it not for the rivalry of Islam and the opposition of the *abuna*, he estimated that some million and a half Abyssinian Christians, "heretics by birth alone", might be led to embrace the Catholic faith of their own free will.[3] But even so, he saw the significance of the mission less in the number of such converts than in the strategic situation Abyssinia offered to the Roman Catholic Church for an advance into interior Africa.[4]

The missionaries who had meanwhile reached Gallaland found little welcome. "Had you come thirty years ago," said Abba Baghibo, who himself later turned Muslim, "not only I, but all my countrymen might have embraced your religion; but now it is impossible."[5] Even the few converts won in course of time seem to have been very unstable.[6] By 1853 Massaja was himself able at last to reach his appointed field among the Gallas.[7] But this was on the eve of decisive political events.

With Kassa's coronation as Theodore II a fresh wind blew in Abyssinia and blew to some purpose. There was discomfiture for many. The Muslims were no longer in favour as they had been

[1] *Ibid.*, 448–51. The companion of Massaja who reported these adventures wrote of Ras Ali: "Bien qu'il soit baptisé, il a cependant reçu une éducation toute musulmane. Aussi fut-il impossible à Mgr Massaia de l'entretenir sérieusement de la religion chrétienne, pour laquelle il n'a que de l'indifference."

[2] *Ibid.*, 452–3.

[3] *Ibid.*, 455–6.

[4] *Ibid.*, 454. The Church Missionary Society saw a Protestant mission in Abyssinia similarly in strategic terms, as a link between operations in Egypt and East Africa.—*Proceedings of the C.M.S.* (1855), 58.

[5] Massaja, *I miei trentacinque anni di missione nell' Alta Etiopia* (1885), IV, 103, quoted in T. W. Arnold, *The Preaching of Islam* (1913), 348, n 5.

[6] They are reported to have "either embraced Islam or ended by believing neither in Christ nor in Allah".—T. W. Arnold, *op. cit.*, 349.

[7] K. S. Latourette, *op. cit.*, VI, 32.

with Ras Ali, baptized Christian though he was. Theodore was their "implacable enemy".[1] His attitude to the Christian missionaries was determined on political rather than on theological grounds. The Roman Catholics he saw as backed by France while the Protestants had their links with Britain. His own political preference was without hesitation for the British. The French consulate, as well as the Roman missionaries, had cultivated his rival Ubié, and this naturally had its effect.[2] The mistrust of missionary purpose is well expressed in his saying of precoronation days, that he granted missionaries liberty of action "on condition that my subjects do not say, 'I am French because I am a Catholic,' or 'I am British because I am a Protestant' ".[3] With his accession the combination of his distrust of the Romans with the *abuna* Salama's intense hostility sufficed to expel them from his dominions.[4] De Jacobis, compelled to retire precipitately from Gondar, worked on in his settlement near Massawa, where he died in 1861 from sunstroke the day after setting out on a re-entry of Abyssinia.[5] Massaja, seeking to prosecute his calling despite the imperial decree, was imprisoned but later released. The Catholic cause now reached almost its lowest ebb.[6]

Bishop Gobat of Jerusalem, himself a former missionary to Abyssinia, determined to use the opportunity that appeared to offer through the revolutionary changes taking place, and sent four German Protestant mechanics who had been trained at the St. Chrischona Institution near Basel and had resided with him for a year in Jerusalem where Arabic was acquired. Coming under the aegis of an English bishop, they were welcome to Theodore, and doubly so as trained mechanics.[7] Theodore's bitter disappointment at a later date through unfulfilled hopes of Britain's help, and the tragic climax to his career, when a British expedition invaded his country to end the tyranny he had then imposed, relate to a subsequent period.

[1] I. Guidi in *Ency. Islam*, I (1913), 120.

[2] D. Mathew *op. cit.*, 187–8. Cf. J. L. Krapf, *Travels, Researches and Missionary Labours* (1860), 440–2.

[3] Quoted by J. S. Trimingham in *The Christian Church and Missions in Ethiopia* (1950), 27. He adds: "At a later date bitter experience forced out of him the celebrated saying, 'First the missionary, then the consul, then the soldier.' "

[4] *Cath. Ency.*, I (1907), 76; J. L. Krapf, *op. cit.* (1860), 440–2.

[5] *Annales*, XXXIII (1861), 78–9; D. Mathew, *op. cit*, 228.

[6] *Cath. Ency.*, I, 77.

[7] *Proceedings of the C.M.S.* (1856), 53; D. Mathew, *op. cit.*, 188. Gobat sent the four men on his own responsibility and as a charge on his diocesan fund. They were Martin Flad, Bender, John Mayer, and Gottlieb Keinzlen. A further party was sent in 1858.—*The Autobiography of Theophilus Waldmeier* (1886), 45–6.

(3) *The Sultanate of Zanzibar*

Beyond these lands of the early Church to the southward lay a coastal strip that had known Portuguese control, with a hinterland unknown to Europe. Before the mid-eighteenth century, however, the Portuguese had accepted as permanent the recession in their East African affairs that pinned them below Cape Delgado.[1] The Arabs of Oman had ejected them from the Persian Gulf by 1650, and a century later were in possession of the East African coast to the River Rovuma. As Coupland has put it: "East Africa, in fact, to use a phrase of later days, was 'partitioned' between colonists from Europe and colonists from Asia."[2] The colonists from Asia were Arabs and Muslims, and any Christian missionary attempts at probing along this coastline had to take account of the fact. There were external political influences operating in due course by means of consuls appointed to Zanzibar, but the Sultanate of Muscat, with Zanzibar at first but a distant settlement within its orbit, was nevertheless a sovereign state. As the general alignment of the time would lead one to anticipate, France and Britain were the natural rivals in the Indian Ocean in the latter part of the eighteenth century, with the United States playing an exceedingly active role in its own commercial interest in the nineteenth. The German intervention, which by the 'eighties had won a spectacular colonial territory, was a later development.

Seyyid Said had established himself in 1806 as Sultan of Muscat by methods not unknown to oriental courts.[3] He ruled for half a century first in Muscat and then in Zanzibar. The geographical position of his territory of Oman brought him into active relations with the British Government of India, for they shared a common interest in the maintenance of peace in the Persian Gulf. Nevertheless, as Coupland points out, Said was shrewd enough to realize that their interests might not always coincide. Zanzibar was not only a desirable residence for the court, but the British at the time were apparently little interested in East Africa. Above all, the desire to escape from the unceasing feuds of Muscat with its neighbours, together with Said's overriding interest in trade rather than in war, proved

---

[1] Approximately 10° S. lat.
[2] R. Coupland, *East Africa and its Invaders* (1938), 70.
[3] R. Coupland, *op. cit.*, 108.

decisive.[1] By 1840 the transfer had been made to the new home and capital 2,500 miles away by sea.[2]

The Indian merchant and banker had a centuries-old reputation, and Said found them indispensable to the economic development he sought. His welcome to them was wholehearted. By 1844 there were more than a thousand of them at Zanzibar, and by 1860 five times as many.[3] They came as British subjects, and to that extent gave Britain a stake in the fortunes of Zanzibar. But Britain was also committed to a stern and vigorous crusade: the ending of the slave-trade; and this was active between the East African and Asian ports. Clearly the cross currents of interest would demand careful navigation.

Said's economic ambition depended for its realization not on the limited range of products which the island of Zanzibar could supply but on the extensive resources of the mainland opposite, brought by caravan to the coast. There was some Arab activity here before 1840, but after that the pace quickened. Travel routes to the interior were extended, new trading quarters established, and more caravans set on the road. Ujiji on the shores of Lake Tanganyika was a regular outpost by the eighteen-fifties. To the north they had then reached Kampala, the capital of Buganda, and a decade later were on the upper reaches of the Congo. A flag, plain blood-red, was a token that the caravan hailed from Zanzibar and was under Said's protection.[4]

If the extension of trade connexions on the mainland was one aspect of Said's economic enterprise, the fostering of friendly relations not only with the markets of Asia but also with those of the West was its essential counterpart. Starting while still resident in Muscat, within a decade he had secured commercial treaties with the United States (1833), Great Britain (1839) and France (1844).[5] The appointment of consuls was a natural sequel.[6] The Americans held the lead in commerce at

---

[1] *Ibid.*, 153, 296–7, 299–300. "It was trade above all else," says Coupland, "that drew Said to Zanzibar."

[2] *Ibid.*, 295.

[3] *Ibid.*, 303.

[4] *Ibid.*, 305–7, 311. Coupland outlines the three principal routes to the interior.

[5] *Ibid.*, 315, 367–70, 423–4, 480–2. The priority of the treaty with the United States was the natural result of the early American interest in East Africa. In addition to the sections in Coupland's classic narrative a comprehensive and well-documented account is Sir John Gray's "Early Connections between the United States and East Africa" in *Tanganyika Notes and Records*, No. 22 (December 1946), 55–86.

[6] American in 1837, British in 1841, and French in 1844.—*Ibid.*, 378, 482; 471, 482, 484; 424; John Gray, *loc. cit.*, 62. There had been a British Resident in Muscat from the beginning of the century, and the French had established a consulate there in 1840.—Coupland, *op. cit.*, 103, 422.

Zanzibar, and traders from Salem, Massachusetts, at first enjoyed a monopoly. Among their imports plain unbleached cotton cloth headed the list, and was in such universal demand that the name by which it was known, *merikani*, became installed in vernacular vocabularies.[1] Rumours during the 'thirties that the United States had colonial ambitions in East Africa proved baseless, though when the first British Consul to Zanzibar arrived in 1841 he found the Americans pointedly, not to say aggressively, applauded.[2] Relations with the French involved for Said and his subjects more than the interests of normal commerce, for "they were linked in Arab eyes with the restoration of the Slave Trade".[3] The fact that despite this attraction the friendship of the British was preferred, indissolubly linked as it was with their policy to suppress the slave trade, indicated a realization that self-interest was in the end more likely to be satisfied in this connexion. As Coupland again makes clear, Said saw in British friendship the best security of his sovereign status.[4] Such was the political situation at Zanzibar when the first missionary ventures were attempted in Said's dominions.

The American Board was the first to consider entry. The missionary party which sailed from Salem, Mass., in April 1839 for the Mahratta mission, touched at Zanzibar and Muscat in the course of their voyage. At Zanzibar, as guests of the American Consul, they were courteously received by Said, to whom they explained the object of their journey.[5] E. Burgess, who wrote to the Board an interesting account of the mainland tribes which he had gathered from those who had been on trading expeditions, reported favourably on the missionary opportunity. "The probability is", he said, "that a missionary would be permitted to reside in the sultan's dominions, . . . even introducing the

---

[1] *Ibid.*, 378–9. In 1859 American cotton imports were nearly three times those of English cotton.—Rigby's Consular Report of 1860, in C. E. B. Russell, *General Rigby, Zanzibar and the Slave Trade* (1935), Appendix II, 344. The only surviving portrait of Seyyid Said is in the Peabody Museum, Salem, Mass.—Coupland, *op. cit.*, 378–9.

[2] Coupland, *op. cit.*, 372–6, 477–8.

[3] *Ibid.*, 478.

[4] *Ibid.*, 478.

[5] *The Missionary Herald of the A.B.C.F.M.*, XXXVI (1840), 42, 60–2. Dr. E. H. Hume, grandson of Robert Wilson Hume who was one of the party, reports an amusing incident on the occasion in which his grandparents figured. He relates that Said had received from Queen Victoria two years before the gift of a piano which had since lain undisturbed. On Said's enquiry as to its use Mrs. Hume began to play her simple pieces and so charmed him that he offered Hume half a dozen Zanzibar damsels if Mrs. Hume could remain with him as court musician!—*Third Quarry Article* (Tambaram Conference, 1938), 15–16.

principles of Christianity, until instances of conversion to the Christian faith should occur. This would create a disturbance. Yet owing to the commercial relations of the two nations, such disturbance would probably not result in anything very serious."[1] This coincided with the earlier report of Captain Edmund Roberts who had carried through the negotiations at Muscat that resulted in the commercial treaty of 1833: "All religions are not merely tolerated but protected by his highness, and there is no obstacle whatever, to prevent the Christian, the Jew, or the gentile from preaching their peculiar doctrines, or erecting temples."[2] As Burgess, however, was quick to realize, what was a policy of tolerance under one ruler might, under a despotic form of government, be reversed without apology by his successor. After further inquiries addressed to the American Consul at Zanzibar, the Board announced that they were seeking "a competent missionary to be placed there as soon as may be".[3] But the appointment was never made.

(4) Achievement of Krapf and Rebmann

The pioneer work of missions in Said's East African dominions was carried out by Germans in the service of the Church Missionary Society of whom Krapf and Rebmann are the most distinguished. Their journeys on the mainland were outstanding contributions to geographical science, while their linguistic labours proved a rich heritage for their successors.

Johann Ludwig Krapf was born January 11, 1810 near Tübingen in Württemberg. He came of farming stock, but his parents valued education and sought to give him an opportunity superior to their own. Geography became his favourite subject, and at fourteen his ambition was to be a sea captain so as to see the world. One day there was read to the class a pamphlet about missionary work overseas, on which they were then directed to write an essay. This raised a new question in Krapf's mind: "Shall I be a missionary and go to the heathen?" This idea sank in. So it transpired that at seventeen he appeared at Basel, offering himself as a missionary student. A year later he was admitted but his extra-curricular reading of the mystics so unsettled his mind that after two years he withdrew. He then entered on a university course with a view to the home ministry. At twenty-four he had qualified in his theological studies and

[1] *The Missionary Herald*, XXXVI (1840), 118–21.
[2] *Ibid.*, 118; Coupland, *op. cit.*, 367.
[3] *The Missionary Herald*, XXXVII (1814), 4.

was appointed to a parish; but his forthright utterances were displeasing to authority and he lost his living. The sad state of his parish, he says, had made him think again of the heathen world, and thus the idea of a missionary vocation overseas was revived. He followed the example of numbers of Basel men before him and from Basel offered to the Church Missionary Society. His credentials being approved he was accepted for service and designated to Abyssinia. He was one of the few who went straight from Basel to the field.[1]

In 1837 he left for Abyssinia, reaching Massawa in December. *En route* he had spent some six months at Cairo with Krusé and Lieder, acquiring a working knowledge of colloquial Arabic which enabled him to dispense with an interpreter on arrival. His first destination was Adowa in Tigré where Isenberg and Blumhardt were already at work. Together they visited Ubié "who received me very kindly, and gave me promises of protection, which were not kept".[2] Within three months the mission was expelled, through the influence of recently arrived Roman Catholic priests (in advance of de Jacobis) and of the Abyssinian clerics who preferred them. Krapf decided to attempt the journey to Shoa, while his companions retired to Cairo to await developments.[3] Early in June 1839 Krapf, with Isenberg who had now joined him, entered Ankober the Shoan capital, and was well received by Sahela Selassie. Isenberg, who was occupied with various works in Amharic, returned to Europe within six months to see them through the press.[4] Krapf stayed on for three years, seeking to enrich the impoverished Christianity of Shoa and developing a concern for a mission to the pagan Gallas which he came to regard as the key to successful advance in East Africa. It was during this period that the British mission from India, led by Major Harris, reached Ankober. Krapf with his knowledge of Amharic was enlisted as interpreter, and Sahela Selassie retained him as his adviser for the period of the negotiations.[5] While not dissatisfied with the success of his work

---

[1] J. L. Krapf, *Travels, Researches and Missionary Labours* (1860), 1-12.
[2] *Ibid.*, 18.
[3] *Ibid.*, 19-20.
[4] *Proceedings of the C.M.S.* (1850), xix.
[5] Krapf, *op. cit.*, 29-33. The objects of the treaty, says Krapf, were attained only on paper, and this he regretted. "I gave up much time and thought to the cause of the embassy, and wished for it prosperity and success, as likely to promote the spread of the Gospel, as well as the prosperity of Shoa itself." Had Sahela Selassie appreciated his opportunity, Krapf judged he might have become sovereign of a greatly extended Abyssinia. Much material in Harris's *The Highlands of Ethiopia* was contributed by Krapf.

among the Christians of Shoa, yet other concerns now demanded attention: contact with the newly appointed *abuna*, inquiry as to the possibility of a return to Adowa, and last but not least, the meeting of the lady who had come to Egypt to be his bride. In March 1842 he left Ankober, little thinking he would be refused permission by Sahela Selassie to re-enter the country.[1] Thus his advance was again deflected, this time however to the land where he was to write his name as undaunted pioneer: he now entered the domain of the Sultan of Zanzibar. Krapf, with his wife, finally set sail from Aden[2] on November 23, 1843 and after a slow coastal voyage reached Zanzibar on January 7, 1844. The East Africa mission of the Church Missionary Society had begun.[3]

Krapf was well received by Captain Hamerton the British and R. P. Waters the American Consul, who both showed him much kindness. Hamerton introduced him to Said who gave a friendly welcome. Krapf, conversing in Arabic, offered some account of his Abyssinian adventures and stated his proposals for the conversion of the Gallas. Said showed attentive interest and supplied a letter of introduction to his mainland governors: "This comes from Said Sultan, to all our subjects, friends, and governors, our greeting. This Note is given in favour of Dr. Krapf, the German, a good man, who desires to convert the world to God. Behave ye well toward him, and render him services everywhere. This has been written by Ahmed, the Secretary and Servant, at the order of your Lord."[4] Thus after two months at Zanzibar Krapf set out on an exploratory tour to the north, visiting Pemba, Tanga and Mombasa. The last named he considered an eligible missionary station from which to advance to the Galla or other pagan tribes. Accordingly he was back at Zanzibar within a fortnight, and a few weeks later he and his wife reached Mombasa, on May 5, 1844, to commence missionary operations.[5] Waters, the American Consul, who had encouraged the American Board to consider a post at Zanzibar, had sought to persuade Krapf to make it his headquarters. As, however, Krapf's objective was the Galla peoples he preferred a base on the coast from which they would be more accessible

---

[1] Krapf details the reasons for Sahela Selassie's change of attitude.—*Op. cit.*, 107–8.

[2] Aden had been annexed by the British in 1839.—Coupland, *op. cit.*, 465–7.

[3] The C.M.S. had earlier applied the name to the Abyssinia mission, in prospect of work among the Gallas.—*Proceedings* (1841), 57.

[4] *Proceedings* (1845), 49–50; Krapf, *op. cit.*, 122–3, 127.

[5] *Proceedings* (1845), 50; Krapf, *op. cit.*, 126–30.

(he had originally thought of Lamu) and naturally could scarcely consider being anchored in Zanzibar.[1]

The happy prospect of May was heavily overclouded in July. Mrs. Krapf died on the 9th while Krapf was himself incapacitated by malaria, and six days later the new-born babe was laid by her side.[2] Rosine Krapf's was the first life given on the East Africa mission. Waters generously had a monument erected over her grave.[3] When Krapf had recovered in a measure from this stunning blow he devoted himself with renewed zeal to the study of Swahili, the lingua franca of the East African coastlands and beyond. Within the next two years he had almost completed the translation of the New Testament into Swahili, and entered 4,000 words under the first two letters of a comprehensive Swahili dictionary.[4] A beginning had also been made with Nyika, Pokomo and Kamba, and he had done some prospecting among the Nyika and Kamba peoples.[5] In June 1846 his loneliness was at last relieved by the arrival of a colleague—Johannes Rebmann, a fellow Württemberger, also from Basel, who was destined to serve for twenty-nine years without a furlough in Europe.[6] We now enter on the period of active exploration, from 1847 to 1852, in which the two men made eight journeys between them into the interior—several of major importance—and for the first time disclosed to Europe the country beyond the coast.

Krapf's excursions in 1844–45 were designed in the first instance to discover a suitable location among the Nyika for a mission station, but he was also brooding over the possibility of penetrating the interior from the east coast. This is reflected in a letter from Mombasa to his friend Captain Graham in Bombay on May 1, 1845 in which he wrote: "As to entering the Centre of Africa from this Quarter, I cannot consider it impossible, but it would be connected with great difficulties. . . . I think a traveller can only by degrees advance towards the Interior, if he studies the languages, and forms connections with

---

[1] Krapf, *op. cit.*, 122. Waters, says Krapf, was the only Westerner in Zanzibar who before his own arrival had distributed Bibles and tracts.—*Ibid.*, 127.

[2] *Ibid.*, 131–2. They had already buried an infant daughter in Abyssinia.—*Ibid.*, 109.

[3] *Ibid.*, 132.

[4] The earliest Swahili word-list appears to have been *Vocabulary of the Soahili* by Samuel K. Masury, an American merchant in Zanzibar from Salem, Mass. It was published in the *Memoirs of the American Academy* in 1845 at Cambridge, Mass.—*Tanganyika Notes and Records*, No. 22 (December, 1946), 63.

[5] *Ibid.*, 136–51; *Proceedings of the C.M.S.* (1846), 52–4; (1847), 50.

[6] Krapf, *op. cit.*, 152; Stock, *History of the Church Missionary Society*, II, 72.

the Natives."[1] The absence of a major waterway north of Cape
Delgado meant that there would be no alternative to overland
travel, and since such physical barriers as the Great Rift Valley,
the great lakes and the equatorial forest regions were still unknown, Krapf's caution was certainly not misplaced!

His first step after Rebmann's arrival was to establish a
station on the mainland among the Nyika. While prospecting
fifteen months before Rebmann joined him he had found what
he believed to be the very spot at Rabai Mpia (New Rabai). He
now returned with Rebmann to negotiate; they were welcomed
by a conference of twelve chiefs convened to meet them, and
promised both a site and a dwelling.[2] They had planned an
early transfer, but both had bad bouts of malaria, and when
they at last arrived it was as tottering convalescents. "Scarcely
ever was a mission begun in such weakness," wrote Krapf. But
they were now nearly 1,000 feet above the sea and could look
down on Mombasa of painful memory.[3] Krapf estimated the
scattered Rabai community (both Old and New) at some 4,000,
about a tenth or less, he imagined, of the whole Nyika tribe. He
itinerated among the Rabai settlements while Rebmann took
charge of domestic arrangements as he was learning the language. It was while thus engaged that they both came to the same
conclusion: "That it was our duty not to limit our missionary
labours to the coast tribes . . . but to keep in mind as well the
spiritual darkness of the tribes and nations of Inner Africa. This
consideration induced us to take those important journeys into
the interior. . . ."[4]

Rebmann was the first to take the road. On the return journey from his prospecting tour to Rabai Mpia Krapf had seen
for the first time Mount Kadiaro, some 4,000 feet high, and it
gave him a thrill of pleasure. He thought of its cooler climate as

[1] *East and West Review*, III (1937), 268. Captain Graham was on the staff of
Sir George Arthur, then Governor of Bombay. A copy of the letter was found
among the papers of Sir George, when examined by the S.P.G. Archives Department. In the same letter Krapf also passes severe strictures on the Arabs for the
way in which they were prosecuting the slave-trade in the interior, and offers his
comments on current speculations regarding an interior river system. Interesting
observations are also made on the resources of East Africa, the local tribes and
related matters.—*Ibid.*, 259–69.

[2] Krapf, *op. cit.*, 148–9, 152–4.

[3] *Ibid.*, 154–6. Rabai Mpia was situated "about four miles to the west of the
extremity of the Bay which extends about eighteen miles inland from Mombasa".—
Proceedings of the C.M.S. (1847), 50. Later experience confirmed the choice.—*Ibid.*
(1851), cxxv; cxxvi.

[4] *Ibid.*, 159–60. The first attempt at a school at Rabai, with some five intermittent
attenders who even then desired encouragement by gifts, tested missionary patience.
—*Proceedings of the C.M.S.* (1848), lxxiv–v.

providing an ideal base for advance to the interior. It was to Kadiaro, accordingly, that Rebmann now wended his way. It was a satisfactory journey: he was away for eleven days (October 14 to 25, 1847), and reported the Taita who inhabited the hilly uplands as possibly numbering some 150,000. A mission to them he regarded as both feasible and desirable.[1] The journey, a straightforward march of some 100 miles each way, was, as Coupland puts it, "only important in history because it is the first recorded intrusion of a European into the interior of mid-East Africa."[2]

Six months passed and Rebmann was on the road again. This time it was a more ambitious venture of twice the distance; the objective was the Chagga country north-west of the Taita. He set out on April 27, 1848, traversed the now familiar road to the Taita uplands, and after five days more reached the Chagga border. He now found himself in country so strongly reminiscent of his home that he wrote: "I could have fancied myself on the Jura mountains, near Basel, or in the region about Cannstatt in the dear fatherland, so beautiful was the country, so delightful the climate."[3] Four days later (on May 11) he recorded: "The mountains of Jagga gradually rose more distinctly to our sight. At about ten o'clock I observed something remarkably white on the top of a high mountain, and first supposed that it was a very white cloud . . . but having gone a few paces more I could no more rest satisfied with that explanation; and while I was asking my guide a second time whether that white thing was indeed a cloud, and scarcely listening to his answer that yonder was a cloud, but what that white thing was he did not know, but supposed it was *coldness*, the most delightful recognition took place in my mind of an old well-known European guest called *snow*. All the strange stories we had so often heard about the gold and silver mountain Kilimandjaro in Jagga, supposed to be inaccessible on account of evil spirits, which had killed a great many of those who had attempted to ascend it, were now at once rendered intelligible to me; . . . Soon after we sat down to rest a little, when I read the 111th Psalm at which I had just arrived in my daily read-

---

[1] Krapf, *op. cit.*, 151, 183; and for Rebmann's narrative (in Krapf), 221–9. Six Nyikas and two "Mohammedans" (?Swahili) completed his party.

[2] R. Coupland, *op. cit.*, 392. This geographical pioneering was incidental to their missionary task. Rebmann wrote of it in 1855: "We came to Africa without a thought or a wish of making geographical discoveries. Our grand aim was but the spreading of the Kingdom of God."—Stock, *op. cit.*, II, 124.

[3] Krapf, *op. cit.*, 232.

ing. It made a singular impression on my mind in the view of the *beautiful snow mountain so near to the Equator*, and gave, especially the sixth verse, the best expression to the feelings and anticipations I was moved with."[1] Rebmann's were the first European eyes to gaze on the highest of African mountains, rising to over 19,000 feet, and to identify it as a snow-capped summit.[2] After six weeks' wanderings Rebmann reached Rabai once again on June 13.[3] His report of a summit covered with perpetual snow so near to the equator was discredited in Europe. Such a phenomenon at the very heart of the torrid zone could not be! Rebmann calmly replied that he had not spent years in view of Alpine scenery for nothing, and Krapf, who later saw the peak several times on his journeys, corroborated Rebmann's report.[4]

The Chagga, by contrast to the Nyika, were found to have a centralized political system with a chief whose authority was acknowledged throughout the tribe. His consent would be required for any missionary's entry. "Let him once secure the friendship of the king", wrote Rebmann, "and all else will quickly follow; . . . To sustain the friendly feeling of the king, he should be accompanied by a good doctor and some useful mechanics, whose presence would be profitable to the king."[5] He was to visit the Chagga again.

Rebmann now "tarried by the stuff"[6] while Krapf explored. A month after Rebmann's return he set out, on July 12, 1848. His own objective was the kingdom of Usambara to the south. It lay immediately west of Tanga (opposite the island of Pemba) with its capital, Vuga, in the Usambara mountains. Its extent in 1848 was some sixty miles north from the River Pangani and about 140 miles along the axis of the Usambara range. At the

---

[1] *Proceedings of the C.M.S.* (1849), lxxxviii–ix. Italics in original. Cf. Krapf, *op. cit.*, 235–6. The Governor of Mombasa had warned Krapf in advance of the risks the journey involved from warlike tribes, among them the Masai, and he cautioned against any attempted ascent of Kilimanjaro which was full of *Djinn*. Those who had tried had "been slain by the spirits, their feet and hands have been stiffened, their powder has hung fire, and all kinds of disasters have befallen them".—Krapf, 192.

[2] Kilimanjaro has a series of glaciers extending to some 15,500 feet.—J. W. Gregory, *The Rift Valleys and Geology of East Africa* (1921), 152, 207.

[3] Krapf, *op. cit.*, 192, 196–7; Rebmann's narrative, *ibid.*, 230–43.

[4] Stock, *History of the C.M.S.*, II, 127. W. D. Cooley, in particular, attained some notoriety as a rampant critic of the armchair variety in his *Inner Africa Laid Open* (1852). Cf. Coupland, *op. cit.*, 393 *n.* 1; *Livingstone's Last Journey* (1945), 108 *n.* Krapf's defence of Rebmann's report is given in an Appendix to his book, pp 543–7.

[5] Krapf., *op. cit.*, 246.

[6] 1 Samuel 30: 24 (R.V.).

time of Krapf's visit Kimweri was king, great-grandson of the founder of the line. It was a centralized government of the despotic order: Kimweri ruled and his district governors were aware of it. Everywhere there was efficiency but at the price of freedom.[1] Krapf set out with high optimism for the accomplishment of his particular mission. He said of Kimweri: "I knew well that he would soon learn to respect any European missionary, and give him leave to reside in his country; adopting such measures for his protection, that he would always have access to him by way of Tanga and Pangani, both in his dominions, without fear of molestation from the Suahili, an object of the greatest importance for spreading the Gospel in East Africa."[2] After a month's travel he reached Kimweri, "the only true lion" as his title ran, and was granted an audience. His favourable reception lifted the ban on general intercourse which was universally observed until the royal wishes were known. In his two interviews Krapf expounded his missionary purpose, and in the second "tried to familiarize him with the chief doctrines of Scripture, describing the fall of man, and then showing the necessity of the atonement by Jesus Christ, both God and man." Some Muslims present (two of the king's sons had also turned Muslim) were about to contest Krapf's message when Kimweri remarked: "I see what his words are; they are words of the Book." The king was willing to admit teachers, but he really wanted skilled artisans and a capable doctor. After four days Krapf returned reaching Rabai on September 1. He was not dissatisfied with the outcome: "On the whole I had reason to be very well satisfied with the king, especially when I considered the pains taken by the Mohammedans to injure me in his estimation."[3] Kimweri had wanted him back in three or four months. It was to be three and a half years before he was able to return.

Ten weeks after Krapf's return to Rabai Rebmann set out on his second visit to Chagga. This was to be twice the length of the first, taking a full three months. He first made his way to Masaki, chief of Kilema, whose guest he had been for a fortnight on the previous journey. His plan was to move on from here to visit Mamkinga of Machame, reputed the most powerful chief of Chaggaland. Masaki was reluctant but durst not offend his virtual overlord. Moving north-westward and ascending

[1] Coupland, *op. cit.*, 345–50.
[2] Krapf, *op. cit.*, 266–7.
[3] Krapf, *op. cit.*, 278–82.

beyond the banana zone, they passed so near to Kilimanjaro that Rebmann could distinctly see the snow-capped summit by moonlight, and reported: "It was as cold as in Germany in November." They descended once more to banana country and at the south-west base of the mountain found themselves in Mamkinga's territory. Protective ritual having been performed by the court magician, Rebmann was admitted to the chief to deliver his presents and declare the object of his coming: "I stretched out my Bible towards him, and told him my only business was with this book, which contained the word of God, and which we wished to teach to all nations." The astute Mamkinga gave Rebmann a favourable impression: "It was evident that he cared more about myself than about my presents . . . he assured me frequently of his great affection for me, and would have kept me much longer with him." He left on January 29, 1849 and reached Rabai again on February 16.[1]

Rebmann's report of Mamkinga's friendliness, together with his expressed willingness to promote journeys beyond his own territory, determined the missionaries to take immediate action in a situation apparently so favourable. Rebmann accordingly set out once more on April 6 to return to Mamkinga and then penetrate beyond to the country of Unyamwezi. "We considered it to be our duty", he wrote, "to make Christians at home acquainted with the unknown countries of the African interior."[2] This time it was a more ambitious expedition of thirty men besides himself, well provided with the necessary presents for tribute demanded in transit. The rainy season however had begun, so that, what with downpours of rain by day and night and swollen rivers to be crossed, they did not reach Machame until May 15. After ten days' delay Mamkinga received the missionary and now appeared in his true colours: "He began to develop his treacherous character promising, in the hope of presents, to promote my journey to Uniamesi, while all the while he had resolved to prevent it. Extortion, too, followed upon extortion. . . . I saw the stock of goods which I had intended for Uniamesi gradually melting away, and when by order of the king I was obliged to part with piece after piece of the calico which I had reserved for my further journey, I could not suppress my tears."[3] Mamkinga promised ivory in exchange, but the ivory

---

[1] Krapf, *op. cit.*, 237–41, 248–56.

[2] *Ibid.*, 257.

[3] *Ibid.*, 260. In reply to Mamkinga's inquiry as to why he wept, he said it was not merely the loss of his goods, but the foiling of the purpose of his Christian friends in providing them "to send the Book of Life to all Africans".

never came—save for an old tusk of little value, with which to buy food on the way home. It was a bitter disillusion. The one concern of all was to get safely back, but that was no easy matter. The usual route by Masaki's Kilema would have been folly under the circumstances, so they plunged into the wilderness, hacked their way through jungle, and after a gruelling experience reached the welcome shelter of Rabai on June 27, three weeks after leaving Machame.[1] So ended Rebmann's fourth and last journey.

Rebmann returned to find their numbers increased: J. J. Erhardt and Johannes Wagner, two fellow-countrymen, were a welcome reinforcement. But they had scarcely landed when both came down with fever; Wagner's took a fatal turn and he passed away on August 1, 1849.

Krapf now decided to explore in a new direction. His long-cherished desire to move towards the Galla country decided it: he would make for the north-west towards Ukamba, or Kambaland. Setting out from Mombasa on November 1, 1849 his first objective was Kivoi's settlement, a friendly Kamba chief who had come trading to Mombasa. It was a hard march through desert country with water at rare intervals and the imminent risk of running into a Masai foraging party. They once did thirty-three miles in a single day. Three weeks' travel brought them to the plain of Yatta, an extensive lava plateau some 3,200 feet high.[2] From this elevation they had an almost constant view of Kilimanjaro, and were traversing rolling grass-land. They at length reached Kivoi's on November 26. Krapf's statement of his missionary object met with a sincere welcome: "I fully understand your purpose, and you shall have all your requests," said Kivoi. He invited Krapf to go with him into the interior, returning to the coast in four or five months, but this had to be declined. Meanwhile Krapf met some Kikuyu for the first time, who wanted to take him back with them. And more: Kivoi told him of another "Mountain of Whiteness", and a few days later Krapf saw Mount Kenya for the first time: "The sky being clear, I got a full sight of this snow mountain. . . . It appeared to be like a gigantic wall, on whose summit I observed two immense towers, or horns. . . . These, at a short distance from each other, give the mountain a grand and majestic appearance, which raised in my mind overwhelming feelings."[3]

[1] *Ibid.*, 261–4.
[2] J. W. Gregory, *op. cit.*, 184–9.
[3] *Proceedings of the C.M.S.* (1851), cxx. "Although Kenya stands actually on the Equator, the summit being 8 miles S. of it, the peak bears a system of about fifteen glaciers."—J. W. Gregory, *op. cit.*, 149.

He was the first European to see this the second highest peak in Africa, rising to a height of over 17,000 feet. After an absence of fifty-one days Krapf was once more back at Rabai on December 21, 1849.[1]

It was now more than twelve years since Krapf had been in Europe, and both on grounds of health and for purposes of consultation he decided on a visit in the spring of 1850. But before setting out he carried through with Erhardt a project he had long cherished: a coasting voyage southwards to the limit of the Sultan's dominions. This was done in February and March 1850. It was part of the programme of probing all possible avenues of approach to the interior: "The friends of missionary labour . . . should also obtain some knowledge of this unexplored portion of the East African coast, and thus become better acquainted with the various routes by which messengers of the Gospel may press forward to some common centre."[2] Travelling in a small Swahili vessel whose captain was told to hug the shore as closely as possible, they made their survey, landing at every place of any importance. They found the Arab slave-trade in full swing. At Kilwa Kivinje, which was the most important town between Zanzibar and Mozambique, with a population which they estimated at over 12,000, the annual transit of slaves was almost equal to the population.[3] They found the Sultan's prohibition of the slave-trade with Arabia (under British pressure) craftily evaded by methods they report. Kilwa Kivinje they discovered to be the coast terminus of roads to Lake Nyasa and to the country of Unyamwezi which Rebmann had tried to reach by way of Chagga territory. Cape Delgado and the River Rovuma[4] at the Portuguese border were the limit of the voyage. They were back at Rabai on March 26.[5] Krapf left for Europe on April 10, arriving two months later.

In Europe Krapf was honoured and his work given recognition in high quarters. At Windsor he was received by the Prince Consort, and in Berlin granted interviews with the King of Prussia and Baron Humboldt.[6] He met the Committee of the

---

[1] *Proceedings of the C.M.S.* (1851), cxviii–xxi; Krapf, *op. cit.*, 283–99.

[2] Krapf, *op. cit.*, 411–12.

[3] This is to be distinguished from Kilwa Kisiwani, famous in Portuguese times, but now in decay.—*Ibid.*, 425–7. Krapf suggested that the island would be useful for a settlement for freed slaves, comparable to that of Sierra Leone.

[4] The Rovuma, they were assured by their captain, had its source in Lake Nyasa. This led Krapf to think it important to ascend it to the lake. Later exploration, however, was to show the Rovuma to rise some distance to the east of Lake Nyasa.

[5] *Proceedings of the C.M.S.* (1851), cxxiv–v; Krapf, *op. cit.*, 411–31.

[6] Stock, *History of the C.M.S.*, II, 129–30.

Church Missionary Society and advocated the scheme, over which he had long brooded, of a chain of mission stations across the continent from east to west. This they accepted to the extent of authorizing the establishment of two new stations, one in Usambara and one in Ukamba, and commissioned five recruits to accompany him.[1] Thus when, on the eve of Krapf's return in January 1851, Henry Venn delivered "Instructions" to the outgoing party, he saw the East Africa Mission as providing an entry to the interior: "It was not merely a lodgment upon the coast, or the evangelization of one tribe, at which the Mission aimed; but . . . to open in faith the Continent of Africa."[2] Krapf's companions were all Germans: C. Diehlmann and C. Pfefferle who left England with him were both Basel men; they were joined at Trieste by three lay helpers—a carpenter, an agriculturist and a smith. But the hope inspired by this accession of strength soon faded. Diehlmann withdrew at Aden; Pfefferle was buried within a month of arrival; and soon after two of the three mechanics were invalided to save their lives. It was a heavy blow for the pioneers to bear. However, nothing daunted, Krapf prepared to set out alone once more for Ukamba some 200 miles inland where a station in the projected chain was to be founded.

On July 11, 1851 he set out and by August 4 had arrived at Kivoi's, not without adventure. Here he met a visitor who lived near Mount Kenya and had often been to the mountain but had not ascended it because of *kirira*, "a white substance, producing very great cold". This substance, he said, continually produced water which formed a lake in which the River Tana took its rise.[3] Three weeks later, on August 23, Krapf set out with Kivoi in an expedition to the Tana River. Four days after setting out they were attacked by robbers and Kivoi was killed. This was the crowning calamity for Krapf. Kivoi's people fled and he was left a lonely wanderer in the wilderness. In panting search for water he at last struck the Tana. At least he had accomplished the objective of the expedition but in circumstances that gave him little satisfaction. Hiding from possible wandering marauders by day and seeking shelter from wild beasts by night (for he was in what later travellers described as "big game country") he reached a Kamba village three days later. Here he found himself in a predicament of another order:

[1] Krapf, *op. cit.*, 210.
[2] Stock, *op. cit.*, II, 131.
[3] Krapf, *op. cit.*, 311.

he had had a gun and yet had not protected Kivoi; said some, he should die.[1] He decided his only safety lay in escape, but before his plan could be carried out he was transferred to another village. On the fifth night he determined on immediate action for people were saying he should have died with Kivoi, with a plain determination to compensate for that oversight. Creeping stealthily from his hut he managed to clear the enclosure, leapt over a couple of thorn hedges and found himself at liberty but a virtual outlaw, hiding by day and travelling painfully by night. He eventually had no alternative but to report to Kivoi's village and throw himself on their mercy: "I was now in a painful plight; one, so to speak, rejected of men, and forced to be content if I escaped with my life. . . . Nobody would procure me any food, or even fetch me water, or kindle me a fire." Whether it was from fear of reprisals from Said's governor on the coast, or desire of the goods Krapf had left at Yatta and promised to Kivoi, he was at length escorted out of their territory, joined a small Nyika caravan that was returning to the coast, and after a further eleven days' travel reached Rabai on September 28. So ended his valiant attempt to found a mission among the Kamba.[2] He wrote concisely of the total experience: "On the whole, I understand this man of God [Paul] better when he speaks of hunger and thirst, of nakedness and robbers."[3]

Krapf now realized that it was hopeless to begin a mission station in Ukamba under the existing circumstances. The extremely dangerous route, together with the distance (over 200 miles) would make regular communication next to impossible, while the lack of even comparative security which his personal experience had just revealed would mean that any mission establishment was in constant jeopardy. He reluctantly came to the conclusion that the projected mission must be postponed, though he hoped not abandoned.[4]

There remained the task of finding out what opportunity there might be in Usambara where his first journey had been

---

[1] He records of his own conduct during the attack: "I fired twice, but in the air; for I could not bring myself to shed the blood of a man."—*Ibid.*, 320.

[2] *Proceedings of the C.M.S.* (1852), 61–4; Krapf, *op. cit.*, 300–50.

[3] *Proceedings of the C.M.S.* (1852), 64.

[4] Krapf, *op. cit.*, 350–1. Krapf wrote to the Committee: "You will now ask what I intend to do in the future. My answer is, that we must put off the Mission to Ukambani for three or four years more, and first possess a nearer Station. This could be at Kadiaro. . . ."—*Proceedings of the C.M.S.* (1852), 64. To the name Ukamba (=Kamba country) Krapf added the locative suffix—*ni*.

made in 1848. Kimweri had then received him favourably and given his consent to a missionary establishment. Perhaps here the next link in the chain of stations might be forged. Accordingly after some four and a half months for recuperation, he set out on his journey southward on February 10, 1852. On this occasion he decided to proceed by sea to Tanga and thence inland, but the governor there would not permit the journey without Said's written authorization. Returning to Zanzibar to secure it, he was back at Tanga by February 20, and found an escort from Kimweri awaiting him. The effect of this mark of royal favour was highly gratifying: "Never before had a journey been made so easy for me; . . . I had no trouble either with the chiefs . . . or about baggage-bearers." The efficiency of this personal monarchy impressed Krapf by contrast with the "republicanism" of the Nyika and Kamba. On March 8 they entered Vuga the capital. It was a week before Kimweri himself arrived, but then his reception of the missionary was cordial. Krapf explained his long-delayed return to the king's satisfaction, and delivered the presents he had brought, in accordance with African etiquette, equally to Kimweri's satisfaction. No interest whatever was shown in his missionary message, and this saddened him, but his request for a site was granted, despite the warnings of two Muslim courtiers to the chief that "wherever a European once plants his foot, the whole country must soon fall into his hands".[1] Before he left Kimweri's promise was officially sealed, according to traditional custom, and an officer at the court was appointed as Krapf's representative before the king. On March 19 Krapf took his leave. He was reasonably well satisfied with the result of the visit: Kimweri had not vacillated, though his preoccupation was indeed exclusively with material interests, but had confirmed his earlier promise that a missionary would be admitted. On the other hand Krapf saw quite clearly that any mission in Usambara could only continue for as long as it enjoyed the royal favour. He reached Rabai again on April 14, 1852.[2] This was his last journey. His health had now failed under the strain to which he had been putting it, and on September 25, 1853 he took farewell of his colleagues and returned to Europe. Erhardt was to follow two years later. Reb-

---

[1] Krapf, *op. cit.*, 396. Krapf warned those who reported this to him that if the Muslims intrigued against him, he would denounce them to the English Consul at Zanzibar, who would see that they were suitably punished. As Coupland remarks, Krapf in this may have overestimated the Consul's power.—Coupland, *op. cit.*, 407.

[2] *Proceedings of the C.M.S.* (1853), 52–7; Krapf, *op. cit.*, 367–408.

mann held on devotedly for another twenty years, until he, too, blind and shattered, had no option but to leave.[1]

(5) *Hopes and Realities*

It has already been indicated that behind the journeys of these men, for ever notable in the annals of African exploration, lay a high missionary strategy. They were insistently probing to discover a way into the interior, and knew quite well what their next step was then to be: an advance as rapid as circumstances might permit, establishing a series of missionary posts that should cross the heart of Africa from east to west.

Krapf's original idea of a chain of missionary stations connecting East and West was born in the period following his bereavement, before the arrival of Rebmann: "I used to calculate how many missionaries and how much money would be required. . . . I estimated at some 900 leagues the distance from Mombaz to the river Gabun in Western Africa, where the Americans . . . had founded a mission. . . . Now, if stations with four missionaries were established at intervals of 100 leagues, nine stations and thirty-six missionaries would be needed, probably at an annual expense of from £4,000 to £5,000. If every year progress were made both from west and east, I calculated that the chain of missions would be completed in from four to five years."[2] This optimistic estimate and time-table soon faded, but the idea remained though dormant. In 1850 it arose again and was presented, as we have seen, to the Committee of the Church Missionary Society.[3] It now appeared, after its incubation period, shorn of its precise calculations, but the more effective for that, as the master plan to determine missionary advance. Krapf wrote of it, in a letter of June 20, 1851 to Dr. Barth of Württemberg, after referring to death and illness among the new recruits: "And yet I keep to my purpose. Africa must be conquered by Missions; a chain of Missions must be effected between the east and west though a thousand warriors should fall to the left, and ten thousand to the right. . . . The idea of a chain of missions between East and West Africa will yet be taken up by succeeding generations, and carried out; for the idea is always conceived tens of years before the deed comes to pass. This idea I bequeath to every Missionary coming to East

[1] Stock, *History of the C.M.S.*, II, 135.
[2] Krapf, *op. cit.*, 133–4.
[3] *Ibid.*, 210, 300.

Africa."[1] Even the disastrous second journey to Ukamba did not shake his faith: "The chain of missions will yet be completed when the Lord's own hour is come. His mills grind slowly, indeed, but beautifully fine."[2] Missionaries in West Africa saw their own work in terms of the same grand strategy. The devoted Van Cooten, who reached Badagry in March 1850 only to pass away twelve months later, was inspired by the conception: "Dr. Krapf's letter to the Committee warmed my heart; . . . I should like to go half way and meet him. I have afresh dedicated myself to this work."[3] David Hinderer, also of Yorubaland, saw the missionary programme in the same generous terms: "That we are aiming at the Missionary chain through Central Africa is no longer a question. It only appears that our mode of procedure here in the West has been, and perhaps ever will be, of a different character from that of our brethren in the East. . . . And now for our chain again. Two good links we have already towards it—Badagry and Aḅbeokuta; and I am sure God will graciously hear our prayers and give us Ibadan, about two days' journey N.E., as a third. Next to that Ilorin may, by the providence of God, in time constitute a fourth; and a fifth will bring us to the Niger; and the same number again, if not less, to the Tchad, where we shall soon shake hands with our brethren in the East."[4]

Krapf had at one time seen as an alternative plan the use of rivers as lines of advance, on the assumption that their sources were not far apart. As he then saw it (December 21, 1849): "The Niger will carry the messengers of peace to the various states of Nigritia, whilst the Tchadda, the large branch of that river, together with the Congo, will convey them to the western centre of Africa, toward the northern tribes of Uniamesi. The different branches of the Nile will lead the Missionaries toward the same centre from the north and north-east, whilst the Jub and the Dana will bring them in from Eastern Africa; and, finally, the Kilimani will usher them in from the south."[5] He then put it squarely to those concerned: a chain across the

---

[1] *Proceedings of the C.M.S.* (1852), 60–1.

[2] *Ibid.* (1852), 64.

[3] Tucker, *Abbeokuta* (1853), 266.

[4] *Proceedings of the C.M.S.* (1852), 55–6.

[5] *Ibid.* (1851), cxxiii. He was confident of his assumption: "Certain it is, that he who reaches the sources of the Nile will have a more than probable chance of reaching the sources of the Tschadda [Benue], of the Congo, and of the Kilimani [an estuary of the Zambezi]. All of them verge toward the equator—toward the extensive country of Uniamesi [Unyamwezi]."—*Ibid.*, cxxiv. Cf. Krapf, *op. cit.*, 496–7.

continent linking east and west, or follow up the water-courses? He seems at a later date to have combined, to some extent, these two proposals, for he became concerned, after his return to Europe, with a project of the St. Chrischona Institution, near Basel, to locate twelve mission stations along the Nile, from Alexandria to Gondar, from which centre in Abyssinia they were to radiate south, east and west. This was to be named "Apostles' Street" from the names given.[1] Krapf admits the modification of his earlier plan: "Thus the African continental mission chain will be started from the north instead of from east to west, as I had originally contemplated."

So much for the hopes—and noble they were—of a vigorous advance into the continent. What of the realities? The first steps of an advance from the east in geographical terms were now far better understood, thanks to the journeys of Krapf and Rebmann. In addition, information had been gathered about a great lake in the interior. Krapf first heard of it on his arrival in 1843. Erhardt gathered more information and with Rebmann prepared a provisional map on the basis of it in 1855, showing what Speke called "that monster slug of an inland sea". Rebmann sent the map to Europe, it was published, and produced the historic expedition of Burton and Speke in 1857.[2] This was a major event in geographical discovery. Richard Francis Burton and John Hanning Speke were both officers of the Indian Army, commissioned by the British Government to find out the truth of this "Sea of Ujiji or Unyamwezi Lake" in Central Africa.[3] They set out from England in September 1856, were at Zanzibar by way of India in December, and on June 16, 1857 left for the mainland and the plunge into the interior. From Bagamoyo on the coast they followed the route taken by the Arab slave caravans. At Zungomero, "that hot-bed of pesti-

---

[1] Krapf, op. cit., 133 n., 214 n. The term apostle was not strictly correct for the first three stations planned were to be, St. Matthew, at Alexandria; St. Mark, at Cairo; and St. Luke, at Aswan.

[2] Stock, History of the C.M.S., II, 136–7, where a facsimile of the famous map is given. Thirty years earlier Lieut. J. B. Emery, Governor of Mombasa during "Owen's Protectorate" (cf. Coupland, op. cit., 217–70), had heard of the lake and planned an expedition to it, which the liquidation of the Protectorate prevented. Emery then passed on his information to the armchair critic, W. D. Cooley, who pooh-poohed it.—J. M. Gray, "A Precursor of Krapf and Rebmann" in The Uganda Journal, I (1934), 71.

[3] Burton was already famous through his visit to Mecca of 1853, and in 1854–5 was exploring in Somaliland behind the horn of Africa, Speke being a companion at the end and having a marvellous escape from death.—Burton, First Footsteps in East Africa (Everyman ed., 1910), 296–8.

lence" as Burton described it, the caravan of 132 persons was finally made up, and they then climbed into highland country. Traversing Ugogo and Unyamwezi—they were at Unyanyembe (Tabora) 600 miles from the coast by November 7—they reached Ujiji on the lake shore on February 13, 1858, the first Europeans to gaze on the waters of the first of the Great Lakes to be discovered. As Burton recorded it: "The whole scene suddenly burst upon my view, filling me with wonder, admiration, and delight. Nothing, in sooth, could be more picturesque than this first view of the Tanganyika Lake, as it lay in the lap of the mountains, basking in the gorgeous tropical sunshine . . . in front stretch the waters, an expanse of the lightest and softest blue, in breadth varying from thirty to thirty-five miles, and sprinkled by the crisp east-wind with tiny crescents of snowy foam."[1] The reality behind Erhardt's map was revealed at last. After some exploration of the lake, on May 26 they bade its waters farewell and set out for Zanzibar. A halt was made at Tabora where Speke was detached to ascertain the truth of the report that a second lake lay to the north. He set out on July 10 and on August 25 he reappeared, having seen the vast, expansive waters of Victoria Nyanza which he believed to be the sources of the White Nile.[2] On July 30 he first glimpsed it but on August 3, says Speke, "the pale-blue waters of the N'yanza burst suddenly upon my gaze. It was early morning. The distant sea-line of the north horizon was defined in the calm atmosphere. . . . This view was one which, even in a well-known and explored country, would have arrested the traveller by its peaceful beauty. . . . But the pleasure of the mere view vanished in the presence of those more intense and exciting emotions which are called up by the consideration of the commercial and geographical importance of the prospect before me. . . . The Arabs' tale was proved to the letter."[3]

In addition to these advances in geographical knowledge stimulated by the missionaries' and other reports, the necessary linguistic preparations for any missionary move inland were well in hand. While still on the Abyssinian mission Krapf had completed versions in Galla of the Gospels, Acts and Genesis; and his researches in Swahili and several tribal vernaculars had produced various translations, Biblical and other, together with

---

[1] R. F. Burton, *The Lake Regions of Central Africa* (1860), II, 42–3.

[2] *Ibid.*, II, 156, 173, 204. Burton commented on Speke's assurance: "The fortunate discoverer's conviction was strong; his reasons were weak."

[3] E. W. Smith, *Exploration in Africa* (1929), 104–5, quoted from Speke, *What led to the Discovery of the Source of the Nile* (1864), 266 *et seq.*

grammar, dictionary and other language tools.[1] On his visit to Europe in 1850 he saw through the press at Tübingen an Outline of the Elements of Swahili, the Gospel of St. Mark in a Kamba version, and a comparative vocabulary of Swahili, Nyika, Kamba, Pokomo, Hiau and Galla.[2] Such were the conditions that may be called favourable. But the overriding factors were political; and here there was another story to tell.

There was, of course, the ever-recurrent problem of health, and while the mortality and invaliding rate was not as high as on the West, yet it was daunting enough. This and other hardships, however, were willingly accepted and patiently borne.[3] But political conditions were another matter—and they were decisive. There was first the situation which Krapf termed "republican" where local chiefs were not subject to any central control of a paramount. This was the case in Ukamba with a consequent lack of security, as Krapf had found to his cost. He realized that advance must here be by shorter stages and at longer time intervals. Concerning the proposed station at Kadiaro, only some three days' from Rabai, he said: "This station must first be established and bear fruit, before we can plant a Missionary tree in Ukambani."[4] The other situation among the tribes was of monarchical type, where a strong central control was exercised, depending inevitably on the personality of the king, whose wishes, not to say whims, were decisive. Krapf found this system in Usambara, and for its convenience to the traveller he welcomed it. But as he realized, and Erhardt later discovered, the will of the king was the single thread on which the mission hung. The king must therefore be cultivated and humoured, as by the customary gifts at intervals, in order to secure admission to the country.[5] When in August 1853 Erhardt visited Usambara with the intention of establishing the mission for which Krapf had arranged, he found Kimweri of another mind. After a three months' delay the king told

[1] W. Canton, *History of the British and Foreign Bible Society*, II (1904), 276–7; Krapf, *op. cit.*, 188, 198, 205. Some were printed in Bombay.

[2] *Proceedings of the C.M.S.* (1851), cxxv; Stock, *op. cit.*, II, 129.

[3] "A missionary and a cross are closely connected," wrote Krapf.—*Proceedings of the C.M.S.* (1848), lxxvii.

[4] *Proceedings of the C.M.S.* (1852), 64.

[5] "A missionary has, therefore, to choose between two courses:" said Krapf, "either he gives a present and is admitted into the country, or he refuses a present, and is consequently excluded from it."—Krapf, *op. cit.*, 397–8. Krapf strongly deprecated, however, as a missionary method the attempt to make of the king the first convert and so through him seek to establish the mission "by the force of edicts and military power".—*Proceedings of the C.M.S.* (1853), 57.

Erhardt to leave, and of course there was no alternative.[1] Erhardt rejoined his colleague Rebmann. The second string to the bow—Usambara after Ukamba—had now also snapped. "Both Missionaries concur in the opinion", ran the next Report, "that all the roads into the interior are for the present closed against them."[2]

There was yet another, and that a finally controlling, factor in the political situation—the will of the Sultan of Zanzibar. The decision of Kimweri was underlined by Said on Erhardt's return: he made it clear that he would not consent to a mission beyond his own coastal territory in that direction.[3] Since any mission to East Africa north of Mozambique must secure the right of entry from the Sultan, his was the deciding voice. This was clearly demonstrated in the case of the projected Hermannsburg mission to the Galla country.

Louis Harms, Lutheran minister at Hermannsburg in Hanover, established in 1849 a mission which should embody those principles he regarded as essential to evangelism overseas. A seminary to train missionary candidates was begun, and then a destination decided upon.[4] Louis Harms' heart was with the Gallas in East Africa. He had been inspired by Krapf's reports about this people, and so the Galla Mission became the great objective.[5] The problem of transport proved so intractable that at last the only way out was to commission the building of their own ship, and this they did. She was christened the *Candace* in view of her destination, and bore an appropriate figurehead.[6] On October 28, 1853 she set out on her first voyage with eight missionaries and eight colonists on board from the Hermannsburg community—for the idea was to found a Christian colony. Official recognition of the enterprise had been secured, and the British Government commended it to the Governor at the Cape and their Consul at Zanzibar. The *Candace* arrived at Cape Town on January 21, 1854 and after a call at Durban

---

[1] Political jealousies and a threat of war by Said are said to have been the effective reason.—*Proceedings of the C.M.S.* (1854), 53.

[2] *Ibid.* (1854), 54.

[3] *Ibid.* (1854), 54.

[4] Harms wrote to Bishop Gobat, then in Jerusalem, and to Krapf in East Africa, but the letters seem to have miscarried. His attention was then directed to Bonny, east of the Niger, but a proposal of six young sailors to go out and start a settlement by arrangement with a local chief where slavery should be abolished, and then return for missionaries, proved on inquiry to be entirely visionary.—Haccius, *Hannoversche Missionsgeschichte*, II (1907), 162–3.

[5] Haccius, *op. cit.*, II, 164, 247–51.

[6] Cf. Acts 8: 27.

reached Zanzibar in April.[1] Here the travellers received a shock: they were refused permission to proceed to Mombasa. Eventually this was modified to permission to go to Mombasa but not under any circumstances to set foot on the mainland. This was truly disheartening, but they thought if once they could consult with Rebmann (Krapf had now left) they might find a way out. They left Zanzibar on April 25, but were carried far north by a strong current and driven about for a month, finally making Mombasa on May 30. In an interview with the Governor, Rebmann being present, they set out their purpose and asked for permission to go to the Gallas, or failing that, to settle elsewhere on the mainland. The Governor asked for their written authorization from the Sultan, but they had none. His refusal was therefore inevitable. Rebmann paid the Governor visit after visit but all to no effect. He then told the Hanoverians there was only one thing to do: return to South Africa. They were reluctant and thought they might find a piece of coast to the northward, beyond the Sultan's domain. Rebmann assured them it was a vain hope; they must return south. He himself might only have a short time longer on the mainland, British citizen as he was. They should get to Port Natal (Durban) and there begin work, waiting for any door that might open farther north. However, some were obdurate, and three of their number set out for the mainland despite the Sultan's prohibition. After aimless wanderings they decided to make for Rabai where Rebmann gave them shelter. Meanwhile the Governor was, not unnaturally, incensed at their conduct and served the whole party with notice to quit immediately. Indeed, their ship was at once towed out of harbour. On August 2 they reached Durban.[2]

There was bitter disappointment at Hermannsburg. Louis Harms attributed the Sultan's refusal, first, to the fact that he was a Muslim, and so "the arch enemy of Christ"; and second, to his being an Arab with a trade monopoly in East Africa and hence jealous of all intruders. Harms would have preferred the brethren to hold to their resolution to go ashore despite the prohibition, and then penetrate fifty miles or so inland, not realizing how impossible such a proposal was.[3] On his instructions a second attempt was made at a later date, this time with six people only who were to seek a settlement among the

[1] Haccius, *op. cit.*, II, 176, 238, 241–52.
[2] Haccius, *op. cit.*, II, 253–6, 262.
[3] *Ibid.*, II, 260.

Pokomo as being next-door neighbours of the Gallas. On March 31, 1858 the *Candace* set out once more from Durban, by mid-April was over against Zanzibar and Mombasa, and then explored the coast from the Tana River to Cape Guardafui, with frequent landings to prospect for a settlement. But all was of no avail, and on May 31 they turned south. They now called at Zanzibar, where Rebmann was living, and tried again to secure permission, but gained nothing by it. The vision of a Galla Mission faded away, while the work in Natal went on from strength to strength.[1]

Surprising as it may sound, Krapf was the cause of the Sultan's refusal. It happened in this way. In conformity with his expressed policy of cultivating African rulers whose fiat determined the life or death of a mission, he had favoured Kimweri of Usambara by furnishing to his officer names of European and American firms in Zanzibar with whom he might trade direct. This cutting out of the Swahili middlemen bitterly antagonized them, and Krapf was so far aware of it: "I was naturally a thorn in the side of the Suahili, because I had taken an unbeliever to Zanzibar, where he could see with his own eyes things as they were."[2] What he seems not to have been aware of was the weapon he unwittingly put into their hands. While in Zanzibar with Erhardt in April 1852 on the return from Usambara, he was asked, in conversation with the French Consul, whether a certain stretch of coast he had just visited was in reality under Said's authority. It would seem that Erhardt realized the risk of answering but Krapf would not be warned, and reported how Kimweri had actually levied tribute on the coast. There were listening ears and it was soon noised abroad that Krapf had said the Sultan's writ did not run on a stretch of coast of considerable commercial importance. Further, there were already fears of a French colonizing venture on the coast and now Krapf's journey to Usambara was seen as a thread in the tangled diplomatic web. Krapf was meddling in politics. Said had been in Muscat during these events, but on his return six months later he heard it all, and doubtless with some embroidery at Krapf's expense. So it came about that when the Foreign Office desired Hamerton, the British Consul, to render any necessary assistance to the Hanoverian missionaries, he replied: "I have cause to believe that this or any other missionary expedition will not be well received by the Imam or his people." The change in the attitude to missionaries was due to a

[1] *Ibid.*, II, 262–9.　　　　　[2] Krapf, *op. cit.*, 404.

different view of their intentions, "which I regret to say, has been caused by Dr. Krapf".[1] Small wonder that the refusal to permit the *Candace's* passengers to settle on the mainland and found a "Christian colony" was rigid and unbending.

With the return of Krapf to Europe in 1853 and of Erhardt in 1855 Rebmann alone of the famous trio was left to hold the fort, but events soon compelled his withdrawal to a restricted sphere. In 1856 Seyyid Said died, after fifty years of rule in Muscat and Zanzibar. The work at Rabai was suspended: "Upon the death of the Imam of Muscat, the unsettled state of the country obliged the Missionaries to remove to a place of safety."[2] The year 1857 found Rebmann pursuing his linguistic researches in Mombasa; and then, sometimes at Rabai, sometimes in Zanzibar, in hope of the better day he did not live to see.

The probings on the east had still left interior Africa largely a land of the unknown. But 1856 was a significant year in its unveiling. When Seyyid Said died at sea off the Seychelles on October 19, David Livingstone was recuperating in Mauritius after emerging from the heart of Africa.

---

[1] Coupland, *op. cit.*, 414–15. Krapf's error lay in his indiscretion when conversing with the representative of a foreign power. The ripples occasioned by this diplomatic incident spread far and wide; the Government of India was annoyed, to say the least, and asked Whitehall to deal suitably with the C.M.S., as a sequel to which Krapf and Venn submitted appropriate apologies.—*Ibid.*, 417. Cf. Burton, *The Lake Regions of Central Africa*, I, 7.

[2] *Proceedings of the C.M.S.* (1857), 50.

CHAPTER 5

THE THRUST FROM THE SOUTH

By CONTRAST with the persistent missionary drive in the west, and in the east the insistent search for possible points of entry—to break into "Inner Africa" as the phrase then went—the south appeared in the 'forties and early 'fifties placid and undisturbed. Undisturbed, that is, in respect of any comparable impulse to move into the interior, for there were political disturbances enough, what with the claim of the emigrant Boers to independence, and recurring wars on the eastern frontier—the War of the Axe in 1846, and the disastrous irruption of the Bantu in 1850 in a conflict of unprecedented length and ferocity. This last outbreak, indeed, was deemed sufficiently serious to demand the appointment of a Select Committee of inquiry by the Home Government.

In respect of missionary development, however, the regions south of the Vaal and Orange Rivers, already in a measure occupied, remained for the most part the accepted field of endeavour. Here existing Societies consolidated, and on occasion expanded, their work; and new partners in the missionary enterprise arrived. But "Inner Africa" was not a lodestar—except to a rather lonely figure whose eager spirit, harnessed to a grim determination whenever conscience approved, was destined to lead him to resounding achievement. Silently and for the most part unobserved, David Livingstone during the 'forties underwent a steady discipline of preparation that, in the mid-'fifties, issued in the first grand trans-continental journey, which commanded the attention of the world.

(1) *The Apprenticeship*

David Livingstone[1] was born at Blantyre on March 19, 1813. Although born in the Lowlands he came on his father's side of Highland stock. The quality of his home may be judged from words he chose for his parents' tombstone: ". . . to express the thankfulness to God of their children . . . for poor and pious parents."[2] At the age of ten he passed from school to factory,

---

[1] It is tempting to link his name with his character (as a friend once did with his career), and see in it the combination of eager vitality with rock-like determination and stability.

[2] True to his simplicity of character Livingstone resisted a suggestion that "and" should be "but".—Blaikie, *The Life of David Livingstone* (11th impression, 1906), 8.

but not from mental activity to inertia. Out of his first week's wages he bought a Latin Grammar, though time for study was now severely limited by his working day—six in the morning to eight at night, with two breaks for meals. Attendance at an evening school from eight to ten, for the study of Latin, followed by what he terms "the dictionary part of my labours" till midnight completed a working day of some sixteen hours. He was soon reading many of the Latin classics in the original. He devoured books voraciously, scientific studies and records of travel being his favourites. At twenty-three he entered as a student at the University of Glasgow, paying his own way by dint of summer labour, his elder brother John, in traditional Scottish fashion, supplementing his resources when necessary. It was a stern and severe discipline, but he never regretted having borne the yoke in his youth. Twenty years later he wrote of it: "Were it possible, I should like to begin life over again in the same lowly style, and to pass through the same hardy training."[1]

His concern to study medicine was linked with his sense of missionary vocation. It is interesting how this came about. A predisposing cause is to be seen in his father's enthusiasm for all good Christian works, including the support of missions. So much so, that after his self-committal as a Christian believer in about his twentieth year, David Livingstone resolved to devote to missions the margin of his earnings beyond a subsistence allowance.[2] It was at about the same time, in 1833, that a distinguished missionary pioneer in China, Karl Gützlaff, who had just completed three coasting voyages, issued one of his appeals to the Christian public of the West. A copy came into David Livingstone's hands and deeply impressed him. Gützlaff, who was an individual missionary from 1828 and whose medical work had proved a valuable asset in his enterprise, sought like-minded men to join him at their own expense.[3] The force of this appeal led to Livingstone's decision to study medicine with the object of becoming a medical missionary to China.[4]

---

[1] D. Livingstone, *Missionary Travels and Researches in South Africa* (1857), 3–4, 6. On his brother's help, cf. R. J. Campbell, *Livingstone* (1929), 49.

[2] Blaikie, *op. cit.*, 12.

[3] H. Schlyter, *Karl Gützlaff als Missionar in China* (1946), 83–6, 123. The inception of the China Inland Mission under Hudson Taylor, who was first sent to China by the Gützlaff Association in London in 1853, is traceable to Gützlaff, the real father of the C.I.M., as Hudson Taylor called him.—*Ibid.*, 287–90.

[4] There is direct evidence for this connexion of a missionary vocation with the practice of medicine in a letter of Livingstone's father to the Secretary of the London Missionary Society, quoted in Campbell, *op. cit.*, 59.

After two sessions at the University of Glasgow (1836–38) Livingstone submitted an offer of service to the London Missionary Society.[1] He was provisionally accepted and after a prescribed course of preparation along with other candidates of the Society, had an opportunity of completing his medical studies and becoming qualified. But meanwhile the Opium War of 1839–41 had made the possibility of service in China recede indefinitely.[2] Coincident with this was an encounter with Robert Moffat who was then on his first visit to England. After opportunities of meeting and hearing him, Livingstone inquired whether he would do for Africa, and Moffat records his reply: "I said I believed he would, if he would not go to an old station, but would advance to unoccupied ground, specifying the vast plain to the north, where I had sometimes seen, in the morning sun, the smoke of a thousand villages, where no missionary had ever been."[3] His own decision now coincided with that of the Directors and he was appointed to the Society's South African field. On December 8, 1840 he sailed from London, reaching Cape Town on March 15, 1841. A month was spent there before the resumed voyage to Algoa Bay, where from Port Elizabeth a trek overland brought him by July 31 to Kuruman, the mission station then lying farthest north. David Livingstone had reached his base.

That his work should lie at the outpost and beyond was confirmed for him by what he saw of missions at the Cape. He admitted his limited field of observation, but he had seen enough to lead him to think that region sufficiently, if not excessively, well supplied with missionaries—indeed, he hazarded that there were three times too many.[4] When he found a concentration, not to say congestion, of workers in centres of limited population—Dutch Reformed, Anglican, Wesleyan, and Independent, with a Government schoolmaster in addition, cheek by jowl in places of some thousand or so inhabitants—he naturally grudged the starving of the regions beyond.[5] He further held that such a situation encouraged that deterioration in personal

---

[1] Blaikie, *op. cit.*, 19.

[2] *Ibid.*, 25–6. In November, 1840, he was admitted a Licentiate of the Faculty of Physicians and Surgeons (Glasgow).—Livingstone, *op. cit.*, 7. His decision on a change of field was taken before the war actually broke out.—Campbell, *op. cit.*, 63.

[3] Blaikie, *op. cit.*, 28.

[4] Blaikie, *op. cit.*, 68.

[5] Chamberlin, *Some Letters from Livingstone, 1840–1872* (1940), 108–9. "The Colonial market is literally glutted with missionaries," he wrote to Tidman in 1847. Cf. Blaikie, *op. cit.*, 31, 47–8; Chamberlin, *op. cit.*, 200.

relations between missionaries which had given him an un-expected shock on his arrival, while the same cause seriously limited the field of activity for African converts.[1] There was little enough inducement, then, for Livingstone to modify his original plan of service on the missionary frontier.[2]

The Directors had appointed him to the mission staff at Kuruman where he found himself with four colleagues: Hamil-ton, Ross and Edwards, and Moffat who was still in England. The limited population around Kuruman was a disappoint-ment, and within a couple of months Edwards and Livingstone set out for the north, prospecting for new fields. They reached a point they estimated to be some 250 miles north-east of Kuru-man, though their double journey covered 700 miles. The people they came upon were the Kwenas located in the Bechu-analand Protectorate of to-day. They found chiefs and people eager for missionaries, though from mixed motives. This was the occasion of Livingstone's introduction to the chief Sechele.[3] In preparation for service among them he now withdrew from Kuruman for six months and lived the only European among a section of the Kwena at Molepolole, to the study of whose language and tribal life he devoted himself with the same assiduity that had marked his student days in Glasgow. This strenuous self-discipline produced its own rich reward. "I gained", he says, "by this ordeal an insight into the habits, ways of thinking, laws and language of that section of the Bechuanas, called Bakwains, which has proved of incalculable advantage in my intercourse with them ever since."[4] Before returning to Kuruman he pushed farther north and visited the Ngwato tribe. He was then but ten days' journey from the lower Zuga, a river flowing south-eastwards from the neighbourhood of Lake Ngami, and somewhat laconically remarks later: "I might then (in 1842) have discovered that lake, had discovery alone been my object."[5] The intention to settle among the Kwena being foiled by tribal war, a centre was selected among the

---

[1] Blaikie, *op. cit.*, 47; Chamberlin, *op. cit.*, 109.

[2] Blaikie states that he had been invited on arrival to supply for Dr. Philip in Cape Town during the latter's absence in England.—*Op. cit.*, 31. But there seems to be reason to doubt this.—Chamberlin, *op. cit.*, 23 *n.*

[3] Fifty-eighth *Report of the Directors* (1842), 16, 85. Kwena is the form of the name now in use by ethnologists for the tribe described by the missionaries as Bakwains.

[4] Livingstone, *op. cit.*, 9. He approached his study of African languages with an independent mind. He produced a Sechuana Grammar of which he said: "Mine is on the principle of an analysis of the language, without reference to any other."— J. I. Macnair, *Livingstone the Liberator* (1940), 112–13 and *n.*

[5] Livingstone, *op. cit.*, 10.

now more accessible Khatla tribe at Mabotsa to the south-east of the Kwena, but still some 250 miles north of Kuruman. Here Livingstone and Edwards removed in August 1843, and here Livingstone had his well-nigh fatal adventure with a lion.[1] To Mabotsa early in 1845 Livingstone brought his bride Mary, eldest daughter of Robert Moffat.[2] It had taken five visits, says Livingstone, to win sufficient confidence for the Khatla to offer the missionary a cordial invitation to settle among them, so that now a thriving centre serving the dozen or so villages around was hoped for.[3] But as far as the Livingstones were concerned this hope was denied them. Rogers Edwards, the senior colleague, found himself in harness with a man of initiative and resented what he regarded as a reflection on himself. In the end Livingstone felt the only way to avoid the scandal of open disagreement was to remove.[4] Thus it was that he came to settle among the Kwena at Chonuane, the residence of Sechele, some fifty miles north-east of Mabotsa. The cordial relations with the chief developed into a fast friendship, so much so that when there arose necessity for removal Sechele declared: "Though all my people should leave me, I am determined to cleave to you wherever it may be needful to go." The water supply had proved inadequate, though the tribe found good garden ground for their particular crops. The decision was taken to remove some forty miles to the north-west on the Kolobeng River, after which the settlement took its name. Here Sechele and his people came and set about building a new town.[5] This proved to be the last settled station Livingstone ever had.

The personal relations that existed between the missionary and the chief can only be characterized as those of a true friendship founded on mutual respect. It has been suggested that Livingstone's Highland ancestry naturally led him to an appre-

---

[1] *Ibid.*, 11–13; Blaikie, *op. cit.*, 55–6; Macnair, *op. cit.*, 82–5. His matter-of-fact treatment of the incident is shown in his reply to the inquirer who asked what his thoughts were with the lion above him: "I was thinking what part of me he would eat first!" The injury was serious and his left arm remained permanently crippled.

[2] Chamberlin, *op. cit.*, 76 n. He had earlier written with some hesitation about the advisability of marriage, despite the good advice that he says was showered upon him. Apparently his encounter with Mary Moffat on the family's return in 1843 settled the point.—*Ibid.*, 8; Blaikie, *op. cit.*, 57. Concerning his friendship with Catherine Ridley during the training period at Chipping Ongar in Essex; see Macnair, *op. cit.*, 53–6.

[3] Fifty-first *Report of the Directors* (1845), 124–5.

[4] On the correspondence which took place, see Chamberlin, *op. cit.*, 82. Cf. Blaikie, *op. cit.*, 62–3; Macnair, *op. cit.*, 89–92.

[5] Fifty-fourth *Report of the Directors* (1848), 116–17; Chamberlin, *op. cit.*, 110–11.

ciation of chieftainship.[1] Be that as it may, his capacity for establishing happy relations with chiefs who enjoyed full independence in the Africa of their day was characteristic of his progress through the continent. Sechele was a chief of outstanding qualities. He speedily learnt to read, mastering the alphabet in a day, and made the Bible his regular manual. Livingstone records that Isaiah was a great favourite with him, and that he would say: "He was a fine man, that Isaiah; he knew how to speak." At Kolobeng Sechele spontaneously offered "to build a house for God, the Defender of my town". When his own house was completed he asked the missionary to conduct daily prayer: "I greatly desire to have prayer in my house every evening." Sechele was a polygamist, and as such not eligible for Christian baptism. Livingstone, with a fine sympathy for those involved, was careful not to bring pressure to bear; but when Sechele was resolute to fulfil the requirement of monogamy, with due regard for those being separated from him, Livingstone accepted his decision. The chief became a baptized convert.[2] News travels fast in Africa. Hearing that Sechele had embraced "the word of peace", the tribe of the Kaa some 1,000 strong, who had suffered from repeated Ngwato attacks, trekked the 150 miles south to Kolobeng to place themselves under Sechele. They said they came "to enjoy sleep as they had none at home".[3] Such attachments to a trusted protector were not infrequent in periods of tribal commotion.

Livingstone had from the first been an advocate of a policy of African agency for expanding evangelism, and he now sought to act upon it. His attempt to advance to the east to locate a teacher first brought him into collision with the Boers. A commando against the tribe concerned was threatened, the allegation being that Livingstone was an advance agent of the British Government and was supplying the tribes with firearms. In consultation with some ministers of the Dutch Reformed Church, who proved more reasonable, he was persuaded to hold his hand. But the hostility did not abate, and Livingstone soon found that any advance to the east was permanently

[1] Blaikie, *op. cit.*, 4.
[2] Fifty-fourth *Report of the Directors* (1848), 117; Livingstone, *op. cit.*, 15–18; Chamberlin, *op. cit.*, 121. Livingstone wrote to the Directors at some length on the circumstances of Sechele's conversion and baptism.—Fifty-fifth *Report* (1849), 106–7. To Livingstone's great sorrow, Sechele had later to be placed under discipline; he details the circumstances in a letter to W. Thompson.—Chamberlin, *op. cit.*, 181–2. Robert Moffat was also critical at a later date.—J. P. R. Wallis, *The Matabele Journals of Robert Moffat* (1945), II, 29–30, 33, 35. Cf. Macnair, *op. cit.*, 102–3.
[3] Fifty-sixth *Report of the Directors* (1850), 92.

blocked. The hostility was further driven home by the disaster that was shortly to overtake the mission at Kolobeng. That only left open the north.[1]

On his arrival at the Cape Livingstone heard talk of a large fresh-water lake in the interior. He had now heard more of it, and Sechele had told him of a great chief to the north of the lake, Sebitwane. Here was a double incentive to prospect in that direction. So it came about that on June 1, 1849 David Livingstone accompanied by two friends, Oswell and Murray who were travelling in the country as hunters, set out to find the lake. After two months' travel across the Kalahari desert they sighted Lake Ngami, the first Europeans to do so, on August 1, 1849. This event and the discovery of Kilimanjaro in 1848 have been acclaimed as marking the beginning of the exploration of Central Africa.[2] A fine river flowing into the lake from the north stirred Livingstone's imagination: "What think you of a navigable highway into a large section of the interior? . . . Is it not the Niger of this part of Africa?"[3] Memories of Exeter Hall, June 1, 1840! The Directors of the London Mission concurred: "The discovery of large inland rivers running from the north—that hitherto *terra incognita*—seems to open a highway for the progress of the gospel in the interior of Africa."[4] This was not to prove the means, but the event was to happen. Meanwhile the appetite of the intrepid missionary pioneer was whetted for more.

A second visit was planned with little delay. A main object on the first journey had been to pass beyond the lake and make contact with Sebitwane, chief of the Makololo.[5] This he now set out to do. In April 1850, accompanied by Mrs. Livingstone and

[1] *Ibid.*, 92–3; Blaikie, *op. cit.*, 64–7, 74–6, 88; Chamberlin, *op. cit.*, 97–8, 126. For Livingstone's early advocacy of African agency, as soon as he had some knowledge of the country, see his letter to the Directors.—Forty-ninth *Report* (1843), 13–14.

[2] Livingstone, *op. cit.*, 65–8; Blaikie, *op. cit.*, 82–6. When the discovery was reported to the Royal Geographical Society, the President gave frank recognition of the fact that a missionary, possessing the essential requirement of the confidence of the tribes, had accomplished what others had failed to do. With this Livingstone concurred: "The lake belongs to missionary enterprise." This was true in a double sense, for the discovery was not only made by a missionary, but in the course of missionary prospecting for advance. Speaking of discoveries, Livingstone wrote later: "I never need to go much or at all out of my way to make them."—Blaikie, *op. cit.*, 85; Chamberlin, *op. cit.*, 194. At Lake Ngami he had reached a point some 870 miles north of the mission base at Kuruman. On Livingstone's right to be recognized as the discoverer, see H. H. Johnston, *Livingstone and the Exploration of Central Africa* (1891), 98 *n.* 1.

[3] In a letter to D. G. Watt.—Blaikie, *op. cit.*, 84.

[4] Fifty-sixth *Report of the Directors* (1850), 8.

[5] This form is so embedded in the literature that it is retained for the modern ethnologist's Kololo.

their three children and the chief Sechele, he once more journeyed to the lake. But tsetse fly was found on the banks of the river they had hoped to ascend, so their wagons had to turn back.[1] Livingstone was prepared to push on alone but, the children coming down with fever, that proposal had to be abandoned, and the whole party returned to Kolobeng.[2] News had meanwhile reached Sebitwane that a white man was seeking to visit him, but his efforts to facilitate Livingstone's progress were foiled by the commercial jealousy of intervening chiefs. A year after the second attempt, in April 1851, Livingstone again set out with his family, and this time with Mr. Oswell also, who proved a valued friend on this as on other occasions. Success attended them. Sebitwane gave Livingstone a warm welcome, and deeply appreciated the confidence shown by the presence of Mrs. Livingstone and the children, for in Africa men travelled alone when doubtful of public security. But the intercourse was short-lived. Sebitwane fell ill with inflammation of the lungs, starting in an old wound, and within a fortnight he was dead. Livingstone had wisely refrained from treatment lest in the event of death he should be accused—a view that was confirmed by those around.[3] To Livingstone it came as a heavy personal loss: "He was decidedly the best specimen of a native chief I ever met. I never felt so much grieved by the loss of a black man before."[4] With the permission of Sebitwane's daughter who now acceded to the chieftainship, Livingstone and Oswell travelled in the country and in June 1851, 130 miles or so to the north-east, discovered the Zambezi flowing in the heart of the continent. Livingstone comments: "This was a most important point, for that river was not previously known to exist there at all."[5] In August 1851 the party set out for Kolobeng. In October Livingstone had formed his plan and wrote to the Directors proposing the return of his wife and children to England, while he set out to open up the new territory: "This arrangement would enable me to proceed, and devote about two or perhaps three years to this new region; but I must beg your sanction. . . . To orphanise my

---

[1] The fly was *glossina morsitans*, says Livingstone, the vector of nagana in cattle. The first specimens of the fly had been brought to England from the Limpopo in 1848.—Livingstone, *op. cit.*, 75 *n.*

[2] Fifty-seventh *Report of the Directors* (1851), 94; Livingstone, *op. cit.*, 74–6.

[3] Dr. E. W. Smith informs me: "Old men have told me that Sebitwane died after falling from Livingstone's horse. This may have caused an old wound to break out."

[4] Livingstone, *op. cit.*, 90.

[5] *Ibid.*, 90.

children will be like tearing out my bowels, but . . . it is the only way, except giving up that region altogether." The Directors gave their sanction.[1] On April 23, 1852 Mrs. Livingstone and their four children sailed from Cape Town. On June 8 Livingstone left Cape Town for the north, a lonely man. But his loneliness was the price of a master plan for Africa. The apprenticeship was over.

(2) *Contemporary Enterprise*—(a) *Within Colonial Territory*

During these years missionary enterprise had been proceeding within and beyond the Colony, and this it is now necessary to review to the limit of our present period. The political uneasiness of the time, often flaring up into acute distress at the two points of inflammatory contact—Colony and emigrant Boers on the one hand, and Colony and Bantu tribes on the other—provided the sombre, when not somewhat lurid, background to their work.

The Boer farmers who had established a republic east of the Drakensberg in Natal under Pretorius, successor to the murdered Retief, had seen their flag hoisted in December 1839. The trekkers were anxious for the privileges without the responsibilities of British subjects—a request the hard-pressed Sir George Napier found it scarcely convenient to concede. But when the Boers began to unload unwanted Bantu to the south in the Pondoland of to-day, colonial peace was threatened and in the ensuing clash Port Natal was occupied by British troops in May 1842. Napier was prepared to discuss a modified form of independence on terms the trekkers found unacceptable: "No colour bar, no encroachment on native lands and no slavery." The frail remains of the republic crumbled, and the trekkers began to move across the Drakensberg to the Vaal and beyond. Natal was finally annexed as a district of the Cape in 1845, and eleven years later was erected into a Crown Colony.[2]

When Sir Harry Smith arrived as Governor at the Cape in December 1847, "bursting as ever with vigour and good intentions", the political pace quickened. He was already experi-

---

[1] Blaikie, *op. cit.*, 99–100; Fifty-eighth *Report of the Directors* (1852), 15–16; Chamberlin, *op. cit.*, 165.

[2] E. A. Walker, *A History of South Africa* (1947 edition), 218–19, 223–4, 229–30, 278. There was a high political concern in these events, in that the British Government could scarcely consent to independent republics having uncontrolled access to the sea where they might provide entry for a foreign power. The Natal Republic had mistakenly claimed Dutch intervention ("the seventeenth century Holland of their imagination"), but the hand of France was actually suspect.—*Ibid.*, 224, 229.

enced in South African affairs and *persona grata* to both Dutch and English colonists. He crossed the Orange River and finding, as he believed, emigrant Boers and African chiefs both agreeable to the Queen's sovereignty, he proclaimed it in February 1848 for the region west of the Drakensberg lying between the Orange and Vaal rivers. The Orange River Sovereignty carried on a precarious existence for half a dozen years. Meanwhile the emigrant farmers beyond the Vaal, in a territory of 100,000 square miles or so, were feeling their way to some kind of political order. In the nature of the case the type of Boer here was distinctive: they had come farthest because they resented interference most, and as always, malcontents and outlaws found the distance from civil authority congenial. By 1849 they had secured a Volksraad for the Transvaal, and by 1852 had been recognized by the British Government in the Sand River Convention as free to manage their own affairs. The Boers guaranteed no slavery, and on their side the British undertook to refrain from any alliance with African chiefs beyond the Vaal. It was perhaps inevitable that after this the Orange River Sovereignty should be abandoned and the Orange Free State be born in the Bloemfontein Convention of 1854, with a similar undertaking concerning chiefs north of the Orange River.[1]

Relations with the Bantu tribes on the eastern frontier had improved for a period under the change of policy following the disastrous war of 1834–5. What became known as the Stockenstrom system[2]—security for the frontier by treaty—functioned for a time, whereby reprisal by patrol and commando for cattle stealing was replaced by recourse to reason, as recognized in Bantu law.[3] But with failure on both sides to observe the treaties, and the loss of confidence in the Government's good faith which Stockenstrom's withdrawal produced, the system eventually broke down.[4] The increasing tension in relations between colonists and tribes provided the atmosphere in which open conflict again loomed on the horizon. When the War of the Axe broke out early in 1846 Sir Peregrine Maitland decided on

---

[1] *Ibid.*, 237, 240–1, 255–7, 261, 266.

[2] Andries Stockenstrom, who had retired after twenty years' frontier service, was appointed by Lord Glenelg in 1836 Lieutenant-Governor of the Eastern Districts. At the end of the year the treaty system had been inaugurated.—Macmillan, *Bantu, Boer and Briton* (1929), 151, 158. For his trials and frustration; cf. *ibid.*, 153–7, 234–43.

[3] Walker, *op. cit.*, 220; Macmillan, *op. cit.*, 228–31, 234.

[4] Walker, *op. cit.*, 220, 232–3; Macmillan, *op. cit.*, 234, 238–40.

immediate action and colonial forces crossed the frontier. But he made clear that no land would be handed out for farms at the end of it, and the colonists for the most part remained apathetic.[1] Upon the agreed signal—the firing by the troops of the first Kafir hut—the frontier tribes raided the Colony and did much damage before they were contained. By the end of the year the fighting was over and the territory between the Keiskamma and the Kei then remained under colonial control. Within a year it had been annexed by the newly arrived Governor, Sir Harry Smith. Colonists were given farms and protection was planned for mission stations.[2] The fundamental causes of Bantu discontent, however, remained and there was not long to wait for the explosion. The war of 1850 proved the longest and the most costly of the whole disastrous series. "The root weakness of the settlement", says Walker of Sir Harry Smith's arrangements, "was that too much was expected of the chiefs and too little given in exchange for their loss of power."[3] The war, in which the loss of the *Birkenhead* was a long-remembered episode, dragged on for a couple of years and cost the British Exchequer two millions sterling.[4] Sir George Cathcart, who had succeeded Sir Harry Smith, finally cleaned up affairs early in 1853. In the following year he was succeeded as Governor of the Cape by Sir George Grey, whose seven years' administration was rendered notable by high statesmanship and as genuine a concern for African as for European interests.

The year 1854 also marked a political milestone in the history of South Africa. The grant of representative government was then made to Cape Colony, the first Cape Parliament meeting in June of that year. There was no colour bar. All adult male British subjects enjoyed the franchise on terms intended to be

---

[1] The so-called Seventh Kafir War was popularly known as the War of the Axe from the attack on a police escort and rescue of the prisoner who was accused of the theft of an axe. The rescue involved the killing of a Hottentot, and the chiefs, on demand, declined to surrender the murderers.—Walker, *op. cit.*, 235–6; Macmillan, *op. cit.*, 228, 255–63.

[2] Walker, *op. cit.*, 237–8. Sir Harry exhorted the chiefs: "So be good and believe your father as you used to call me. . . . You *shall* be good and I *will* have peace that my people may plough."—*Ibid.*, 238, *n.* 1. Italics in original.

[3] *Ibid.*, 258–9.

[4] *Ibid.*, 263. The War of the Axe had cost the British taxpayer a million sterling.—*Ibid.*, 242. The Rev. J. J. Freeman, a Director of the London Mission deputed to survey the field, reported on his return, before the outbreak, that he found among frontier chiefs and tribes a deep-seated sense of wrong, and that several among them besought him "to seek for them that justice from the Government of Britain which they had sought in vain from its local representatives."—Fifty-seventh *Report of the Directors* (1851), 15.

reasonable for all.[1] The various political units that now complicated the South African scene—Cape Colony with its Parliament, the Transvaal Republic recognized in 1852, and the
Orange Free State in 1854, together with Natal shortly to receive Crown Colony status (in 1856)—raised large issues of
political and racial relationship, for the background to the
whole was constituted by the African tribes, not infrequently
led by chiefs of ability among whom Moshesh of the Basuto was
outstanding. When the then Colonial Secretary, Sir Bulmer
Lytton, invited Sir George Grey to state his views on the major
political issues, he replied in a masterly review of the situation
with a closely reasoned case for federation—a state document
that remains a classic.[2] Unhappily his proposals were not to
determine policy in the 'sixties (he retired in 1861), but half a
century later were destined to find their essential realization in
the Union Act of 1909. Such were some of the conditions of the
period—a necessarily extreme simplification of a highly complex
situation—under which the Christian missionary enterprise was
carried forward.

The Dutch Reformed Church, from the nature of the case,
bore the major responsibility in ministering to the religious
needs of the colonists. To supply their pastorates with qualified
clergymen was difficult, but recruitment both from Scottish
Presbyterianism and the ranks of the London Mission relieved
the pressure created by moving frontiers.[3] With the achievement of self-government for the Church in 1843 there came a
new concern for active evangelism, and the Synod of that year
appointed a Committee whose responsibility was the field of
home missions. Travelling missionaries, to serve in the existing
parishes, were in due course appointed.[4]

[1] "Occupation for twelve months of premises worth £25 per annum or a salary
of £50 or, with board and lodging, £25."—Walker, *op. cit.*, 252 n. 1. On the constitution governing the Cape Parliament, see Walker, 251–2. The war of 1850 has-
tened rather than retarded the grant, on the ground that the colonists should bear
the burden of their wars, with the possibility that this might produce more restraint
in inflammable situations. Gladstone told Bishop Gray that he favoured the grant
of representative government (which Gray did not) on the same ground.—C. Gray,
Life of Robert Gray, Bishop of Cape Town (1876), I, 359.
[2] His despatch, dated November 19, 1858, was printed in Parliamentary Paper,
No. 216, of April, 1860. It is reprinted in F. R. Cana, *South Africa from the Great
Trek to the Union* (1909), Appendix II. A substantial extract is quoted by Walker,
op. cit., 280.
[3] Du Plessis names some of the more notable recruits.—*A History of Christian
Missions in South Africa* (1911), 254 n. 1, 2; G. M. Theal, *History of South Africa,
1834–1854* (1893), 577.
[4] Theal, *op. cit.*, 577; Walker, *op. cit.*, 246; Du Plessis, *op. cit.*, 254–5.

The problem of the voortrekkers was a special one. The Church had not approved of the Great Trek, and for long the emigrants were without help from their own ministers. The action of the Church Synod in issuing a pastoral letter in 1837 condemning the Trek may have restrained some, but left an unpleasant memory with many of the trekkers.[1] Meanwhile, in default of their own clergy help was received from J. Archbell of the Wesleyan station at Thaba Nchu and Daniel Lindley of the American Board. Lindley's ministry was outstanding: already serving the Boers in Port Natal, he was in 1841 called to be exclusively their minister in Pietermaritzburg, and gave them devoted service until, in 1847, he returned to the Zulu Mission.[2] After a decade (from 1847 onwards), however, those in the Transvaal received periodical visits from Dutch Reformed ministers as those in Natal and the Orange River Sovereignty had already done. When at length a minister from Holland arrived in the Transvaal it was decreed by their General Church Assembly that they should remain independent of the Cape Synod, in contrast to Natal and the Sovereignty.[3]

The Moravian Mission continued its distinctive service to Hottentots in the pioneer settlement at Genadendal and at other centres, but opened no new stations in the west of the Colony between 1839 and 1859. In the east Shiloh, founded in 1828, was a similar settlement for both Hottentots and the Bantu of the frontier region. It had a chequered career. In the War of 1847 Shiloh became a military camp, with such unhappy results for the mission as might be expected. In the war of 1850 British troops, imagining the Hottentots there to be rebels, beseiged the place and destroyed it. It was, however, rebuilt by the Government.[4] The work of the Moravian missionaries was much valued by the authorities, and Bishop Gray regarded it, despite certain criticisms, as the best of its kind in the Colony.[5]

The London Mission lost in this period the distinguished leader who had guided its affairs for thirty years. John Philip died at Hankey on August 27, 1851 aged seventy-six.[6] In-

---

[1] E. A. Walker, *The Great Trek* (1934), 182–3; E. W. Smith, *The Life and Times of Daniel Lindley* (1949), 178–9.
[2] E. W. Smith, *op. cit.*, 180–206.
[3] Walker, *History of South Africa*, 268, 274.
[4] J. E. Hutton, *A History of Moravian Missions* (1923), 281, 290–2. Shiloh lay between the Great Fish and the Kei Rivers; see Walker, *op. cit.*, map at p. 240.
[5] C. Gray, *op. cit.*, I, 192, 269, 318.
[6] Fifty-eighth *Report of the Directors* (1852), 3.

creasing infirmity had weakened his hold on affairs in later years, and the death of his son William in 1845 by drowning while in the service of the Mission came as a shattering blow. There were those who had resented his superintendency and created prejudice against him, but fair-minded men who met him paid tribute to the man and his notable achievements for the Hottentots.[1] Together with the death of the aged James Read in 1852, an earlier generation was thus seen to be passing. These events speeded decision on an issue that had already been a matter of concern: the question of self-support for the churches of the Colony. A circular letter from the Board in 1853 raised the question officially, and in 1856 the Directors passed a series of resolutions initiating the policy of self-support at the Cape. A beginning had already been made, so that in 1857 the Directors were thankfully able to record that their hopes had been more than realized.[2]

Of the Institutions which the Mission had developed for Hottentot welfare two examples may be taken. Hankey was situated on the Gamtoos River, claimed to be one of the finest in the Colony, emptying itself into St. Francis Bay to the west of Port Elizabeth. Bearing down silt from the Karroo, the river was of great fertility value, but irrigation facilities were limited. W. Philip (Dr. Philip's son), though an amateur, engineered a tunnel some 260 yards long through a sandstone ridge, thus leading the fertilizing waters to the Institution lands which, from serving a population of 300, now became capable of supporting 3,000. Thus the wedding of the Bible and the plough received practical demonstration.[3] The Kat River Settlement was the leading London Mission enterprise in the east. Its position on the frontier exposed it to peril and eventually to disaster. Here the Reads, father and son, devoted themselves to the welfare of the Hottentots, prepared teachers for surrounding villages, and

---

[1] David Livingstone's estimate is perhaps of special interest: "I came to the Cape full of prejudice against him, but after living a month at his house and carefully scrutinizing his character that prejudice was entirely dissolved and affection and the greatest respect took its place."—Chamberlin, *op. cit.*, 22; cf. 20, 23; T. Hughes, *David Livingstone* (1889), 12–13. Such critical appraisals as those of Du Plessis (*op. cit.*, 152–3) and Findlay and Holdsworth (*History of the Wesleyan Methodist Missionary Society*, IV, 272–4) need to be read in the light of W. M. Macmillan's more recent researches.

[2] Sixty-third *Report* (1857), 10. For the official resolutions, see Sixty-second *Report* (1856), 11–12; also A. J. Haile, *A Brief Historical Survey of the London Missionary Society in Southern Africa* (1951), 7–8.

[3] Fiftieth *Report* (1844), 88; Fifty-first *Report* (1845), 102–3. Quaker friends, James Backhouse among them, contributed liberally towards the cost.

even directed a mission to Bushmen. The Superintendent General of Education early paid a tribute to its educational service, and added: "In no part of the colony have I seen cultivation carried on to the same extent . . . the Kat River is one of the most interesting sights in South Africa."[1] The Bushman mission arose from the spontaneous desire of the Christian Hottentots at Kat River. At their own expense they maintained a teacher with two assistants for agriculture, and supplied a plough and seeds. The problem was to get the shy Bushmen to come in and settle at the selected centre, but their confidence was won and the work among them began. James Read the younger reported that the chief and his people "say they now begin to think they belong to the human race, because there are men who seem concerned about them". Surely there could be no more Christ-like work than this. The station was christened New Bethelsdorp, and numbers began to swell as cautious Bushmen crept out of their hiding-places among the rocks. The people of Kat River had presented them with ten oxen in addition to other equipment. Some of the children and even a few adults had begun to read the New Testament when the war of 1846 burst upon them and broke up this promising work.[2] The Kat River Settlement itself suffered severely in a conflict in which some twenty mission stations of the London and other Societies were abandoned and destroyed.[3] Many Hottentots of the Settlement served with the colonial forces, and being deprived of pastoral care and exposed to the corroding influences of a military camp for more than a year, were in no condition to return and assist the Settlement to resume its normal life. It was this moral and spiritual decline rather than the tale of material loss, heavy as that was, which constituted the scars of war for this as for other stations. The sad story was repeated in fuller measure three years later, with this difference—that part of the hitherto loyal Hottentot population of the Kat River now joined the Bantu invaders of the Colony. This was fateful news for the colonial press, and rumour soon multiplied the number of centres of disaffection in their midst. Passion usurped the throne of reason, and the real perils of a conflict between black

[1] Forty-sixth *Report* (1840), 83.
[2] Forty-sixth *Report* (1840), 83–5; Forty-seventh *Report* (1841), 84; Forty-ninth *Report* (1843), 93; Fifty-third *Report* (1847), 101.
[3] Fifty-third *Report* (1847), 106. Calderwood wrote to the L.M.S. (August 13, 1846): "Except near Peddie and Block Drift, all stations of London, Scottish, Wesleyan and German societies this side the Kei have been destroyed. It is a sad blow to us all."—Macmillan, *Bantu, Boer and Briton*, 257 n. 2.

and white were needlessly increased.[1] The Directors of the London Mission, emphatically condemning the acts of cruelty and rapine perpetrated against the colonists, yet were courageously outspoken: "The Kaffirs are charged with robbery and encroachment; but whose lands have they sought but the lands of their fathers? What soil have they claimed but the soil that gave them birth? Why should the love of home and the love of country be eulogised as the virtues of patriotism in the civilized, and be branded as crimes and rebellion in the savage? . . . How could Christianity be more awfully blasphemed or rendered more hateful to the heathen than when the blessing of its Author is invoked to sanction these sanguinary counsels and prosper this purpose of desolation and death?"[2] The bitterness of colonial feeling against the London Mission in particular may be gauged from the fact that when the Society raised a relief fund in Great Britain to meet the urgent needs of destitute missionaries and "the relief of the afflicted and homeless poor" they were stigmatized by a portion of the colonists as "sympathizers with traitors, and friends of rebellion".[3] The cloud under which the London Mission had worked in the Colony, since John Philip's championship of the Hottentot, was rolling up again in redoubled anger.

The Wesleyan work pioneered by William Shaw had included both colonists and Bantu peoples. The first three links in the chain of stations he began in Bantuland—Wesleyville, Mount Coke and Butterworth—proved the most vulnerable, as nearest to the frontier. All three were destroyed in the wars of 1835 and 1846, and rebuilt on each occasion.[4] In 1851 Wesleyville and Butterworth were destroyed for the third time in half a generation, and Mount Coke attacked. Wesleyville remained a ruin. Clarkebury in Tembuland, though attacked in 1851, escaped destruction; Morley and Buntingville in Pondoland

[1] Fifty-seventh *Report* (1851), 15–16; Fifty-eighth *Report* (1852), 10–11. An outrage at Grahamstown calculated to inflame racial feeling, perpetrated against the Hottentot location, was reported by the London missionary there who, refusing to be intimidated, remained as an eyewitness. Innocent and loyal people lost homes and possessions, for many houses were burned. In some cases the Hottentot men of the family were serving at the front.—Fifty-eighth *Report* (1852), 12; cf. 58–9.

[2] Fifty-seventh *Report* (1851), 15. This last point was brought vividly home by an officer's account of the terrible carnage inflicted between the Keiskamma and Fish Rivers, quoted in the Fifty-ninth *Report* (1853), 12. Cf. J. Whiteside, *History of the Wesleyan Methodist Church of South Africa* (1906), 222.

[3] Fifty-eighth *Report* (1852), 14.

[4] For the losses in the war of 1846, see Whiteside, *op. cit.* (1906), 221–6.

were also spared, as was Shawbury in the north Transkei.[1] But the losses in physical equipment were the least to be regretted. More ominous was the change in atmosphere among hitherto friendly peoples. The war, says Whiteside, had "embittered the natives against Europeans, and the missionaries had to suffer. . . . The same hostile influence was felt in places so far apart as Butterworth and Shawbury. There was everywhere a resuscitated antagonism to Christian teaching; the missionary was not welcomed as he had formerly been".[2] The depression lasted for half a generation. Where fourteen workers—half of them ministers—had served before the war, there were but four (two of them ministers) in 1854. This sharp decline disheartened the faithful few who held on despite the now strongly flowing tide of paganism that threatened to overwhelm them.[3] A reinforcement of four missionaries in 1857 brought some relief, but the up-surging paganism received its heaviest blow from an unparalleled disaster that overtook the Xhosa peoples. This was the famous cattle-killing delusion of 1857.

Nongqawuse, a young girl of about sixteen, professed to have seen strange people with cattle, including departed ancestors of renown who, moved by the sufferings of their people, would rise again to help them; but there was a hard condition: all their cattle must be destroyed and all their corn consumed. The girl reported to her uncle (some say father) Mhlakaza, a diviner, who duly made public the revelation. Kreli, paramount of the Galekas, accepted the message from the ancestors, and instructed his people accordingly. Sandile of the Gaikas held off for a time, under the influence of Commissioner Charles Brownlee, but finally succumbed. From March 1856 the story of the message rolled on like a snowball, accumulating lavish rumours of European destruction and a glorious future of prosperity in store for the Xhosa peoples. The killing of cattle which began in 1856 moved on to a climax in 1857, accompanied by the consumption of the stocks of corn and the refusal to plant for the next season. The inevitable penalty of famine fell upon the deluded people in place of the golden harvest of their dreams. Thus stabbed to a rude awakening, such as managed to survive

---

[1] Whiteside, *op. cit.*, 226–9. When Sir George Grey visited the eastern frontier and found Butterworth still in ruins, he urged its rebuilding. "But it has been burned down three times," said Shaw. Sir George countered: "I have never heard of a mission station being burned down four times." The rebuilding was begun.— *Ibid.*, 236.

[2] *Ibid.*, 245.

[3] *Ibid.*, 231–3.

wandered in search of food and work. Brownlee estimated that some 20,000 died while 30,000 or so crossed over into the Colony and found work there, and that the number of cattle killed was at least 150,000.[1] One who held back his people from this self-destruction was the Christian chief, Kama, baptized with his wife, a daughter of the great chief Gaika, by William Shaw in 1825. He remained a staunch Christian throughout his life, despite pressure from heathen chiefs, his brothers and others, to abandon his faith. In 1857, therefore, he was found firm as a rock in opposition to the tribal madness. He reaped his reward in seeing his people, the Gunukwebe, from one of the smaller tribal units grow to be the largest in British Kaffraria. He was the brightest ornament of the Wesleyan Mission, in the steadfastness of his Christian profession and the consistency of his life. His own people said of him: "When God's Word came to Kama he held out his hand, and it fell right into the middle of it, and he has held it fast ever since."[2]

The Glasgow Missionary Society, with its five stations in Kaffraria by 1840, felt the need of a training institution for African agents. It was decided to establish a seminary at Lovedale, and this now famous Institution opened its doors on July 21, 1841 under William Govan as principal, who was to direct the work until 1870, when James Stewart succeeded him. Two decisions of importance he made at the outset: the Institution should be at the service of all Christian bodies; and white and black should be taught together, and dine in the same dining-hall though at different tables.[3] Within five years the Society's work was handed over to a new authority. In 1843 Scottish Presbyterianism was rent in twain, and a "Free Church of Scotland" emerged, to which the Scottish missionaries of the Glasgow Society determined to adhere. In 1844 the Society

---

[1] Brownlee's material is supplied in J. A. Chalmers, *Tiyo Soga* (1878, 2nd ed.), 101–29. An abridgment of this is given in C. Brownlee, *Reminiscences of Kaffir Life and History* (1896), 135–70. Cf. Whiteside, *op. cit.*, 234–5. Valuable comment from the social anthropologist's angle is offered by M. Hunter, *Reaction to Conquest* (1936), 561; cf. 344; who remarks: "The visions of Nongqawuse have been echoed again and again"—as in the "Israelite" movement of 1918–20, and the belief of a following in 1921 that squadrons of aeroplanes would bring American Negroes to their deliverance.—*Ibid.*, 565, 571. The view sometimes advanced that, in 1857, a deliberate policy of the chiefs to precipitate war lay behind does not seem borne out by such evidence as is available. Brownlee doubted it and Hunter and others are sceptical. When news of the reverses suffered by the English in the Crimea filtered through, it was claimed that the ancestors were there fighting the English overseas.—Brownlee, *op. cit.*, 154.

[2] Whiteside, *op. cit.*, 210; W. C. Holden, *A Brief History of Methodism and of Methodist Missions in South Africa* (1877), 308–34; Du Plessis, *op. cit.*, 296–8.

[3] R. H. W. Shepherd, *Lovedale, South Africa, 1841–1941* (1941), 93–5, 97–8.

transferred its work to the Foreign Missions Committee of this Church.[1] The opportunity for development which this seemed to promise was nipped in the bud by war. In 1846 the Institution ceased to function and was occupied by the military. In expectation of a lengthy conflict Govan returned to Scotland. He took with him a bright Bantu lad, Tiyo Soga, one of the thirty-nine children of Soga, a councillor of the chief Sandile. During the progress of the war there was established, a mile from Lovedale, the largest fort on the frontier, Fort Hare,[2] and to this the military in Lovedale removed in 1847. After the war Lovedale's land tenure was no longer from a Xhosa chief but by grant from the Crown.[3] Early in 1850 Govan returned to his post; before the end of the year war had again broken out. This time the proximity of Fort Hare served as a shield, and Lovedale continued its work with but brief interruption. With the arrival of Sir George Grey as Governor a new epoch dawned in the educational work of missions. The Constitution Ordinance granting Representative Government to the Cape in 1854 had laid it down that from colonial revenue a fund was to be supplied for the Aborigines' (Border) Department. Sir George Grey announced that the resources of this fund would be available "to subsidise missionary institutions that would undertake to train Bantu youth in industrial occupations and to fit them to act as interpreters, evangelists and schoolmasters amongst their own people".[4] Lovedale not only benefited in its existing work but added an industrial department which developed into the leading centre of its kind. Beginning with masonry, carpentry, wagon-making, and smithing it had added by 1861 printing and bookbinding.[5] As a sequel to the war of 1850–53 a link with the early days of the Glasgow Society was snapped.

[1] *Ibid.*, 104. The change was from an interdominational to a denominational body. In 1838 a division had occurred in the G.M.S., reflecting current dispute in Scotland over the state and the voluntary principle, and there emerged "The G.M.S. adhering to the principles of the Church of Scotland" and "The G. South African M.S.". In South Africa the missionaries of three stations (including Lovedale) elected to serve under the former, and of two under the latter. The former, in 1844, passed to "The Free Church of Scotland", the latter to "The United Presbyterian Church", a union of the United Secession Church with the Relief Synod in 1847.—*Ibid.*, 91–2; *E.R.E.*, X, 255.

[2] Named after Colonel John Hare, Lieutenant-Governor of the Eastern Province, 1838–47.

[3] R. H. W. Shepherd, *op. cit.*, 117.

[4] *Report of the Interdepartmental Committee on Native Education* (Union of South Africa, 1936), 10. In the period 1855–62 eight training institutions received regular grants: Lovedale, Shiloh (Moravian) and six Wesleyan centres. In addition Presbyterian, Wesleyan and Anglican schools received assistance.—*Ibid.*, 10–11.

[5] R. H. W. Shepherd, *op. cit.*, 132–5.

The pioneer Chumie station "this Iona of the Scottish Church in Southern Africa", as it has been termed, was abandoned. It had been largely destroyed in 1846, and completely so in 1851. By 1854 colonial farmers had received grants of the land.[1] Tiyo Soga had completed his first visit to Scotland in October 1848, when he returned as a catechist of the United Presbyterian Church to the Chumie station. When the war brought ruin to it and his work was thus suspended he was brought once more to Britain. Leaving his own land torn with the horrors of war he arrived in England to find a nation rejoicing in the Great Exhibition of 1851. After one session in the University of Glasgow, where he had matriculated, he was admitted to the Divinity Hall of the United Presbyterian Church in Edinburgh. In due course he was licensed to preach and on December 23, 1856 was ordained to the ministry, the first Xhosa to be so. He returned with his Scottish wife to his own country in a fateful year, 1857, to be faced with destruction and desolation, the aftermath of the cattle-killing. But he braced himself to enter on the service of his people. To the credit of colonial churches, be it said, they welcomed him to their pulpits when once they had discovered his quality. But he was dedicated to the Christian service of his own people, and he served them with ability and devotion until his death in 1871.[2]

The work of the Berlin Mission in Kaffraria suffered heavily in the frontier wars. The stations of Bethel, Itemba, and Emmaus were in stormy territory: in the war of 1846 the work came to a halt and the missionaries Döhne, Güldenpfennig, and Posselt retired to Bethany on the Koranna mission. The plan to build up once more the stations broken down was frustrated by the catastrophic war of 1850–53, the cattle-killing of 1857 supervening as the climax. In the event two of the stations were rebuilt: Bethel and Emmaus (renamed Wartburg to distinguish it from the Emmaus now begun in Natal). Meanwhile these serious setbacks early encouraged the Society to contemplate work in the more secure neighbouring territory of Natal. The opportunity was presented in an invitation from Theophilus Shepstone the Native Commissioner, with the promise of suitable sites and generous subsidy. The invitation was accepted and in 1847 Döhne, Güldenpfennig, and Posselt established the first station at the source of the Tugela in the Drakensberg and named it Emmaus. Even here it was by no means all plain sail-

[1] *Ibid.*, 126–8.
[2] J. A. Chalmers, *Tiyo Soga: A Page of South African Mission Work* (1877), *passim.*

ing. A competitive interest was that of the service of those Boers who had remained behind on the high plateau of the Drakensberg when the general exodus from Natal took place. Döhne and Güldenpfennig before long found their vocation among Boers at Pietermaritzburg and Weenen respectively. Posselt meanwhile combined mission work with the service of a community of German immigrants established near to Durban and calling their settlement Neudeutschland. When this community was threatened with dispersion through the failure of the cotton plantation, Posselt returned to Emmaus for a couple of years (1852–54). On resuming work among the settlers he also began a Zulu mission naming the estate he acquired for the purpose Christianenburg. Thus a highland station, Emmaus, and a coastal centre, Neudeutschland-Christianenburg, became the twin though distant stations of the Society in Natal.[1]

The work of the American Board in Natal had not been surrendered on account of the Retief tragedy. Dr. Adams continued at his station of Umlazi near Port Natal, and Aldin Grout even accepted an invitation to Zululand where, however, the attempted station at Inkanyezi, 100 miles from Port Natal, proved abortive. He was back at Umlazi within a year. British intervention in Natal assured the missionaries, so they believed, of wider opportunities. But the Board thought otherwise, and in 1843 determined on withdrawal. They gave their reasons.[2] The determined protest, however, came from other Christian leaders in South Africa who urged the "necessity of the Board's continuing its operations in that important missionary field". Dr. Philip even offered, despite his age, to visit the States to beg for the mission if funds were the difficulty. The decision to abandon the mission was reversed.[3] Reinforcements were now needed and of these the first were James C. Bryant and Lewis Grout and their wives, who sailed in 1846. Both became language students, Bryant producing Biblical translations and Zulu hymns and Lewis Grout the first Zulu Grammar. Bryant, never robust, died in 1850, the first loss on the field.[4]

---

[1] J. Richter, *Geschichte der Berliner Missionsgesellschaft, 1824–1924* (1924), 116–17, 124–6. J. L. Döhne transferred his services to the American Board in 1850.—*The Missionary Herald*, A.B.C.F.M. (1850), 139; (1852), 3; J. Richter, *op. cit.*, 171.

[2] *The Missionary Herald* (1842), 131, 337–9; (1843), 78; (1844), 2. In consideration of the pressure on their resources, the Board regarded Natal as a less eligible field in view of "our disadvantages as foreigners in prosecuting a mission in the presence of a young English colony and the strong probability that the English Wesleyan missionaries will spread themselves over the ground".

[3] *Ibid.* (1844), 182.

[4] *Ibid.* (1846), 213, 394; (1850), 173–6; (1851), 150–1, 203.

With the annexation of Natal as a district of the Cape in 1845, the problem of the 100,000 Zulus resident there faced the authorities. A Commission was appointed in March 1846 to make recommendations about possible locations. Newton Adams and Daniel Lindley were two of the five members. Within a year it was reported that progress was very satisfactory, "the policy of the government being marked with great liberality".[1] Before long, however, there was cause for disquiet. Opposition from British colonists brought about a suspense of operations, the Board remarking that they exhibited "no great degree of friendly feeling towards the native population, and far too little regard for their interests or rights; but a strong desire to obtain for themselves the best lands, and all the advantages the country affords, irrespective of these interests".[2] Happily, the worst fears were not realized, though for some time the more liberal location policy was in jeopardy and there was serious misgiving when "a sudden desolating wave of civilization threatened, for a time, to sweep over the native race".[3] The Board's operations now became stabilized for some years at twelve head stations, with a staff of some twelve to fourteen missionaries and their wives. They reported in 1858: "Ten years ago, there were no churches, and not more than two converts; now, eight Churches contain nearly two hundred members. . . . The prospects of the mission have never appeared more cheering."[4]

The Church of England was late in the field but by the 'fifties was making rapid strides to a position of commanding influence. In the late 'forties there were but thirteen Anglican congregations—and no mission—in the whole of the colony.[5] Within a decade growth had been such that there were three dioceses, with the beginning of missions in Kaffraria and Natal. The transformation was due to the vigorous leadership of Robert

[1] *Ibid.* (1847), 145, 394; (1848), 197–8. Of the first five locations reported, the Board was in missionary possession of three: Umlazi (Adams), Umvoti (Aldin Grout), and Inanda (Lindley).

[2] *Ibid.* (1850), 319.

[3] *Ibid.* (1851), 3; (1852), 3; (1853), 33. "The danger is", they remarked with insight in 1853, "that the prosperity of the colony will be kept in view, as the leading object of all legislation, and that whatever seems to interfere with this, will be forced to assume a subordinate position"—a comment unhappily applicable to more than that place and time. An admirable account of the whole location question is supplied by E. W. Smith, *The Life and Times of Daniel Lindley*, 250–71. On colonists' demands and threatened restrictions; cf. 260–1, 263, 265.

[4] *The Missionary Herald* (1858), 3. The labours of Daniel Lindley reflect the perils and progress of the mission.—E. W. Smith, *op. cit., passim.*

[5] E. A. Walker, *op. cit.*, 246.

Gray, first Bishop of Cape Town. Born October 3, 1809, he was the seventh son (and twelfth child) of Robert Gray, from 1827 the Bishop of Bristol. A peculiar accident at Eton, together with constitutional frailty, made him an invalid whose survival was at times despaired of. Nevertheless, after four years at Oxford he went forward to ordination, a vocation he was long prepared for—"the desire grew up with me". He was a devoted son of the Church, and the appeal of the Oxford Movement for a revival of High Church principles found in him a convinced disciple. When invited early in 1847 to proceed to a colonial bishopric at the Cape of Good Hope he accepted in obedience to a call, but having accepted, took up his heavy task with the single-hearted devotion that was characteristic of the man, becoming "the founder of the English Church in South Africa".[1]

He landed at Cape Town on February 20, 1848. The position of the Church as he found it distressed him. With but a handful of clergy for a diocese that extended 600 miles from west to east, marked weakness if not actual absence of instruction in Church principles, and no dependable revenue from local sources, there faced him a truly gigantic task.[2] It was inevitable that his ecclesiastical predilections should make him regret the number and activity of other Communions in so young a country. But staunch as was his Churchmanship, he studiously refrained from any aggressive attempt to proselytize, though he had suspicious critics enough. "Now as to other religious bodies", he wrote soon after arrival, "they are all in some confusion. If we can . . . let it be seen that we are anxious to do the work of God without attacking others, I believe in time they will seek rest in our fold."[3] In the nature of the case financial affairs pressed heavily, and as he had been warned that representative government might come within a couple of years, and the colonial temper was not too friendly to his activities (for as Colonial Bishop he ranked as a state official), such help as he thought it reasonable for the Colonial Exchequer to give had to be sought without delay, all having to receive confirmation, of course, from the Home Government. This insistent problem of finance when he sought to increase the number of clergy in the

[1] C. Lewis and G. E. Edwards, *Historical Records of the Church of the Province of South Africa* (1934), 31.

[2] He wrote at Easter, 1848: "We are *now*, with my staff included, only 17 clergy to 200 ministers of all sorts. I could weep to see the havoc made, the ground lost, through past indifference and neglect."—C. Gray, *Life of Robert Gray, Bishop of Cape Town* (1876), I, 174. Italics in original.

[3] *Ibid.*, I, 159.

diocese is reflected in his request to his brother-in-law[1] to secure a clergyman for Port Elizabeth: "No man would be too good, but there is nothing to tempt any one. . . . He shall have bread and cheese; I can promise him nothing more."[2] Within a few months of arrival he had set out on his first visitation of the diocese. It was a strenuous seventeen weeks' journey to the Great Fish River in the east and Colesberg, the last colonial town in the north. The physical difficulties of such a journey at that date were serious enough but added to them were the stress and strain of services, interviews, and conferences all along the way. The bishop, for example, confirmed 900 persons during the visitation. On reaching Cape Town he had travelled 3,000 miles.[3] In 1850 he set out once more on his extensive travels, devoting nine months to this visitation, which is described as "perhaps the most important ever made by a bishop of the Church of England".[4] It took him beyond the Cape and the Eastern Province into Kaffraria, Natal, and the Free State. As ever, he gave himself lavishly to his people, being personally available to any who might seek spiritual counsel. He wrote on his return: "The state of the Diocese as a whole is encouraging. There is scarce a parish where a real work is not going on. The people are exerting themselves to build their churches, and help to maintain their clergy. . . . But everywhere there is a growing jealousy and opposition shown on the part of those who are not of us. . . . The anti-English spirit, the Colonial spirit, the dissenting spirit, all raise up enemies against us, and the press is almost exclusively in their hands."[5] He came into direct contact on this journey with the work of other Societies (not all for the first time)—Moravian, London, Wesleyan, Paris, Berlin, American—frequently being their guest. Much as he longed for the unity of the Church he could be generous in appreciation of the work others were doing. He had already expressed himself about their Christian contribution to the life of the country: "I can rejoice to see Christianity, however imperfect in its form, making way at all. If there is a mote in our brethren's eye, there is a beam, I well know, in ours. It is better to do the work as they do it than not to do it at all, as is

---

[1] Dr. R. Williamson, head master of Westminster School.
[2] C. Gray, *op. cit.*, I, 316.
[3] *Ibid.*, I, 209.
[4] Lewis and Edwards, *op. cit.*, 52. This ranks as the bishop's third visitation, the second being to St. Helena in 1849.—*Ibid.*, 45.
[5] C. Gray, *op. cit.*, I, 324–5.

the case with ourselves."[1] He was determined, however, that his Church also should realize its missionary duty. But first the diocesan house must be put in order. It was clear the original diocese was hopelessly unwieldy; a division into three was successfully negotiated, and Bishops of Grahamstown and of Natal respectively were consecrated on St. Andrew's Day, 1853. Bishop Gray wrote of this event: "The Church will now, I think, fix her roots deep in South Africa."[2] Bishop Armstrong of Grahamstown had served barely two years in his diocese when he died. Bishop Colenso took up his work in Natal with enthusiasm and survived to become the central figure of stormy debate. With three episcopal centres whence activity might radiate, Anglican missions appeared on the scene and before long took a worthy place in South Africa. From Grahamstown there was work begun in Kaffraria, the original centre being Umhalla's kraal, some thirty miles to the east of King William's Town, where in 1850 Gray had accepted the invitation to enter, though war prevented his doing so.[3] In Natal Gray had submitted a scheme for Mission Institutions as early as 1850, in connexion with the locations policy, but the first of them did not mature until 1856, a farm of 4,000 acres having been assigned for the purpose in 1854 at Ekukanyeni, some six miles from Pietermaritzburg. By 1858 missionary work had been begun at half a dozen other centres in the diocese.[4] With these eastern areas in the capable hands of his episcopal colleagues, Bishop Gray turned his attention to the "stranger within the gates" of his own diocese, and wrote in 1857: "Henceforth, if my life is spared, it will be chiefly devoted to Hottentot Missions."[5] The Society for the Propagation of the Gospel was actively interested in all these enterprises.

[1] In February, 1850. *Ibid.*, I, 269.

[2] *Ibid.*, I, 372.

[3] *Ibid.*, I, 272. Gray had interviewed Umhalla on the 1850 visitation, when the latter wanted as his missionary Archdeacon Merriman on whom he had set his heart: "This he repeated twenty times during the course of our conversation, which lasted two hours."—*Ibid.*, I, 308.

[4] *Ibid.*, I, 288–9, 291–3; Pascoe, *Two Hundred Years of the S.P.G.* (1901), I, 330.

[5] C. Gray, *op. cit.*, I, 425. Gray was also concerned for the Muslims in Cape Town who were winning converts, he said (1848), "chiefly from among the liberated Africans, but occasionally also from the ranks of the Christians. . . . I am resolved, God helping, to make some effort for their conversion—very little has hitherto been done for them."—*Ibid.*, I, 169–70; cf. 178, 237. The London Mission had work among them in Malay and Arabic by 1848, and before this had reported more than a dozen baptized converts. They estimated the total number of Muslims in Cape Town in 1848 as about 6,000.—Forty-seventh *Report of the Directors* (1841), 76; Fiftieth *Report* (1844), 83; Fifty-fourth *Report* (1848), 95.

Concurrently with these developments the Roman Catholic Church was also expanding its interests in southern Africa. It anticipated the Anglican initiative by a decade, when the vicariate apostolic of the Cape of Good Hope was erected by Gregory XVI in 1837, distinct from that of Mauritius under which it had hitherto been included. In August of that year the Dominican, Patrick Raymond Griffith, was consecrated Bishop of Paleopolis and appointed the first Vicar Apostolic of the Cape. His first visitation, which took him by ox-wagon from Cape Town to Port Elizabeth and Grahamstown, brought to light a Roman Catholic community of but 500 or so, and these for the most part so easy-going that measures of discipline were called for which produced secessions but purified the body Catholic.[1] Missions were begun at Grahamstown and Port Elizabeth in the east, and by 1841 a third at George, 300 miles from Cape Town. There were then some 200 communicants in the vicariate.[2] Within a decade a division of the field was seen to be necessary, largely owing to great distances and difficulty of travel; in 1847 therefore there appeared the western and eastern vicariates of the Cape of Good Hope. Griffith continued as Vicar Apostolic of the western, serving altogether for a quarter of a century. A priest who had been his colleague for nine years, Aidan Devereux, was consecrated by Griffith in December 1847 Bishop of Paneas and appointed first Vicar Apostolic of the eastern vicariate. The Dhanis family of Belgium gave him liberal support at the outset, but the destruction and confusion of the frontier wars, coupled with paucity of staff, severely crippled the work.[3] Devereux had attempted some contact with Natal in 1850, but it was clear that a separate vicariate was necessary there.[4] In that year, therefore, Pius IX established Natal and the Orange Free State as a new vicariate. Allard, the first Vicar Apostolic, left Europe in November 1851 with five members of his own French Order, the Oblates of Mary Immaculate, and reached Natal four months later. He made his headquarters at Pietermaritzburg where the largest number of Roman Catholics, some 200, was to be found, Durban and Bloemfontein having about 100 each. These were mostly Irish, a number being among the troops. A second centre in the Free State was begun at Smithfield. No convert was re-

---

[1] *Cath. Ency.*, VI (1909), 645–6.
[2] *Annales de la Propagation de la Foi*, XIII (1841), 351, 352; XV (1843), 325.
[3] *Cath. Ency.*, VI, 645.
[4] *Annales*, XXIX (1857), 91.

ceived for seven years.[1] With a deep concern for the African peoples, Allard launched the St. Michael Mission in 1855, but it met with severe setbacks due to tribal rivalries. When numbers of orphan refugees appeared, the victims of tribal war beyond the Colony, Allard's offer to receive forty under the age of ten, to be cared for until they were sixteen to eighteen, was accepted.[2] Thus the Romans, as the Anglicans, were by the mid-'fifties operating in three episcopal units. But progress was disappointing. Schmidlin grants that in South Africa "the Catholic mission has been most backward, and has been far outstripped by the Protestant".[3] The Protestants, for their part, regretted what they regarded as an intrusion with not infrequent experience of proselytizing, but such statistics as are available do not suggest any serious defection at that time.[4]

(3) *Contemporary Enterprise*—(b) *Beyond Colonial Frontiers*

Beyond the colonial frontiers we are concerned with four areas: Zululand, Basutoland, Namaqualand and Bechuanaland. Zululand was the field chosen by the Norwegian Missionary Society, a union in 1842 of various mission groups, in which to begin its work. Hans Palludan Smith Schreuder, who had produced a stirring pamphlet addressed to the Church of Norway and offered himself for the service, was appointed the pioneer in 1843. Setting out from Norway on July 9 he arrived at Cape Town on November 10 and on New Year's Day 1844 set foot

---

[1] *Cath. Ency.*, X (1911), 708; *Annales*, XXIX (1857), 91; XXX (1858), 32.

[2] *Annales*, XXX (1858), 35–8.

[3] *Catholic Mission History* (1933), 656. He assigns as reasons neglect of the pagan field, concentration on a few centres, and inadequate methods.

[4] Griffith reported that by April, 1841, there had been thirty-eight renunciations of "heresy", and Devereux, in 1847, some forty-five "snatched from infidelity or heresy" at George in the previous six years.—*Annales*, XV (1843), 325; XX (1848), 164. Dr. Philip viewed their advent with disquiet but wrote in 1845: "We cannot deny to the Roman Catholic missionaries the liberty which we claim for ourselves, and I should even rejoice in their prosperity, could I see that their chief concern was to increase their Church from among the heathen."—Fifty-second *Report of the Directors* (1846), 8–9; cf. Fifty-first *Report* (1845), 16; Fifty-fourth *Report* (1848), 98; *Missionary Herald*, A.B.C.F.M. (1853), 230. The Dutch were implacably hostile. Devereux reports that some of the more ignorant confused them with the Romans who crucified Christ.—*Annales*, XX (1848), 165–6. Bishop Gray reports an occasion on his 1850 visitation when he was refused hospitality—a rare experience—because as a "bishop" it was assumed he was of the Roman persuasion.—C. Gray, *op. cit.*, I, 319.

on the soil of Natal.[1] Having arrived in Natal, which he found well served with missions, he applied himself to the Zulu language and in due course sought permission from Mpande, paramount chief of the Zulus, to commence work in his country, but this was not granted.[2] Schreuder accepted this as a closing of the door, and sailed for China to join Karl Gützlaff by whose missionary ideas he had been much inspired. But arrived at Hong Kong, he met with little encouragement from Gützlaff: the obstacles in China would be no whit less than those of Zululand, whose speech he already had as an asset; and in particular, his light reddish hair and blue eyes could never be camouflaged to make him acceptable in China! In 1848, therefore, he was once more in Natal.[3] Here a party of three recruits joined him, and a renewed attempt to establish work was made. In 1850 the first permanent station was begun at Umpumulo, north of Mapumulo a station of the American Board, in the recently demarcated Umvoti location just south of the River Tugela which was the boundary with Zululand.[4] Before long Mpande sent for Schreuder to help him in an illness; Schreuder took the risk of prescribing and his patient recovered. He received ten cows and, for him best of all, an invitation to reside in the country. The first station in Zululand was at Empangeni, and the second at Entumeni.[5] Despite the favour of the court, the furrow was a hard one to plough and progress was slow. Jealousy between Mpande's first-born, Cetshwayo, and his brother, Mbulazi, son of Mpande's favourite wife, broke into open conflict and in December 1856 there was war to the death between them. Mbulazi and his five full brothers (all but one) were killed, and his people mercilessly slaughtered. Schreuder had warned Shepstone of what was afoot, but before he could intervene the tragedy was complete. The one surviving brother of Mbulazi was smuggled across the Tugela into

[1] *Det norske misjonsselskaps historie i hundre år*, III (1949), 11, 13. Dosent O. G. Myklebust, to whom I am indebted for this and subsequent references to the centenary history of the Norwegian Missionary Society, is the author of the South Africa section of the history (III, 5–187).

[2] While not explicitly refusing, Mpande "shunned a direct answer": so Schreuder reported to Aldin Grout.—*Missionary Herald* (1846), 159.

[3] Herman Schlyter, *Karl Gützlaff als Missionar in China* (1946), 200.

[4] *Missionary Herald* (1851), 146–7. An earlier attempt, on Schreuder's return in 1848, to establish a mission at Uitkomst (midway between Durban and Pietermaritzburg) did not meet with success and this station was abandoned in 1854.— O. G. Myklebust, *op. cit.*, 29–30.

[5] *Missionary Herald* (1851), 305; O. G. Myklebust, *op. cit.*, 30–2.

the care of Bishop Colenso.[1] Schreuder was an able language student and in 1850 published an outline Zulu Grammar.[2] The hunter, W. C. Baldwin, who knew him in Zululand, paid him high tribute saying he was "thoroughly acquainted with the language, manners, and customs of the nation. . . . the Zulus respect and look up to him, and would on no account injure him".[3] His further career belongs to a later period.

When in 1854 the Hermannsburgers on the *Candace* were back in Port Natal after their abortive attempt to reach the Gallas, they were in touch once again with Posselt of the Berlin Mission. He proposed a mission to Zululand, and advised for that purpose an introduction through Schreuder. The missionaries Schröder and Hohls and the colonist Schütte then set out to see him. Schreuder was quite prepared to present them to Mpande but saw little likelihood at best of more than three or four of their total number being admitted. He therefore recommended a settlement just inside Natal which could become the base for any later move into Zululand. They took his advice and time proved it right. Being unable to secure a grant of Crown land (Posselt had warned them the Governor was no friend to missions), they had no alternative but to purchase a place of their own. This they did from a German named Behrens whose place of some 6,000 acres, named "Perseverance" (an apt name for the new régime!) they secured for £630. They took possession on September 19, 1854 and with happy optimism renamed the place New Hermannsburg.[4]

As fellow Lutherans they were in very friendly relations with their Berlin and Norwegian missionary neighbours who lay partly to the north, and partly south and south-west. Posselt and Döhne in particular were of direct assistance in language study as the missionary brethren prepared for the new Zulu mission. The British authorities in Greytown proved well-disposed, and even with the Boers they were in friendly relations. Their emphasis on practical training pleased the Boers well, as

[1] A. T. Bryant, *Olden Times in Zululand and Natal* (1929), 679–80; E. W. Smith, *Life and Times of Daniel Lindley* (1949), 297.

[2] *Grammatik for Zulu-Sproget*, forfattet af H. P. S. Schreuder (88 pp., Christiania, 1850). This was a pioneer venture in writing a scholarly grammar of Zulu and has been acclaimed by Dr. C. M. Doke as a remarkable achievement.—C. M. Doke, "H. P. S. Schreuder som Språkforsker" in *Norsk Tidsskrift for Misjon*, IV (1950), 222–6. A facsimile of the title-page is reproduced at p. 223. I owe this reference to O. G. Myklebust.

[3] W. C. Baldwin, *African Hunting and Adventure from Natal to the Zambesi* (1863), quoted in Mendelssohn, *South African Bibliography* (1910), II, 287; cf. I, 73–4.

[4] G. Haccius, *Hannoversche Missionsgeschichte*, II (1907), 294–6, 299.

the work of the Moravians had done, although as a Reformed Church the Boers had less in common, and in addition, as the Hermannsburgers soon discovered, they "lived more in the Old than in the New Testament". Nevertheless, the brethren often preached in Dutch in their farmhouses.[1] Within the first five years they had founded four new stations in Natal: Ehlanzeni, New Hanover, Etembeni, and Müden. Within the same period they had secured an entry at last into Zululand, establishing their first settlement of seventeen persons, for the original principle was that colonists and missionaries should be complementary members of the Christian fellowship. This was at Umlalazi, so named from the river on which it stood. A second, with Cetshwayo's consent, was begun at Inyezane in the neighbourhood of his military kraal at Ngingindhlovu. At the end of the five-year period they were able to report for the four stations in Natal fifty baptized converts, and fifteen for the two in Zululand.[2]

In Basutoland as elsewhere in this period the missionary undertaking was seriously affected by political complications and military measures. The pioneers of the Paris Mission, who had begun their work in 1833, enjoyed an early period of prosperity. Until 1848 all went with a swing. For fifteen years converts had been received in their hundreds, churches had grown in effective witness, and chiefs had become obedient to the faith. It was small wonder that the missionaries faced the future with an eager optimism in the hope that one day the nation would be Christian. Pellissier at Bethulie, Rolland at Beersheba, Arbousset at Morija, and Casalis at Thaba Bosiu where he served as sagacious counsellor to Moshesh, successfully carried forward the work they had begun, labouring with joy for a future that seemed assured. True, even in the heyday of success the cloud no bigger than a man's hand was appearing on the horizon. The emigrant Boers were on the move. At first numbers were few and land resources ample. Moreover, Moshesh seems to have assumed that land, occupied with his consent as paramount chief, was taken on the customary terms of African land tenure—an occupation right conferred, but with no alienation of land as property. He is reported to have remarked, believing the farmers would one day move on: "They will not cart off my land in their wagons."[3]

[1] *Ibid.*, II, 301–2.
[2] *Ibid.*, II, 313–17, 318–19, 329.
[3] E. Jacottet, "Histoire de la Mission du Lessouto" in *Livre d'Or de la Mission du Lessouto* (1912), 207. Cf. Walker, *op. cit.*, 212; G. Lagden, *The Basutos* (1909), I, 64, 66–7.

In 1841–42 Dr. Philip was on tour for the London Mission and visited Basutoland. "The future peace of the country", he wrote prophetically, appeared to be "involved in the future relations between Moshesh and the Boers." He interviewed Moshesh and transmitted to the Government at the Cape his desire for diplomatic relations.[1] Sir George Napier took action and on October 5, 1843 concluded a treaty with Moshesh recognizing him as paramount over territory between the Orange and Caledon rivers and beyond the latter where his people lived.[2] But now a tribal complication arose. The Wesleyan missionaries, J. Archbell and J. Edwards, had arrived here a decade before, in 1833, with some 12,000 Barolong seeking a new home, and with the consent of Moshesh had settled at Thaba Nchu within territory where he was the acknowledged suzerain. It became the contention of Moroko, chief of the Barolong, supported by the Wesleyan missionaries in his claim, that the land had been ceded to them in full by Moshesh, a claim which he strenuously denied. In this denial Moshesh was stoutly supported by the French missionaries; indeed, Jacottet affirms that it was at this point that a political concern first arose among them. An uneasy situation supervened in which each side smarted from a sense of grievance.[3]

[1] W. M. Macmillan, *Bantu, Boer and Briton*, 195–6; E. Jacottet, *op. cit.*, 208; Walker, *op. cit.*, 227. On the occasion of his visit Philip discovered a striking example of the significance of personal influence as a factor in missionary success, where the widow of a former Basuto chief had become a Christian at the Cape, and then sent urging chiefs and people to attend to the French missionaries—a message that appears to have marked the turning point from apathy to interest and response.— Forty-ninth *Report of the Directors* (1843), 92–3.

[2] The text of the treaty is given in Lagden, *op. cit.*, I, 70–1; cf. Walker, *op. cit.*, 228–9.

[3] Findlay and Holdsworth, *History of the Wesleyan Methodist Missionary Society*, IV, 266; L. A. Hewson, *An Introduction to South African Methodists* (1951), 17–18. The Wesleyans had early reported the purchase of the land the Barolong occupied.—*Report of the Wesleyan Methodist Missionary Society for the Year ending April 1835* (1835), 41. John Edwards wrote of the transaction: "A document was then drawn up, a kind of deed of sale, showing the various beacons agreed upon, and the amount and manner of payment were fixed. This was signed by the chiefs who ceded the territory."—Quoted in J. Whiteside, *History of the Wesleyan Methodist Church in South Africa* (1906), 335. Other stations under Wesleyan auspices followed; by 1836 Jenkins was at Plaatberg with a settlement of Griquas, and Edwards with Korannas at Umpukani. By 1843 there were also Wesleyan stations at Lishuane, Merumetsu where Taaibosch was chief of the Korannas, and at Imparani among the Batlokua in Sikonyela's territory beyond Moshesh's domain where James Allison was distinguished pioneer.—*Report of the W.M.M.S.* (1836), 39; (1844), 64. On the Moroko-Moshesh dispute, see further: Lagden, *op. cit.*, I, 62–4, 72; Walker, *op. cit.*, 255; E. Jacottet, *op. cit.*, 209; E. W. Smith, *The Blessed Missionaries* (1950), 79–80. For a map showing the disputed territory and the stations involved, see Lagden, *op. cit.*, I, at p. 72; and E. W. Smith, *The Mabilles of Basutoland* (1939), front endpaper. Dr. E. W. Smith has supplied me with the following note: "Moshesh allowed the

The year 1848 was the turning point in the fortunes of the mission. At the home base it opened with a financial crisis at the Mission House; there followed hot on its heels the Paris Revolution of February which still further depressed the affairs of the Society. The three stations recently begun (Cana, Hebron, Hermon) were to be abandoned; the missionaries must now look to their own resources, and hope of any reinforcement from Europe need not be entertained. Indeed, two recruits only were to sail in the next decade: Théophile Jousse in 1850 and François Coillard in 1857.[1] Coupled with this heavy blow there came critical developments politically in local affairs. Sir Harry Smith, newly arrived as Governor of the Cape, in a visit to the north met Moshesh, and told him he was about to proclaim the Queen's sovereignty over territories north of the Orange River, including his own. As Jacottet laconically remarks: "Une conversation de quelques minutes, et tout fut réglé."[2] But the solution was not so simple, and Moshesh was caught up in the entanglements of following events.[3]

To cut a long story short, Moshesh, who had accepted under duress the so-called Warden Line as a boundary in 1849[4]—indeed his concessions threatened revolt among his own people, for the Line cut off a hundred Basuto villages—received in 1851 an ultimatum from the Resident, Warden himself. The British authorities were sadly underestimating the patience and power of the Basuto paramount, seemingly taking it for granted that Moshesh would not dare to resist without the support of the French missionaries. These on their part were in ill-odour with both sides: with the Boers and British, on this very assumption (when they protested to the British on behalf of Moshesh they were told they were not impartial); and with the Basuto who charged them with lining up with their fellow-Europeans.[5] The

Barolong to settle around the mountain Thaba Nchu and they acknowledged his suzerainty by paying the *peho*. The Wesleyans claimed to have *bought* the land and produced a deed to that effect. Some mystery attaches to this document: it was not countersigned by the French missionaries, Moshesh's advisers; and Moshesh denied that he had *sold* the land. The Wesleyan claim was the basis on which Napier cut off the Thaba Nchu area from Moshesh's territory." Italics in original.

[1] E. Jacottet, *op. cit.*, 226–7.

[2] *Ibid.*, 228. The text of the Proclamation is given by Lagden, *op. cit.*, I, 83–8.

[3] From the Boer revolt of July 1848, in refusal of the Queen's sovereignty, to the British representative's attempts to draw boundaries for the tribes. Cf. Lagden, *op. cit.*, I, 88–114.

[4] Walker, *op. cit.*, 225. Walker's comment on the British Resident's decision is: "Warden . . . fell in with the Wesleyan view completely," which denied to Moshesh the paramountcy over lands he had permitted them and their chiefs to occupy.

[5] E. Jacottet, *op. cit.*, 232.

deep strength of patriotic feeling, held in leash by Moshesh, was a factor that had to be reckoned with. Indeed, the missionaries were already suffering a heavy blow for the position they took when Sikonyela of the Batlokua had attacked Moshesh whose patience was then at an end and who in 1849 hit back to good effect. When the warriors returned in triumph with much cattle, the missionaries protested and placed under discipline all Christians who had taken part. The missionaries had, in a sense, been accepted as chiefs of the Christians. But they were now legislating, so the Basuto felt, in the realm of civil power. The expedition was a spontaneous expression of patriotic feeling; by intertribal tradition cattle-lifting was the legitimate perquisite of the victor, and Moshesh had sanctioned the whole proceeding. There began a considerable defection from the Church, not as a sudden landslide, but a steady withdrawal from its ranks. Of most serious significance was the fact that the greater part of the Christian chiefs and the Christian youth were involved. The event marked a rupture between the Church and the tribe which never really healed.[1] To return to Warden's ultimatum of 1851, which demanded restitution of cattle taken in retaliation and payment of fines imposed: before the expiry date the Resident's inadequate levies which included vassals of Moshesh were badly thrashed in a clash with Basuto outposts, put to flight, and the country overrun by Moshesh up to the boundary he claimed. Not Moshesh but Warden had been humbled.[2] The French missionaries then addressed a memorial to the Imperial Government, giving the Basuto side of the picture, in the course of which they said: "Moshesh has been placed on a level with chieftains whom he had received in the land. . . . This astounding mode of government has been crowned by employing one tribe against another. . . ."[3] The next act in the drama speedily unfolded. In 1852 Sir George Cathcart, who had now succeeded the recalled Sir Harry Smith, sent in his turn an ultimatum to Moshesh: Moshesh pleaded for time to collect the cattle demanded, but was refused. Cathcart advanced and received so severe a check in the engagement of the Berea mountain and was also so rebuffed before the fortress of Thaba Bosiu that he withdrew. Moshesh, always restrained

---

[1] E. Jacottet, *op. cit.*, 232–5. The blow fell when the Mission was least able to bear it—in 1848. Jacottet remarks that Casalis was on leave in France at the time. Had he been present, his wisdom might have averted the catastrophe.

[2] Walker, *op. cit.*, 260; Lagden, *op. cit.*, 118–19 (ultimatum), 119–21; E. Jacottet, *op. cit.*, 235–6.

[3] Lagden, *op. cit.*, I, 121–4.

and wise in the hour of success, neither conceded his opponent victory nor claimed his own, but at midnight on the day of the battle sent to Cathcart what has been called "the most politic document that has ever been penned in South Africa", offering the Governor a way out of the impasse which he gladly took, though to the dismay of those who wished to see Moshesh humbled in the dust.[1] Cathcart regarded the Warden Line in the Caledon region as unjust to the Basuto, but mainly through lack of Boer co-operation an effort to secure a revised boundary did not succeed. Meanwhile Moshesh held his hand until his northern neighbours—Sikonyela an avowed antagonist and Taaibosch of Merumetsu in territory Moshesh held to be his own—in their audacious raiding went just too far for his patience. He then fell upon them and administered such a castigation that the lands of both were occupied, the Wesleyan work suffering severely in the process. The stations of Imparani and Merumetsu disappeared, and further losses reduced their centres to two only—Thaba Nchu and Plaatberg.[2] The wheel soon turned full circle for the Boers: by the Bloemfontein Convention of 1854 the British Sovereignty was renounced and the Orange Free State was born. For four years the Boers and Moshesh lived in uneasy peace. In 1858 the storm broke; on March 22 President Boshof declared war. The Boer commandos attacked the Basuto on two fronts; the mission stations of Beersheba and Morija were involved. Beersheba was fired, though mission property was respected while Rolland was interned as prisoner of war. At Morija Arbousset and his family judged it wise to take refuge in the mountain behind the station; the station was destroyed.[3] When the commandos were arrayed be-

---

[1] Walker, *op. cit*, 263, 265-6; Lagden, *op. cit.*, I, 136-60; E. Jacottet, *op. cit.*, 237-9. Lagden's account of the battle of Berea is subjected to criticism by E. A. T. Dutton, *The Basuto of Basutoland* (1923), Appendix A. Moshesh's famous letter ran as follows: "Your Excellency, This day you have fought against my people and taken much cattle. As the object for which you have come is to have compensation for Boers, I beg you will be satisfied with what you have taken. I entreat peace from you—you have chastised—let it be enough; and let me no longer be considered an enemy to the Queen. I will try all I can to keep my people in order in the future.—Your humble servant, Moshesh."—G. M. Theal, *Basutoland Records* (1883), I, 627; quoted in Dutton, *op. cit.*, 110.

[2] Walker, *op. cit.*, 265-6. For a rebuke of the Wesleyan missionary James Cameron of Thaba Nchu as over-active politically, which was administered by the Commissioners Hogge and Owen, cf. Lagden, *op. cit.*, I, 130; Walker, *op. cit.*, 262. For Cameron's report of these events; cf. *The Wesleyan Missionary Notices* (1851), 61-2, 193-6. Cameron was honoured in Wesleyan circles as "one of the princes of his people".—Whiteside, *op. cit.*, 375. Cf. Report from Plaatberg, 30.1.1853, in the *Wesleyan Missionary Notices* (1854), 10.

[3] E. Jacottet, *op. cit.*, 252-4. The Boer account of events is recorded by Lagden, *op. cit.*, I, 225-6; 233-5.

fore the stronghold of Thaba Bosiu grave news reached the Boer camp: Moshesh's warriors had carried the war to their own domestic front. The commandos hurriedly dispersed, each man to defend his hearth and home. Again Moshesh had won. President Boshof proposed a parley: Moshesh accepted. He always knew where to stop. Sir George Grey, Governor of the Cape, now mediated, and peace returned with the First Treaty of Aliwal North, September 29, 1858. The Warden Line was confirmed, though with some extension in favour of the Basuto.[1]

The mere recital, in however truncated a form, of such a sequence of events in the decade 1848–58 provides the indispensable background for an appreciation of the work of the French Mission. The missionaries had no friendly colony at their rear to which to retreat had they been inclined to do so, though to have left the nation in time of crisis would have been to forfeit for good the confidence of chief and people. That the mission continued at all in such a period of storm was itself a tribute to the devotion of the missionaries and their converts. Changes in the personnel of the mission now marked the end of an era: Casalis retired in 1855 to take up in Paris the Directorship of the Society. His wise counsel had been much valued by Moshesh whose confidence he had to a degree unequalled by any successor. The Basuto long cherished his memory. In 1860 Arbousset retired; the destruction of Morija was a blow from which he never really recovered. As Casalis was rather *l'homme de cabinet* so Arbousset was man of action. He was a great evangelist, and trained his Christians to itinerate among their own people. With the passing of the old guard, there came on the scene the leaders to be. François Coillard, to achieve fame as Zambezi pioneer, arrived in 1858, and Adolphe Mabille followed as Arbousset's successor. A new generation now held the reins.[2]

Namaqualand, astride the Orange River by the Atlantic coast, was spared the problems produced by expanding colonization; its sandy wastes offered no attraction to immigrant farmers. The Namaquas, some south and some north of the Orange River, were Hottentots. Beyond them to the north lay the Hereros, a

---

[1] E. Jacottet, *op. cit.*, 254–6; Lagden, *op. cit.*, I, 237–8, 253–75; Walker, *op. cit.*, 301.

[2] E. Jacottet, *op. cit.*, 245–6, 257–60. Coillard reached the Cape in November, 1857, but did not arrive in Basutoland until the following year. Mabille was at the Cape by October, 1859, and entered Basutoland in January, 1860.—E. Favre, *Francois Coillard* I (1908), 266, 275; E. W. Smith, *The Mabilles of Basutoland* (1939), 91, 97.

Bantu people.[1] It was in this as their main field that the Rhenish missionaries developed their work. They had been preceded among the Namaquas by the London Mission, under whose wing indeed they first entered the country, and by the Wesleyans under Barnabas Shaw. But these had worked principally south of the river whereas the Rhenish Society was to develop its work north of it.

Johann Heinrich Schmelen will long be remembered as devoted pioneer of the London Mission among the Namaquas where he wielded great influence. To him Barnabas Shaw owed his introduction to the country, and when the London Mission meditated withdrawal from an apparently unfruitful field, since so many other claims were pressing upon its limited resources, Schmelen sounded the Rhenish missionaries then at the Cape, seeking their co-operation. When in 1840 Kleinschmidt and J. F. Budler arrived in South Africa for the Rhenish Society, Kleinschmidt joined Schmelen at Kommaggas south of the Orange. In due course the Society took over the remaining London stations in Little Namaqualand (Steinkopf, Pella, Concordia), Kommaggas remaining on the London list until Schmelen's death in 1848.[2]

The northern Namaquas were divided into various tribes, each being composed of a number of clans. Clan loyalty was stronger than tribal, and on occasion a clan would develop into a new tribe. Members of a clan formed a single community. Numbers were not large; reliable figures are not available but in 1876 the settlements were reported as being from 600 to 2,500 each.[3] The chief of the tribe was important in such a country, where holding together under recognized leadership was essential for survival. The Swedish traveller Charles John Andersson who was in the country in 1850–54 reported as the

[1] The early Dutch settlers called those south of the Orange River the Little Namaqua and north of it the Great Namaqua. The latter, it is thought, "may have formed the rearguard of their invasion of South Africa."—I. Schapera, *The Khoisan Peoples of South Africa* (1930), 48. The Hereros belong to the western section of the southern Bantu which includes the Ambo and Mbundu peoples.—I. Schapera, *The Bantu-Speaking Tribes of South Africa* (1937), 23.

[2] H. Driessler, *Die Rheinische Mission in Südwestafrika* (1932), 18–19; Forty-seventh *Report of the Directors* (1841), 92; Forty-eighth *Report* (1842), 86; Forty-ninth *Report* (1843), 85, 103; Fifty-fourth *Report* (1848), 96; Fifty-fifth *Report* (1849), 108–9. Sir James Edward Alexander made a pioneer journey north of the Orange River as far as Walfish Bay in 1837, and met Schmelen to whom he paid high tribute.— *An Expedition of Discovery into the Interior of Africa* (1838), I, 89–91, 101, 137–8, 141, 167–8, 249–54; II, 48–9, 252–3. He also wrote with appreciation of Wesleyan missions as he saw them.—*Ibid.*, I, 148–9, 181, 196, 201, 217; cf. II, 188–9.

[3] I. Schapera, *The Khoisan Peoples*, 224–8.

principal chiefs among the northern Namaqua Jonker Afri-
caner, Cornelius, Amral, Zwartbooi, Jan Boois, William Frans-
man, Paul Goliath, David Christian, and Bondel Zwartz.[1]
These were the men representing authority in the country
with whom the Rhenish missionaries had to deal. Clearly much
would depend on the individual missionary's wisdom and personal tact.

Kleinschmidt soon moved across the Orange to the northern
tribes and was first located at Bethany, an early London Mission station, lying inland from the later Lüderitz Bay. He had
hoped to move farther north to Windhuk but discovering a
Wesleyan missionary had anticipated him, told the chief Jonker
Afrikaner he would not remain. The chief, however, replied
that he accepted the missionary sent by "Father Schmelen",
and the Wesleyan perforce retired to Warmbad. Kleinschmidt
then sent for Hugo Hahn, who had recently arrived, and together at Windhuk they rejoiced in all the glad encouragement
of the early days—spring with the promise of summer to follow.
The chief showed himself so helpful that in their misplaced optimism the missionaries even dubbed him "a little King David".
But the response was emotional and superficial; Christian
character was far from being formed even in embryo. The spring
was as shortlived as Jonker Afrikaner's attitude of favour, with
which it was perforce bound up. In a couple of years his attitude
changed, and the missionaries reported: "There fell a frost on
the sprouting seed." In 1844 the opportunity for Wesleyan
entry was taken, and Kleinschmidt and Hahn retired. After a
couple of years so did the Wesleyans. Traders from the Cape
were bringing in spirits and firearms, and Afrikaner resumed
cattle-raiding to secure the means to pay for them. Perhaps the
greatest gain was the experience obtained to guide the missionaries in future operations. Kleinschmidt now went in 1845
to Rehoboth, south of Windhuk and lying almost on the southern tropic; while Hahn resumed his original objective, the
Bantu Hereros to the north.[2]

Meanwhile H. C. Knudsen, who had come out with Hahn,
had taken up the work at Bethany in 1842. Here again an
eager emotional response to his preaching proved deceptive. In
three years he had baptized some 500, but the inner change did

[1] C. J. Andersson, *Lake Ngami; Explorations and Discoveries in South Western Africa*
(New York ed., 1857), 253. Andersson paid tribute to Schmelen as being "one of
the most gifted and most enterprising of missionaries that ever set foot on African
soil".—*Ibid.*, 93; cf. 261 *n.*

[2] H. Driessler, *op. cit.*, 19–23.

not match the outward excitement. The alarming dangers in-
herent in such a situation were flashed across Knudsen's startled
vision by one who declared: "Jesus is coming to make sinners
happy; then let us sin that we may be happy." The inevitable
reaction set in, encouraged once again by the arrival of white
traders. Knudsen had painfully to admit that what he had regarded as the period of grace was, like the Northern Lights,
slowly fading away. He was embittered by the relapse and unhappily let his feelings get the better of him with the result of a
rift between missionary and community. David Christian and
his people asked Knudsen to leave, and he did so in 1851. There
were successors, but David Christian no longer proved co-
operative.[1]

While still at Bethany Knudsen had begun work with the
small clan of Paul Goliath, and been well received. Samuel
Hahn in due course took over the work, with Christopher Tibot,
Knudsen's trusted helper who had been baptized by Schmelen.
Hahn paid him a high tribute: a child among children, a
manly Christian among the young, a father in Christ among
heads of families, a priest of God in public assembly. In 1850
Hahn removed with the clan to a more attractive site which he
named Beersheba, and the following year J. Krönlein joined
him there. He was the first to devote himself assiduously to the
study of the language. Knudsen had prepared some tentative
translations, but it was left for Krönlein to do adequate work
in this field. He held the palm among the early missionaries as
language student. In 1860 he could report that the Christian
community at Beersheba still held firm.[2]

Kleinschmidt had been invited to Rehoboth by the chief,
William Zwaartbooi, at the instance of his wife Anatje (he was
monogamist at the time), who had been baptized by Schmelen.
Events moved swiftly in true Nama fashion, and within a
couple of years the baptized Christian community numbered
200, out of a total population of 1,000 or so, the chief himself
receiving baptism. Anatje was a great influence for good.
Kleinschmidt even started a missionary society to which the
first gifts were of necessity in kind: nine oxen, fifty-four small
stock, two bundles of ostrich feathers and over one hundred
loads of wood! In the true parlance of a hunting people, a little

[1] *Ibid.*, 24–7.
[2] *Ibid.*, 28–30, 45. Krönlein first translated the New Testament, and by 1883 had
completed the Old. He had also produced hymns and a liturgy. For dates of
publication of the Scriptures, see E. M. North, *The Book of a Thousand Tongues*
(1938), 247.

old woman who was invited to seek Jesus made reply: "I am already out on the hunt for him, but I have not fallen in with him yet." The omens were undeniably favourable: the site was fertile and the people settled (stone buildings even began to appear); but the attempt at a democratic form of self-government proved premature, and the Nama nature was not yet really changed. Only too soon the backward pull was felt which the coming of white traders made even stronger; it came to the point when the forbidden cattle-raiding was revived and an expedition against the Hereros triumphantly carried out. Thereupon Kleinschmidt disciplined the Christian community with the result that only six persons were eligible to attend communion. The chief turned polygamist and encouraged others to follow him. Through many vicissitudes there was a long uphill climb, but the end was tragedy: in 1864 Rehoboth was attacked and almost completely wiped out. Kleinschmidt led a remnant to found a new settlement, but they were pursued and attacked, and he died soon after, a broken-hearted man.[1]

On the border of Damaraland where dwelt the Hereros were a couple of small stations, typical of one aspect of pioneer work. There lived not far from Walfish Bay a poor little Nama tribe of some 800 persons, among whom the missionary Scheppmann was the first to settle in 1845. In self-denying obedience to his missionary vocation he forged ahead with the language, faithfully served his people, and was gladdened by their response. When he died in 1847 the place was named after him, Scheppmannsdorf.[2] In the same latitude, but 140 miles east of Windhuk on the Bechuanaland border, lay Gobabis where the chief Amral Lamberts lived with his people. He was one of Schmelen's converts, who had baptized him, and he had remained loyal to his profession. It was not till 1856 that the Rhenish Mission was able to allow him a missionary; then Eggert established the station of Gobabis in a country abounding in wild life, with elephant and rhinoceros the lords of the land.[3] Thus

[1] Driessler, op. cit., 30-4. The attack in 1864 was carried out by the Nama chiefs Jan Jonker and Oasib. Jonker Afrikaner had died in 1861. Andersson visited Rehoboth in 1852, and wrote prophetically of the station: "Should it be abandoned, ten years of unremitted labour and exertion will be entirely lost; and I sadly fear it will break the heart of its founder—the worthy and venerable Kleinschmidt."—Op. cit., 229.

[2] Driessler, op. cit., 39-40. Andersson and Galton were both guests at Scheppmannsdorf and have described it.—Andersson, op. cit., 19-21; Francis Galton, Narrative of an Explorer in Tropical South Africa (Minerva ed., 1889), 15-18. Galton's Narrative was first published in 1853.

[3] Driessler, op. cit., 36-7.

the work in Great Namaqualand was steadily carried forward amidst manifold difficulties. Some were physical: it was a land of vast desert tracts intersected by more fertile regions so that to encourage a traditionally wandering people to a settled life with farms and gardens was not always possible. Some of the problems were created by the Nama character, which demanded much patience and wise nurture; and some were produced by the half-breed and white traders who began to press into a country rich in ivory.[1] Yet despite them all, by 1851 some 1,000 baptized persons could be reported, and from among these had come teachers and evangelists, church elders and deaconesses.[2]

The pioneer of the mission to the Hereros was Hugo Hahn, and the year of his entry 1844. At Otjikango on the banks of the Swakop the first station was begun and called in faith New Barmen as the future centre of the mission.[3] A second at Otjimbingue was opened in 1849 with J. Rath as missionary, and a third at Okhandja in 1850 where F. W. Kolbe was stationed. This last had also been named Schmelen's Hope, because after once visiting it he had longed to establish a mission there.[4] The Hereros were at first extremely reserved and for this they might seem to have cause: if Jonker Afrikaner had allowed these white men through Namaqualand, were they not his spies?[5] The barrier of language proved serious when the Dutch of Hahn had to pass through the medium of Nama to reach an incompetent interpreter into Herero. But within three years the missionaries were making their own halting attempts in the local speech. Hahn laid the foundation for future students with grammar and dictionary and was honoured with a doctorate for his pioneer work by the University of Berlin.[6] But even so Herero hearts proved stony ground. Material interests absorbed their attention, yet they were so far oblivious of the missionaries' material needs as never to offer them a basin of milk, much less a cut from the joint. When there was no alternative, once Bam and once

[1] It is said that in one year about 300 such adventurers crossed the Orange River into the district east of Beersheba. Many took up residence on mission stations as the most attractive centres.—*Ibid.*, 46.

[2] *Ibid.*, 46.

[3] The Rhenish Society's headquarters in Europe were at Barmen. The Swakop, emptying itself north of Walfish Bay, was only a river at certain seasons, like others in the territory. Cf. Galton, *op. cit.*, 53.

[4] It is so called by the travellers Andersson and Galton, both of whom visited it. Andersson, *op. cit.*, 92–4; Galton, *op. cit.*, 68.

[5] Galton, *op. cit.*, 44.

[6] Driessler, *op. cit.*, 53–6; Andersson, *op. cit.*, 77. For Scripture translations; cf. E. M. North, *op. cit.*, 164.

Rath made the long journey to Cape Town by ox-wagon (Bam took a year for the double journey), to replenish their supplies.[1] But the supreme frustration came from the persistent hostility between aggressive Namas from the south and raided Hereros in the north. The Namas, with their firearms and with robber chiefs to lead them, found the attractive herds of the Hereros an easy prey in the unequal conflict. Both sides were guilty of shocking cruelties, and the missionaries found themselves helpless in the passionate struggle. At first the combatants respected the mission stations, but that self-restraint wore off. Okhandja (Schmelen's Hope) was first hit, in the course of Jonker Afrikaner's pursuit of Herero chiefs in 1850. Kolbe fled with his family from the nauseating carnage of Okhandja only to discover at Otjikango the same cruel scenes. Despairing of success, and with a distraught family on his hands, he retired to the Cape in 1853.[2]

Francis Galton the explorer, who had now entered the country, had been commissioned by the Cape Government to establish friendly relations with the Herero chiefs. In this connexion he got into touch with Jonker Afrikaner and so far succeeded in impressing him that he undertook not to molest the Hereros in future and even wrote apologetically to Kolbe for the destruction of his station.[3] But the reform was only temporary. As soon as his repentance had faded his promises were forgotten and he was back at the old game of raid and plunder. Otjimbingue was now the target and Rath the victim: when the people were all dispersed, he too retired to the Cape and the station was then destroyed by fire.[4] Hahn now visited Europe, and Schöneberg in desolating loneliness at New Barmen was forced by Jonker Afrikaner to get out. The Herero field was now denuded. But Hahn and Rath had not yet surrendered: Rath was back at Otjimbingue in 1854 and Hahn in 1856 at Otjikango. A few faithful souls gathered round them and Jonker Afrikaner forbore to interfere. In 1857 they travelled north to Ovamboland, seeking a new field, and barely escaped with their lives. The results of fourteen years' devoted work among the Hereros were, in 1858, as meagre as could be. Hahn had one baptized convert who had served him in the house from a child and was only half Herero; Rath had one under instruction he regarded as ready

[1] Driessler, *op. cit.*, 57. Andersson wrote very understandingly of Hahn and his colleagues in their uphill task.—*Op. cit.*, 77–8.

[2] *Ibid.*, 59–60.

[3] Galton, *op. cit.*, 45–6, 51, 70–1.

[4] Driessler, *op. cit.*, 61.

but who said she would be killed forthwith were she ever baptized. In March 1862 Hahn and Rath left Hereroland with heavy hearts and took up work at the Cape.[1]

In Bechuanaland, where London Mission developments under Robert Moffat's colleagues have already been recorded, Kuruman remained the base. Here Robert Moffat assiduously pursued his translation labours. Indeed, so engrossed had he become in the task that his health was seriously affected, and he took the opportunity that offered of a third journey to his friend Umsiligazi in 1854.[2] The chief Mothibi, who had first consented in Campbell's day to receive the missionaries, as an old man became a believer. After forty years of waiting, Mothibi, "though the rightful chief of 20,000 Bechuanas, stood with as much humility as others of his people beside him, whom he formerly considered as his 'servants' or 'dogs', to receive the ordinance of baptism".[3]

The advance of the emigrant Boers beyond the Vaal was now imposing new handicaps on the Bechuana Mission. The so-called Missionaries' Road pointing to Central Africa, though some seventy miles to the west of any Boer settlement, fell with the Bechuana country, they claimed, under their control. The western border of the Transvaal had not yet been defined.[4] The London Mission, thanks to Dr. Philip's campaign for Hottentot freedom, was in especial ill odour with the emigrants. Moreover, the missionaries were astride the road that led to the interior, and who could tell what unhappy developments might take place if the tribes were encouraged in their resistance to being made vassals to the superior race.[5] The inescapable hardships of a pioneer community which has inherited the Christian tradition have more than once in history led them to see in the

---

[1] *Ibid.*, 61–5.

[2] J. P. R. Wallis, *The Matabele Journals of Robert Moffat* (1945), I, 139. The text of the Journal is given on pp. 144–356. Livingstone reported on Moffat's health as seriously impaired by his intense application to translation work (To Dr. Tidman, 2.11.52).—Chamberlin, *op. cit.*, 184–5.

[3] Forty-eighth *Report of the Directors* (1842), 16.

[4] Walker, *A History of South Africa* (2nd ed., 1947), 185, 287–8.

[5] There were Boers among the Transvaalers who "had no objection to the Gospel being preached to natives, though some of them would have felt happier if only the missionaries would have consented to teach that the Boers were a superior race."
—*Ibid.*, 288; cf. Fifty-sixth *Report* (1850), 93; Livingstone, *Missionary Travels*, 37. As early as 1843 the Wesleyan Methodist Missionary Society submitted to Lord Stanley, Secretary of State for the Colonies, a "Memorandum on the perilous circumstances in which the Wesleyan Missionaries, at the Bechuana stations in South Africa, are placed by the proceedings of the emigrant Boors".—*Wesleyan Missionary Notices*, X (1843), 298–300.

wanderings of ancient Israel the prototype of their own pilgrimage to a promised land. But such self-identification as a
chosen people carries its own peculiar perils, of which a sense
of divinely bestowed superiority is not the least. Small wonder,
with their favourite narratives of Exodus and Joshua at hand,
that the emigrants should find history very literally repeating
itself, and yielding, as they sincerely believed, religious warrant
for armed attack on the tribes, and their subjugation to the
victors' service.[1] The London Mission agents had been the
pioneers beyond the Colony of Christianity and civilization
among the peoples of Bechuanaland. It was therefore with real
alarm that the missionaries received news of the Sand River
Convention of 1852 by which the Transvaalers were recognized
as independent, with an undertaking on their part not to prac-
tise slavery, but otherwise with no safeguard whatever either
for the missionary or the Bechuana north of the Vaal river.
Indeed, the emigrants are alleged to have said they were told
by one of the Commissioners that "they might do with the
Missionaries as they pleased".[2] They were not long in taking
action. In August 1852 (the Convention had been signed in
January) a commando attacked Sechele and his people at
Dimawe, a few miles from Kolobeng, to which Sechele had
removed on account of water failure. In October the missionaries Inglis and Edwards were hailed before Pretorius, accused
of having issued defamatory reports to the effect that the
farmers had treated as slaves the women and children captured,
and banished forthwith from their stations. "Substantially", says
Walker, "the charges were true. Traffic in indentures, and
therefore in apprentices did go on."[3] The Directors of the Society
made urgent representations to the British Government seeking
some modification of the treaty, only to be told that it had

---

[1] The wars of Joshua, with such a narrative as that of the Gibeonites, condemned for their duplicity to be hewers of wood and drawers of water (Joshua 9:
21, 27), are an example of such (as they took it) scriptural warrant. Cf. Livingstone, *Missionary Travels*, 119. Walker points out that this identification with their
own experience went so far that Andrew Murray in 1849 even found *Jeruzalem-
gangers* prepared to trek down a river they believed would lead to Zion!—*A History
of South Africa*, 271, 274; *The Great Trek*, 54–6.

[2] Fifty-ninth *Report of the Directors* (1853), 15; Livingstone, *Missionary Travels*,
38–9.

[3] Fifty-ninth *Report*, 15; Walker, *A History of South Africa*, 291–2. Walker pro-
ceeds: "Who then were these apprentices? Starving children, it was said, abandoned after a battle like Magongo or the fight with Secheli; children willingly exchanged for goods by their parents; prisoners in inter-tribal fights, who would
otherwise have been killed. . . . Maybe, said the critics, but the supply of orphans
on the frontiers was singularly abundant and steady."

already been confirmed and was no longer subject to revision. With grief and dismay the Directors received a letter of January, 1853 from the field: "Mamusa is vacated—the Missionaries of Matebe and Mabotsa are driven out of the country—Kolobeng is destroyed. Kuruman and Lekatlong are the only stations of our Society that yet exist in the Bechuana country."[1] Any prospect of advance to the interior from this the most forward base was diminishing to vanishing point.

(4) *The Quest*

It was thus a deeply troubled South Africa that Livingstone left behind him when he set his face once more to the north. It was during the stormy period of the 1850–53 war that he had visited Cape Town to speed home his family and prepare for his expedition. As a London Society missionary he incurred the full odium of the colonists, fanned into a flame by the defection of the Kat River Hottentots and various supporting rumours. Only with great difficulty could he secure the ammunition necessary for the expedition, and in other ways he was subject to petty annoyance.[2] One valued friend, however, he made before leaving; Sir Thomas Maclear as he later became, the Astronomer Royal, instructed him in the taking of observations for the accurate recording of his journeys.[3]

Livingstone left Cape Town on June 8, 1852 and reached Kuruman at the end of August. Here he learned of the recent Boer attack on Kolobeng, involving the plundering of his home at Kolobeng and the destruction of Sechele's nearby town at Dimawe. Livingstone estimated his personal losses at over £300. The Boers were reported to be disappointed at not finding the missionary in residence. Sechele was eager to visit England to appeal in person to the Queen, but got no farther than Cape Town. Livingstone did all he could by means of a detailed re-

[1] Fifty-ninth *Report*, 16. The Directors had memorialized the Government for modification of the treaty on three points: (1) That the Article on slavery be more explicit and more strictly enforced; (2) that the new Republic should be delimited to north and west, thus preventing limitless Boer claims in those directions; (3) that the Article by which the British Government bound itself not to enter into alliance with any tribe to the north of the Vaal should be cancelled. For Robert Moffat's comment and his report of a chief's poignant pleading, cf. Sixty-second *Report* (1856), 9–10.

[2] Blaikie, *op. cit.*, 107–9, 147–8. "They longed to hook me in from mere hatred to London Missionaries," he wrote later to Mrs. Livingstone.

[3] Livingstone's first instructor had been Captain Donaldson on his outward-bound voyage.—Blaikie, *op. cit.*, 30, 110.

port of the attack to the Lieutenant-Governor.[1] The Boer attempt to block the road to the interior produced an effect the reverse of that which they intended: it made Livingstone more than ever determined to open it up, and by snapping the last tangible link with the Kwena mission left him single-hearted in the enterprise. He wrote of it five years later: "The plundering only set me entirely free for my expedition to the north, and I have never since had a moment's concern for anything I left behind. The Boers resolved to shut up the interior, and I determined to open the country; and we shall see who have been most successful in resolution—they or I."[2] Thus ended his mission among the Kwenas. For eleven years David Livingstone had served in the Bechuana country, and a century later he is still remembered: "His name still lives and will live amongst the Bechuana—Nnake, the Doctor."[3]

Robert Moffat, on his third journey to Umsiligazi in 1854, visited Sechele at Lithubaruba, his new settlement some thirty miles north of Kolobeng. He found that Andries Pretorius, Commandant-General of the western Transvaal Republic, had repeatedly invited Sechele to visit him, but the latter had replied he must first receive back all his children as a token of the Boers' desire for peace.[4] Some three years later, however, the situation would seem to have eased, since Sechele received a missionary from Pretorius.[5] The latter, not able to secure Moravian help, turned to the German Lutherans of the Hermannsburg Society, recently arrived in Natal. They welcomed the invitation and by July 1857 were in Sechele's capital. A month later Robert Moffat found them there, on his fourth journey to Umsiligazi. He used his influence to commend

[1] This report, the most precise, is printed in Campbell, *op. cit.*, 145–8. The account written to his wife is supplied by Blaikie, *op. cit.*, 111–12; cf. Livingstone, *Missionary Travels*, 38–9; Chamberlin, *op. cit.*, 178–9, 187–8. Sechele's letter to Moffat is reproduced by Livingstone, *op. cit.*, 118–19. On Sechele's attempt to visit England, see *ibid.*, 120–1. The Boer version is given in the official report by the commando leader (Du Plessis, *op. cit.*, 443–6; cf. 252) and by Paul Kruger (who was present) in his *Memoirs* (1902), 42–5. Walker regards Livingstone's charge of wanton damage as not proven, but the looting as having taken place.—*History of South Africa*, 289 n. 5. The Boer claim that Livingstone was arming the Kwenas is almost too fantastic to be noticed, but has been examined.—Campbell, *op. cit.*, 149–51; cf. Chamberlin, *op. cit.*, 188, for Livingstone's counter-charge.

[2] Livingstone, *Missionary Travels*, 39. He laconically remarked that the Boers had saved him the trouble of making a will.—*Ibid.*, 229.

[3] A. J. Haile, *A Brief Historical Survey of the L.M.S. in Southern Africa* (1951), 6.

[4] J. P. R. Wallis, *The Matabele Journals of Robert Moffat 1829-1860* (1945), I, 174; Chamberlin, *op. cit.*, 195–6.

[5] Dr. E. W. Smith tells me: "I think the medium was Jan Viljoen, the Fieldcornet in the Marico, who is often mentioned in Moffat's Journals and who was friendly with Sechele."

C. Schröder with his two colleagues to Sechele and his people who appeared rather disgruntled over the business.[1] A second party under H. C. Schulenberg reached Shoshong, the Ngwato capital some 100 miles north of Lithubaruba, in 1858, at the invitation of the chief Sekhome who had seen their work on a visit to Shoshong. He granted the missionaries facilities and his own sons came to school, Khama his eldest among them. Khama Boikano, later to become the most distinguished of Ngwato chiefs, was baptized by Schulenburg on confession of faith, May 6, 1862.[2] The London Mission later occupied Shoshong as a European station where before they had only had an evangelist for a brief period.

When Livingstone left Kuruman for the north in December 1852[3] he was without a European companion. The Society had urged him to take one, but Moffat was the only person he favoured for such an expedition, and he was too heavily committed to translation work to contemplate the proposal.[4] Travelling by a more westerly route than before, to avoid collision with the Boers, Livingstone was at Linyanti, the Makololo capital, by May 23, 1853. He found that Sebitwane's daughter had now surrendered the chieftainship to her brother Sekeletu, a youth of eighteen. Happily he proved as well-disposed as his father had been. Livingstone had written while at Cape Town of the objects of his journey: to establish a mission in Barotseland or beyond, to throw some light on the problem of the slave-trade, and "also find a way to the sea on either the East or West coast".[5] In pursuit of the first he explored the Barotse region in search of a healthy locality in the company of Sekeletu and his considerable entourage for a period of nine weeks, but without success. He therefore turned to the task of finding an outlet to the sea. The commercial advantages of direct trade

[1] G. Haccius, *Hannoversche Missionsgeschichte*, II (1907), 321–2, 324–5; J. P. R. Wallis, *Matabele Journals*, II, 28–41. Moffat wrote of them to his wife: "The missionaries appear to be estimable men, and I only fear that neither Sechele nor the Bakuena are able to appreciate their value." They entered the country with the goodwill of the L.M.S.

[2] G. Haccius, *op. cit.*, II, 327–8; J. C. Harris, *Khama* (1922), 25–6. Du Plessis by identifying Liteyane with Shoshong, appears to have treated the two missions as one.—*Op. cit.*, 372. The date given above is that of the actual entry in the baptismal register, according to Harris, and corrects Haccius.

[3] Blaikie, *op. cit.*, 113. Cf. Livingstone, *op. cit.*, 120; Chamberlin, *op. cit.*, 189.

[4] Chamberlin, *op. cit.*, 163 n. 2; Blaikie, *op. cit.*, 115.

[5] Livingstone to Tidman, 17.3.52.—Chamberlin, *op. cit.*, 165; cf. Blaikie, *op. cit.*, 102. It is a tribute to the liberal outlook of the London Directors that they sanctioned so cordially these proposals.—Livingstone, *Missionary Travels*, 93; cf. Sixtieth *Report* (1854), 11.

with Europeans were clear to the Makololo, and in full assembly they appointed a party of twenty-seven to go with Livingstone to the west: "These men were not hired, but sent to enable me to accomplish an object as much desired by the chief and most of his people as by me."[1] They were to become famous in history as the loyal, if not always resolute, followers of their distinguished leader.

There could be no thought of comfort, much less of any luxuries, in the traveller's equipment. His severely limited financial resources alone determined that, for he had nothing but his personal means to go upon, supplemented by a small grant to meet the exigencies of the case.[2] But it was partly a matter of policy: "I had a secret conviction that if I did not succeed it would not be for lack of the 'nicknacks' advertised as indispensable for travellers, but from want of 'pluck', or because a large array of baggage excited the cupidity of the tribes through whose country we wished to pass."[3] This self-imposed austerity reduced equipment and supplies to the following minimum: "I had three muskets for my people, a rifle and double-barrelled smooth bore for myself. . . . I took only a few biscuits, a few pounds of tea and sugar, and about twenty of coffee . . . one small tin canister, about fifteen inches square filled with spare shirting, trowsers, and shoes, to be used when we reached civilised life, and others in a bag, which were ex-expected to wear out on the way; another of the same size for medicines; and a third for my books, my stock being a Nautical Almanac, Thomson's Logarithm Tables, and a Bible; a fourth box contained a magic lantern, which we found of much use. The sextant and artificial horizon, thermometer and compasses, were carried apart. My ammunition was distributed in portions through the whole luggage. . . . Our chief hopes for food were upon that, but in case of failure I took about 20 lbs. of beads, worth 40s.; . . . a small gipsy tent, just sufficient to sleep in; a

---

[1] Livingstone, *Missionary Travels*, 222, 228. He says of them: "I was entirely dependent on my twenty-seven men, whom I might name Zambesians, for there were two Makololo only, while the rest consisted of Barotse, Batoka, Bashubia, and two of the Ambonda."

[2] He wrote to Tidman from Cape Town, 17.3.52: "The expenses incurred in Cape Town will leave nothing remaining of the salary of 1853. I have now to crave your indulgence with respect to this overdrawing. I cannot possibly pay my people and go back with supplies of meal, tea and coffee unless I draw the salaries of /53 & /54. We have used no delicacies of any kind. . . . I have been a teetotaller for 20 years."—Chamberlin, *op. cit.*, 166. The Directors thereupon made an outright grant of £150, in addition to a further £120 annually for Mrs. Livingstone and the family at home.—*Ibid.*, 169 n. Livingstone's salary was £100 per year.

[3] Livingstone, *Missionary Travels*, 230-1.

sheepskin mantle as a blanket, and a horse-rug as a bed."[1] On November 11, 1853 the little expedition set out from Linyanti, Sekeletu and his elders going with them to the Chobe to see them safely embarked.

The shortest route to the coast would have been that to Benguella in Portuguese Angola, but as this would have meant traversing country used by slavers from the coast, and so involving him and his men in suspicion of a similar purpose, Livingstone chose the more northerly route to Loanda. The hardships of the journey it is difficult to appreciate:[2] drenching rain for days and weeks together, with the inevitable damage to clothes, instruments, and bedding, not to mention health; repeated attacks of malaria (in the *Travels* Livingstone admits some twenty bouts of fever);[3] tact in negotiation with chiefs of uncertain temper and firm control of greedy guides; maintenance of food supplies when game was scarce and local charges were exorbitant; the easing of friction among the Makololo and the strengthening of their spirits, always ready to fail before the actual dangers of the journey and to quail before the imaginary perils of the unknown—these were obstacles calculated to daunt the most stout-hearted traveller committed to an uncharted journey in the very heart of darkest Africa. But the traveller in this case was possessed of the sternest resolution—"I was determined to succeed or perish in the attempt"[4]—under-girded by a sense of Divine commission that supported him when all seemed desperate. The party reached San Paulo de Loanda without loss of a man on May 31, 1854.

The stay in Loanda was considerably longer than intended. Livingstone arrived suffering from chronic dysentery with an accompanying depression of spirits that was severe. Happily he was welcomed by Edmund Gabriel, British Commissioner in Loanda for the suppression of the slave-trade, and nursed back to health, though suffering a severe relapse before he was fit to take the road again. British cruisers were visiting Loanda and Livingstone was offered passage home, but this, though exceedingly tempting, he declined in view of the obligation he felt to take his Makololo to their home again. And further: the country

---

[1] *Ibid.*, 230.

[2] Blaikie remarks that Livingstone's unpublished Journal of some 800 pages is more explicit than the printed account in respect of the obstacles met with: on the latter "the record of many a bad deed and many a bad character is toned down".—*Op. cit.*, 129.

[3] *Op. cit.*, 236, 244, 247, 283, 287, 289, 294, 295, 296, 323, 343, 347, 348, 350, 352, 357, 376, 380, 381, 384.

[4] *Ibid.*, 229.

traversed, crossed by forest and intersected by river and marsh, offered no highway along which trade could flow. It remained therefore to ascertain whether the Zambezi itself might serve as an artery for trade to the eastern coast. As he wrote while travelling through Angola on his way back: "I return because I feel that the work to which I set myself is only half accomplished. The way out to the Eastern Coast may be less difficult than I have found that to the West. If I succeed we shall at least have a choice."[1]

During their stay of some three and a half months in Loanda he and his men received much kindness from the Portuguese, including the Roman Catholic Bishop of Angola to whom Livingstone paid tribute for his personal kindness and general influence for good. Friends both Portuguese and British replenished their supplies and renewed their equipment to such good purpose that they were now far better furnished than on the outward journey. On September 19, 1854 they set out from Loanda. The return journey had its trials no less severe than before: passage through hostile tribes whose cupidity was aroused by the goods now carried; stoppages due to sickness so that there were sometimes but ten travelling days a month, though twenty was the normal number; heavy rains which soaked the earth on which they had to sleep, and produced in Livingstone severe rheumatic fever;[2] the problem of food, on which they had to expend all the goods secured in Loanda in order to get home again. The outward journey had taken six and a half months; the return took nearly twelve. They reached Libonta on July 27 and were welcomed as men risen from the dead. On the following day a service of thanksgiving was held for their safe return. The whole party reached Linyanti again safe and sound on September 11, 1855. Despite their acquisitions at Loanda, they returned as poor as they had left, but none the less they had a glorious reception. They had been away for two months short of two years, and had travelled some 3,000 miles on the double journey.[3]

A month after arrival Livingstone submitted a full report of the inland region he had traversed, "between 18° and 10°

[1] Livingstone to Tidman, 14.1.55.—Chamberlin, *op. cit.*, 230; cf. *Missionary Travels*, 390–1.

[2] "This was brought on by being obliged to sleep on an extensive plain covered with water. The rain poured down incessantly, but we formed our beds by dragging up the earth into oblong mounds . . . and then placing grass upon them."—*Missionary Travels*, 444.

[3] The usual rate of travel by traders was seventy miles a month; on this journey Livingstone's party performed some 200 miles a month.—Blaikie, *op. cit.*, 142 n.

South Latitude, and situated towards the centre of the Continent", regarded as a missionary field.[1] He had formed the view of a central plateau, flanked by eastern and western ridges, the northern part of this basin having its waters discharged by the Congo (though he was unaware of its source and extent) and the southern by the Zambezi. This view of the general configuration proved correct and had already been advanced by Sir Roderick Murchison of the Royal Geographical Society.[2] The greatest obstacle to missionary settlement he held to be malaria, from Lake Ngami to the Equator and beyond. He had found a large population; chiefs would feel honoured by the residence of a European, and Christian instruction could be begun without hindrance.

Preparations for the journey to the east coast were soon under way. Arabs from Zanzibar described their route by way of Lake Tanganyika, but the Makololo recommended that by the Zambezi as preferable.[3] This time an escort of 120 Makololo was provided together with riding oxen, cattle for food, a liberal supply of butter and honey, and even hoes and beads with which to purchase what might be necessary. Livingstone was deeply touched by Sekeletu's liberal provision: "I was entirely dependent on his generosity, for the goods I originally brought from the Cape were all expended by the time I set off from Linyanti to the west coast . . . the Makololo again fitted me out, and sent me on to the east coast. I was thus dependent on their bounty, and that of other Africans, for the means of going from Linyanti to Loanda, and again from Linyanti to the east coast, and I feel deeply grateful to them."[4] This notable co-operation between white and black should never be forgotten. On November 3, 1855 the new expedition set out, accompanied by Sekeletu and some 200 of his people. On November 15 they reached the famous Falls which Livingstone's were the first European eyes to see, and to which he gave the name of the Queen—the first name he bestowed as a discoverer. On November 20 Sekeletu and his people returned, while Livingstone and his men pursued their journey, first to the north of the river over the Batoka plateau to the Kafue, and then along the north bank of the Zambezi to the east of Zumbo where they crossed

---

[1] Livingstone to Tidman, 12.10.55—Chamberlin, *op. cit.*, 240–55; cf. *Missionary Travels*, 504–6.

[2] Chamberlin, *op. cit.*, 242; Livingstone, *op. cit.*, 473–5. Sir Roderick Murchison's view was communicated to the Royal Geographical Society in 1852.—*Missionary Travels*, 475 n.

[3] *Missionary Travels*, 506–7. *Ibid.*, 516.

to the south, through very unfriendly country. This hostility of the tribes was the already known disadvantage of this route compared with that to Zanzibar, but was more than counter-balanced, in Livingstone's opinion, by the necessity to ascertain the usefulness of the Zambezi as an avenue for commerce. However the risks were heavy. In prospect of one crossing at the confluence of the Loangwa and Zambezi he wrote in his journal, January 14, 1856: "Felt much turmoil of spirit in view of having all my plans for the welfare of this great region and teeming population knocked on the head by savages to-morrow. But I read that Jesus came and said, 'All power is given unto me in heaven and in earth. Go ye therefore, and teach all nations—and lo, *I am with you alway, even unto the end of the world.*' It is the word of a gentleman of the most sacred and strictest honour, and there is an end on't. I will not cross furtively by night as I intended. It would appear as flight. . . . Nay, verily, I shall take observations for latitude and longitude to-night, though they may be my last."[1]

Tete, the farthest inland settlement of the Portuguese on the Zambezi, was reached on March 3, 1856. Here the traveller remained until April 23, once again detained by fever and receiving every kindness from his host, the Portuguese Commandant, Major Sicard. Here he decided to leave, until his return, most of his Makololo followers on land assigned them by the Commandant; then, on again down the Zambezi past Sena to Quilimane on the coast which was reached on May 20, 1856 —a point 1,300 miles east of Linyanti. The great transcontinental journey had been performed at last; the thrust from the south had achieved a penetration of the heart of Africa not granted either to attempts in the west or to probings on the east, valiant as these efforts had been. It was an achievement that marks a watershed in the history of the continent, and which, together with Livingstone's total contribution, has meant more for the expansion of Christian missions in Africa than any other single exploit. It was a breaking of the lock that opened a door inviting to advance. It was thus that Livingstone himself regarded it:[2] "I am not so elated in having performed what has not to my knowledge been done before in traversing the continent, because the end of the geographical feat is but the beginning of the missionary enterprise. May God grant me life to do some more good to this poor Africa."

[1] Blaikie, *op. cit.*, 151. Italics in original.
[2] Livingstone to Tidman from Tete, 2.3.56 [*sic*].—Chamberlin, *op. cit.*, 258.

168

II. PRESSING THE ADVANTAGE
1858–1878

CHAPTER 6

PRELUDE TO PROGRESS

NOT SINCE the Niger Expedition of 1841 had such publicity been given to African affairs as they now received through the man who had tramped across Africa. As the story became more fully known the popular imagination was kindled by the courage and tenacity of the pioneer who had braved the perils of the unknown; while the learned were profoundly impressed by the scientific accuracy of his work and his notable contributions to knowledge.

David Livingstone arrived in England on December 9, 1856. Within a week, on December 15, the Royal Geographical Society held a special meeting of welcome. They had already awarded him their gold medal, the highest honour at their disposal, in May 1855, for his journey from Linyanti to Loanda. It was computed that his African travels had now covered some 11,000 miles. Sir Roderick Murchison, as President, reviewed some of the traveller's achievements—his accurate determination of positions on his line of march, the ascertaining of the general contour of the interior as that of a plateau flanked by ridges east and west, the careful observation and recording of the natural history of the regions traversed—but pride of place was yielded to the moral integrity of a man who kept his promise to his African followers and conducted them safely home again: "How much indeed must the moral influence of the British name be enhanced throughout Africa, where it has been promulgated that our missionary has thus kept his plighted word to the poor natives who faithfully stood by him!"[1] The next day it was the turn of the London Missionary Society, with Lord Shaftesbury presiding. Early in the New Year a meeting was convened at the Mansion House by the Lord Mayor for the purpose of raising a testimonial in recognition of the traveller's great achievements. In due course the University of Oxford conferred its D.C.L. and of Glasgow its LL.D., while the Royal Society elected Livingstone a Fellow. He was early given a personal interview by the Prince Consort, whose interest in African affairs had been shown at the Niger Expedition meeting over which he presided in 1840, little thinking at the time that a young man then in the audience would win lasting fame by his African travels. And before he

[1] *Proceedings of the Royal Geographical Society*, I (1857), 233–5.

sailed again he was received in personal audience by the Queen, saying he would now be able to declare that he had seen his chief.[1] Africa was without doubt once more in the news, and this in a year when Asian affairs claimed public attention: war with China terminated by the Treaty of Tientsin that opened the country to Europeans; and the Indian Mutiny, as a sequel to which the government of India was transferred to the British Crown. That African affairs remained in the foreground of public interest was significant of the mark the missionary traveller had already made on his generation. So also was the success of his first book. After the initial welcomes Livingstone devoted himself to preparing for the press, under Sir Roderick Murchison's encouragement, the record of his sixteen years in Africa. It was published in November 1857 in a first edition of 12,000, but orders for 13,800 had been received before publication.[2] There was no doubt about it: Africa was placed fairly and squarely on the map of the world, no longer as to its outline merely, but now with something more than guesswork as to its interior.

It was during these months that decisions were taken which re-directed the manner of Livingstone's African service though not his missionary vocation. He found himself at the end of the year the appointed leader of an expedition to the Zambezi.

(1) *A Zambezi Expedition*

Livingstone had first come seriously to question his continuance with the London Missionary Society on receipt of a letter from Dr. Tidman placing in doubt the ability of the Society "within any definite period, to enter upon untried, remote, and difficult fields of labour".[3] This appeared to Livingstone to be a refusal to enter the door that had been flung open: "The proposition to leave the untried, remote, and difficult fields of labour as they have been ever since our Saviour died

---

[1] Blaikie, *op. cit.*, 198. It was a deep personal sorrow to Livingstone that his father had died just before his homecoming. He had much wanted to see his son, and said at the end: "But I think I'll know whatever is worth knowing about him. When you see him, tell him I think so."—*Ibid.*, 165.

[2] *Missionary Travels and Researches in South Africa; including a sketch of sixteen years' residence in the interior of Africa, and a journey from the Cape of Good Hope to Loanda on the West Coast; thence across the continent, down the River Zambesi, to the eastern ocean* (London, John Murray). On the writing of the book and its reception, see Blaikie, *op. cit.*, 174–81.

[3] Campbell, *op. cit.*, 233, where the full context is given, with the secretary's wish "for conferring with you fully on your future plans".

for the poor sinners who inhabit them involves my certain severance from the L.M.S. and the attempt to support myself and return in the best way I can."[1]

Livingstone's experiences in Central Africa had intensified his desire to counter the Portuguese and Arab slave-trade by opening up the country to legitimate commerce in advance of that desolating invasion. It is perhaps worth while to recall that at the Exeter Hall meeting on June 1, 1840 his attention had been directed to this evil in eastern Africa. Sir Robert Peel, in his speech on the occasion, had quoted from the current Cape *Shipping List* the callous conduct of slave-traders: "On the 24th of January 1840, during a hurricane from the South-east, two slavers, a ship and a brig, were wrecked at Mozambique harbour, but the crews of both and 200 slaves on board the brig were saved. It was reported that the brig had originally 900 slaves on board, but during the hurricane the hatches had been battened down, and on opening them 300 were found to have died from suffocation. Again the hurricane came on; the hatches were battened down a second time, and the consequence was that 300 more of the slaves perished from the same cause, and 100 of the remaining 300 died on the passage to Mozambique harbour; and what was the conduct of the parties to this mortality—what course did the vessel pursue? Why, they returned for the purpose of getting a fresh supply. Until this country rescues Christianity and the character of the white people from the grievous infamy of these sins, it will never be able to convince the black population of Africa of the moral superiority of their European fellow-men; scarcely can it convince them of the truths of Christianity, which continue to tolerate such monstrous sins."[2] David Livingstone, as we know him, cannot have listened to these words unmoved. Long lying dormant, they would be invoked to life by what he had himself discovered to be taking place on the Zambezi. On his contact with Sebitwane of the Makololo in 1851 he found that the slave-trade had only penetrated to this central region the year before, coming simultaneously from both west and east. From the west came a party of people called Mambari, with Ambonda affiliations, domiciled to the south-east of Angola. They had some old Portuguese guns which Sebitwane coveted for defence against his

---

[1] Livingstone to W. Thompson, from Mauritius, 17.9.56.—Chamberlin, *op. cit.*, 263. He had inferred: "I suppose that it is intended to send me to some of the tried, near and easy fields where I may wax fat and kick like Jeshurun." Cf. Deut. 32: 15.

[2] *The Times*, June 2, 1840.

doughty southern neighbours the Matebele, but one commodity only was sought in exchange: "The Mambari refused everything except boys about fourteen years of age. The Makololo declare they never heard of people being bought and sold till then, and disliked it, but the desire to possess the guns prevailed, and eight old guns were exchanged for as many boys."[1] These were captives from conquered peoples. The Mambari then proposed a joint expedition against the Mashukulumbwe (the name given by the Barotse to the Ila people),[2] the Makololo to take the cattle and the Mambari the people. On this expedition the Makololo first met Arab slave-traders from Zanzibar who traded three English guns, this time for some thirty slaves. Guns began it, but much more followed, with Lancashire textiles soon in brisk demand, and all for slaves—cattle were offered but refused. By 1853 half-caste Portuguese were entering the new market. In Coupland's expressive phrase, Livingstone "had raised a corner of the veil that hid the heart of Africa and seen the Arab Slave Trade feeding on it".[3] Small wonder then if any opportunity to open up the country for legitimate commerce, offering the wide range of manufactured goods from Europe for the natural resources of Africa, thus enriching and not ravishing her people, would be eagerly welcomed as a genuine Christian vocation.

The opportunity was soon presented. Sir Roderick Murchison, President of the Royal Geographical Society, made the first move by directing the attention of the Earl of Clarendon, Foreign Secretary in Aberdeen's Administration, to Livingstone's exceptional qualifications for official service in Africa. This he did as early as January 5, 1857. An introduction to Lord Clarendon followed and on January 26, in a letter Murchison had evidently invited, Livingstone outlined his proposals for Christian and commercial development in Central Africa—a task, he said, he had already decided to undertake on his own responsibility.[4]

[1] Livingstone, *Missionary Travels*, 92.
[2] Livingstone spelt the name Bashukolompo. It was apparently bestowed on account of their characteristic coiffure.—Smith and Dale, *The Ila-speaking Peoples of Northern Rhodesia* (1920), I, xxv; cf. 42.
[3] Livingstone, *op. cit.*, 91–2, 180–1, 271; Chamberlin, *op. cit.*, 151–2; R. Coupland, *Kirk on the Zambesi* (1928), 45. On further activities of the Mambari; cf. Livingstone, *op. cit.*, 215–16, 218.
[4] This new information on the initiative that led to Livingstone's employment in an official capacity is derived from the Clarendon papers in the Bodleian. These have been investigated (apparently for the first time on this issue) by Dr. E. W. Smith who has generously placed his notes at my disposal. He himself discusses the whole question in *Roger Price: His Life and Times*, chap. iii, section (2), and has presented photostats of the more important letters concerned to the Blantyre Memorial.

Meanwhile the Board of the London Missionary Society adopted on January 26 a recommendation of its Southern Committee in consultation with Livingstone, to which the question had been remitted, that missions north and south of the Zambezi should be attempted. This was put before a special meeting of the Directors, both Town and Country, on February 10 when it was resolved: "That in accordance with the recommendation of the Southern Committee efforts be forthwith made with a view to the establishment of Missions upon the North and South of the river Zambese." Livingstone had thus been called in as consultant, but any active participation as leader of a Makololo mission was precluded by his concern with those wider issues which by this time he had already been invited to submit to Lord Clarendon.[1]

Murchison continued to press Livingstone's claims on the Foreign Secretary and on May 2, 1857 Livingstone himself, in a letter to Lord Clarendon, outlined the policy of development he proposed to pursue on the Zambezi, and indicated that as

[1] There has been some confusion over Livingstone's responsibility in relation to the Makololo mission. The *Report of the Directors* for 1857 states the resolution of February 10, at the special meeting above referred to, as follows: "That the two new Mission Stations should be opened—the one among the Makololo, north of the Zambese, under the charge of Dr. Livingston, assisted by another Missionary; and the other among the Matabele, to the south of that river, under the superintendence, in the first instance, of Mr. Moffat . . .". It is this statement, which he quotes, on which Lovett relies in *The History of the London Missionary Society, 1795–1895* (1899), I, 618. The exact entry in the Minute Book, however, which is given above, and which must claim prior authority, makes no such reference to Livingstone's leadership. The record of the Minute Book of the Board on this point (to which Dr. E. W. Smith has directed my attention and for which I am indebted to Miss Fletcher, Librarian of the London Missionary Society) runs as follows:—*January 12* —After a statement by Livingstone on a Makololo mission north of the Zambezi, in the course of which he is recorded as saying "that in his judgment the result would be promoted by the residence of himself and Mrs. Livingston amongst them and with God's blessing almost certainly secured were Mr. Moffat to commence a Mission at the town of Moselekatse", the Board referred the matter to the Southern Committee with a few other Directors in further consultation with Livingstone (Board Minutes, p. 373). *January 26*—Report of the Southern Committee of January 22 received, which recommended the opening of two new mission stations among the Makololo and Matebele respectively, and which added: "That . . Mr. Moffat be invited to commence the proposed new Mission among the Matabele. . . . That a Missionary be appointed to assist Dr. Livingston in the organization of the intended Mission among the Makololo. . . ." (Board Minutes, p. 385). *February 10*— The special meeting of Directors endorsing the recommendation to establish the two new missions, the resolution of which is quoted above. (Board Minutes, p. 391). It would appear therefore that the statement in the *Report* represents a conflation of the Southern Committee (January 22) recommendation, with "organization" enlarged to "in charge of", and the resolution of the meeting of the Directors of February 10. The Clarendon papers provide collateral evidence of Livingstone's preoccupation with wider issues in the month that followed his review of the situation on January 12.

he would no longer be in the service of the London Missionary Society he would be available for official appointment should the Government see fit to accept his services.[1] In August he was in Dublin, lecturing at the meeting of the British Association for the Advancement of Science, where influential friends approved his proposals, so that he wrote to Mrs. Livingstone: "I think the visit to Dublin will be beneficial to our cause, which, I think, is the cause of Christ in Africa."[2] The official response was favourable. Lord Clarendon, in personal consultation with Livingstone, ascertained with more precision what the proposal involved, and thereupon commended the scheme to the Cabinet, so that before Christmas it was announced in Parliament that £5,000 would be voted for a Zambezi Expedition under Livingstone's personal direction. The essential programme of the Niger Expedition of 1841 was to be tried again on the Zambezi: "Livingstone, in fact, had taken the old positive policy from the shelf where it had lain for a decade in disrepute."[3] Early in the New Year the plan of operations was decided upon, but meanwhile Livingstone had visited Cambridge and delivered two lectures, in each of which he ended on this note. On December 4 in a crowded Senate House before an audience representative of the university he concluded: "I beg to direct your attention to Africa;—I know that in a few years I shall be cut off in that country, which is now open; do not let it be shut again! I go back to Africa to make an open path for commerce and Christianity; do you carry out the work which I have begun. I leave it with you!" On the following day in the Town Hall his closing words contained the same emphasis on a positive policy: "My object in labouring as I have in Africa, is to open up the country to commerce and Christianity. This is my object in returning thither. . . . I propose in my next expedition to visit the Zambesi, and to propitiate the different chiefs along its banks, endeavouring to induce them to cultivate cotton, and to abolish the slave-trade."[4]

The Admiralty drafted a scheme which Livingstone found over-elaborate: his own memorandum, which was accepted, proposed a steam-launch, half a dozen qualified Europeans and

[1] R. J. Campbell by error gives the date as May 22.—Campbell, *Livingstone*, 244. It was written in response to a request for it from Clarendon which Murchison, in an undated letter among the Clarendon papers above mentioned, promised to transmit. He forwarded Livingstone's letter to Clarendon on May 6.
[2] Blaikie, *op. cit.*, 183; cf. Coupland, *op. cit.*, 76.
[3] Coupland, *op. cit.*, 46, 76.
[4] W. Monk (ed.), *Dr. Livingstone's Cambridge Lectures* (1858), 24, 46–7.

a company of Krumen. His suggestions as to who five of the Europeans should be were accepted: among these were Dr. (later Sir) John Kirk, who was to rise to distinction as Consul at Zanzibar, and Thomas Baines, artist and explorer, later to be actively concerned in the gold-fields in Matebele territory.[1] Livingstone himself was to be accredited as British Consul but the precise designation involved some diplomatic exchange with Lisbon. Indeed, permission for the expedition to pass through Portuguese coastal territory was necessary and this was secured, though Portuguese sensitiveness was evident in respect of an expedition, even by a Power in ancient and honourable alliance, to a territory where little more than a façade of government existed. Thus it was that when Livingstone's commission was proposed as British Consul at Quilimane, Sena and Tete, Lisbon accepted it for Quilimane only. Livingstone, when informed, was quick to appreciate the implication: "In reference to the refusal of the Portuguese Government to recognize the right of free intercourse up the Zambesi, I beg to suggest that it is very undesirable to admit the claim as it involves the admission of their power over the independent tribes on its banks." He suggested that he should be accredited to Sekeletu and other chiefs beyond the boundary of Portuguese authority; this was done and an appropriate letter sent by Livingstone to the chief "thanking him in the Queen's name for his previous assistance to her servant, condemning the Slave Trade, and asking him to keep 'God's highway', the Zambesi, open to the free traffic of all peoples".[2]

On the eve of the Expedition's departure a "Farewell Livingstone Festival" as it was styled was held under the auspices of the Royal Geographical Society on February 13, 1858. A distinguished company met to do the traveller honour, in which Mrs. Livingstone, who was present, was accorded generous recognition. Livingstone's statement of his objective, in his speech on the occasion, is deserving of record: "I do hope to find in that part of the country which I have partially explored, a pathway by means of the river Zambesi which may lead to highlands where Europeans may form a healthful settlement, and where by opening up communication and establishing commercial intercourse with the natives of Africa they may slowly,

---

[1] Coupland, *op. cit.*, 76–8. For Kirk at Zanzibar, see Coupland, *The Exploitation of East Africa, 1856–1890* (1939); and for Baines in Matebeleland; Wallis (ed.), *The Northern Goldfields Diaries of Thomas Baines*, I–III (1946).

[2] Coupland, *op. cit.*, 89–91.

but not the less surely, impart to the people of that country the knowledge and the inestimable blessings of Christianity."[1] This frank and forthright avowal of his ultimate Christian purpose illustrates his contention that the severance of his connexion with a recognized Missionary Society involved no essential discontinuity in Christian vocation or missionary labour. He was capable of giving the reply direct to those who sought to determine for him what "missionary" meant, as he did to one such well-intentioned lady: "My views of what is *missionary* duty are not so contracted as those whose ideal is a dumpy sort of man with a Bible under his arm."[2] He anticipated no speedy result from what was to be attempted, but in the same farewell speech stated his conviction that if successful it would have the most far-reaching effects: "I feel convinced that if we can establish a system of free labour in Africa, it will have a most decided influence upon slavery throughout the world."[3]

The members of the Expedition set sail on March 10, 1858 calling at Sierra Leone *en route* to the Cape. Livingstone was much impressed by what he found of an orderly Christian community and wrote that "the man even 'who has no nonsense about him' would be obliged to confess that England has done some good by her philanthropy."[4] The purpose in calling was to embark a dozen men of the Kru tribe to serve with the launch they were carrying for service on the Zambezi. They proved unsuited, however, to the Expedition's purpose as they were unequal to the land marches that were involved, and were soon shipped home by a naval vessel.[5] A crew of Livingstone's loyal Makololo took their place.

---

[1] *Proceedings of the Royal Geographical Society*, II (1858), 125.

[2] Blaikie, *op. cit.*, 181–2. Italics in original. In a more generous spirit and with greater depth of understanding his action was questioned by a close and trusted Quaker friend, Mr. J. B. Braithwaite of Lincoln's Inn: "To dissolve thy connection with the Missionary Society would at once place thee before the public in an aspect wholly distinct from that in which thou art at present, and, what is yet more important, would in a greater or less degree, and, perhaps, very gradually and almost insensibly to thyself, turn the current of thy own thoughts and feelings away from those channels of usefulness and service, as a minister of the gospel, with which I cannot doubt thy deepest interest and highest aspirations are inseparably associated."—*Ibid.*, 193.

[3] *Proceedings of the Royal Geographical Society*, II, 126.

[4] Livingstone to Sir R. Murchison, 30.3.58.—*Proceedings of the Church Missionary Society* (1858), 36.

[5] Domiciled on the so-called Kru Coast at the eastern end of Liberia, the Krus were a seafaring people that proved of great service to both naval and trading vessels on the West Coast. They were usually embarked at Sierra Leone where they had a settlement.—W. Monk (ed.), *Dr. Livingstone's Cambridge Lectures* (2nd ed., 1860), 28, 370; D. and C. Livingstone, *Narrative of an Expedition to the Zambesi and its Tributaries* (1865), 84. Cf. H. H. Johnston, *Liberia* (1906), I, 294.

Difficulties on such a venture were only to be expected. They were not long in appearing. Scarcely had the Expedition arrived when a leading member of it resigned. Commander Bedingfeld, R.N., who had been appointed the naval officer with appropriate duties, after some altercation with Livingstone decided to withdraw.[1] This left Livingstone with the additional responsibility of navigation. Disease was soon busy with the European members, malaria as usual being the bane of most. The effect of this on the nervous system is noted in a passage of *The Zambesi and its Tributaries* thought to be penned under the influence of Dr. Kirk.[2] It would partially explain the unhappy personal friction that marred the Expedition. This resulted in two dismissals towards the end of 1859, that of Thomas Baines securing some disturbing publicity.[3] The sinister influence at work is now seen to have been that of David's brother Charles whom he had recommended for appointment as general assistant and "fully qualified to act as moral agent". But as time went on Charles's failures in duty and his stinging provocations —Kirk wrote in his diary of a narrowly averted tragedy—compelled even his long-suffering brother to turn, as a painful entry in the locked Journal reveals. If, in Kirk's words, it was "an unfortunate Expedition for quarrels", it is only fair to all concerned to note, with Coupland, "the clear fact that the mainspring of those quarrels was the mischief-making of the Expedition's 'Moral Agent' ".[4]

As if the handicap of disease and the deterioration of personal relations were not enough, there was the added frustration of the failure of the essential arm of river transport: the steam launch *Ma Robert* proved hopelessly unserviceable.[5] The fact that it took all hands one and a half days to cut the fuel for one day's travel was a sore trial, but added to this was the defective

---

[1] The dispute has been examined by Coupland, *op. cit.*, 114–17. Cf. Campbell's comments, *op. cit.*, 250–1; Macnair, *op. cit.*, 221. "Bedingfield" has crept into certain accounts.

[2] *Op. cit.*, 73–4; Coupland, *op. cit.*, 273; Campbell, *op. cit.*, 260. The use of quinine as a prophylactic was reported on jointly by Livingstone and Kirk in a letter to Sir James Clark of July, 1859.—W. Monk (ed.), *Dr. Livingstone's Cambridge Lectures* (2nd ed., 1860), 370–5.

[3] Coupland, with relevant letters and Kirk's diaries at his disposal, has offered a judicial estimate of Baines's case.—*Op. cit.*, 158–62. H. H. Johnston's earlier judgment must now be read in the light of this.—Johnston, *Livingstone and the Exploration of Central Africa* (1891), 248–50. Cf. Macnair, *op. cit.*, 233–7.

[4] Coupland, *op. cit.*, 78, 180–1; Campbell, *Livingstone*, 259, where the relevant entry in the locked Journal is quoted.

[5] The name was Mrs. Livingstone's bestowed, by tribal custom, on the birth of her first-born.

hull, so that by March 1860 Livingstone reported "a worn-out steamer with 35 patches, covering at least 100 holes". Small wonder that he had soon christened her the old *Asthmatic*, and even reported the humiliation of her being out-distanced by canoes![1]

Against the resistance of these inhibiting conditions Livingstone pursued his purpose: to open a pathway by means of the Zambezi for settlement and commerce. It was necessary as a preliminary step to ascertain the navigability of the river through to the interior. The crucial section, as Livingstone already knew, was the Kebrabasa gorge and rapids some fifty miles above Tete, which he had skirted on his journey to the coast in 1856. If the launch could pass at a season of high water this obstacle to navigation, the river would prove to be that highway to the interior on which so much depended—at least, such was the hope. Kirk reports that Livingstone was even prepared to blast a channel through the obstruction if necessary. But the obstruction proved more daunting than he had imagined. He tried hard to hold on to his original idea, but in the end had reluctantly to admit that the Zambezi was no thoroughfare. Reluctantly? It was a bitter disillusion. There is an agonizing entry in his private Journal for December 1858: "Things look dark for our enterprise. This Kebrabasa is what I never expected. What we shall do if this is to be the end of the navigation I cannot now divine, but here I am, and I am trusting him who never made ashamed those who did so. . . . Spare me, good Lord . . ."; and there follows the poignant heartcry of a strong man in anguish.[2]

Frustration on the main Zambezi led to investigation of its principal tributary, the River Shiré, entering from the north between Sena and the sea. Kirk was now proving the one member of the Expedition suited to accompany Livingstone in these arduous undertakings; together they puffed into the Shiré on the old *Asthmatic* on December 29, 1858. They were cheered by what they found: "All the way the river had continued clear

---

[1] Blaikie, *op. cit.*, 218 *n.*, 224, 227, 234–5; Coupland, *op. cit.*, 115, 147, 184; W. Monk (ed.), *op. cit.* (2nd ed.), 347. On December 21, 1860, she stuck on a sandbank and forthwith filled and had to be abandoned. The plates were at first only 1/16 inch thick! Livingstone wrote scathingly of the professed philanthropy and worthless assurances of her builder.—*Zambesi and its Tributaries*, 92–3, 149; Blaikie, *op. cit.*, 223–4.

[2] Coupland, *op. cit.*, 104, 129, 135–6; Campbell, *op. cit.*, 253–5. A sketch of the gorge by Kirk is reproduced in Coupland, at p. 134. At Tete, which became the base of this exploratory enterprise, Livingstone had been rapturously welcomed by the Makololo who had been left there.—Macnair, *op. cit.*, 222.

and deep," wrote Kirk on January 3; "under proper care this
would be a splendid plain, far before that of the Nile, with a
fine navigable river winding through it." The people were shy
if not hostile; slave-raids had made them suspicious. On
January 8, 1859 some 150 miles upstream they reached the
settlement of a chief Chibisa, and heard tell of two lakes to the
north. They were on the threshold of discovery. One day's
journey, however, and the river road was blocked: the Shiré too
had its rapids. Naming these the Murchison Cataracts in honour
of the President of the Royal Geographical Society, they returned to base. On a second journey in March they pushed beyond Chibisa's, passed Mount Zomba, rising to 6,000 feet, and
on April 16 sighted Lake Shirwa. It was the Expedition's first
discovery. But more to their purpose was the fact that in reaching it they had traversed the Shiré Highlands, the very type of
country for colonization of which they were in search. They
were the first Europeans to be seen in the land. Again a return
to base, and a third journey to Chibisa's, with nearly three
weeks' march beyond, handicapped by hostile because suspicious villagers, when on September 17 the shimmering waters of
Lake Nyasa rejoiced their eyes—"Ninyessi", the Lake of Stars.
It stretched so far north, they had been told, that no one had
reached the end of it. This was a major discovery indeed. The
Expedition's achievements were positive at last.[1]

The impulse to explore further the major new discovery had
for the moment to be restrained. Livingstone had deferred
going home with the Makololo he had left at Tete in 1856 until
the main task of the Expedition had first been put in hand. He
now returned by land with such of them as wished to go—for
some preferred to remain on the Lower Zambezi. He received
his customary warmth of welcome on arrival, and now first
learned of the tragedy of the attempted London Mission. The
double journey, on foot in the old manner, occupied from May
15 to November 23, 1860—within a week of the six months
Livingstone had estimated. He reported of it to Sir Roderick
Murchison: "We have kept faith with the Makololo though we
have done nothing else."[2]

[1] Livingstone, *Zambesi and its Tributaries*, 81, 123; Blaikie, *op. cit.*, 215, 218–20;
Coupland, *op. cit.*, 137–44, 151–7. Where discrepancies in dates occur Coupland
has been followed. Cf. *ibid.*, 156 n. The German explorer Roscher was at the lake
in November, 1859, but was murdered on the return journey. Livingstone later
discovered that *Nyassa* was a Portuguese abbreviation of *Nyanza ia Nyinyesi*=Lake
of Stars.—(Livingstone to Maclear), Blaikie, *op. cit.*, 372.

[2] Coupland, *op. cit.*, 170–82, largely based on Kirk's diary and letters. Livingstone was accompanied by Kirk and his brother Charles.

The way was now clear for those exploratory journeys consequent on the discovery of Lake Nyasa which might bring the
objectives of the Expedition nearer to realization. The new
steamer which Livingstone had requested, the *Pioneer*, was on
the scene early in 1861. The first party of the Universities' Mission arrived about the same time and became in a measure his
responsibility as we shall see in due course. The first journey in
the *Pioneer* was to be an ascent of the River Rovuma (northern
boundary of Portuguese territory) to ascertain whether it rose
from Lake Nyasa, as African report maintained. This, if true,
would obviate the necessity of using the Lower Zambezi, for
the Portuguese were now proving difficult. The Zambezi Expedition had never been to their liking, despite smooth words
from Lisbon, and local officials were scarcely likely to promote
what, if successful, would sound the death knell to their own
profits from dominating the traffic with the interior. Indeed,
Livingstone soon realized that the discovery of the Shiré Highlands had but opened a new territory to slave-traders and
raiders. Hence the attempt to by-pass the Portuguese by the
Rovuma route if feasible. But it was not feasible. Some 150
miles from the sea there were cataracts again; and the river
did not rise from Lake Nyasa.[1]

The lake itself claimed attention as soon as Livingstone's
duties with Bishop Mackenzie's party were discharged. The
plan was to take the *Pioneer* to Chibisa's at the foot of the
cataracts, and then carry up a boat in which to explore the lake.
Leaving Chibisa's on August 6 they entered Lake Nyasa on
September 2, 1861 the colour of which indicated great depth:
"the deep blue or indigo tint of the Indian Ocean". The grand
promontory projecting into the southern end of the lake they
named Cape Maclear.[2] Proceeding northwards they caught the
beauty of magnificent mountain ranges when the heavy haze
permitted and were impressed by the density of the lake-
side population. But there was a destructive blight over the
whole: the slave-trader was ever busy and an Arab dhow had
even begun to ply upon the lake. For a month they crept
steadily northwards, covering some 250 miles, and then turned
because they must. They thought they were near the end, but
that was still 100 miles beyond! This was the high-water mark

---

[1] The first ascent of the Rovuma in 1861 was limited by the necessity of returning
to the Universities' Mission party. It was the second in the following year which
proved decisive.—Livingstone, *The Zambesi and its Tributaries*, 348–50, 427–44. On
the stiffening Portuguese attitude, see Coupland, *op. cit.*, 162–3, 234–5.

[2] After the Astronomer Royal at the Cape.

of the Expedition's achievement, in both senses of the term. By November 8 they had rejoined the *Pioneer*.[1]

The Expedition was now drawing to its close. Within three months there were arrivals that seemed to promise further life, but in reality the climax had been reached. On January 30, 1862 there came by H.M.S. *Gorgon* Mrs. Livingstone, the *Lady Nyassa* and James Stewart of the Free Church of Scotland to investigate the possibilities of an industrial mission. All was stimulating to Livingstone. But the satisfaction was short-lived. Stewart's decision was negative. Mrs. Livingstone fell ill on April 21, and within six days had passed away. James Stewart was with them at the end, and wrote: "The man who had faced so many deaths, and braved so many dangers, was now utterly broken down and weeping like a child." The bereaved husband confided his grief to his private journal, and the entry for May 11 concluded: "For the first time in my life I feel willing to die."[2]

The *Lady Nyassa* was the steamer built at Livingstone's own charges with which he had expected to navigate Lake Nyasa. His personal hopes were now shattered, but he kept his hand to the plough: "I work with as much vigour as I can, and mean to do so till the change comes; but the prospect of a home is all dispelled."[3] The *Lady Nyassa* reached the foot of the Murchison Cataracts by April 1863, there to be dismantled and conveyed in sections for reassembly and launching on the lake. But that proud moment never came. The same month Kirk and Charles Livingstone were invalided and in June came the despatch from the Foreign Office, recalling the Expedition.[4] Livingstone was at Quilimane with the *Pioneer* and the *Lady Nyassa* by mid-February 1864. The *Pioneer* was delivered to the Royal Navy; the *Lady Nyassa* he took on a perilous voyage to Bombay where he left her, and embarked for England, landing on this his second visit home on July 23, 1864.[5]

After six years of striving and frustration the Zambezi Expedition was over. What results could be claimed? Livingstone himself indicated three: settling the question of the navigability of the Zambezi; revealing the capacity of the highland regions for

---

[1] Livingstone, *op. cit.*, 365–87; Coupland, *op. cit.*, 202–11.
[2] Blaikie, *op. cit.*, 251–3. This occurred at Shupanga some fifty miles from the delta in heavily malarious country. For the reason for delay at that point, see Macnair, *op. cit.*, 262.
[3] Letter to Sir Thomas Maclear, 27.10.62.—Blaikie, *op. cit.*, 261.
[4] Coupland, *op. cit.*, 251, 254.
[5] Blaikie, *op. cit.*, 276–83.

producing valuable export crops; and above all, the exposure of the growing devastation by the slave-trade of a region by nature so beautiful and for development so promising.[1] This dark human tragedy was the dominating feature of the whole: "We confess we do not attempt to describe the productions of the country with that fulness they deserve, nor with that hopeful heartiness we once felt. Nor do we cite the discoveries of Lakes Shirwa and Nyassa . . . with any degree of pride. These were all incidental to our main design. What we have seen of the slave-trade has thrown a gloom over all . . . the rich upland plateaux like open prairies . . . the deep gorges and ravines leading down from the edges of the tablelands to lower levels where the Shiré meanders in green meadows like a silver thread, or the broad lake, backed with its mountain masses . . . all their natural beauties are now inseparably associated with human sorrow and woe."[2]

The main object of the Expedition remained unachieved. The project dear to the heart of Livingstone of a settlement which should at once encourage legitimate commerce and radiate a Christian witness remained unrealized. Sir Roderick Murchison had reported little enthusiasm for it, and James Stewart on the spot had turned it down.[3] Livingstone, who followed West African developments with keen interest, had regretted the absence in Central Africa of an African agency comparable to that supplied from Sierra Leone.[4] In letters to influential friends he reiterated time and again his conviction that Christian and commercial enterprise should be simultaneous, and by the former he meant settlements of Christian families: "It does not need connexion with a Society to be a Missionary"; "If we have Christian poor they will shine as lights in the darkness, and hold up the teacher's hands when the heathen are against him. Hitherto we have sent our paupers, our ragamuffin poor to colonize."[5] But the Government was not to be drawn into colonial adventure, as witness Lord John Russell's

[1] Livingstone, op. cit., 585-95.

[2] Ibid., 591. It has been suggested with reference to the Expedition as a whole that Livingstone was happier as leader among Africans than among men of his own race. Coupland, on the basis of Kirk's diaries, makes some relevant comments on this limitation.—Op. cit., 161, 246, 252. Kirk has an amusing reference to the warning conveyed whenever Livingstone began to sing to himself!—Ibid., 240.

[3] Stewart's Journal, with a selection from his correspondence, has been published.—J. P. R. Wallis (ed.), The Zambesi Journal of James Stewart, 1862-1863 (1952).

[4] Monk, op. cit. (2nd ed.), 362, 365; Livingstone, op. cit., 353.

[5] Monk, op. cit. (2nd ed.), 353, 378; cf. 369, 376, 377.

note on the first despatch about the Highlands: "I am unwilling to embark on new schemes of British possessions. Dr. Livingstone's information is valuable, but he must not be allowed to tempt us to form colonies only to be reached by forcing steamers up cataracts."[1] If there was disappointment at the official level, was there not hope for settlement from missionary enterprise? There had been, but this hope had also failed.

(2) *Two Inner Africa Missions*

During Livingstone's visit to England in 1857–58 two missions had been projected to the interior region he had explored. The first was that of his own Society.

In an early conference with the Directors his recommendations were as follows: that a mission to the Makololo be commenced in the elevated open country north of the Zambezi between that river and the Kafue, which the tribe had already occupied before being driven out by the Matebele, and to which he was confident they would return if under safeguard against further molestation; and also that adequate security against any such aggression by the foe they feared would be practically guaranteed by a simultaneous mission to the Matebele led by Robert Moffat, well known for his established friendship with Umsiligazi. At a special meeting convened for the purpose on February 10, 1857 the two new missions were agreed to and later confirmed by the Annual Meeting of the Society. Simultaneous preparations for the two missions were undertaken; only that to the north of the Zambezi concerns us here.[2]

There was appointed to the responsible post of leader of the pioneer party Holloway Helmore, a tested missionary of seventeen years' experience in Bechuanaland. Accompanying him with his wife and four children were to be two recruits fresh from their theological studies, Roger Price and John Mackenzie, with their wives. These recruits, with those for the Matebele mission, were met on arrival at Cape Town in July 1858 by Robert Moffat who communicated to the Secretary on the occasion his misgivings about the Makololo enterprise. He much doubted the willingness of Sekeletu and his people to return to territory exposed to Matebele attack without some

---

[1] Coupland, *op. cit.*, 271.
[2] Sixty-third *Report of the Directors* (1857), 28–9; Sixty-fourth *Report* (1858), 2. On the question of Livingstone's leadership, *vide supra* p. 175 *n*.

acceptable assurance against molestation from that quarter: "This they will require to know through a source upon which they can place the fullest reliance—i.e. either from Livingstone or myself. That they will break up their town and remove some hundred miles immediately on the arrival of the missionaries without some such assurance, we can hardly expect." Further, report had reached Moffat that Umsiligazi had been preparing a fleet of canoes on the Zambezi, and that Sekeletu had sent warriors to disperse them without success. This would intensify his reluctance to move.[1]

John Mackenzie on learning of this uncertain situation proposed, with that wisdom which was to characterize his later distinguished career, that a "bachelor party" should first go forward and, providing the Makololo were prepared to remove, set up a station at the new site and then return for their wives and families. Price approved, Helmore hesitated, the wives disliked it, and finally Mrs. Helmore's "quiet determination" decided it. In view of later criticism of the men for taking wives and families on an untried (to them) journey of a thousand miles largely through desert country, these facts are worthy of record.[2]

On July 8, 1859 the party set out; the Helmores with four children, together with African helpers. The Mackenzies were detained at Kuruman by Mrs. Mackenzie's health. The journey was a gruelling experience. Water was their insistent problem, both for themselves and their oxen, for they travelled by ox-wagon. Roger Price reported in a letter to the Society: "For more than a week every drop of water we used had to be walked for about thirty-five miles. You may imagine dear Mrs. Helmore's feelings when, one afternoon, the thermometer standing at 107 deg. in the shade, she was saving just *one spoonful* of water for each of the dear children, for the next morning, not thinking of taking a drop herself."[3] After seven months on the road,

---

[1] Moffat to Tidman, Cape Town, 20.7.58.—Campbell, *Livingstone*, 267–8.

[2] Mackenzie to Tidman, Kuruman, 1.3.59.—J. Mackenzie, *Ten Years North of the Orange River* (1871), 32–3. Kirk was critical of the Society for having sent so large a party into notoriously unhealthy country without medical assistance.— Coupland, *op. cit.*, 176. The party was late in setting out owing to Boer threats to close the road (*vide infra*, p. 281) and this delay contributed to the disaster.—E. W. Smith, *Roger Price: His Life and Times*, chap. iv, section 3.

[3] Sixty-seventh *Report of the Directors* (1861), 10. Italics in original. Extracts from letters of Mrs. Helmore recounting the sufferings of the desert crossing are given by Mackenzie, *op. cit.*, 121–7, 160–5. One of Mackenzie's own experiences is also recorded.—*Ibid.*, 167–73. A detailed account, based on the Roger Price papers, of the intense and prolonged suffering to which all were exposed on the lengthy journey is given by E. W. Smith, *op. cit.*, chap. iv.

greatly weakened by the vicissitudes of the journey, they reached Linyanti, Sekeletu's headquarters, on February 14, 1860.

Tragedy quickly followed. Sekeletu received them and made the customary presents of food, but declined to consider removal or to permit them to reside elsewhere than at Linyanti.[1] There was no word of Livingstone. In the course of a week virulent fever broke out among them. Children were the first casualties: Henry Helmore died on March 7, the Prices' infant on March 9, and Selina Helmore on March 11, with Mrs. Helmore on the following day. Holloway Helmore struggled on until April 21. The Prices and two Helmore orphans alone survived of the European contingent. At this point Sekeletu appeared in an ugly guise: his people without restraint pilfered the party's property by day and by night, and he himself claimed the Helmores' new wagon with much else. As the Prices eventually struggled away they were practically stripped of their remaining possessions. Barely were they at last set going on their journey south when on July 5 Mrs. Price collapsed under the strain she could no longer bear: "A little after midday her spirit took its flight to God who gave it. I buried her the same evening, under a tree—the only tree on the whole of the immense plain of the Matabe." Two months later on September 8, in the neighbourhood of Lake Ngami, Roger Price and the Helmore orphans were met by the Mackenzies now travelling north to Linyanti, unaware of the disaster that had overtaken the mission. They were back at Kuruman again by February 20, 1861.[2] Livingstone, delayed as we have seen by one frustration after another on the Zambezi Expedition, had not set out with the returning Makololo on the 600-mile tramp until May 15, 1860 reaching Linyanti in August. He then first learned of the fatal termination of the mission. In a letter to the Society he expressed his sorrow at arriving too late to be of use.[3]

Roger Price had left Linyanti under the impression that poison, not fever, was the cause of death, an impression shared

[1] Livingstone's subsequent report did not quite tally with this.—*Zambesi and its Tributaries*, 279.

[2] Sixty-seventh *Report of the Directors* (1861), 10–13; Mackenzie, *op. cit.*, 186–203.

[3] Livingstone to Tidman, dated Chicova, Zambesi, 10.11.60.—Sixty-seventh *Report of the Directors* (1861), 15–16. Livingstone stated he found Sekeletu quite willing to remove; Tidman notes this as in direct contradiction to the chief's conduct. It is doubtless resolved by remembering that Helmore was a complete stranger, Livingstone the trusted friend, in the difficult situation Moffat had correctly foreseen. On the question of an appointment for Livingstone to meet the mission party at Linyanti, see Blaikie, *op. cit.*, 231 *n.*, with Campbell, *op. cit.*, 270.

by the Bechuana who with them, are well on the basis of a report by a certain Makololo. The same report was given to Mackenzie by an old Bushman who had travelled south and whom he had encountered before his meeting with Roger Price. Was the story true? As Mackenzie points out, but for the sad sequel of Sekeletu's rapacity such a charge, not only against Livingstone's friend but involving a cardinal failure in the chief's sacred duty of hospitality, would never have been credited. There were thus two issues: the cause of death, and the explanation of Sekeletu's conduct.[1]

The view that poison was the cause of death depended on circumstantial evidence: Makololo rumour and Sekeletu's subsequent cruel treatment of those received as guests. Price was also of the opinion that Mambari slave-traders, who disliked nothing so much as a European mission among their Makololo clients, had brought pressure to bear on the chief. But nowhere was there any proof. On the other hand, those who could speak with any authority on the symptoms of the disease that ravaged the little party regarded them as entirely consistent with a virulent malaria. Sir George Grey, Governor of the Cape, and others there were of this opinion on the basis of reports reaching them. Livingstone's verdict was definite: "The spear, and not poison, is their weapon. There is no occasion for suspecting other poison than malaria, that being more than enough. We have witnessed all the symptoms of this poison scores of times, and, from the survivors' description, believe the deaths to have been caused by severe African fever, and nothing else." Mackenzie, with all the information at his disposal, was of the same opinion.[2]

What of Sekeletu's degradation of his office in the spoliation of his powerless guests? Here Mackenzie seems to have supplied the clue. The villain of the piece was a certain Mahuse, in the service of Tabe, the African teacher, and thus a member of the mission party. Moffat, who knew the man, recommended his expulsion but Helmore, more charitably than wisely, yielded to Tabe's request to take him. Mahuse, posing as an authority on the way chiefs down south handled white men, asserted that when a white man died all his property fell to the chief. Covetous courtiers took up the cry, and the weak Sekeletu stifled the voice of conscience (must it not have spoken when he

[1] Sixty-seventh *Report of the Directors* (1861), 13; Mackenzie, *op. cit.*, 158–9, 197.
[2] Sixty-seventh *Report of the Directors* (1861), 13; Livingstone, *The Zambesi and its Tributaries*, 280; Mackenzie, *op. cit.*, 187–8, 193–4, 216. E. W. Smith has made an exhaustive inquiry into this question.—*Op. cit.*, chap. vi, and Appendix, "What caused the Deaths?". He tells me that in later life Price changed his opinion.

remembered these were friends of Livingstone?) and played with fire. And the fire, so local legend affirmed, destroyed his people. For the Barotse, their vassals in the Zambezi valley, rose and massacred them all just five years later. The proud Makololo were no more. Such was the tragic history of the first mission to inner Africa.[1]

Livingstone's lecture before the University in the Senate House at Cambridge on December 4, 1857 had been given at the instance of William Monk, on whose proposal the lectures were edited with the avowed object of encouraging a Cambridge mission to Africa.[2] This served to maintain the interest the visit had aroused. In November 1858 Robert Gray, Bishop of Cape Town (who had met Livingstone in the previous February), went to Cambridge and took up the question of a university mission to Central Africa. The Makololo mission was a spur: he urged "that the Church should do at least as much as the Independents, who have already raised £7,000, and sent forth six missionaries". He proposed that Cambridge should take the lead in sending six men to the Zambezi, one to be consecrated bishop as leader of the mission.[3] This set the ball rolling. A Cambridge Committee for the purpose was constituted the same month; Oxford followed suit in March 1859, and soon after the "Oxford and Cambridge Mission to Central Africa" was fairly launched. On November 1, 1859 a notable meeting in support of the new enterprise was held in the Senate House in Cambridge, addressed, among others, by W. E. Gladstone then Chancellor of the Exchequer, Sir George Grey Governor of the Cape, and Samuel Wilberforce Bishop of Oxford. Archdeacon Mackenzie of Natal attended the "Great Zambesi Meeting" as it came to be called, but had his reservations: "I am *afraid* of this," he said to a friend, "most great works of this kind have been carried on by one or two men in a quieter way, and have had a more humble beginning." The

---

[1] Mackenzie, *op. cit.*, 194–5; 199–200, 243–8. The influence of these events was lasting and far-reaching. Mackenzie reports of the Ngwatos: "In some of our difficulties at Shoshong, when sinister councils had well-nigh prevailed, some Gamaliel was sure to stand up and advise, 'Let the missionary alone: the Makololo injured the missionaries and where are the Makololo?'"—Mackenzie, *op. cit.*, 248.

[2] W. Monk (ed.), *Dr. Livingstone's Cambridge Lectures*, with Prefatory Letter by Professor Sedgwick, and Appendix (1858). The appendix runs to some 120 pages, fifty of which are devoted to the question of missions.

[3] C. Gray, *Life of Robert Gray*, I, 438. A detailed account of the origin of the Mission is provided by W. Monk, *op. cit.* (2nd ed., 1860), 326–34. The constitution agreed upon is given in *Report of the Oxford, Cambridge, Dublin, and Durham Mission to Central Africa for 1860* (1861), 9–11.

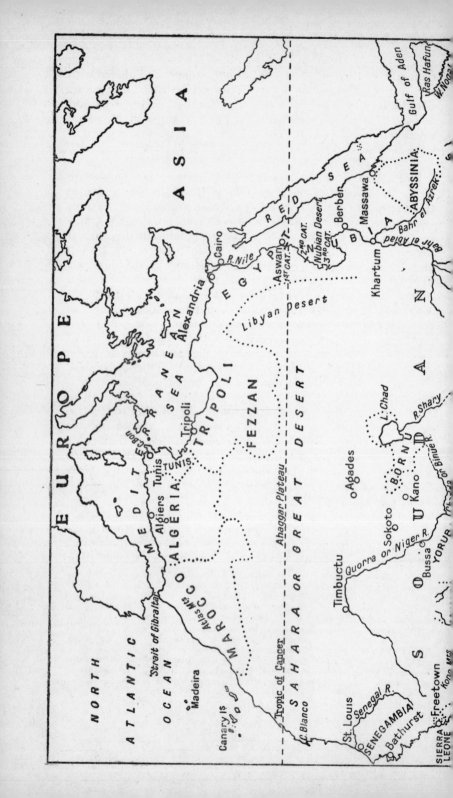

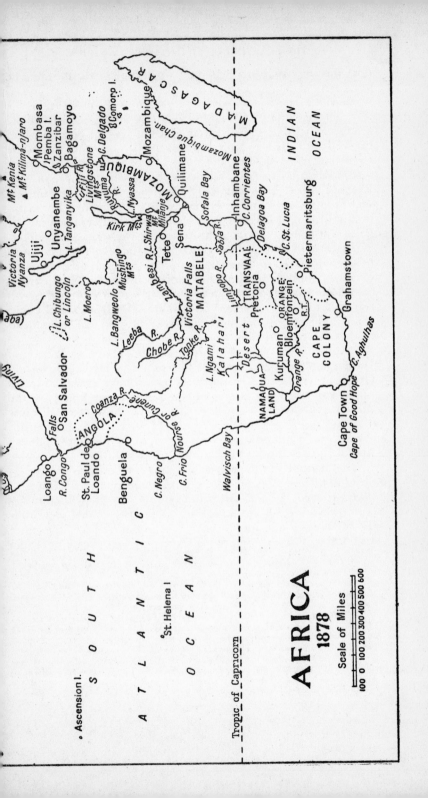

AFRICA
1878

Scale of Miles

100 0 100 200 300 400 500 600

next day he was himself invited to lead the new mission; he accepted.[1]

Charles Frederick Mackenzie was born in 1825 and at the age of nineteen came into residence at Cambridge. In 1848 he graduated with mathematical honours as Second Wrangler and proceeded to a fellowship at his college, Gonville and Caius. He seemed marked out for the career of tutor in the academic seclusion of his university when, in 1854, Bishop Selwyn of New Zealand visited Cambridge. The impression made on him was such that he revoked a recent decision and accepted the invitation of Bishop Colenso to go to Natal. For the next five years he had served, not without vicissitudes, as Archdeacon of Pietermaritzburg in that diocese. When his friend, Dr. Paget of Cambridge, remarked to Miss Mackenzie that an insurance company would be unlikely to allow her brother more than a two years' expectation of life in the new Zambezi venture, and this was reported to him, he replied he had considered it carefully and come to the same conclusion. Such was the man selected as head of the Zambezi Mission.[2]

Meanwhile developments were afoot. The Universities of Dublin and Durham agreed to co-operate.[3] The plea by Bishop Gray that the head of the mission should have episcopal status raised constitutional issues, but a solution was found by the consent of Gray and his comprovincials to consecrate. This was done at Cape Town on New Year's Day 1861. The Mission thus fell within the ecclesiastical jurisdiction of the Province of South Africa.[4]

The question of the precise location of the mission was recognized to be largely dependent upon Livingstone's recommendations. Indeed, Bishop Gray had kept in touch with him by correspondence for this purpose, and reported his view that the mission should operate in the neighbourhood of the Shiré and Lake Nyasa. Livingstone's offer of co-operation in the

[1] H. Goodwin, *Memoir of Bishop Mackenzie* (1864), 216–19. Italics in original.
[2] H. Goodwin, *op. cit., passim.*
[3] This expanded the name to "The Oxford, Cambridge, Dublin and Durham Mission to Central Africa", happily compressed in due course to "The Universities' Mission to Central Africa". Dublin did not long continue in the team.
[4] A "Missionary Bishop" in a territory beyond the Queen's Dominions was a new idea. The issues involved were discussed in Convocation, and the Law Officers of the Crown indicated no objection, provided such bishops were recognized not to have legal powers within the Queen's Dominions. The Foreign Office was concerned about the limits of the proposed diocese. Gray suggested to Bishop Wilberforce that to be on the safe side they might name the Mountains of the Moon!— A. E. M. Anderson-Morshead, *A History of the Universities' Mission to Central Africa* (1909), 411–20; H. Goodwin, *op. cit.*, 228–35; C. Gray, *op. cit.*, I, 440, 454, 465–70.

introduction of the pioneer party was welcomed, as he on his side rejoiced in the opportunity to effect a settlement on the Shiré highlands. Moreover, the objective tallied with Livingstone's own conceptions: "It will be understood that the great object of this Mission is to make known the Gospel of Christ; but as the Committees are well aware that, in Dr. Livingstone's own words, 'civilization and Christianity must go on together', they think it advisable to state that it will be their aim to encourage the advancement of science and the useful arts, and to direct especial attention to all questions connected with the slave-trade as carried on in the interior of Africa." This last feature was to prove more ominous for the mission than its promoters realized.[1]

On February 7, 1861 Mackenzie was at the Kongone mouth of the Zambezi, eager to proceed upcountry and commence the work already too long delayed. To his chagrin Livingstone counselled waiting: the season was unhealthy, and it was first desirable to test the usefulness of the Rovuma as a waterway to the lake. Mackenzie then proposed that he and his party should proceed inland independently, but to this Livingstone, with a knowledge of the situation, could not consent. Mackenzie perforce had to submit: "He had not yet learned", comments Coupland, "how long it could take to carry out a simple plan in Africa." But Livingstone and Mackenzie speedily took to one another and developed each for the other a deep personal esteem. By May 1 the mission party were ascending the Zambezi and the Shiré in the *Pioneer* along with Livingstone, Kirk, and others of the Expedition, and two months later on July 8 were at Chibisa's. Towards the end of the month Mackenzie and his colleagues were settled at Magomero, some sixty miles north-east of Chibisa's towards Lake Shirwa at an altitude of some 1,000 feet, a temporary location until the land could be surveyed.[2] They reached Magomero not as the simple mission party they had been on setting out but with a following of some one hundred Africans for whose welfare, as freed slaves, they had accepted responsibility. They arrived therefore in the eyes of neighbouring tribesmen not so much as preachers and teachers as slave-liberators, a role for which they had scarcely been cast. How had events taken this unexpected turn?

The people inhabiting the Shiré valley south of Lake Nyasa

---

[1] C. Gray, *op. cit.*, I, 451, 465; Coupland, *op. cit.*, 182, 186; *Report of the O.C.D.D.M.C.A. for 1860* (1861), 9.

[2] Goodwin, *op. cit.*, 288, 305–17, 330–1; Coupland, *op. cit.*, 187–8, 191–2, 201–2.

were the Nyanjas, the "people of the Lake". Their northern neighbours to the east of Lake Nyasa south of the Rovuma were the Yaos who at this time were aggressively inclined and were preying upon Nyanja villages in the interests of the Portuguese slave-trade.[1] On reaching Chibisa's the combined expedition and mission parties heard there was now war in the Nyanja country on this account. During a halt at Mbame's village on the way up from the Shiré they were informed by the chief that a slave-gang bound for Tete would shortly pass through. They came to an immediate decision. In Livingstone's own words: " 'Shall we interfere?' we inquired of each other. We remembered that all our valuable private baggage was in Tette, which, if we freed the slaves, might, together with some Government property, be destroyed in retaliation; but this system of slave-hunters dogging us where previously they durst not venture, and, on pretence of being 'our children', setting one tribe against another, to furnish themselves with slaves, would so inevitably thwart all the efforts, for which we had the sanction of the Portuguese Government, that we resolved to run all risks, and put a stop, if possible, to the slave-trade, which had now followed on the footsteps of our discoveries."[2] Interference, therefore, was a deliberate policy. Scarcely had the decision been taken when the line of manacled men, women, and children appeared, jauntily conducted by their African captors "blowing exultant notes out of long tin horns". No sooner had they caught sight of Livingstone and his party, however, than they took to their heels at top speed. The slaves were thereupon set free, many being "mere children, five years of age and under. One little boy, with the simplicity of childhood, said to our men, 'The others tied and starved us, you cut the ropes and tell us to eat; what sort of people are you? Where did you come from?"[3]

Mackenzie, with his colleagues Procter and Scudamore, was absent at the time, but on his return "warmly approved of what had been done; he at first had doubts, but now felt that, had he been present, he would have joined us in the good work".[4] The

[1] In contemporary accounts the terms Manganja and Ajawa are current for the respective peoples. For a summary ethnological account, see Seligman, *Races of Africa*, 230–2.

[2] Livingstone, *The Zambesi and its Tributaries*, 355–6; Coupland, *op. cit.*, 195–6, who endorses Livingstone's decision as the right one.

[3] *Ibid.*, 356–7. A picture of the slave-gang in marching order is given by Livingstone. There had been losses *en route* through killing by the slavers.

[4] *Ibid.*, 357. For Mackenzie's own report in a letter to Bishop Wilberforce, see Goodwin, *op. cit.*, 324–6.

eighty-four liberated Africans, given the opportunity of doing as they wished, chose to stay with their liberators, and were thereupon received by Mackenzie as the nucleus of a mission settlement. Some further successful interception of slavers brought the number to well over a hundred. Hence their arrival at Magomero almost as a chief with his own following. Indeed, the chief Chigunda who invited Mackenzie to Magomero said there was room enough for both.[1] Mackenzie was later exposed to some criticism for having settled in a land distraught by slavers, but if the mission was to be established in the Shiré country at all there was now no option. Horace Waller, an able colleague of Mackenzie, wrote of it later: "It should be remembered that before we left England we were quite prepared to find the slave-trade in the field of our mission: nay more, I do not say too much when I state that a large proportion of the funds subscribed to carry out the scheme was given with the special hope that we should be able to undermine the slave-trade, though no one could foresee how completely we should be brought at once face to face with it."[2]

Scarcely had the decision to locate at Magomero been taken when an ominous incident occurred. It was learned that the Yaos were scourging the countryside near at hand. Livingstone determined to seek an interview with them and was himself unarmed, though not his party. Unhappily the attempt at parley was a failure, the Yaos sought to cut them off, and only by firing in self-defence were they able to withdraw. Livingstone notes with sadness: "It was the first time we had ever been attacked by the natives or come into collision with them." But the prospect for the mission was becoming more clouded: they now appeared compromised as the friends of the Nyanjas and therefore as hostile to the Yaos.[3]

Mackenzie, who had earlier considered with his colleagues the question of resort to force and rejected it for self-defence, now accepted it as in keeping with his vocation when in the defence of others. Face to face with the havoc wrought by the superior Yaos on the defenceless Nyanja villages, he proposed to take immediate steps to eject the Yao marauders. It was thought at

[1] Livingstone, *op. cit.*, 359.

[2] Waller to Goodwin, April, 1865.—Goodwin, *Memoir* (2nd ed., 1865), Appendix 2.

[3] Livingstone, *op. cit.*, 360–2. During the attempt at an interview, some Nyanja followers had called out exultingly, "Our Chibisa (i.e. champion) is come!", whereupon the Yaos near at hand fled, calling, "War, war!". This may unhappily have turned the scale. For Mackenzie's account, see *Report of the O.C.D.D.M.C.A. for 1861* (1862), 6–7.

the time that Yao aggression was due solely to the encouragement of Portuguese slavers or those in their employ, whereas a major factor in the situation was Makua pressure on the Yao from the north, thus forcing them down upon their Nyanja neighbours. It was in the course of this that the slavers took their profit. Livingstone advised Mackenzie not to act as he proposed. But if the Nyanjas sought his aid against the Yao oppressors, ought he not to give it? "No," said Livingstone, "you will be oppressed by their importunities, but do not interfere in native quarrels."[1] No sooner had Livingstone left on his exploration of Lake Nyasa than, as he had predicted, requests for help flowed in. Early in August two leading chiefs, however, requested a conference to state their case. Once granted, it was difficult to refuse to help, but it was decided that help would only be available on the missionaries' terms: captives of the Yaos when released to be free, no more buying and selling of men by the Nyanja themselves, punishment of any chief who might attempt it, and no traffic with slavers. The chiefs accepted, and under the leadership of the mission party, advanced to the Yao villages. Parley having failed, the conflict began and the Yaos were successfully driven off within the hour. The missionaries saw that the terms as to rescued captives were carried out. The expedition added some forty people to the mission settlement. Livingstone was disturbed on hearing the news, as contradicting the assurances he had given the people of the peaceable objects of the mission, and "a friendly disapproval of a bishop's engaging in war was ventured on".[2] The bitter attacks, however, to which the bishop's action exposed him at home led Livingstone to sympathize more deeply with a man who, in full consultation with his associates, had discharged what he believed to be his duty. Their action appeared to have held in check the Yao menace for the time being, but this proved illusory. A further expedition in October was finally undertaken as a result of which the number of protected persons at Magomero exceeded 200. The care of this growing community proved a considerable responsibility.[3]

Mackenzie's team at this time consisted of L. J. Procter

[1] Livingstone, *op. cit.*, 363; Goodwin, *op. cit.* (1st ed., 1864), 334. Livingstone was none the less blamed by many for the issue.—Livingstone, *op. cit.*, 416; Blaikie, *op. cit.*, 249–50. For his attitude on the resort to force, see his letter to J. W. Sturge, Tete, 11.12.58.—Chamberlin, *op. cit.*, 268–70. For Mackenzie's attitude, Goodwin, *op. cit.*, 254–5, 319–20.

[2] Livingstone, *op. cit.*, 416. Kirk was likewise concerned: "The policy of attacking the Ajawa is very doubtful."—Coupland, *op. cit.*, 215.

[3] Goodwin, *op. cit.*, 355–6; *Report of the O.C.D.D.M.C.A. for 1861* (1862), 7–8.

(Durham), H. C. Scudamore (Cambridge), with Horace Waller and Henry Rowley, lay members. In November 1861 the first reinforcements arrived: H. de Wint Burrup (Oxford), John Dickinson (Durham) as medical officer, and R. M. Clark a craftsman. Miss Mackenzie and Mrs. Burrup, to follow later from the Cape, were to be met by Livingstone in the *Pioneer*, who arranged to pick up Mackenzie at the mouth of the Ruo, eastern tributary of the Shiré, early in the New Year. The proposal was for the bishop to proceed overland from Magomero. Mackenzie suggested two journeys, the first to be exploratory. Livingstone advised a single journey by a more westerly route; unhappily his advice was not followed. Mackenzie records: "On returning home, I considered the whole matter, and, after consulting the others, I determined to abide by my own opinion." The sequel is briefly told. Procter and Scudamore were despatched on the exploratory trip but after three days reached a village where an ugly temper was displayed and in the end had to run for their lives. After an eighty-five-mile tramp as fugitives they were back in Magomero. African members of the party were still missing. An expedition was decided upon, with the help of Makololo now settled on the Shiré; the offending village was found deserted and fired. The attempt to pass down the Ruo at this point was resisted by a friendly chief in their own interest because of these events and they returned to Magomero.[1] This threw out the time-table for the rendezvous with Livingstone. By January 8, 1862 however, Mackenzie accompanied by Burrup was at Chibisa's. It was a comfortless journey downstream by canoe in teeming rain, and when their canoe sank and drenched their few possessions their supply of medicine was not recovered. They reached the Ruo mouth to learn that Livingstone, himself delayed, had only recently gone downstream. Mackenzie's last writing, dated January 13 at the Ruo mouth, records: "So matters stand at present. Burrup is very low and we have no medicine. Quinine, which we ought to be taking every day, there is none." He determined to remain on the island at the mouth of the Ruo, and Burrup concurred. Happily a couple of faithful Makololo were with them throughout. Both men had hitherto seemed almost immune to malaria and apparently did not realize the serious risks they now ran. They both fell victims. On January 31 Mackenzie died and Burrup struggled to bury him, reading as much of the burial service as the fading light allowed. The Makololo got Burrup

[1] Goodwin, *op. cit.*, 376–400; *Report of the O.C.D.D.M.C.A. for 1861* (1862), 34–8.

back to Chibisa's suffering with dysentery whence he was carried to Magomero, to expire on February 22. Ten days later Miss Mackenzie and Mrs. Burrup reached Chibisa's only to have the sad news broken.[1]

Further troubles now beset the mission. Kirk seems to have felt they had sent exaggerated reports of famine and disease, though he admits sanitation had been sadly neglected.[2] The decision was taken to remove nearer the Shiré. The Yaos interpreted this as retreat and acted accordingly. There was nothing for it but to move on, and they now settled in the Shiré valley itself opposite Chibisa's, waiting for the arrival of their new bishop. But the sickle was now busy: Scudamore died on New Year's Day 1863 and Dr. Dickinson on March 17. William George Tozer, who had been consecrated as Mackenzie's successor, arrived on the Shiré in June. He found in the situation in which he was called upon to act so little hope that he ultimately took the decision in November 1863, with the approval of his superior at Cape Town, to remove from the Zambezi region altogether. "The Zambezi has proved in every way a miserable failure," he wrote to Bishop Gray (rather testily, says Coupland), "and the selection of it for English missionary work can only be due to the blindest enthusiasm." The mission was thereupon transferred to Zanzibar, a decision in characteristic British tradition, as Coupland notes, to settle on a coastal island secured by sea-power as a jumping-off point for the mainland. It was long however before the jumping-off took place. One mainland station was opened in the next decade, and it was not until the twenty-fourth anniversary of Mackenzie's death that the mission steamer for which he had planned was at last sailing on Lake Nyasa.[3]

Meanwhile the withdrawal to Zanzibar came as a heavy blow to Livingstone. To him it was a sad defection from the front line. The second inner-Africa mission had also failed.[4]

[1] Goodwin, op. cit., 406, 413–16. For L. J. Procter's report to the Society, see Report for 1861 (1862), 40–4.

[2] Coupland, op. cit., 221–2, 227.

[3] G. Ward (ed.), Letters of Bishop Tozer (1902), 43; Coupland, op. cit., 257–8. The transfer to Zanzibar removed the diocese from the Province of South Africa to that of Canterbury.—A. E. M. Anderson-Morshead, op. cit., 419. Livingstone relieved Tozer of the orphans in the mission's care, and Horace Waller generously made himself responsible for conveying some twenty boys and one girl to Cape Town for education.—G. Ward, op. cit., 44; Anderson-Morshead, op. cit., 41; Goodwin, op. cit. (2nd ed., 1865), Appendix 6. Tozer's alleged remark on the removal to Zanzibar, "one black face is as good as another to me", cut Livingstone to the quick.—Zambesi and its Tributaries, 576.

[4] Livingstone, op. cit., 574, 576; Coupland, op. cit., 258–9.

(3) *Return to the Road*

On his return to England in July 1864 Livingstone's future plans were undetermined, but one immediate purpose was at least clear: there must be no mincing matters about Portuguese interest in the slave-trade. He was so forthright on the matter in addressing the British Association at Bath in September, that he stimulated a Portuguese counterblast, of which he wrote to a friend that they were "cussin' and swearin' dreadful"![1] A major responsibility was the writing of a book which should report on the Expedition and paint the slave-trade picture in its true colours. This he did as the guest of an old friend of Kolobeng days, W. F. Webb, who with his wife pressed Livingstone to accept the hospitality of their home, Newstead Abbey, one-time residence of the Byrons.[2] The book which took some seven months to complete received its *finis* on April 15, 1865.[3]

Meanwhile he had received in January a proposal from Sir Roderick Murchison that he should undertake a geographical commission in respect of "the watershed, or watersheds, of South Africa". He accepted, with a significant qualification as his Journal entry for January 7, 1865 reveals: "Answered Sir Roderick about going out. Said I could only feel in the way of duty by working as a missionary."[4] When he came to write the preface to his book on April 16 he was able to formulate his purpose: "I propose to go inland, north of the territory, which the Portuguese in Europe claim, and endeavour to commence that system on the East which has been so eminently successful on the West Coast; a system combining the repressive efforts of H.M. Cruisers with lawful trade and Christian Missions —the moral and material results of which have been so gratifying."[5]

---

[1] Blaikie, *op. cit.*, 289, 290. Livingstone replied in a "Postscript to Preface" in his book on the Zambezi Expedition, pp. vii–x.

[2] A. Z. Fraser, *Livingstone and Newstead* (1913), *passim*. A plaque commemorating the visit was placed in Newstead Abbey in 1949.—*The Times*, September 10, 1949.

[3] *Narrative of an Expedition to the Zambesi and its Tributaries; and of the discovery of the Lakes Shirwa and Nyassa, 1858–1864*, by David and Charles Livingstone (1865).

[4] Blaikie, *op. cit.*, 293–5. In his letter to Sir Roderick he was quite precise: "What my inclination leads me to prefer is to have intercourse with the people, and do what I can by talking, to enlighten them on the slave-trade, and give them some idea of our religion. It may not be much that I can do, but I feel when doing that I am not living in vain."—*Ibid.*, 294.

[5] *Op. cit.*, vi.

The return was by way of Bombay and Zanzibar. At Bombay he was generously assisted by the Governor, Sir Bartle Frere, and at Zanzibar called on the Sultan to whom Frere had warmly commended him, and from whom he received a letter of introduction for the mainland. On the voyage from Bombay he had again affirmed his missionary purpose, as his Journal bears witness, in reference to evening prayers on board: "I mean to keep up this, and make this a Christian expedition, telling a little about Christ wherever we go."[1]

Zanzibar was reached on January 28, 1866 and after a couple of months the party was ready: "I have thirteen Sepoys, ten Johanna men, nine Nassick boys, two Shupanga men, and two Wayaus, Wekatani and Chuma."[2] As it was Livingstone's intention to strike inland to Lake Nyasa, they made by sea for the Rovuma which they reached on March 22. They were a considerable cavalcade with the young menagerie included: six camels, three buffaloes and a calf, two mules, and four donkeys; by these it was hoped to secure some further evidence of reaction to the bite of the tsetse fly. The trials of the road however soon reduced their number. Striking across difficult country with sinister evidence of the slave-trade they had reached by mid-July Mataka's town of 1,000 houses at an altitude of 2,700 feet. Might this not be an eligible mission centre? "Nearly as desirable a residence as Magomero," the Journal comments, but the very name recalls painful memories: "I shall never cease bitterly to lament the abandonment of the Magomero mission."[3] Within a decade Bishop Steere of the Universities' Mission visited Mataka—the second white man to arrive at this Yao town.

From Mataka's to Lake Nyasa was some seventy miles but Livingstone struck south-west reaching the lake on August 8 and then, passing round its southern end, crossing the base of Cape Maclear. As he entered familiar territory memories of the past surged up once more: "It is impossible not to regret the loss of good Bishop Mackenzie, who sleeps far down the Shiré,

[1] Blaikie, op. cit., 309. One task in Bombay was the sad one of disposing of the Lady Nyassa which had cost him £6,000. He had to sell for £2,300, and even this he lost through the failure of the bank in which it was deposited.—Ibid., 307.

[2] The Last Journals of David Livingstone, ed. Waller (1874), I, 9. Johanna was one of the Comoro Islands. At Nassick, Bombay, was a training school where Africans as well as Indians were received. Shupanga on the Zambezi was the last resting-place of Mrs. Livingstone. Several of these men had already served Livingstone on the Zambezi Expedition, while the two Yaos had been among the liberated of 1861.

[3] Last Journals, I, 81.

and with him all hope of the Gospel being introduced into Central Africa . . . but all will come right some day, though I may not live to participate in the joy, or even see the commencement of better times."[1] Arrived at the western base of Cape Maclear there were rumours of marauding Mazitu; they were far enough away for safety, but the Johanna men took the opportunity to withdraw. The Sepoys had already been dismissed. The Johanna leader Musa, seeking to justify their return to Zanzibar without their master, put about a tale of Livingstone's murder with such circumstantial detail that it was officially accepted and flags were flown at half-mast. But E. D. Young in England, who had known Musa and other Johanna men on the Zambezi Expedition, had more than doubts—he refused to believe a word of it. He headed a small expedition promoted by the Royal Geographical Society and the Government, and while not meeting Livingstone, got satisfactory evidence that he was still alive and the tale a fabrication.[2]

Moving north-west and north Livingstone slowly advanced towards the southern end of Lake Tanganyika. Food was proving a difficult problem even for their reduced company. On Christmas Day 1866 their four goats were lost, and his only milk supply vanished with them. This was a serious blow. Repressed desire through food shortage now sought its revenge in dreams: on December 30 "I dreamed the night long of dinners I had eaten".[3] The heaviest blow however was yet to come. On January 20, 1867 the precious medicine chest was lost through desertion: "I felt as if I had now received the sentence of death, like poor Bishop Mackenzie"—words that were to prove truer than he knew. Coupland, pointing out that malaria and dysentery, unchecked by drugs, would undermine even his incomparable constitution, passes judgment: "It is not too much to say that Livingstone's decision to go on into the unknown without his medicine chest proved, in the long run, suicidal."[4] The first of April 1867 found him at Lake Tanganyika, the sight of which enchanted him: "I never saw anything so still and peaceful"; and a fortnight later the charm still held: "This Lake still appears one of surpassing loveliness. Its peacefulness is remarkable." He was susceptible just then to peaceful scenes,

---

[1] *Ibid.*, I, 100–1.
[2] *Ibid.*, I, 114–15, for Livingstone's account of the defection; Coupland, *Livingstone's Last Journey* (1945), 60–6, for the sequel.
[3] *Last Journals*, I, 163, 167; cf. 169 ("am constantly dreaming of better food when I should be sleeping"), 172, 181.
[4] *Ibid.*, I, 177; Coupland, *op. cit.*, 52–3, 259–60.

for his lack of medicines was telling. Excessive weakness and even fits of insensibility kept him here for a month.[1]

In pursuit of the watershed problem he reached Lake Mweru on November 8, 1867 thus adding another item to his list of discoveries. After some exploration of the lake and a visit to the Lualaba which issued from it on the north (actually the headwaters of the Congo), he struck south towards another lake of which he had heard. He reached it on July 18, 1868 and Lake Bangweolu was now added to the central water system, being linked by the River Luapula to Lake Mweru.[2] The discoveries were mounting. But the cost was severe beyond calculation. He now made for Ujiji where he expected supplies: he reached it on March 14, 1869 suffering acutely from want of food and medicine, only to find that the major part of the stores had been plundered and some were still held up on the journey from the coast. And there was no mail. He had been in the society of Arab slavers on his travels, but at Ujiji, which he now saw for the first time, he found once more a ruthless traffic in progress: "This is a den of the worst kind of slave-traders: those whom I met in Urungu and Itawa were gentlemen slavers: the Ujiji slavers like the Kilwa and the Portuguese, are the vilest of the vile. It is not a trade, but a system of consecutive murders; they go to plunder and kidnap, and every trading trip is nothing but a foray."[3] He was before long to find these words ring true in bitter experience.

After four months' recuperation at Ujiji the traveller was on the move once more, this time westward towards the Lualaba as possibly the western arm of the Nile—"if this arm is indeed that of the Nile, and not of the Congo".[4] Setting out in July 1869 he had hoped in a few months to be back again, but forecasts in the Africa of that day were all too often belied: he actually returned to Ujiji in October 1871. Bambarré, some 100 miles west of Tanganyika, was reached on September 21, 1869.[5] This had until recently been the farthest west of the Arab traders.

[1] *Last Journals*, I, 203–4, 206. Lake Tanganyika had been first seen by western eyes when Burton and Speke, following the route of Arab slave-traders, struck it at Ujiji in its northern sector, on February 14, 1858.—*Vide supra*, p. 112. Its southern shores had not been visited.

[2] *Ibid.*, I, 242–3, 261, 313–14. Lake Mweru lies athwart the boundary of the Belgian Congo and Northern Rhodesia; Lake Bangweolu lies within Northern Rhodesia. Through the proximity of the Bemba people the latter had been called Lake Bemba. Livingstone corrects this. *Ibid.*, I, 308–9.

[3] *Ibid.*, II, 6, 11. Writing three years later of "the enormous open sore of the world," he quotes the remark of an English sailor on seeing slave-traders actually at work: "Shiver my timbers, mate, if the devil don't catch these fellows, we might as well have no devil at all."—*Ibid.*, II, 214.

[4] *Ibid.*, II, 15; cf. 102.   [5] *Ibid.*, II, 26.

Here the traveller was detained by illness but entered in the Journal for November 1: "Being now well rested, I resolved to go west to Lualaba and buy a canoe for its exploration."[1] But one obstacle followed another and again and again he found himself back in Bambarré. And when in July 1870 he "limped back to Bambarré on 22nd" it was to be held there in idleness for eight weary months.[2] On February 16, 1871 a start was made at last, and this time the river he sought was reached. By March 31, 1871 he was at Nyangwe on the Lualaba, his farthest west. A fortnight later we read: "I have been writing part of a despatch in case of meeting people from the French settlement on the Gaboon."[3] It was at Nyangwe that a slaver's massacre occurred, so terrible that Livingstone's unvarnished account makes the reader recoil with horror. It was plain, cold-blooded murder, mainly of women assembled under the safe-conduct of market day, universally respected by African tribes. Of the 1,500 people assembled at least a quarter perished. "The open murder perpetrated on hundreds of unsuspecting women fills me with unspeakable horror"; two days later: "The murderous assault on the market people felt to me like Gehenna. . . . The terrible scenes of man's inhumanity to man brought on severe headache. . . . I cannot stay here in agony." The massacre occurred on July 15; on July 20 he set out for Ujiji.[4] On October 23 he arrived, to find his expected supplies had been shamelessly disposed of: "I felt in my destitution as if I were the man who went down from Jerusalem to Jericho, and fell among thieves. . . . But when my spirits were at their lowest ebb, the good Samaritan was close at hand." Henry Morton Stanley had got through to Livingstone at last.[5]

[1] *Ibid.*, II, 32.

[2] *Ibid.*, II, 47, 100; Coupland, *Livingstone's Last Journey*, 82, 91.

[3] *Ibid.*, II, 111, 116.

[4] *Ibid.*, II, 132–9, 141.

[5] *Ibid.*, II, 154–6; H. M. Stanley, *How I Found Livingstone* (2nd ed., 1872), 409–13; On the initiative of James Gordon Bennett of the *New York Herald*, who sensed the publicity value of any direct news of Livingstone who for three years had been "lost" to the world of the West, Stanley had been commissioned, as journalist in the service of the paper, to "find" Livingstone. But the commission, given in October, 1869, was apparently not urgent, for intervening engagements took Stanley to Egypt, Jerusalem, Constantinople, the Crimea, Persia, and India. He finally reached Zanzibar on January 6, 1871, took prompt measures to form an expedition and won through to Ujiji in little more than seven months.—Stanley, *op. cit.*, xvii–xxi, 68. Livingstone records the date as October 28, only five days after his return. Stanley gives November 10.—*Op. cit.*, 405. The last eyewitness of the famous meeting survived, it would seem, until October 13, 1949. This was Sheikh Ali bin Said, who claimed to have accompanied Stanley to Ujiji.—*The Times*, October 15, 1949.

The meeting of two such men in the heart of Africa could not fail to be momentous for each. To Livingstone it meant a new lease of life—tonic for the mind as well as food and medicines for the body. To Stanley, hard-bitten journalist of the world, there came the discovery of a man of simple goodness—religion without parade and achievement without pride—that made a mark on him for life. When the emotions of the time had died down, he wrote six months later: "God grant that if ever you take to travelling in Africa you will get as noble and true a man for your companion as David Livingstone! For four months and four days I lived with him in the same house, or in the same boat, or in the same tent, and I never found a fault in him. I am a man of quick temper, and often without sufficient cause, I dare say, have broken ties of friendship; but with Livingstone I never had cause for resentment, but each day's life with him added to my admiration for him."[1]

In vain Stanley sought to persuade Livingstone to return home—Livingstone admits they were "very strong arguments" —but he must stay to finish his task. He estimated that six or seven months might do it but the estimate had risen to eighteen before they parted.[2] The two men therefore travelled together to Unyanyembe (the modern Tabora) on the road to Zanzibar, where Livingstone was to await the supplies and men Stanley had promised to send him.[3] On March 14, 1872 they said "Good-bye!" It was Livingstone's last greeting to a man of his own race. Three weeks later, while waiting at Unyanyembe, he met a party of 150 Baganda on their way to Zanzibar, taking a gift from Mutesa, king of Buganda, to the Sultan—evidence of the contact of that kingdom with the outside world.[4] At last on August 14, 1872 the men sent by Stanley arrived. Notable among them was Jacob Wainwright who as a literate African was to play an active part in the final drama.

The plan was now to tramp south to Lake Bangweolu and complete a circuit round it, thus settling the question of any

[1] Stanley, *op. cit.*, 627–8.

[2] *Last Journals*, II, 169; Stanley, *op. cit.*, 436, 626.

[3] Supplies sent by Kirk, then British Consul at Zanzibar, to Livingstone had failed to reach him. Stanley's public report of this was unfortunate and reflected seriously on Kirk. Coupland, with relevant documents at his disposal, has thoroughly examined the question and acquitted Kirk of negligence.—*Livingstone's Last Journey*, 182–202, 212–16.

[4] *Last Journals*, II, 176–7. The earliest references to Uganda in the Journals are on January 30 and December 25, 1868. A convenient summary of all such references is supplied by G. Masefield, "Livingstone and the Baganda", in *The Bulletin of the Uganda Society* (June, 1945), 14–17; reprinted in *The Uganda Journal*, X (1946), 79–83.

feeding streams coming from farther south. They reached the lake but became entangled in its dreary marshes, exposed to drenching rains, and suffered much. An entry for February 14, 1873 is revealing: "If the good Lord gives me favour, and permits me to finish my work, I shall thank and bless Him, though it has cost me untold toil, pain, and travel; this trip has made my hair all grey." But on March 25 the iron determination speaks once more: "Nothing earthly will make me give up my work in despair. I encourage myself in the Lord my God, and go forward."[1] Within a month his men were having to carry him; April 27 saw the last entry in the Journal: "Knocked up quite." On April 29 they reached Chitambo's village, near the southern end of Lake Bangweolu. On the morning of the first of May, at about 4 a.m., his band of faithfuls found him apparently engaged in prayer: "A candle stuck by its own wax to the top of the box shed a light sufficient for them to see his form. Livingstone was kneeling by the side of his bed, his body stretched forward, his head buried in his hands upon the pillow. For a minute they watched him: he did not stir, there was no sign of breathing; then one of them, Matthew, advanced softly to him and placed his hands to his cheeks. It was sufficient; life had been extinct for some time, and the body was almost cold: Livingstone was dead."[2]

The behaviour of Livingstone's men at this tragic juncture was remarkable. With all their wits about them they prepared the body and bore it to the sea, together with every instrument, article, and scrap of paper that was his. They were loyal to the end, worthy servants of so great a master. "The story stands alone in history. The ten thousand had Xenophon still alive to lead them back, and they were soldiers and Greeks; but Livingstone was dead, and his men negroes, and most of them recently freed slaves."[3]

Thus the last journey ended. And Christian Missions seemingly little more advanced for all his effort. But it was not in vain. It was but the prelude to expanding progress.

---

[1] *Last Journals*, II, 276, 289.

[2] H. Waller in *Last Journals*, II, 308. The date carved by Jacob Wainwright on the tree where his heart was buried was May 4. Cf. Blaikie, *op. cit.*, 382 n. A new narrative of Livingstone's last days by one of his African followers has come to light in the archives of the Church Missionary Society. It corroborates in many ways the story secured by Horace Waller from Susi and Chuma, two of the "faithfuls".— H. B. Thomas, "The Death of Dr. Livingstone: Carus Farrar's Narrative", in *The Uganda Journal* XIV (1950), 115–28.

[3] T. Hughes, *David Livingstone* (1889), 194.

CHAPTER 7

DEVELOPMENTS IN THE NORTH AND WEST

WHILE THE south was growing politically and the east was being explored, the north and west of the continent remained upon the map much as before. On the Mediterranean shore France had set foot in Algeria in 1830, but "once there she wanted to leave, and vacillated for decades".[1] It took thirty years to reach Kabylia and not till 1870 was there any substantial success in this extension of France into Africa. In the west a few French trading-posts had long existed around the Senegal, but not till the mid-'fifties did that energetic direction of affairs appear that eventually added French West Africa to the colonial empire. General Faidherbe, who came to the Senegal as Governor in 1854, was the first to set the pace. Meanwhile British interests remained few and scattered—the Gambia, Sierra Leone, some forts on the Gold Coast, and the island of Lagos—all mere footholds, and there was no desire to extend them. Indeed, a select Committee of the House of Commons in 1865, that had inquired into their condition, reported "that all further extension of territory, or assumption of government, or new treaties offering any protection to native tribes would be inexpedient; and that the object of our policy should be to encourage in the natives the exercise of those qualities, which may render it possible for us more and more to transfer to them the administration of all the governments, with a view to an ultimate withdrawal from all, except, probably, Sierra Leone".[2] In 1866 the consulate on the Niger was abolished and further, Sierra Leone became the seat of government for all the settlements; but the march of events led once again to decentralization and further development, much as this was regretted at the time. For the rest, the Dutch still retained a line of forts on the Gold Coast and the Danes their solitary holding at Christiansborg until bought out by the British in 1850, while the United States held a watching brief over the Republic of Liberia. For the most part therefore missions would continue to be in relation with African political authorities and dependent on their goodwill for entry and continuance. Moreover, malaria was still the

---

[1] S. H. Roberts, *History of French Colonial Policy*, I, 177.
[2] C. P. Lucas, *Historical Geography of the British Colonies*, III (2nd ed., 1900), 115–16.

deadly scourge of the coast, with periodic outbreaks of yellow fever as an even heavier lash.

The period is not noteworthy for any spectacular development of Protestant missions which had been the pioneers. Indeed, there were heavy handicaps that made for limitation of activity if not actual recession, so that for the decade 1862–72 Eugene Stock, for example, speaks of an ebb-tide in Anglican affairs.[1] Roman Catholic missions, however, had been stirred to new interest in Africa, and now re-entered with resolution the field where they had once been the first to carry the Christian mission. The beginnings of the renewed effort were small at first and often interrupted, but in due course the work got under way and vicariates apostolic were successfully set up from the Senegal to the Congo.

The initiative came from the United States when in 1833, in view of the Negro emigrations to Liberia, the bishops desired the Propaganda to promote a mission there. In due course the Bishop of Philadelphia was authorized to proceed, and selected from his own diocese Edward Barron who, with two companions, set out for Monrovia in December 1841. A preliminary survey suggested Cape Palmas as a suitable centre for the work which it was hoped would extend beyond Liberia. There followed a visit to Rome where in 1842 Barron was appointed Vicar Apostolic of the Two Guineas, Upper and Lower; and then to France in search of missionaries. It so happened that in 1841 a new society, the Congregation of the Sacred Heart of Mary, had been established by a converted Jew, Francis Libermann, at Neuville near Amiens, for the specific service of the Negro race. Barron here secured his needed helpers, seven priests and three lay brothers. The situation at Cape Palmas on their arrival had so deteriorated through local feuds that Barron decided to disperse his workers. Two priests were sent to Senegal where the French Government had requested them, two each to Assinie and Grand Bassam on the Ivory Coast, and the seventh to far-away Gabon, but recently claimed for France. In a few months five were casualties from malaria, one had returned to Europe, and Jean Remi Bessieux, who had gone to Gabon alone survived. Over him silence reigned for two years, all letters going astray, so that his demise was assumed and the last rites of the church performed in Paris on his behalf. Meanwhile, events having taken such an unexpected turn, Barron secured release from his alarming responsibilities

[1] Stock, *History of the Church Missionary Society* (1899), II, 427.

and returned to the States. The Society of the Sacred Heart of Mary now accepted the charge and provided in 1845 reinforcements for Senegal and Gabon, but again there was tragedy: Tisserand, appointed prefect apostolic, was shipwrecked and lost at sea; Truffet his successor, with the rank of vicar apostolic, was quickly a casualty. Steps were taken however to strengthen the work by an amalgamation of the Society with the Fathers of the Holy Ghost in 1848,[1] and in the following year Bessieux was appointed as Vicar Apostolic of Senegambia and the Two Guineas, supported by Aloyse Kobès as prefect apostolic. Bessieux retained his residence in Gabon while Kobès settled in Senegal. Thus affairs stood on the Guinea Coast at the mid-century.[2]

(1) *From Barbary to Senegambia*

The original episcopal see of Algiers founded at Icosium, which existed from the second century to the Arab conquest, was re-established by papal bull in 1837, as a suffragan of the diocese of Aix. In 1838 the Abbé Antoine Adolph Dupuch was consecrated the first bishop.[3] At his accession he reported some 10,000 Catholics in Algiers alone, not counting the troops; two years later there were 12,000, together with another 5,000 each at Oran and Constantine. He also claimed Protestants returning to the fold. Such accessions as were thus reported however were among European, mainly French, colonists who soon formed a sensible proportion of the population in the fertile coastal strip.[4] Algeria was never regarded as a colony in the usual sense so much as "a prolongation of France, separated from France by a geographical accident of thirty hours by sea, but otherwise an integral portion of the mainland".[5] Nevertheless there were, lying behind, the people of the land with their own centuries-long tradition; the toughness of the Muslim-Berber problem remained, whether for church or state. The usual benevolent service through schools, orphanages, and hospitals was soon in

---

[1] The two Societies, *Congrégation du Saint-Cœur de Marie* and *Congrégation du Saint-Esprit* were united under the name *Congrégation du Saint-Esprit et de l'Immaculé Cœur de Marie*.

[2] *Annales de la Propagation de la Foi*, XV (1843), 314–16; XIX (1847), 100–3; XXXVI (1864), 101–4. The terms Upper and Lower Guinea were current for the stretches of coast from the Senegal to the Niger, and thence to the Congo respectively.

[3] *Cath. Ency.*, I, 311; A. Pons, *La Nouvelle Église d'Afrique* (1930), 18.

[4] *Annales*, XI (1839), 446; XII (1840), 591–2, 595; XIV (1842), 5–8.

[5] S. H. Roberts, *op. cit.*, I, 175.

being, but there was rigid official prohibition of any attempt at Christian propaganda among Muslims.[1] Of necessity therefore Dupuch devoted himself to the troops and the colonists. During his episcopacy the Lazarist, Jesuit and Trappist orders were encouraged to establish themselves in North Africa.[2]

Dupuch retired in 1845 and was succeeded the following year by Louis Antoine Augustin Pavy who presided over the diocese for twenty years. A scholar as well as a man of affairs—he had been, as abbé, Dean of the Theological Faculty at Lyons—his personal ascendancy infused new life into the North African Church. New parishes were steadily set up year by year in the three provinces of Algiers, Oran, and Constantine until by 1862 he had added to the thirty-five he inherited no fewer than 152.[3] But any attempt at securing converts from the Muslim population was as sternly prohibited as ever by both civil and military authorities. Nevertheless, Pavy's organizational development of his diocese was so impressive that Rome decided on division; on July 18, 1865 it was announced that Algiers would become an archbishopric and Oran and Constantine suffragan sees. On July 25, 1866 Pavy was named by papal bull the first archbishop; on November 16, he died.[4]

Elsewhere on the North African coast there were ecclesiastical jurisdictions in Tunis, Tripoli, and Morocco. With the extension of French influence in Tunis colonists from France, Italy, Sicily, and Malta began to arrive, and the earlier prefecture apostolic was elevated to a vicariate by Gregory XVI on March 21, 1843 with Fidèle Sutter of the Capuchins of Bologna as first vicar. By 1867 nine active centres were in being with a staff of twenty-two missionaries, and an increase of Catholic membership in a quarter of a century from 3,000 to 15,550.[5] The prefecture apostolic of Tripoli, in charge of the Franciscans Minor, saw an increase in the Catholic population from some 1,300 in 1843 to 4,000 in 1866 through European immigration. Ten missionaries, eight of whom resided in Tripoli the capital, and five stations were then reported. In 1859 the prefecture apostolic of Morocco was restored, under the administration of Spanish

---

[1] A. Pons, *op. cit.*, 105–9. Surprisingly, the first Catholic church in Algiers was a converted mosque. The story of its acquisition, on official initiative in 1832, is told by A. Pons.—*Ibid.*, 7–8.

[2] *Ibid.*, 25–9, 39–45.

[3] *Ibid.*, 65–6, 76–7.

[4] *Ibid.*, 78–9; Schmidlin, *Catholic Mission History*, 589–90; *Annales*, XXXIX (1867), 74; *Cath. Ency.*, IV, 295; XI, 266.

[5] *Annales*, XXXIX (1867), 345–58.

Franciscans, once again the Catholic population being of European origin. José Lerchundi, arriving in 1862, was an outstanding missionary at Tangier.[1]

The year 1867 was notable in North Africa for the arrival of Pavy's successor: Lavigerie, Bishop of Nancy. Charles Martial Allemand Lavigerie was born October 31, 1825 at Bayonne. He was ordained priest in 1849, won his doctorate at the Sorbonne in the following year, and in 1853 was appointed to the Chair of Ecclesiastical History and Discipline at that university. The sufferings of Christians in the Near East called forth a movement for their relief in which he became actively engaged. In 1863 he was consecrated Bishop of Nancy and three years later was called to the archdiocese of Algiers. On May 15, 1867 he stepped ashore. With his coming a new wind blew in Algiers, and blew with some vigour.

When Lavigerie accepted the appointment, which had been proposed by Marshal MacMahon the Governor-General, he was not unaware of official policy regarding the Muslim population, and was not prepared to capitulate to it.[2] He is said to have remarked to a friend at the time: "Algeria is but an open door to an untamed continent of two hundred million souls."[3] The clash was not long in coming. A desolating famine following a visitation of locusts was soon sweeping the country, and Lavigerie gathered together some 1,800 orphans suffering from the disaster. These were placed in the care of sisters in the diocese to be clothed and fed and educated. Any who wished to do so were free to leave; very few did. In a letter of April 16, 1868 he made plain his intention in this situation: these poor children, having in their ignorance no prejudice against their teachers, would under their influence in all probability ask to be baptized. Thus would begin the regeneration of the people and an assimilation which could never be achieved while the

---

[1] *Annales*, XXXVIII (1866), 319; *Cath. Ency.*, X, 575; XV, 60; K. S. Latourette, *A History of the Expansion of Christianity*, VI, 10.

[2] MacMahon's letter was dated November 17, 1866, the day after Pavy's decease. The nomination was made public, January 14, 1867. Lavigerie said in the course of his reply: "Vous me proposez une mission pénible, laborieuse, un siège épiscopal de tous points inférieur au mien, et qui entraîne avec lui l'exil, l'abandon de tout ce qui m'est cher. . . . Un évêque catholique, monsieur le Maréchal, ne peut répondre qu'une seule chose à une semblable proposition: J'accepte le douloureux sacrifice qui m'est offert."—MacMahon's letter conveying the proposal and Lavigerie's reply are printed in *Œuvres Choisies de son Éminence le Cardinal Lavigerie, Archevêque d'Alger* (1884), I, 184–6.

[3] J. Perraudin, *Lavigerie, Ses Principes Missionnaires* (1941), 12; A. Pons, *op. cit.*, 123–4.

teaching of the Koran was not countered.[1] This provoked a vigorous protest from MacMahon; Lavigerie appealed to Napoleon III, and was granted his orphanages.[2]

Meanwhile there was a missionary stirring in the diocesan seminary. Three offers of service in 1867 were augmented by four the following year. With these seven Lavigerie founded in 1868 the novitiate of a missionary society. It was not to be a regular religious order in the strict sense of the term since there were no vows but only an oath of obedience.[3] Lavigerie's master word was adaptation: the missionaries must conform in every way except to vice and error. This meant a mastery of Arabic, an appreciation of the Arab point of view, even a garb like theirs. He therefore chose for his novices the white Arab robe and mantle, and it was this that led to the missionaries being dubbed the White Fathers.[4] Rules for the Society having received papal approval, on October 1, 1872 the first twelve missionaries took the solemn oath of obedience that devoted them for life to the service of Africa.

In the following year there was begun a pioneer mission to the Kabyles in their highland fastnesses in the hinterland. It was an inflexible rule that always and everywhere there must be at least three missionaries living in community: *Funiculus triplex difficile rumpiter*.[5] This was practised in Kabylia. The tactics of missionary approach as developed by Lavigerie envisaged eventually three stages. In the first, which was a preparatory period only, there were both negative and positive aspects. On the negative side there was to be no preaching of specific Christian doctrine and no baptism of individual adults. But

---

[1] "Ces pauvres enfants, profondément ignorants de toutes choses, de celles de leur religion comme de toutes les autres, n'ont, en effet, même à ce point de vue, aucun prejugé, aucune répulsion contre nous, et je ne doute pas qu'instruits par nos paroles, par nos exemples, plusieurs ne demandent, eux-mêmes, un jour, le baptême. Ce sera le commencement de la régénération de ce peuple et de cette *assimilation* véritable que l'on cherche sans la trouver jamais, parce qu'on la cherche jusqu'ici avec le Coran, et qu'avec le Coran, dans mille ans comme aujourd'hui, nous serons les chiens de chrétiens, et il sera méritoire et saint de nous égorger et de nous jeter à la mer."—Lavigerie, *Œuvres Choises*, I, 161–2. Italics in original.

[2] For the letter to the Emperor, *ibid.*, I, 187–9; for Lavigerie's letters in the ensuing public discussion, *ibid.*, I, 191–204. See also on the whole affair: A. Pons, *op. cit.*, 305–6; Schmidlin, *op. cit.*, 590, n 38, 39; J. Bouniol, *The White Fathers and their Missions* (1929), 27–8.

[3] *Cath. Ency.*, XII, 758; A. Pons, *op. cit.*, 310, where the form of the oath is cited.

[4] The new Society was first named The Society of Missionaries of the Venerable Geronimo. Geronimo was a Christian martyr of Algiers in the sixteenth century.— Bouniol, *op. cit.*, 32; *Annales*, XXVI (1854), 327–52; A. Pons, *op. cit.*, 87–9. As however Our Lady of Africa was the patroness of the Society its members became known as the Missionaries of Our Lady of Africa.—A. Pons, *op. cit.*, 308–9.

[5] *Annales*, LIII (1881), 195.

there were to be positive works of mercy—care of the sick, provision of schools, relief of orphans—which would commend the
missionaries to the people as their friends. At the second stage,
when this goodwill was assured, there might be intimate personal talks with individual inquirers. Such converts as these
might supply would then become the nucleus of small Christian
communities; and only at this stage with local Christian believers already able to witness among their own people, would
open and unfettered evangelism be advisable.[1]

In 1868 Pius IX appointed Lavigerie Delegate Apostolic of
the Sahara and the Sudan. In the same year a Jesuit mission at
his invitation established itself at Laghouat, at the limit of
French occupation. In 1872 they were replaced by White
Fathers, then first available, and other desert posts were also
occupied. It was a vast, if desert, territory which Lavigerie now
had committed to his care—from the Atlantic to the Libyan
desert and from the inhabited northern strip to the Senegal and
Guinea.[2] Circumstances occurred in 1875 which seemed to
offer an opening among the Tuareg and even the entry to
Timbuktu of medieval fame. The great adventure was undertaken by Fathers Paulmier, Bouchand and Menoret. They left
Metlili, one of the Fathers' desert outposts, on January 15, 1876
only to meet their end in a tragedy of the desert. All three were
murdered, the first Christian martyrs of the Sahara.[3] But the
White Fathers did not limit their mission to the Muslim lands of
Africa. They soon moved into pagan Negro regions and eventually were established in East and Central Africa from Victoria
Nyanza to the Zambezi. But by 1878 they were only on the eve
of this advance.

While these developments were taking place on Africa's
Mediterranean shore, the Atlantic coast also became the scene
of some missionary activity. The region of Senegambia, lying
north and south of Cape Verde, was at the northern end of the
extensive vicariate apostolic of the Two Guineas. It was in this
region of the Senegal that Ibn Yasin had established the re-

[1] *Annales*, XLVI (1874), 426–8; J. Perraudin, *op. cit.*, 69–81; L. Massignon, "The
Missionary Method of the White Fathers", in *The Moslem World*, V (1915), 138–42;
A. Pons, *op. cit.*, 310, 315–16. "Ce serait une faute de baptiser ouvertement avant
dix ans en Kabylie, avant cent ans au Sahara."—Lavigerie to his missionaries in
1876.—Quoted by Perraudin from *Les Instructions de son Eminence le Cardinal Lavigerie à ses Missionnaires* (1927), 395.
[2] *Annales*, XL (1868), 485–6; XLI (1869), 20–36, where Lavigerie wrote of the
new opportunity; *Cath. Ency.*, XIII, 327–8.
[3] Bouniol, *op. cit.*, 41–3.

forming movement among the Sanhadja, Berbers of the desert, whence sprang the Almoravides that in the eleventh century dominated the western Sahara.[1] It was therefore to be expected that any Christian mission would here again be face to face with Islam. That it had degenerated from those early days of reform was also to be anticipated, but at least it was a rival faith with an established prestige. Thus when two of the early missionaries, M. Arragon and M. Briot of the Sacred Heart of Mary, once went on a visit from the island of Goree, the mission headquarters at the time, to the village of Dakar on the mainland opposite to interview the chief and seek permission to open a school, he replied that he already had one where Arabic was taught and he did not want their teaching to upset his religion. In reply it was pointed out that the missionaries would teach French as well, and that as for Christian conversion, freedom of conscience would be respected. He replied he could take no decision on the matter without consulting his people. During the interview he produced a very beautiful Arabic manuscript of the Koran, consisting of some 300 loose sheets simply placed one on the other and protected by a leather case, which he displayed with pride, calling attention to such skilful line-drawings as those of Mecca and Medina and of the prophet's tomb.[2] These early missionaries soon distinguished between peoples of the interior with some sort of moral standard and those of the coast corrupted by their contact with the type of European they had met. Indeed they came to the conclusion that all obstacles considered—Islam, polygamy, influence of degenerate Europeans—their one hope lay in the children and their most rewarding work in their education.[3]

These early efforts might easily have been nipped in the bud and the whole mission swept away had not General Faidherbe appeared on the scene in 1854. In that very year a returned pilgrim from Mecca, the Tuculor Omar Tal, henceforward called al-Hadj Omar, who had started on a career of missionary and military conquest in 1838, took Kaarta on the upper Senegal and proclaimed his intention of marching down the river to St. Louis where he would set up the capital of his empire.

[1] See Vol. I, 90–1.
[2] *Annales*, XIX (1847), 118–19. Some years later one of the missionaries visiting this chief felt he was responsive, at the bottom of his heart, to Christian truth, and urged him to decide between Islam and Christianity. "We shall find out after death on which side the truth lies," he answered. The missionary made an appropriate reply.—*Ibid.*, XXIV (1852), 390–1.
[3] *Ibid.*, XX (1848), 317, 319; XXIII (1851), 7.

European foes of the faith would be liquidated and their hoarded wealth given to his followers. A terrible holy war, unleashed against the French, was happily halted at Faidherbe's fortified post of Medina on the river. Al-Hadj Omar then turned against Muslim cities and took Segou on the Niger (1861) and Masina (1862). At his death in 1864 he left a vast inland empire which however was later to crumble before the French advance. Delivered from this immediate danger, the missionaries developed their centres on the coast.[1]

When Bessieux of Gabon was in 1849 appointed Vicar Apostolic of Senegambia and the Two Guineas he continued to reside in Gabon and was granted as coadjutor Aloyse Kobès who became virtual vicar apostolic of the work in Senegambia. This was recognized in fact in 1863 when he was given charge of Senegambia as a distinct vicariate apostolic. It was his policy that shaped the work of the mission, supported by a loyal band of missionaries from the Fathers of the Holy Ghost, with Sisters of the Immaculate Conception. He made Dakar his headquarters until 1860. It was only in 1847 that this section was annexed by the French, and once Dakar became a port of call in place of St. Vincent its future was assured. The first outpost from Dakar, and the only one that succeeded in the early days in maintaining itself, was Joal. The local suzerain was not encouraging; he prohibited the erection of any stone structure here on the ground that it could only too easily be turned into a fort, but when Faidherbe, having deflected the armies of al-Hadj Omar, cast his eye on Joal as a point of strategic value and promptly ran up the tricolour, the embargo was lifted and the long-desired stone church appeared at last. The mission centre of outstanding interest was that of Saint Joseph de N'gazobil; the station was Kobès' creation and here the main activities were centred. His first concern, once Faidherbe's use of the military arm had guaranteed security from marauding tribes, was to develop an agricultural settlement with which industrial training was to be associated. Kobès applied to the French Government for a concession of 1,000 hectares in the neighbourhood of Sine and Joal on the coast, and in 1863 the application was granted. The American Civil War had cut off cotton exports from the States, so Kobès with commendable enthusiasm determined to attempt a cotton plantation. The idea caught on;

---

[1] Delafosse in *Ency. Islam*, IV (1934), 496; H. H. Johnston, *A History of the Colonization of Africa by Alien Races* (1913), 201–2 n.; *Annales*, XXVIII (1856), 299–300. The Tuculor were a caste of the Torodbe of Takrur; cf. Delafosse, *loc. cit.*

an industrialist in Alsace and a merchant at Goree co-operated in the enterprise. In the course of a couple of years six new villages of workers in the scheme appeared, all under Kobès' supervision. By 1864 four priests and seven lay brothers in charge of various departments in the industrial school were in residence. Agricultural and industrial apprentices were received —100 in the first group and 25 in the second—and some 200 African workers were employed. But a heavy blow was soon to fall: in 1865 hordes of locusts devastated the land and the cotton crop, as well as food supplies, was destroyed. The staff was withdrawn to Joal. Plucky attempts were made to renew the enterprise, but when for nine consecutive years the locust plague returned, there was no alternative but to abandon the project. No such visitation had been experienced within living memory.[1]

Kobès gave particular attention to the training of an African ministry, claiming that success in this was the real test of missionary progress and the surest guarantee of the future of the Church. A curriculum of studies was carefully prepared, and those who in the elementary stage manifested a suitable disposition and showed capacity for Latin studies were separated as a clan of "young Levites". In 1852 the first African was ordained to the priesthood, and two others at Rome and Paris in 1862 and 1869 respectively; but in 1870–71 six received the clerical tonsure and others were admitted to minor orders. In 1871 there were five African priests on the mission and twenty-seven students of theology. Kobès had been eager to give opportunity to African women with a suitable vocation to enter a religious order, and for this purpose established the Congregation of the Daughters of the Sacred Heart of Mary. In 1871 twenty members were reported, with a dozen others as novitiates and postulants. With all his practical concerns, Kobès was aware of the importance of language studies, and in 1869 completed his Wolof grammar. His devoted life came to an end at Dakar on October 11, 1872 in the fifty-third year of his age. With his passing the pioneer period of the mission drew to a close.[2] The Catholic population, reported as 4,000 in 1864, had risen to 5,000 by 1871.[3]

A solitary Protestant attempt at work in Senegal was made by

---

[1] *Annales*, XXVII (1856), 297; XXXV (1863), 264–7; XXXVIII (1866), 32–7, 400–2; XLIV (1872), 100–1, 102, 103–4.
[2] *Annales*, XLIV (1872), 106–13, 116–17; XLV (1873), 72–5.
[3] *Annales*, XXXVIII (1866); XLIV (1872), 106.

the Paris Missionary Society. As early as 1830 an inquiry had been voiced as to the suitability of Senegal for a mission of the Society, but it was thirty years before the opening occurred. Then in 1861 the Protestant Governor of Senegal, Jauréguibéry, invited the Committee to enter. The invitation was accepted. The first missionary, Jacques, a Swiss, sailed in December 1862 to St. Louis and settled at Sédhiou where he was joined in 1863 by Andrault. Not long after came two further recruits from Paris, Lauga and Guindet. But soon after their arrival yellow fever swept them away, one after the other. The Society abandoned Sédhiou and held in suspense the post at St. Louis.[1]

Within the ambit of Senegambia lay the small British colony of the Gambia, an enclave astride the estuary of the river of that name. Here the Wesleyan Methodists had pioneered in 1821 but after the early period the work had been almost stationary.[2] William F. Fox, who joined the Gambia mission in 1833, saw opportunities of advance and nine years later pleaded that the mission, though small, should not be overlooked: "The River Gambia, too, *is in Africa*; and I still maintain that it is one of the most important, direct, and safe entrances into the interior. . . . Send us sufficient help, and, ere many years have elapsed, you will, I trust, have a missionary station at the great emporium of Africa, Timbuctoo."[3] But the help was not forthcoming. Deaths, invalidings, and removals continually depleted the European staff, so that more than once only one remained, and the African agents from Sierra Leone were of necessity left without the oversight their status required. A decennial comparison of membership shows the numbers little more than maintained: 612 (1850), 812 (1860), 715 (1870), while by 1870 only two stations, those at St. Mary's and McCarthy's Island, remained open. A hopeful step was taken however in 1875 with the setting up of a training institution.[4] A continuing weakness was the dependence of the missionaries on interpreters—unavoidable in the case of brief periods of service—when seeking to serve other than the liberated African population. In this respect the missionaries themselves admitted the advantage lay with the Roman Catholic missionaries in the Colony.[5]

[1] J. Bianquis, *Les Origines de la Société des Missions Evangéliques de Paris*, III (1935), 328, 329, 354-5.
[2] See Vol. I, 283-5.
[3] Letter dated Gambia, 13.1.42.—W. F. Fox, *A Brief History of the Wesleyan Missions on the Western Coast of Africa* (1851), 543. Italics in original.
[4] Findlay and Holdsworth, *The History of the Wesleyan Methodist Missionary Society*, IV (1922), 135, 138, 139, 140.
[5] *Ibid.*, 138-9.

The British Colony was an enclave in French territory (indeed, there had been talk of an exchange with France with which the events of 1870 in Europe interfered), and it thus fell within the vicariate apostolic of Senegambia. Fathers of the Holy Ghost and Sisters of the Immaculate Conception were established here in the 'sixties, and served with customary devotion. In an epidemic of cholera that swept the Colony (as well as Senegal) in 1869 their conduct won a special citation of heartfelt gratitude from the Governor. Their schools too were valued and given Government grants. In 1872 there were three priests, two brothers at boys' schools and several sisters at schools for girls, established at St. Mary's.[1]

(2) *In Colonies of the Liberated*

In two areas of the West Coast—Sierra Leone and Liberia—Africans had been settled who were not native to the region, while in the hinterland of each colony lay truly local tribes. We now turn to consider the state of affairs in them in respect of the Christian Church.

In Sierra Leone the main burden had been borne by the Church Missionary Society and in 1854 a step had been taken towards local devolution.[2] This now demands further attention. The classic statement on the whole subject as a part of missionary policy is the paper of Henry Venn, which was circulated to missionaries of the Society in 1851, entitled "Minute upon the Employment and Ordination of Native Teachers". It concludes: "Regarding the ultimate object of a Mission, viewed under its ecclesiastical result, to be the settlement of a Native Church under Native Pastors upon a self-supporting system, it should be borne in mind that the progress of a Mission mainly depends upon the training up and the location of Native Pastors; and that, as it has been happily expressed, the '*euthanasia* of a Mission' takes place when a missionary, surrounded by well-

---

[1] *Annales*, XXXVI (1864), 108–9; XLII (1870), 40–1; XLIV (1872), 105. One report gave a minimum of 2,000 deaths from cholera in the Gambia alone.—*Ibid.*, XLII (1870), 43. An account of the outbreak is given in J. M. Gray, *A History of Gambia* (1940), 444–6. When in 1816 British merchants removed from the Senegal and Goree, then restored to France, they settled on St. Mary's Island at the mouth of the Gambia. The new settlement was then named Bathurst after the Secretary of State for the Colonies; thus St. Mary's and Bathurst became equivalent terms.—C. P. Lucas, *op. cit.*, 117.

[2] The support of the village schools was then transferred from the Society to the Sierra Leone Church.—Stock, *History of the Church Missionary Society*, II, 101. *Vide supra*, p. 58, *n.* 2.

trained Native congregations under Native Pastors, is able to resign all pastoral work into their hands, and gradually relax his superintendence over the pastors themselves, till it insensibly ceases; and so the Mission passes into a settled Christian community. Then the missionary and all missionary agency should be transferred to the 'regions beyond'."[1] When in the following year 1852 the first bishop was appointed to Sierra Leone it was hoped that this policy would be implemented for the Anglican Church of the Colony, but the tragic loss in quick succession of Bishops Vidal, Weeks, and Bowen delayed this development of ecclesiastical organization until the arrival of E. H. Beckles as bishop in 1860. He had oversight of the diocese until 1869 so that a real beginning could at last be made. A Native Pastorate organization was set up consisting of a Council and a Church Committee under the direction of the bishop, to which nine parishes under African pastors were at once transferred. The function of the Council, in co-operation with the bishop, was administrative; that of the Committee, responsibility for finance. Bishop Cheetham, who took over the diocese in 1870, carried forward the new development. The educational institutions remained under the Society, as well as those parishes that were still mission stations. Such was the situation in the Sierra Leone Church when the jubilee of the mission was celebrated in 1866, for it was in 1816 that Bickersteth had first organized it. In so far as figures can dramatize the situation, it is enough to say that the six communicants of his day had now become 6,000.[2]

An attempt to reach beyond the Colony to tribes of the hinterland had been made a generation before this. In particular, the Rev. C. L. F. Hänsel, an able and devoted Basel man who gave ten years in Sierra Leone before proceeding to Jamaica, went to reside among the Temne tribe in 1833–34 in hope of establishing a mission among them, but health failed and he had to retire from the outpost.[3] In 1840 the attempt was resumed and a station begun at Port Lokkoh, a trading centre of some importance, but the people were mostly Muslim and the Sierra Leone traders proved unhelpful. At Magbele however, twenty-four miles higher up the River Rokelle and sixty miles from Freetown, a better atmosphere prevailed: the people were

[1] *Ibid.* (1899), II, 415.
[2] *Ibid.*, II, 415–17, 445–6, 447–8.
[3] His journals were published in *The Church Missionary Record*, July and August, 1834. He later became Principal of Fourah Bay.

largely pagan and the traders well disposed. In 1853 mission premises were erected and this became the headquarters of the Temne Mission. But in seven years' time the place was plundered and the African agent fled for his life. The Temne Mission was then suspended until 1875.[1] The surrounding paganism was not entirely ignored however, the Bulloms to the north and the Sherbros to the south receiving attention.[2]

Wesleyan Methodist affairs during the double decade 1858–78 proceeded steadily though severely handicapped by shortage of European staff, as on the Gambia, and by restricted grants from home funds. Both factors were in a measure due to decreased income through stirrings for reform in the Church at home which absorbed much interest and energy, and to increased demands from other fields overseas. In the year of the Sierra Leone Jubilee of the Anglican Church the Wesleyan Secretary, George Osborn, wrote to the District: "We must regard Sierra Leone as advancing beyond a mere Mission to the position of a Church, in a great measure self-supporting, though for the present assisted by grants from the Mission House Fund." In 1880 the membership stood at nearly 6,000.[3]

The Countess of Huntingdon's Connexion in Sierra Leone continued to maintain its work under African leadership, though from the 'forties the home Conference began to take a steady interest in it. In 1845 a series of eleven questions on the state and conduct of their churches was addressed to the Sierra Leone leaders by the British Conference. Anthony Elliott was the African leader at the time.[4] The Conference was concerned that some missionary activity should proceed from the Sierra Leone churches, in which the British Conference would co-operate, and further questions in this connexion were addressed to the local leaders. These appear to have remained unanswered.[5] In 1848 a series of twenty-two questions on church practice and missionary opportunity received replies, indicating the desire of the local churches for help in "carrying the

---

[1] *Proceedings of the C.M.S.* (1854), 32–3; Stock, *op. cit.*, II, 429–30. Work on the Temne language was started, and a beginning was made with printed books including a Primer, Catechism, Bible Stories, and Temne Traditions.—*Proceedings* (1855), 40.

[2] Stock, *op. cit.*, II, 447.

[3] Findlay and Holdsworth, *op. cit.*, IV, 92, 97–8, 102.

[4] *The Countess of Huntingdon's Connexion Circular*, No. 20 (March, 1846), 197–8, where the questions and Elliott's answers are given. In a further letter Elliott detailed the religious activities of the churches.—*Ibid.*, No. 30 (January, 1847), 53–5.

[5] *Ibid.*, No. 41 (December, 1847), 162–3.

gospel into the interior of Africa".[1] In consequence missions to Sherbro (not included in the Colony until 1862) and on the Scarcies River were put in hand in 1852. In the following year a deputation from the Conference, George Fowler, visited Sierra Leone where he received a warm welcome from Bishop Vidal. He organized a local District of the Connexion, with a constitution acceptable to the local churches.[2] In August 1856 the churches suffered a heavy loss in the death of the senior African minister, Anthony Elliott, at the age of eighty. He had arrived in the country in 1792 with the original Nova Scotia settlers. He was mourned by all the churches.[3] Within a month S. R. Wright, the junior minister ordained at the British Conference in 1853, had also passed away. The Conference at once took steps to provide leadership for the District, and John Trotter went out as minister for the churches. Statistics of membership on his arrival showed a total of 1,044 in ten churches in the Colony. He started a small Training Institution, and by regular visitation and pastoral oversight strengthened the Christian community. In 1859 an epidemic of yellow fever broke on the Colony. Casualties were heavy; half of the eighty to ninety Europeans in Freetown were laid in their graves, Mrs. Trotter among them. It was at this time that good Bishop Bowen passed away. Trotter was now compelled to return on health leave, but before setting out he recorded with joy that he and an Anglican clergyman exchanged pulpits—"real Christian union in our midst" he wrote of it. He paid two further visits to the Colony, but no European superintendent was appointed until the end of the century.[4]

In 1858 an independent Christian community of some 2,300 members and fourteen churches in Sierra Leone, calling themselves "The West African Methodists", applied to the United Methodist Free Churches of Great Britain to be received into their fellowship. The Conference approved and in 1859 Joseph New arrived to serve these churches. He died in 1862 and both his colleagues were invalided. Of two successors, one died within four months. Then came W. Micklethwaite who superintended the work until 1874.[5]

[1] *The Countess of Huntingdon's New Magazine* (1851), 94–6.

[2] *The Harbinger* (1852), 91–3, 122–3; (1853), 151–6, 185–8, 371–4; (1854), 52–3. A survey of stations and the rules of Band Societies (or class meetings) supply information about the nature and extent of the work.—*Ibid.* (1856), 61–3, 77–8.

[3] *Ibid.* (1857), 1–7.

[4] *The Harbinger* (1857), 15, 151; (1859), 180–1, 209, 210. When in England Trotter prepared a survey of the work in Sierra Leone.—*Ibid.*, (1860), 7–13.

[5] J. E. Swallow, *Coast and Hinterland in Africa* (1914), 20, 23.

The Roman Catholic mission was resumed in Sierra Leone in 1858, in which year the vicariate apostolic of Sierra Leone, which included French Guinea and Liberia, was set up with de Marion Brésillac, the founder of the African Fathers of Lyons (1856), as vicar apostolic. Brésillac with three fathers and a lay brother arrived early in 1859, the year of the severe yellow fever epidemic; they were all five speedily swept away. It was a disaster of the first magnitude for the Fathers of the Holy Ghost. In 1864 Fathers Blanchet and Kœberlé of that Congregation arrived to take up the task. Kœberlé soon succumbed but Blanchet settled in to the work; in 1865 he reported fifteen Protestants received into the Roman Catholic Church.[1]

In Liberia the various American missions were hard put to it to maintain their work. Coupled with the threat of disease, an ever-present sword of Damocles, was the uneasy situation to say the least, liable to flare up at any moment into fiery conflict, as between the Negro immigrant settlers and the tribes native to the land. The missionaries had a commission to serve them both but jealousy and distrust made this difficult. The American Baptist Missionary Union closed down their work in 1856. The American Board, as we have seen, had withdrawn to Gabon within a decade and handed over their stations to the Protestant Episcopal Church. This mission held on with fortitude and in 1851 entered on happier times with the consecration of John Payne as bishop in charge of the work. For twenty years he survived to direct a steadily if slowly expanding enterprise.[2] He admitted the difficulty of extending to the interior: "Between the people on the coast of Africa and those in the interior, there exist, and ever have existed, the most jealous feelings. Selfishness is the cause of this." But this very reason should be a spur to missionary effort.[3] An opportunity to establish a station in the interior came with the gift of a legacy from Mrs. Jane Bohlen of Philadelphia. With this the Bohlen station was established on

---

[1] *Cath. Ency.*, XII, 783; *Annales*, XXXI (1859), 246–7, 253, 479; XXXIII (1861), 393–4; XXXVIII (1866), 247–8.

[2] *The Spirit of Missions*, XVI (1851), 486–91, where Payne's survey of the mission is given.

[3] *Ibid.*, 496; XXI (1856), 160–6. Troubles came to a head in 1856 when, to quote Bishop Payne's report: "The Colonists, moved by various provocations, have burned up all the Cape Palmas and Grahway towns—eight in number—and driven their inhabitants—not far below six thousand—into the forest—and the natives, on their part, have burned several unprotected houses in the Colony, and amongst them our first station—Mt. Vaughan."—*Ibid.*, XXII (1857), 187.

the upper Cavalla River.[1] Recruits were encouragingly secured —in 1854 eight arrived on the field—but deaths and invalidings continually thinned the ranks, so that by 1868 there were but three men (including the bishop) and five women on the foreign staff. Ten African ministers (seven Liberian, three tribal) and twenty-five teachers and catechists (five Liberian, sixteen tribal) were the mainstay of station work.[2] Bishop Payne encouraged educational work and was the prime mover in the founding of Liberia College in Monrovia. He had originally made the suggestion of a School of Theology to S. Greenleaf of Boston, but an unsectarian institution was preferred, and eventually in 1862 Liberia College opened its doors with J. J. Roberts, ex-President of the Republic, as its Principal. Three years later the distinguished Negro, Dr. E. W. Blyden, joined the staff.[3] At his retirement Bishop Payne reported 446 communicants, with twenty-two stations (nine Liberian, thirteen tribal) on the mission. He was succeeded as bishop by Johann Gottlieb Auer, a recruit from the Basel Mission who had come to Liberia in 1868.[4]

The Methodist Episcopal Church appointed as its first bishop in Liberia a Negro, Francis Burns, in 1859. He was succeeded in 1866 by John Roberts, also a Negro, who served until 1875. A decline then set in and it was a dozen years before there was a new lease of life.[5] It was in 1875 that the African Methodist Episcopal Zion Church, an all-Negro communion, started work in the country.

In 1854 the American Christian Missionary Society of the Disciples of Christ sent its first missionary for Africa to Liberia. Strange as it may seem, a gifted Christian slave was specially recommended for this pioneer enterprise. His master when approached agreed to let the church have him for $550 though "he could easily have gotten $1,200 elsewhere". Alexander Cross, so named from his master, gave but two months of ardent service and then succumbed. The second missionary sent by the Disciples overseas, he was the first to die. It was half a century before the work was taken up again, but the name of Alexander Cross heads with honour their missionary roll.[6]

[1] *Ibid.*, XXII (1857), 475–6; XXIV (1859), 286–90.
[2] *Ibid.*, XIX (1854), 189; XXXIII (1868), 903.
[3] *Ibid.*, XXXIII (1868), 626; H. H. Johnston, *Liberia* (1906), 231–2, 381–3. Blyden was later Liberian Minister in London. He came to regard Islam as preferable to Christianity for the Negro, and various papers and addresses on this subject were collected under the title *Christianity, Islam and the Negro Race* (1887).
[4] *The Spirit of Missions*, XXXIII (1868), 287, 903; XXXIV (1869), 739.
[5] Du Plessis, *The Evangelisation of Pagan Africa* (1930), 100.
[6] *They Went to Africa* (1945), 5.

The United Lutheran Church of America sent M. Officer and H. Heigard to Liberia in 1860. They settled on the St. Paul's River, twenty-five miles inland, and named the station Muhlenberg after the Lutheran pioneer in America. It was to this station that D. A. Day came in 1874, and put into practice his educational ideas at the Muhlenberg Industrial Mission.[1]

(3) *In Kingdoms of Guinea*

On the Guinea Coast between the Tano and the Niger were to be found peoples more developed and more closely knit politically than elsewhere, often with a strong central authority, as in the kingdoms of Ashanti, Dahomey, and Benin. The disintegration of the Yoruba nation had destroyed their earlier political cohesion yet even here strong political units, if not actual kingdoms, survived. The Fanti on the Gold Coast, the River Pra being the recognized boundary between them and the Ashanti, acted in concert through their chiefs, as in the so-called Bond of 1844 and the Fanti Confederation of 1867. The Bond was a treaty entered into on March 6, 1844 between Governor Hill and the Fanti chiefs to define more clearly the jurisdiction in criminal matters that was customarily exercised by the British authority, more particularly since Maclean's day who had considerably extended it.[2] The Fanti Confederation demonstrated effective unity of action in time of crisis. In 1867 an agreement was reached by the British and Dutch Governments to exchange certain of their forts so that each would have a continuous stretch of coast. The dividing line fell to the east of Elmina. The cession of the forts carried various rights of jurisdiction, and hence the transfer was resented by those people concerned who were losing British protection. They decided to resist, and the Fanti Confederation sprang into being to support the resistance by force of arms. It represented the capacity for united action of the Fanti nation.[3] In the event the Anglo-

---

[1] Du Plessis, *op. cit.*, 105. For Day's statement of principles and practice after a field experience of twenty years (he gave one period of ten years without a furlough), see: David A. Day, "Lutheran Industrial Mission, Liberia, West Africa" in *Missionary Review of the World*, VIII (1895), 47–51. He was far-sighted in his educational outlook: "The harmonious training of heart, head, and hand is the keynote to the redemption of Africa."

[2] W. W. Claridge, *A History of the Gold Coast and Ashanti* (1915), I, 452–3; W. E. F. Ward, *A History of the Gold Coast* (1948), 186–8.

[3] Claridge, *op. cit.*, I, 557–75; W. E. F. Ward, *op. cit.*, 231–9. In 1871 an interesting development was the attempt of some of the chiefs to draft a constitution looking towards self-government.—Claridge, *op. cit.*, I, 614–25; Ward, *op. cit.*, 248–56.

Dutch problem was solved by the transfer of the Dutch settlements to Britain in 1872.[1]

From the Wesleyan Methodist base among the Fantis, with headquarters at Cape Coast, Thomas Birch Freeman had paid visits to Kumasi, Abomey, and Abeokuta, the first contact of a Christian missionary with such peoples beyond the coast. With Kumasi in particular he sought to establish relations. His encouraging pioneer visit of 1839[2] was followed by a second in 1841–42. He was accompanied by Robert Brooking, a missionary who had arrived in January 1840, and by the two Ashanti princes, John Ansah and William Nkwantabissa, recently returned from England, who had been handed over as hostages in connexion with Maclean's treaty of 1831. They had been sent to England for education, and their safe return surprised and gratified their people.[3] The party were the bearers of gifts to the king from Queen Victoria, and of a carriage sent by the Wesleyan Missionary Society. Freeman was cordially welcomed by the monarch and had his request for a mission site granted before he left. The question of being allowed to establish schools was still an open one, and when objections were voiced Freeman acted with characteristic shrewdness: "Fully aware that if I allowed these objections to pass unnoticed, they would say, 'If schools are important, he would vindicate them, and press their claims'; and then if I spoke too strongly, they would say, 'This man is so earnest, and speaks so much, that he has probably some political object in view'; I endeavoured therefore to take the middle course." Brooking was left in charge and after some months was joined by Thomas Rowland who only survived a few weeks, the first missionary to die in Ashanti. Brooking himself was soon to be invalided.[4] In August 1843 Freeman

[1] Claridge, op. cit., I, 626–30. The Dutch had been first on the coast after the Portuguese and counted a continuous settlement of 274 years.

[2] See Vol. I, 304–6.

[3] Claridge, op. cit., I, 410, 412, 433. They were both present at the Coronation of Queen Victoria, and before their return were received by her in private audience. The Rev. Thomas Pyne, who acted as their tutor and guardian, also introduced them to the Board of the S.P.G., "which thereupon voted salaries of £300 a year for two Clergymen to be stationed at Cape Coast Castle," but these posts appear not to have been taken up.—C. F. Pascoe, Two Hundred Years of the S.P.G. (1901), I, 259. Their return voyage to Cape Coast was made with the Niger Expedition in 1841.—The Friend of Africa, I (1841), 123–6, 201–2, 223–4; II (1842), 132–3, where letters about them and from them are given. John Ansah was baptized soon after his return and ordained to the Wesleyan ministry in 1852. Nkwantabissa died in 1859.

[4] T. B. Freeman, Journal of Two Visits to the Kingdom of Ashanti (1843), 167, 168–9; Claridge, op. cit., 433–4. The departure from Cape Coast was on November 6, 1841 and the arrival back February 9, 1842. Freeman's Journal was first printed in Wesleyan Missionary Notices (1842), 162–99.

paid a third visit taking George Chapman to be the resident Wesleyan minister. Chapman earned before long the distinction of averting war between Ashanti and the British Government on the coast. He soon became *persona grata* to the king and chiefs and so was invited to be present at a critical meeting of their Council in 1845. An Ashanti woman trader had been murdered *en route* from the Coast, and her Assin murderer handed to the British Governor. The Ashantis, as an independent nation in treaty relations with the British, had naturally expected to be informed but were ignored. And further, Governor Hill had not reported, as custom demanded, his own assumption of office in succession to Maclean. Feeling ran high and Chapman, about to leave for Cape Coast, was desired to communicate their view of the situation. The fact of his intervention alone restrained the chiefs who were for immediate invasion. The Governor, made wise at last to his oversight, welcomed an embassy from Kumasi, gave the recognition required, and the threat of war died away.[1]

The growth of the Christian community among the Fantis inevitably led to some strain between them and the old religious order. In a case that received much publicity this broke into open conflict in 1849. A small Christian community at Asafa near to Cape Coast lived close by the sacred grove of Brafo, a national god and oracle with priests in attendance. One of the priests became a Christian convert. The priests in charge, sensing the threat to their prestige and revenues, secured the support of the chiefs in defence of their shrine. The breaking point was reached when some of the Christians cut building poles in the sacred grove. The local chief who had been appointed to act for his colleagues arrested ten of the Christians and burned their village. The case, with charge and counter-charge of desecration and assault, came before the Judicial Assessor and aroused great excitement. The Court imposed fines on each side, but it was some time before the excitement died down and the judgment, after a rehearing of the case, was accepted. As a sequel the fraudulent practices of the priests were exposed, but this only produced a temporary lull in the popularity of Brafo. The case however exercised a salutary restraint not only on both parties to the dispute, but farther afield: a warning to the Christians not to be provocative, and a reminder to the pagans that times were changing.[2]

---

[1] Claridge, *op. cit.*, I, 454–6.
[2] *Ibid.*, I, 466–73; Ward, *op. cit.*, 199; F. D. Walker, *Thomas Birch Freeman* (1929), 194–6.

Meanwhile Freeman had not been without his anxieties. A returned missionary who had been opposed to him initiated a correspondence in *The Times* in 1844 in criticism of the man and his work. He was soon in England in his own defence and received the highest expressions of confidence which were not confined to the Methodist Church. Sir Thomas Fowell Buxton sent him £200 for the work, the Lord Provost of Edinburgh presided over a meeting in his behalf, and a total of £5,500 was received for the mission. At the same time a gratifying offer came from the West Indies; Henry Wharton of St. Vincent, a young Negro minister, offered and was accepted for work on the Gold Coast. He was to give twenty-eight years of able and devoted service. Freeman returned fully exonerated, but his indefatigable enterprise gave many a heart-searching to the Home Committee, for while Freeman had the penetrating imaginative eye for opportunity he did not, as the Committee was constrained to do, measure out with painful precision the cost of his undertakings. Moreover the financial situation was a straitened one, for in 1849 the Wesleyan Church, rent with controversy over polity, lost 100,000 members. By 1856 the Committee took drastic action to insist on economy and Freeman was relieved of financial control though not of the superintendency. This he surrendered, feeling he had lost the confidence of the Committee, and soon his resignation followed, with deep sorrow but without a trace of rancour. He showed the finest Christian spirit to the end. The Governor offered him the appointment of civil commandant of Accra, including Christiansborg recently acquired from the Danes, and this he accepted. Thus departed from the active missionary scene in 1857 the most distinguished pioneer of his generation on the Guinea Coast. As one of his biographers has put it: "Thus, after twenty years of magnificent service for the Kingdom of God, Thomas Birch Freeman retired. It was a catastrophe." The day of brilliant enterprise was over.[1]

As the Wesleyan Methodist mission was based on Cape Coast Castle as its headquarters, so the Basel Mission had advanced inland from Accra, having established its work there in the days of the Danish régime. After the tragic record of mortality on the coast Andreas Riis had moved north to Akropong in the Akwapim

---

[1] *Wesleyan Missionary Notices* (1844), 658–78; Findlay and Holdsworth, *op. cit.*, IV, 160–5; F. D. Walker, *op. cit.*, 188–9, 201–5. The most recent biography is by A. N. Birtwhistle, *Thomas Birch Freeman, West African Pioneer* (1950). He survived until 1890, passing away in his eighty-first year. His memory is still treasured among his people.

Mountains in 1835.[1] In the 'forties, with the new policy of West Indian settlers, another station was begun at Aburi in 1847, lying rather more than halfway from Accra to Akropong. In that year the first converts in Akropong were baptized, but not until 1856 did the first adult baptisms take place at Aburi.[2]

Political events led to the founding of the next station. In 1850 the Gold Coast Government was given separate status, independent of Sierra Leone, and in the same year the Danes transferred all their forts and legal rights on the coast to the British in consideration of a payment of £10,000. This brought the Basel missionaries under British jurisdiction. Freeman had the honour of serving the Governor as secretary on his first visit to Christiansborg where later he was himself to hold a civil post. There was no local opposition to the transfer. The Home Government now decided that the peoples on the Gold Coast enjoying British protection should make some contribution to the cost of the establishment. Accordingly in April 1852 a meeting of the chiefs was convened at Cape Coast which, sitting with the powers of a Legislative Assembly, produced a document accepting the principle of African contribution to the revenue and recommending a poll tax for the purpose. This enactment became known in consequence as the Poll Tax Ordinance. The first organized resistance to the payment of the tax was made at Christiansborg in 1854. Commencing with riots, the trouble grew until there was widespread open rebellion. It was decided that extreme measures were necessary, and Christiansborg was bombarded. Casualties were few though the town was left in ruins. Under these circumstances the Basel missionaries there, Johann Zimmermann and August Steinhauser retired to Abokobi, half-way to Aburi, and opened a station there with the little Christian community that had accompanied them. Zimmermann had ideas of agricultural development in so suitable a district, and even of a settlement of European colonists for the purpose, but though the Home Committee was prepared to allow him a free hand, changing circumstances prevented him from carrying out his ideas. It was at this station however that in 1857 a notable convert was won in Mohenu, a leading pagan priest, who was baptized with his family. He proved worthy of his baptismal name of Paul, his effective itinerant preaching ministry being supported by a

[1] See Vol. I, 299–301.
[2] W. Schlatter, *Geschichte der Basler Mission* (1916), III, 64–7.

worthy Christian life. He survived to serve the mission for thirty years.[1]

Kumasi, ever since Riis' visit to the city in 1839-40, had been the lodestar of the mission. In 1853 Johann Simon Süss, then at Akropong to which he had come two years before, determined to strike out north-westward as a free lance in search of the goal. He came to Gyadam, a settlement of emigrants from Ashanti, near the headwaters of the River Humo. In an endeavour to maintain contact with his adventure the Mission sent him a colleague, David Baum, but the individualist Süss became restive and in 1856 moved off eastwards to the Volta, boundary between the so-called Gold and Slave Coasts and then recognized as the limit of British jurisdiction, and established himself at Dauromadam (=here grace is to be found) as he named it. But it was farther north to the east of the Volta that the outpost of Anum was later to be established among a people who had migrated from Akwapim; here Johannes Müller began the work in 1865. Meanwhile by a natural extension north-eastward from Akropong, Odumase among the Krobo people west of the Volta had been occupied in 1857. Before long the chief at Gyadam had moved with his people to the River Berem, tributary of the Pra, and the town was left deserted. The station therefore lapsed. Odumase however was regarded as strategic and in 1859 became a head station with Zimmermann as senior missionary. He regarded the River Volta as the road to the interior. After a decade Zimmermann could declare that the Krobos had been so thoroughly evangelized that no person was without opportunity to embrace the faith. There was then a Christian membership of ninety persons. At that date (1869) the eight mission districts reported twenty-four congregations with a total membership of 1,851. The main strength lay in Akwapim where Akropong (654), Aburi (307), and Abokobi (230) took the lead.[2]

Two notable contributions made by the Basel Society to the Gold Coast must be placed on record: the attention they gave to education, and their vernacular language studies. In 1843 the first school for boys was begun in Akropong, and in 1847 the first for girls. A seminary for the training of catechists was

---

[1] Claridge, op. cit., I, 474-6, 478-81, 496-8; Schlatter, op. cit., III, 53, 55-6, 87-8.

[2] Schlatter, op. cit., III, 57-60, 69-72. A particular enterprise of the Basel Mission was the establishment in 1859 of the Mission Trade Society, a joint-stock company distinct in this respect from the Mission but working in close co-operation with it. Its members were under the discipline of the mission and might share in regular mission activities. Firearms, ammunition and alcoholic spirits were naturally excluded from its stock-in-trade.—Ibid., I, 388-95; III, 91.

opened in 1848. At Abokobi boys' and girls' schools were started soon after the settlement in 1855 while at Odumase a girls' school was opened in 1872. But these are only isolated dates in a vital enterprise competently organized and devotedly maintained.[1] On the linguistic side, while others made their contributions,[2] the name without peer is that of Johann Gottlieb Christaller, the distinguished authority on the Twi or Ashanti language. He served the Basel Mission on the Gold Coast from 1853 to 1868, surviving until 1895. The first Biblical translation from his hand was the Four Gospels in 1859. A steady output followed: the New Testament completed (1864), Psalms and Proverbs (1866), and the whole Bible (completed in manuscript in 1868 when he returned to Europe) in 1871. In addition he produced a standard dictionary and published entirely in the vernacular a collection of 3,600 Twi proverbs (Basel, 1879). Such a royal contribution has continued to serve his successors long after the author's death.[3]

In 1869 an Ashanti invasion of the British Protectorate, in retaliation for unsettled differences, was being prepared. As part of the preliminary strategy an army was despatched across the Volta, and so beyond the frontier of the Protectorate, to subjugate the Krepis and acquire their territory. The Basel station at Anum was in this country, with two recently arrived missionaries in charge: Frederick Augustus Ramseyer (with his wife and child) and Johannes Kühne. The chief offered them carriers to enable them to depart, when the fighting drew near. Unwisely they declined but when the next day they changed their minds it was too late. They were conducted to Kumasi as prisoners of war. They remained such for four and a half years until Sir Garnet Wolseley's force was on the point of taking Kumasi in the war of 1873–4, when they were released.[4]

---

[1] *Ibid.*, III, 91–9.

[2] Hans Nicolai Riis, Andreas Riis's nephew, produced the first Twi Grammar in 1854. Zimmermann made a study of the Ga language and starting with the Four Gospels (1855) had completed the translation of the Bible by 1866, producing in the interval catechisms, grammar and dictionary.—*Ibid.*, III, 60–1, 62.

[3] *Ibid.*,III,62–3; E.M.North, *The Book of a Thousand Tongues* (1938), 58. A selection of 830 of Christaller's Twi proverbs has been translated, with annotations by R. S. Rattray in *Ashanti Proverbs* (1916). Dr. I. C. Ward has said: "Christaller's Dictionary is in the first rank of dictionaries of African languages, or indeed of any languages." —*Report of an Investigation of some Gold Coast Language Problems* (1945), 9 *n*. 2.

[4] Schlatter, *op. cit.*, III, 101–5; Claridge, *op. cit.*, I, 579–80; II, 107, 110, 111. Claridge contends that the prisoners, while suffering acutely on the march to Kumasi, were not cruelly treated by the Ashanti: "From an Ashanti point of view the missionaries were treated extremely well, and they themselves mention numerous acts of kindness that they received, but which it is very unlikely would have been shown to any African."—*Ibid.*, I, 580–2.

The war, into the intricate causes of which it is not necessary to enter here, came to its climax with the occupation of Kumasi, which the confident Ashanti had regarded as inviolate. Wolseley's conditions not being complied with, the royal palace was blown up and the town fired.[1] Wolseley reported in his despatch the next day: "I had done all I could to avoid the necessity, but it was forced upon me."[2]

When in 1876 the Wesleyan missionaries requested permission to resume residence in Kumasi and start schools, they were told in effect: "We will accept the Mission, if you act as Mr. Freeman did to help the peace of the nation and the prosperity of trade, but you must understand that we will not select children for education. . . . The Bible is not a book for us. . . . We will never embrace your religion."[3] It was ten years before the attempt was renewed, and for the Basel Mission not till 1896 was this long-cherished objective realized.

The North German Missionary Society, known as the Bremen Mission from its headquarters, commenced work among the Ewe east of the Volta in 1847 after an abortive attempt to settle in Gabon. Under the leadership of Lorenz Wolf the pioneer party included three others: Luer Bultmann, Carl Flato, and Jens Graff. Malaria soon took heavy toll: they had sailed from Hamburg in March, in November Wolf alone survived. In that month he had begun work at Peki, some ninety miles up the Volta, and despite the loss of his companions carried forward the cause with a stout heart. Two colleagues joined him and in April 1850 Caroline Leist arrived to be his bride. All seemed set fair for the mission when in January 1851 ill health compelled Wolf with his wife to return to Europe. To his chagrin his two colleagues, feeling unequal to the task without him, also sailed for home. There was little joy for him in a homecoming under such conditions: indeed, he died on board on arrival at Hamburg. But his name remains bright among

---

[1] Claridge, *op. cit.*, II, 143-4. Wolseley's instructions from the Home Government had been "to procure an honourable peace, or inflict, in default of such a peace, an effectual chastisement on the Ashanti force". Within a week of these events a treaty of peace had been agreed, and by mid-March had been ratified.—*Ibid.*, II, 145, 151-6, 161. J. H. Glover, of the 1857 Niger Expedition, commanded a column with responsibility for dealing with eastern allies of the Ashantis. He visited Basel mission stations in this connexion, and paid a tribute to their work.—*Life of Sir John Hawley Glover* (1897), 179; cf. 217. H. M. Stanley was war correspondent on the campaign.—H. M. Stanley, *Coomassie and Magdala* (1874), *passim.*

[2] Stanley, *op. cit.*, 236.

[3] Findlay and Holdsworth, *op. cit.*, IV, 175.

Africa's honoured dead. The attempt to resume work at Peki was not successful; it was felt to be too distant from the coast for a first station, but tribal war precipitated the decision to withdraw.[1]

It was now determined to begin with a base on the coast itself, and Keta (or Kitta) was selected, the site of a lonely fort some ninety miles east of Accra on the sea side of an extensive lagoon. Here Däuble and his colleague Plessing established themselves under rather forbidding conditions in September 1853. The plan was now, from this foothold on the seaboard, to advance by stages to Peki and resume there the work so unhappily interrupted. Waya, the first station inland, was selected in 1855 and was soon in action. Anyako followed in 1857 and in 1859 the fourth station was opened at Wegbe, on the parallel of Peki but some twenty-five miles to the east. A sound line of advance was now prepared and regular mission activities were before long in operation. But the simmering turmoil of the tribes boiled over in the Ashanti aggression of 1869, culminating in the war of 1873–74. Wegbe was destroyed in 1869; Waya passed through many vicissitudes, and when in 1871 the missionaries withdrew, the station was plundered. But with the termination of the Ashanti conflict a period of peace ensued and new life and hope began to blossom amidst the ruins of war.[2]

Slightly to the east of the Bremen mission field lay the kingdom of Dahomey. Freeman, who had paid his pioneer visit to Dahomey in 1843 and later accompanied Governor Hill on an official mission, paid a further visit in 1854 with Henry Wharton, evidently intending to place him there, but this was not done. An African agent however was stationed at Whydah on the coast, and from 1857 to 1866 this was P. W. Bernasko who served devotedly in a time of acute distress. In 1860 he was desired by the Society to interview the king who refused to allow the facilities sought and bluntly said he would not give up either war or the slave-trade. In 1862 the Dahomians attacked and destroyed Ishagga, a town in alliance with Abeokuta. Christians were taken prisoner, among them Doherty the African catechist of the Church Missionary Society. A Christian publicly crucified in Abomey was mistakenly thought to be Doherty, but he was later released in 1866. Meanwhile Bernasko

---

[1] G. Müller, *Geschichte der Ewe-Mission* (1904), 1–12.
[2] *Ibid.*, 14–15, 21, 26, 30, 120–2, 131. Keta (German writers) and Kitta (English) is found alternatively as Kwitta and Quittah, the latter being the Portuguese form.

was himself virtually held a prisoner in Abomey. In 1862 it was reported that the king wished to see the Wesleyan superintendent from the Gold Coast: "The King has expressed a wish for a visit from the Rev. William West, that he may see a 'real Englishman'; but Mr. West does not deem it prudent to gratify him." After Bernasko's withdrawal in 1866 Whydah remained for a decade without a Wesleyan representative.[1]

It was in 1860 that Roman Catholics made an attempt to recommence a mission in Dahomey. The Seminary of African Missions at Lyons, established in 1856, had confided to it the vicariate apostolic of Dahomey, erected in 1860, which extended from the Volta to the Niger. Borghero, an Italian, was the first Superior of the Mission. He and his companion Fernandez arrived at Whydah in April 1861 and publicly celebrated mass in the chapel of the disused Portuguese fort, about a hundred people witnessing. Borghero claimed that they were accepted as missionaries and nothing more.[2] He saw in Dahomey the strategic route into interior Africa, reaching to Chad and Timbuktu.[3] In November 1861 Borghero visited the capital. The king desired a processional display and Borghero was nothing loath on his own conditions, the principal one being that no idolatrous object should be visible in the streets and no talisman on the person of any Dahomian. The conditions were accepted and observed, King Gréré (son of Gezo) acknowledging the justice of the demand: "I know well that such things should not be displayed before God's representative, for God is greater than them all." The procession—the five Christians suitably robed and bearing as Christian symbols an ivory crucifix and an image of the Holy Mother, with Borghero in full canonicals—aroused uproarious enthusiasm. The king, not to be outdone, put on military and other displays in return. Then came the vital interview: in a three-hour conference Borghero opened up the aim he had in view; the king was agreeable up to a point and promised full protection for Borghero's own people, with one exception: there must be no baptisms. On that he was adamant. As one whose very position was based on a military

---

[1] Findlay and Holdsworth, *op. cit.*, IV, 162, 171–2; Stock, *op. cit.*, II, 435–6; *Wesleyan Missionary Notices* (1862), 181.

[2] "On sait, au Dahomey, que nous ne sommes ni des agents commerciaux venus pour faire fortune, ni des émissaires politiques envoyés pour explorer le pays afin d'en préparer la conquête, comme on accuse d'agir les protestants anglais."— *Annales*, XXXIV (1862), 209.

[3] *Ibid.*, 231–2.

despotism he was shrewd enough to see that one wife and no more war spelt death to the old régime.[1]

The Roman missionaries began with the nucleus of a Christian community derived from Portuguese days. There were the half-caste descendants of the Portuguese themselves, and there were immigrants from Brazil—slaves who had received baptism, secured their freedom, and returned as traders to the Guinea coast. The king's prohibition of baptism did not apply to this (to him) exotic community.[2] The appropriation of the chapel in the old Portuguese fort to their use the missionaries claimed as a great asset, for this place was the recognized dwelling in Dahomey of the Christians' God. Borghero also contended that the use of Portuguese in teaching commended itself as a familiar tongue by contrast to the use of English by the Protestants.[3] Towards the end of their third year's work Borghero reported they had had 319 baptisms (288 infant, 31 adult), while at Whydah there were twenty-seven catechumens preparing for the rite.[4] In 1870 the name of the vicariate was changed to that of the Coast of Benin as more in keeping with the facts, for Lagos and Abeokuta were now actively within its purview.[5]

The year 1860 heralded a period of distress for missions in Yorubaland. So far prosperity had attended the Christian mission, but with the outbreak of tribal war the tide now turned. The war had an economic cause. The Egbas of Abeokuta had grown prosperous, and were now prepared to give rein to their ambition. They therefore denied to Ibadan a through route to the coast. This automatically produced a state of war with the Ibadans, who desired direct trade with Lagos. The situation increased in complexity when the Egba chiefs, hitherto in cordial relations with the British, grew hostile. It has been alleged that after the annexation of Lagos in 1861 they feared for their own independence; and again, that still having an interest in the slave-trade, British action in clamping down on the export trade through Lagos lost their friendship. Whatever the real reason—probably not a simple one, for sons of liberated Africans

[1] *Ibid.*, 153–6; XXXV (1863), 8–48.

[2] *Ibid.*, XXXVI (1864), 439–42. Borghero says that White, Christian, Free; Black, Pagan, Slave were practically synonymous terms. Africans in the service of Portuguese and Brazilians might be baptized as belonging to their community.—*Ibid.*, 441.

[3] *Ibid.*, XXXVII (1865), 84–5, 95–6.

[4] *Ibid.*, 115–16.

[5] *Ibid.*, XLII (1870), 474.

are accused of fomenting trouble—the Egbas refused the Queen's vice-consul. The missionaries were even accused of encouraging the unco-operative attitude of the Egbas; certainly they were not agreed: Townsend, for example, was for the Egbas, Hinderer for the Ibadans.[1]

The war produced its casualties. Ishagga was destroyed in 1862 by the Dahomians who found the opportunity too good to be missed. The expected advance on Abeokuta did not take place and this was hailed as a great deliverance. However the attack was only postponed; it was delivered in 1864 with an army of 10,000, but the Egbas successfully withstood the assault and won several years' respite from their western enemy. Meanwhile in the same year as Ishagga's fall Ijaye, also in alliance with Abeokuta, was destroyed by the Ibadans. Adolphus Mann and his wife of the C.M.S. were successfully removed to safety by an English naval officer, but Mrs. Mann did not survive the ordeal. A missionary recruit, Edwin Roper, who had come up with Lieutenant Dolben, elected to remain to care for the Christian community. He was carried off to Ibadan as prisoner of war and in vain did David Hinderer in person seek his release. Finally Hinderer appealed to the Alafin of Oyo who generously responded and instructed Ogunmola of Ibadan to release his prisoner without ransom. The order was obeyed.[2]

Ikorodu, a town some nine miles from Lagos, having been willing to serve as transit town for Ibadan traders, was invested in 1865 by the Egbas and their allies. Ibadan being unable to help, Ikorodu turned to the British Government at Lagos. John Hawley Glover, who was then Governor, ordered the Egba chiefs to withdraw. This they ignored, as also an ultimatum which followed. Troops from Lagos then engaged them and scattered them within the hour. Ikorodu was saved.[3] Glover had already reported in a despatch to the Secretary of State: "The exasperation of Abeokuta at the check given to the slave trade by the occupation of Lagos, the wish of this Government for another

---

[1] A. C. Burns, *History of Nigeria* (3rd ed., 1942), 140–1; Stock, *op. cit.*, II, 434–5. In 1860 Henry Venn of the C.M.S. had issued his "Instructions for Missionaries on Missions and Politics", but with a more general reference than Yorubaland.— Stock, *op. cit.*, II, 304.

[2] Stock, *op. cit.*, II, 436–8; S. Johnson, *The History of the Yorubas* (1921), 352–3. Johnson adds: "The good offices of His Majesty the Alafin to the missionaries claim our special notice. This was the second of the kind during this war." Thomas Champness of the Wesleyan Mission was stationed in Abeokuta during the period 1861–3. His account of the year 1862 is given in *The Report of the Wesleyan Methodist Missionary Society* (1863), 121–4.

[3] A. C. Burns, *op. cit.*, 142–3; S. Johnson, *op. cit.*, 360.

road to and from the interior (besides that of Abeokuta), the non-rendering of slaves who sought protection in this settlement, their rejection of Her Majesty's Vice-Consul, and the murders and robberies committed by them on the persons and properties of British subjects, their reverses in the war with Ibadan, and our refusal to allow them to destroy the town of Ikorodu—all these were causes sufficient in themselves to prevent any relations of close friendship existing between them and ourselves."[1] The Egbas smarted from their reverse at Ikorodu. Meanwhile Glover was seeking to relieve the Hinderers who, thanks to the Egbas, had remained shut up in Ibadan for five years. At length an officer cut his way through and brought out Mrs. Hinderer in safety; her husband remained to put affairs in order after peace was made with Abeokuta in 1865.[2]

But the cessation of hostilities did not mean the return of a clear sky. Within two years there fell for Abeokuta the heaviest blow of all: in October 1867 the Egba chiefs suddenly turned on the missionaries: mission premises were looted and destroyed, and all the missionaries, Anglican, Wesleyan, and Baptist, were expelled with nothing but the clothes in which they stood. It was a staggering blow. Eugene Stock has analysed the causes: resentment at the blockade imposed by the Lagos Government; the failure to elect a successor to the deceased Alake with the result that some of the wilder spirits among the chiefs had seized control; the subversive influence of certain Sierra Leone men who were interested in the slave-trade; and the growing influence of Islam in the city.[3] The expelled missionaries were confident of an early recall, but it was 1880 before a permanent return proved possible. This was ebb-tide with a vengeance. The Wesleyan experience a decade after the expulsion was doleful: "Much ingratitude has been shown where we expected better things, and we are almost led to the conclusion that for Abeokuta the day of grace is past. Certainly it would now be a wrong application of the metaphor to speak of it as the 'Sunrise within the Tropics'."[4] But if there was much to lament, there proved also to be some ground for thanksgiving. The Church survived, chastened and purified, a saving remnant faithfully witnessing to Christian truth. In 1870 this was vividly demonstrated; Abeokuta and Ibadan were still in unfriendly relation-

[1] Lady Glover, *Life of Sir John Hawley Glover* (1897), 93; cf. 98–100.
[2] Stock, *op. cit.*, II, 440–1.
[3] *Ibid.*, II, 442–3.
[4] *The Report of the Wesleyan Methodist Missionary Society* (1878), 155. *Vide supra*, p. 64.

ship, when the Christians in each plighted their troth: "However great misunderstandings may be among the Heathen of Abeokuta and Ibadan, let unity and peace be among us Christians of the two rival cities, for we are the followers of the Prince of Peace."[1] Lagos now became the missionary headquarters for Yorubaland.

In 1863 and 1866 Borghero from Whydah made a pilot survey of Lagos and Abeokuta (he vividly describes the ascent of the River Ogun under war conditions) and reported favourably on both as prospective mission centres. In Abeokuta he claimed to find the chiefs favourably disposed, and in Lagos the Government were prepared to help him to find a suitable site. By 1872 Lagos was, with Whydah and Porto Novo, one of the three chief stations in the vicariate of the Coast of Benin.[2]

(4) *From the Niger to the Congo*

The stretch of country from the Niger to the Congo is characterized by many rivers and luxuriant equatorial forest. Here are no coherent kingdoms but peoples of the river and folk of the forest in comparatively small tribal groups and yet living in a well-peopled region as population density goes in Africa. With little of Afric's golden sand but shores thick with mangrove forest, the rivers are the only means of entry and the main arteries of trade.

The Niger Mission, hopefully begun after the 1857–59 Expedition on that river, had soon run into difficulties. In pondering the problem Henry Venn formed a bold resolution: to call Samuel Crowther to head an all-African mission and secure his episcopal consecration for the purpose. The state and ecclesiastical authorities concurring, Crowther was consecrated a bishop of the Church of England in Canterbury Cathedral on June 29, 1864. The University of Oxford had previously entered his name on its roll of divinity graduates by conferring upon him an honorary doctorate.[3] In three weeks he was bound for Lagos

---

[1] Stock, *op. cit.*, II, 444. In the case of the American Baptists the American Civil War was a further factor interrupting their work. Samuel Crowther had occasion to visit their station at Ogbomosho in 1871, ten years after they had temporarily retired, and found a faithful remnant of twenty Christian converts.—J. Page, *The Black Bishop* (1908), 235–7.

[2] *Annales*, XXXVII (1865), 113–14; XXXIX (1867), 235–7; XL (1868), 486–7; XLIV (1872), 261.

[3] Stock, *op. cit.*, II, 454–6; J. Page, *op. cit.*, 183–94. His commission as stated in the royal letter patent read: "to be Bishop of the United Church of England and Ireland, in the said countries of Western Africa beyond the limits of our dominions".

which he made his headquarters. Transport proved a problem, for there was no regular service on the Niger from the Delta to Onitsha and Lokoja, the two principal stations inland. He had to depend on such Government vessels as might ascend the river from time to time, though when trade developed this difficulty disappeared. For staffing his stations he relied largely upon Sierra Leone for catechists and schoolmasters, receiving for ordination those who exhibited the requisite gifts and graces. In seven years he ordained eight such men. His status as bishop commended him to Christian circles, but naturally counted for nothing with the pagan. On one occasion indeed he was kidnapped and £1,000 ransom demanded (his episcopacy apparently counted to that extent!). The British Consul from Lokoja, Mr. Fell, tried without success to secure his release, and then decided they should both run for it. Poisoned arrows followed the boat, and one found its target in the Consul. Crowther wrote: "I would, had such been the will of God, that I had been shot, and my dead body taken to Lokoja instead of his."[1]

Through the extensive Niger Delta and eastwards to the Cross River are many streams with a network of interlacing creeks. These were early known as the Oil Rivers, from the trade in palm-oil that from the sixteenth century took place in their estuaries. At two of these points, Brass and Bonny, Crowther successfully established Christian work. Brass lay in the centre of the Delta seaboard, to the east of Akassa, and Bonny at the Delta's eastern end. In the days of the slave-trade Bonny was a main emporium from which as many as 16,000 slaves a year were exported.[2] Crowther entered Bonny by invitation. Ten years before, in 1854, William Pepple, king of Bonny, had been removed by Consul Beecroft as his life was in danger from the other chiefs. He was brought to England, where he became a Christian, and on his return several men and women, Europeans, went at his request to help in the lifting of his people. These enlisted helpers however, on seeing the local conditions, discovered they had made a mistake and returned by the next boat. In 1864 Pepple prevailed on one of the European traders to send his request to the Bishop of London. Crowther was thereupon advised and arrived at the end of the year. A site was

---

[1] Stock, *op. cit.*, II, 457–60.
[2] Brass is said to have derived its name from the large brass pans, obtained from Europe, used to evaporate seawater to secure the salt.—P. A. Talbot, *The Peoples of Southern Nigeria* (1926), I, 327; A. F. Mockler-Ferryman, *British Nigeria* (n.d.), 107 *n*. 1. Bonny is a corruption of the local *Obane*.—Mockler-Ferryman, *op. cit.*, 113 *n*. 1, 2.

provided and money collected; the European traders gave their support, and despite dissident chiefs and pagan priests the work was set going. In 1871 Crowther's son, who had been ordained (and later became Archdeacon), took charge at Bonny. There was persecution and in 1875 the first Christian was martyred. The leading persecutor among the chiefs, Captain Hart as he was known, in 1877 granted religious liberty, and at his death the following year ordered the family idols to be destroyed. In 1867 a mission was begun at Brass where in 1875 a leading chief became a convert, and two years later the king of Brass himself renounced idolatry.[1]

The Scottish Presbyterian mission at Calabar was in an isolated region as far as other missions were concerned but in a busy centre of trade. It was not surprising therefore that *min makara*[2] was in great demand and proved a serious hindrance to the work. Carousals were all too often the order of the day.[3] Human life was cheap, as always in a slave-owning community, and belief regarding the future life demanded a retinue to follow a departed chief. Further, suspicion of foul play, which meant death from *ifot* or witchcraft, demanded that those accused should submit to trial by ordeal in taking *esere* bean, and this might easily result in a serious death roll.[4] At the decease of Eyo Honesty II in 1858 a holocaust was feared, but he had ordered that no one was to be put to death on his account. Happily there was no human sacrifice, though much anxiety prevailed. But particular crises were always occurring, and the missionaries were continually using their influence to save human life, but did not always succeed.[5] In 1878 David Hopkins, who had just been appointed Consul for the Bights of Benin and Biafra with residence on Fernando Po, visited Calabar on the instructions of the British Foreign Secretary, Lord Salisbury, to secure a treaty with the chiefs that should terminate all such murderous customs. This was secured, thanks to the ability of the Consul in negotiation coupled with his effec-

---

[1] Stock, *op. cit.*, II, 460–4; W. N. M. Geary, *Nigeria under British Rule* (1927), 86–7.

[2] Lit. white man's wine, i.e. rum and other spirits.

[3] W. Marwick, *William and Louisa Anderson* (1897), 446–60; H. Goldie, *Calabar and its Mission* (1901), 204–5.

[4] *Ifot* was regarded as a physical trait to which *esere* was antipathetic. Death from *esere* meant that *ifot* was present; vomiting was, in theory, an acquittal. Eserine (B.P.), the alkaloid of *esere* bean is an active poison, producing death by asphyxiation principally through action on the centre in the brain that controls respiration.

[5] Goldie, *op. cit.*, 197–201, 209–13, 233–4.

tive personal influence. The agreement contained fifteen articles covering, among other matters, exposure of twins, taking or administering of *esere* bean, human sacrifice, and maltreatment of women. Hopkins acknowledged his indebtedness to the previous patient work of the mission for making his successful negotiations possible. He died in the following year at the age of forty-two, universally mourned. His was as truly Christian service as that of the official representatives of the Churches.[1]

The death of a chief and the appointment of his successor was inevitably a time of anxiety for the missionaries because of the influence of these men upon the work of the mission. The chiefs of Creek Town were supporters of it while those of Duke Town were the reverse. In 1860, for example, Archibong II of Duke Town started a movement for the expulsion of the mission from Calabar. The assembled chiefs were to have the missionaries appear before them and then reach a decision about them. Mr. James Irvine, merchant of Liverpool who was in Calabar at the time, witnessed the assembly from a trading hulk in the river. Archibong of Duke Town thundered his charges (the effort of the missionaries to establish stations upriver was a sore point, as the Calabar chiefs feared this would destroy their trade monopoly as middlemen); then Eyo III of Creek Town spoke for the other side. They might as well try to stop the rain, he said, as to prevent God's message from spreading, even if the missionaries went. He had no sooner spoken than a gathering tornado, which in their excitement they had apparently not noticed, crashed down upon them. They never reassembled. A chief later said to Irvine, "For true, your God was there that day."[2] In 1874 when the Creek Town chieftainship was vacant the choice eventually fell on a Christian who became Eyo Honesty VII. When invited he laid down two conditions: that the king should govern and the people consent to be governed by the will of God as revealed in the Bible; and that he should be received as king not by a section but by all. His conditions were accepted, and a written statement embodying them signed

---

[1] Goldie, *op. cit.*, 243–4; D. M. McFarlan, *Calabar* (1946), 65–7; Marwick, *op. cit.*, 564–6. Geary speaks of Consul Hopkins as the "well-beloved" and writes: "He was reputed one of the best, if not the best, Consul on the Coast and settled many a difficult palaver without an expedition. His name is still [1927] a household word. On his death, all the chiefs subscribed either in palm oil or cash many thousands of pounds which was sent to the widow, and a monument erected." He died at Bonny on September 13, 1879.—Geary, *op. cit.*, 85–6.

[2] Goldie, *op. cit.*, 205–8.

in the church by king and chiefs. Well might the missionaries feel so far content.[1]

The mission was happy in its language students: Hugh Goldie who arrived in 1847, William Anderson in 1849, and Alexander Robb in 1858. Anderson translated the first New Testament portions to be printed. Goldie completed the New Testament (1862) and Alexander Robb the Old (1868). Goldie compiled a *Dictionary of the Efik Language* still recognized as a standard work, and Robb made a translation of *Pilgrim's Progress* hailed by the people as the best written book in their language.[2] A significant stage in the work of the mission was reached with the first ministerial ordination in 1872. Esien Esien Ukpabio, the first baptized convert and the first African teacher, was ordained to the ministry on April 9, kept as the anniversary of the beginning of the mission.[3]

When the Baptist missionaries were finally expelled from Fernando Po in 1858 they already had a foothold on the mainland opposite in Cameroons. Here, on the shores of Ambas Bay, Alfred Saker settled as many of the Protestant community as were inclined to accompany him. The new settlement, the land for which had been purchased from local chiefs, was named Victoria. Saker formulated regulations for the little community and laboured for it devotedly with hand and head and heart. Building and printing (with the continuous training of African apprentices), translation and itineration (not till 1875 did he have a launch at disposal), made a crowded life. Some younger colleagues criticized him for the time he gave to what they regarded as "secular" employment. He replied in justification of his methods: "With such, the true work of the missionary is, it seems, to go, book in hand, under a tree here and a shed there, and preach the Gospel to the people. With me the work has ever appeared in a different light. It is to go to the man in his house, to sympathise in his sorrows and cares, to aid him to think of a better condition and of the means to attain it. Then, when his attention has been gained, to speak of that higher life." Nevertheless the Home Committee sent its secretary,

[1] *Ibid.*, 239–40.

[2] Anderson translated St. John's Gospel, Romans, 1 Corinthians 8, 9 and 15, and Hebrews; also Proverbs in the Old Testament.—Marwick, *op. cit.*, 263, 350, 360, 406. The New Testament in Efik, published in 1862 by the National Bible Society of Scotland, was the first missionary publication of that Society.—E. M. North, *op. cit.*, 110.

[3] Goldie, *op. cit.*, 166–7, 196–7, 235.

Dr. E. B. Underhill, to investigate and report; Saker was triumphantly vindicated.[1]

His work on the translation of the Bible he regarded as second to none. The New Testament in Duala was published in 1861 and the whole Bible in 1872. But that was not the end, for until he left Cameroons in 1877 he was constantly engaged on the work of revision.[2] In 1874 there sailed with him as colleague to Cameroons George Grenfell, destined to have his name writ large on the roll of African explorers. Two years later Thomas Comber joined them. Both Grenfell and Comber only served an apprenticeship in the Cameroons before proceeding to the Congo. But all three men had some exploring in Cameroons to their credit. Saker in 1861–62 made the first ascent of the Cameroons Mountain in company with Richard Burton the British Consul at Fernando Po, Gustav Mann the German botanist who had served with the Niger Expedition of 1841, and Señor Calvo a Spanish judge. Merrick, the missionary at Bimbia, had attempted the ascent in 1847 but had not gone higher than 9,200 feet. The volcanic peak is 13,350 feet in height, only exceeded by mountains in East Africa and the Atlas range in the north-west. Comber also ascended the mountain and Grenfell did likewise in 1878.[3]

Alfred Saker bade farewell to Cameroons in 1877. He died on March 12, 1880. When the news reached king Akwa, combatant in many a tribal conflict, he and all the people mourned, and in memory of their missionary and friend the chief decreed that henceforth Sunday should be a weekly day of rest. This was but a symbol of the influence the missionary exercised.[4] Saker has been truly styled the apostle of the Cameroons.

In 1870 a second Protestant mission was begun on the island of Fernando Po. Captain Robinson of the barque *Elgiva* and his carpenter Hands, while their ship was at the island in 1869, made contact with the local Protestant Christian community. On the return voyage Captain Robinson was the bearer of a letter to the Secretary of the Primitive Methodist Missionary Society asking for a missionary, both Robinson and Hands

---

[1] E. M. Saker, *Alfred Saker* (1908), 163, 176–9; H. H. Johnston, *George Grenfell and the Congo* (1908), I, 37, 41.
[2] E. M. Saker, *op. cit.*, 175–6; North, *op. cit.*, 106.
[3] E. M. Saker, *op. cit.*, 216–24; H. H. Johnston, *op. cit.*, I, 38, 41, 43; Fitzgerald, *Africa* (2nd ed., 1936), 11. Comber reported his ascent of the mountain and exploration inland in a paper read to the Royal Geographical Society, 10.2.79.— *Proceedings of the R.G.S.*, I, N.S. (1879), 225–34.
[4] E. M. Saker, *op. cit.*, 213–14.

being members of that denomination. The call was accepted and on February 21, 1870 R. W. Burnett and Henry Roe arrived at Santa Isabel, the capital of the island. While in theory religious liberty was now observed, there were still vexatious restrictions for Protestants, and much depended on the personal attitude of the Spanish Governor. In 1879 W. Holland was banished by the Governor on trivial grounds, but David Hopkins, who was Consul at the time, sustained the missionary, Madrid rescinded the banishment, and the keys of the mission premises were restored. While the core of the work lay among the English-speaking community at Santa Isabel, stations were begun at San Carlos and elsewhere and an attempt made to reach the Bubis, forest folk behind the settlements. Theophilus Parr in the 'seventies prepared a study of the Bubi language. The work on the island has been maintained continuously, though with many vicissitudes.[1]

The Presbyterian Church in the United States, which had already entered Liberia, came further east in 1849 and started work on the island of Corisco north of the Gabon. J. L. Mackey and G. W. Simpson and their wives were the first missionaries; Mackey was soon the sole survivor. But reinforcements were sent and within six years a staff of nine Americans had been assembled. Attempts from their island base to break into territory on the mainland, first by the Rio Muni and then the Benito, produced no result. The successful penetration was finally made by Robert Hamill Nassau who had reached Corisco in 1861. After ten years of language study and itineration, when he returned from furlough in 1874 he made his way up the River Ogowe. At the head of the Ogowe delta, 130 miles inland, lies Lambarene made famous by Albert Schweitzer's hospital; Nassau went twenty miles beyond and established a station at Belambila, but after a couple of years this was abandoned, and in 1877 he settled on Kangwe Hill until the furlough of 1880. Nassau ranks as the effective pioneer of the mission.[2]

The work of the American Board in Gabon had not proceeded without many a struggle and in 1870 they handed over their stations to the American Presbyterian mission.[3]

---

[1] N. Boocock, *Our Fernandian Missions* (n.d.), 6–8, 11–20; Thirty-fifth *Annual Report of the Primitive Methodist Missionary Society* (1878), xxvii. Mr. Parr's study of Bubi, which was never published, came into the hands of H. H. Johnston who gave it high praise.—*Op. cit.*, II, 882, *n.* 1.

[2] J. du Plessis, *op. cit.*, 174; R. H. Nassau, *Fetichism in West Africa* (1904), v–viii.

[3] *The Missionary Herald* (A.B.C.F.M.), LXVII (1871), 1.

In the 'forties a Roman Catholic mission was recommenced in Gabon. The Italian Capuchins who had worked there in the eighteenth century were expelled by the Portuguese Government in 1777.[1] We have already seen that, when Edward Barron's pioneer group of missionaries provided by the new Society of the Sacred Heart of Mary were dispersed in 1843, Jean Remi Bessieux had gone to Gabon where he was lost sight of for two years. When in 1848 the amalgamation of the Society with the Fathers of the Holy Ghost took place there were more ample resources to draw upon for recruits. Also in 1848 Bessieux was given episcopal status as Vicar Apostolic of the Two Guineas, but with a division of this immense sphere in 1863 a separate vicariate apostolic of Senegambia was set up. Sainte-Marie was the headquarters of the mission, and at the latter date there were ten missionaries on the staff (four priests and six brothers). They claimed a Christian community of some 220, with 115 scholars and 75 apprentices in training. There arrived in 1849 the Sisters of the Immaculate Conception of Castres who in 1852 were finally established at Sainte-Pierre, this being the location of the French Government hospital which they were to serve. Here were eleven sisters who in addition to their hospital service had some eighty girl pupils in their care.[2]

In the attempt to gain converts the missionaries discovered a strong resistance to the rite of baptism, and eventually found there was prevalent the idea that by this practice they were capturing the souls of those baptized who would die soon after. Indeed the market women, who came to the gate of the mission with their wares and were not permitted to enter, attributed the prohibition to this fact and thought they had spotted the little hut where the souls were kept! It seemed to confirm these ideas that there were children living on the mission premises much attached to the missionaries. Despite these fears (perhaps first occasioned by administering baptism to the dying), there were converts won, though death-bed repentances, on the missionaries' own showing, were on occasion motivated by fear of hell fire. Not all however were moved by fear alone, as in the case of the old woman's dying prayer: "My God, pardon the evil I have committed; I love you, for I am your child and you are my Father."[3]

[1] Schmidlin, *op. cit.*, 472, *n* 55.
[2] *Annales*, XLI (1869), 100–1, 106–7, 109–10.
[3] *Ibid.*, XLV (1873), 221–5.

When Bessieux died on April 30, 1876 the pioneer era of the mission closed. He had become enfeebled in later years, but had won the esteem of European and African alike; it was reported: "The Christians looked on him as a Saint; the pagans said he was the friend of the Great Spirit." He came to Gabon, the only Christian of his form of the faith; he left a community of 2,000 souls.[1] Ten days after Bessieux's decease came the death of king Denis, one of the leading chiefs of Gabon. He was rumoured to be a centenarian; he claimed to be already paddling a canoe when Louis XVI was King of France. Settled on the south bank of the Gabon, he had much intercourse with Europeans and was said to speak with facility English and Spanish, Portuguese and French. He appreciated the French protectorate and had played a considerable part in bringing it about. Indeed he had had conferred the cross of a Chevalier of the Legion of Honour, and the British Government had also acknowledged his services to its citizens. Nevertheless he was not clear of complicity in the slave-trade, and as a polygamist (he was said to have a hundred wives) remained an obdurate pagan. He had been so distressed by the death of his favourite wife that he devised a new form of salutation as a continual reminder of it. The visitor was to address him, "What is the evil which God has done?" to which he replied, "Death"; "Yes," returned the visitor, "death is the evil God has done." Bessieux on learning of this was so shocked that he remonstrated with the chief and succeeded in persuading him, pagan as he was, to change the formula of salutation: "What is the good which God has done?" "Life"; "Yes, God has given you life." On his death-bed he sent for a missionary, wishing to receive baptism. The missionary not arriving, his Christian son and heir, following the customary questions to which affirmative answers were given, baptized him. And then, before life flickered out, he said to those around in clear and intelligible tones: "Do not ascribe my death to any evildoer, and do not put any slaves to death as a sacrifice on my account." A dying chief for the first time forbidding human sacrifice, and a Christian son succeeding to his father's rule—this surely would have seemed to Bessieux ample reward for his apostolic labours.[2]

In 1866 Roman Catholic missionaries reappeared on the Congo. It was over a century since the Jesuits had been expelled by Pombal, Foreign Affairs Secretary in Portugal, from all the Portuguese dominions (1759); and while in 1766 the

---

[1] *Ibid.*, XLVIII (1876), 445-7.   [2] *Ibid.*, XLIX (1877), 132-8.

prefecture of Loango had been carved out of the Congo territory and entrusted to a French mission, this faded out within
ten years. The second and last Prefect Apostolic of Loango,
M. Descourvières, wrote sadly in 1773 of the work of the Italian
Capuchins in the kingdom of Congo diminishing to vanishing point, and of the pathetic attempts of the African Christians
to hold on to the faith without pastors to feed them.[1] Then came
the final blow from Portugal. In the so-called Miguelite Wars
by which the country had been distraught after the death of
John VI in 1826 the religious orders had supported Miguel
against Dom Pedro. The latter's victory therefore in 1834 was
marked by their suppression, and the last missionary link with
Congo was thereby snapped.[2]

On September 9, 1865 the Holy See issued a decree commit-
ting the prefecture apostolic of the Congo to the Fathers of the
Holy Ghost. On January 25, 1866 Poussot, the vice-prefect,
set out with two companions. As the diocese of Angola claimed a
jurisdiction, if shadowy, over the Congo region, Poussot first
waited on the bishop at Loanda and set his mind at rest by
admitting the claim, with which the bishop was content. The
diocese at the time was practically limited to serving three
centres on the coast, Loanda, Benguella, and Mossamedes,
despite the larger claims sometimes advanced.[3] The few relics
of the earlier Congo missions which the missionaries discovered
saddened their hearts. A chief of Sonyo had been the first in
1491 to receive the missionary party and the first to be baptized.[4] Here they discovered but a few cacao-trees and a giant
tamarind, evidence of the Capuchins' activities. They had been
told of an *igreja* (church), and to their disappointment found it
was but the usual mud and wattle structure recently erected,
with palm-branch roof and sanded floor. However it contained
a large wooden crucifix, a couple of statues of the Virgin the
worse for wear, several small crucifixes and statues of some saint
or other, a copper censer and incense-box in reasonably good
preservation, some worm-eaten wooden candlesticks, and frag-
ments of missals and other books on which insects had been
busy. This then was the church of Saint-Antonio. The people
too, said Poussot, seemed to have lost all vestige of religion.

---

[1] Proyart, *Histoire de Loango, Kakongo, et autres royaumes d'Afrique* (1766), 316–18,
quoted in *Annales* XXVIII (1866), 231–2.

[2] *Cath. Ency.* XIII (1912), 386; *Annales*, XXXVIII (1866), 232–3.

[3] *Annales*, XXXVIII (1866), 233; XXXIX (1867), 66–7; Schmidlin, *op. cit.*,
550.

[4] See Vol. I, p. 128.

Momentarily taken aback, he nevertheless carried out his original intention of saying mass, with some forty respectful Africans to watch. He then waited on the local chief and found him not only seated in an easy chair under a parasol, but with a crucifix in his right hand and supported on his thigh. On a visitor's arrival he would raise the crucifix and move his lips as if in blessing—a garbled version, thought Poussot, of the now vanished blessing of the priest.[1]

In 1877 four stations were reported; three north of the river: Landana on the coast, the first in time and in importance; Banana, the commercial metropolis of the Congo; and Boma, the then limit of navigation for the larger ships. South of the river lay Saint-Antonio at the reoccupied centre of Sonyo. There were eight missionaries on the field. In 1876, 163 baptisms and 70 scholars in the schools were reported. The Congo Mission was once more struggling into life.[2]

As in this survey of developments in the north and west we started from the revival of a second century see, so we conclude with the renewal of the first mission to the Congo in the fifteenth century. Between the two we find a far-flung line, true, little advanced beyond the coast, but providing a base for such advance when the way should open.

But a new feature was now appearing in the situation: the beginnings of a rivalry between the Roman Catholic and the Protestant missionary forces in the continent. Previously the Protestant advance, though so to speak in diverse regiments, had not revealed any exclusive claims, save in the early days at the Cape when the principle *cujus regio ejus religio* was recognized. But with the Roman revival it was now otherwise: there appeared for the first time the implied claim to exclusive rights of Christian evangelization and ecclesiastical jurisdiction. A field occupied by Protestants could not be regarded as occupied. In fairness let it be said that this situation arose from no mere competitive spirit or motive of ecclesiastical aggrandize-

---

[1] *Annales*, XL (1868), 154–9. The missionary Ch. Duparquet visiting the place ten years later, when Sonyo was revived as a mission centre, came across a bell inscribed *Si Deus pro nobis, quis contra nos?*, with the date 1700.—*Ibid.*, XLIX (1877), 384. Also, in 1876, an emigrant settlement from Sonyo was discovered on the northern bank of the river in the neighbourhood of Banana. In memory of the church of St.-Antonio at Sonyo they had built a small chapel in which certain sacred objects —three large copper crucifixes, images, etc.—received from their Christian ancestors had been placed. Moreover they always took their dead to Sonyo to be interred in Christian soil.—*Ibid.*, 377–8.

[2] *Ibid.*, XLIX (1877), 375–85.

ment, but from the conviction that the Roman Church was the sole depository of Christian truth, a conviction sincerely and passionately held. While therefore the exploitation of every opportunity offered by the toleration of others was regarded not only as perfectly legitimate but as morally obligatory, there could on their part be no corresponding toleration of those regarded as the propagandists of error, without involving their own disloyalty to the truth. A hard situation, this, for Protestant missionaries to face who had in the pioneer modern period borne the burden and heat of the day, yet one that is perfectly comprehensible. From now on, complicated by the new political situation shortly to appear, this opposition within the Christian Mission increasingly arises.

CHAPTER 8

ADVANCES IN THE SOUTH AND EAST

DURING THE 'sixties and 'seventies the South was not without its excitements. North of the Orange River in Hereroland and west of the Drakensberg in Basutoland there were protracted wars, while the Cape experienced the last in its series of frontier fightings—the so-called Ninth Kaffir War of 1877—and the discovery of diamonds in 1869 produced the usual hectic fever. Further, a new phase in South African history began with the granting of responsible government to the Cape in 1872.[1]

In the East the Arab slave-trade, as we have seen, still dominated the situation in the interior, and there was but little accession of missionary strength elsewhere. Roman Catholic workers now began to appear however, and the Abyssinian war was a significant event for missions in that country. For the most part therefore as we continue our survey beyond the South it is round the coast that we still move.

(1) *From the Cunene to the Kei*

Between the Cunene and the Orange Rivers lies South West Africa. The fortunes of the Rhenish Mission in their early efforts among the Nama-Hottentots and the Hereros have already been reviewed. In 1861 when Jonker Afrikaner died, the able though untamed chief of the Namaquas, he was succeeded by his son Christian, a weakling by contrast. Nevertheless he was responsible for launching a savage attack upon the Hereros that started a seven-years' war. All preparations made, on August 15, 1863 he fell upon Maharero, the Herero chieftain, who had taken refuge in Otjimbingue. In the fierce battle that followed the Namas retired badly mauled. Christian was among the dead. Jan Jonker, his successor, continued the war against the now united Herero clans who had chosen Maharero as their leader. Andersson, the Swedish traveller, was in Hereroland at the time, and supported Maharero with his counsel. The Hereros remained unsubdued and finally achieved their independence in the decisive battle of Okahandja in 1870. The treaty ending hostilities was a formal affair, for there was no

---

[1] E. A. Walker, *A History of South Africa* (2nd ed., 1949), 348–9; E. A. Walker, *Lord de Villiers and his Times* (1925), 55–6.

restoration of good relations, but at least the country now enjoyed a ten-years' truce.[1]

The state of unrest however still threatened the public peace and in 1872 the missionaries persuaded Maharero to seek advice from the Governor at the Cape, but no action was taken at Cape Town. When in 1874 trek Boers from the Transvaal appeared on the eastern flank of Hereroland, a second letter was sent, seeking British intervention. The outcome was the appointment of W. C. Palgrave as special commissioner to survey the situation. He found the Herero chiefs desirous of British protection on security grounds (a decision they later revoked) and the Namaqua chiefs unwilling to countenance any Colonial intervention. Both groups were extremely sensitive as to possible loss of their land. The net result of the inquiry was the British annexation of Walfish Bay, a total extent of some 400 square miles, in March 1878.[2]

During the war years the missionaries had struggled on. Hugo Hahn had returned from Europe to Hereroland in 1864, and settled at Otjimbingue. He was welcomed by the poor and needy, and was soon besieged by the sick and wounded and crippled, for war casualties were not a few. He had brought with him three colonists from Germany, and others followed later. His policy was now to build up a strong settlement as a central station of the Herero mission. So agricultural and building operations were put in hand at Otjimbingue with some promise of success—the young people at least were keen—and a trading-store was opened which included in its commodities firearms and powder, for when the hostile Namas were well equipped, why should the Hereros fighting for their freedom be deprived? But the scheme did not develop as Hahn had hoped. To begin with, the agricultural project did not, in the long run, succeed. Periodic droughts were a handicap, but perhaps more frustrating was the reluctance of the Hereros to take to tillage. They would taunt the Christian workers in the fields: "There you are like guinea-fowls, grubbing about in the earth the whole day long!" Neither did the blacksmith's anvil nor the carpenter's bench attract them. Then in 1870 the trading concern was detached from the mission and transferred to a joint-stock company. When in 1873 it was decided in Barmen to wind up the settlement scheme the German colonists were released to find

---

[1] H. Driessler, *Die Rheinische Mission in Südwestafrika* (1932), 66–70.
[2] Walker, *History*, 376–7; Theal, *History of South Africa since 1795*, V (1908), 327–38.

alternative employment. Of the five, one became a catechist and two took up trade on their own account. This upshot was a disappointment but it was felt to have been worth while to make the experiment.[1]

Meanwhile an experience of Brincker, one of the ablest linguists of the mission, may be cited as the type of war shock that might fall upon the missionaries without warning. Brincker had been placed in charge of the station at Otjikango on the bank of the Swakop, when out of the blue there descended upon him Jan Jonker and Hendrik Ses, the latter reputed the most arrogant and disagreeable of the Nama chiefs. Ses threateningly asserted: "You teachers baptize with water: I am about to baptize the land with blood, and will see whether the heavens fall or not." Thanks to Jonker's determined interposition Brincker and his family escaped with their lives after three days' terrible suspense. But the Hereros had heard Ses's threat; he was done to death soon after, and smeared with his own blood in inverse fulfilment of his prophecy. The station however could not be effectively protected by Maharero, and on his advice it was closed down.[2]

In 1870, the first year of the peace, partners joined the Rhenish missionaries in South West Africa. In 1859 the Finnish Missionary Society had been founded—it was the 700th anniversary of the conversion of Finland—and at first Swedish missions were supported. But when a decade later a work of their own was desired they were in touch with Hugo Hahn who proposed Ovamboland, north of the Hereros. In company with Rath he had prospected in the country in 1857 and been unceremoniously thrown out. Now however it is said the Ovambo chiefs invited him to return, believing it was due to his magical powers that the Hereros had won the war. Hahn's proposal was gladly embraced by the Finns and a first party of seven missionaries and three lay industrial workers arrived in 1870. However, a normally suspicious people were slow to respond to the missionaries' message, the circumstances of the invitation revealing their motive as the desire for security, not spiritual enlightenment with its concomitant of social change. It was to be twenty years before any substantial progress could be reported.[3]

An abortive attempt was made by a party of Jesuit Fathers to establish themselves in South West Africa in 1878. Fathers

[1] H. Driessler, *op. cit.*, 71–3, 95–7.
[2] *Ibid.*, 74–5.
[3] J. E. Carlyle, *South Africa and its Mission Fields* (1878), 108–9; Du Plessis, *History of Christian Missions in South Africa*, 388–9.

Duparquet and Hogan, soon followed by Father Griffin and a lay brother, landed at Walfish Bay, asserting that Ovamboland and not the Herero country was their objective. They were countenanced by the British official at Walfish Bay and in February 1879 entered Omaruru, a Rhenish station that had been founded since the war, saying they wished to establish here a base for their proposed work farther north. To that there was offered no objection. But when they sought to establish themselves there with school and church the opposition was determined. When Hogan visited Maharero at Okahandja to secure permission to settle it was refused; and more, Maharero ordered the Omaruru chief to turn the fathers out. But they hung on until at last they were ejected by force in September 1881, with a consequent outcry at Herero barbarity and Protestant intolerance.[1]

The ever-extending eastern frontier of the Cape Colony had reached the Kei River by 1866 when British Kaffraria was annexed.[2] The population was sparse at two persons to the square mile.[3] Here were Dutch Reformed, Moravians, London Mission, Wesleyan Methodists, Scottish Presbyterians, German Lutherans, Anglicans and Roman Catholics all more or less busy with more or less tolerance for one another.

The Moravians, who will always hold pride of place as missionary pioneers, were quietly and faithfully maintaining their existing work. A distinguished visitor, Lady Duff Gordon, was at the Cape in 1861–62, and her forthright accounts and skilful delineation offer a valuable contemporary picture. She visited Genadendal and was charmed by the Moravian settlement as was Lady Anne Barnard more than half a century before. There were some 3,000 to 4,000 people all told. When she went to the church "the perfect ear and heavenly voices of a large congregation, about six hundred, all coloured people, made music more beautiful than any chorus-singing I ever heard".[4]

---

[1] Driessler, *op. cit.*, 99, 124–5; Viehe, "Die römischen Missionare in Hereroland und ihre Ausweisung", in *Allgemeine Missions-Zeitschrift*, IX (1882), 66–85; *Cath. Ency.*, IV (1908), 611.

[2] Walker, *History*, 314.

[3] An area of 250,000 square miles inhabited by 496,381 people, of whom some 314,000 were non-European.—*London Missionary Society: Principles and Plans*, letter to the Missionaries in South Africa (1869), 76.

[4] D. Fairbridge, *Letters from the Cape by Lady Duff Gordon* (1927), 101–10; cf. 98–101. This is the first edition to print the letters as they were written. They had already been published in 1864, 1875 and 1921, but in a bowdlerized version. Lady Duff Gordon was a shrewd observer, remarkably free from racial or religious prejudice.

The Directors of the London Missionary Society, with pressing needs besieging them, decided to re-group their forces, and in 1868 forwarded relevant proposals to their missionaries in South Africa. The stations within the Colony were to be reduced to fourteen with an equivalent missionary staff in lieu of the nineteen then in service. This they regarded as generous in view of the population to be served.[1] In 1877 the Congregational Union, Church Aid and Missionary Society of South Africa was constituted, having as its object the establishment and support of churches and missions of the Congregational order in the country. It federated Congregational churches in South Africa, whether under London Mission or American Board auspices.[2]

The principal Wesleyan Methodist work was to be found in the eastern province of the Cape at Grahamstown and beyond, with a series of stations in British Kaffraria that had suffered heavily in repeated frontier wars. An outstanding event in this period was the visit in 1866 of William Taylor, when a remarkable revival of religion took place that transformed the missionary scene. He was an evangelist of considerable experience. As a minister of the Methodist Episcopal Church of the United States he had been in 1848 appointed a missionary to California.[3] He reached San Francisco in September 1849 after a voyage from Baltimore round Cape Horn of 155 days. The California gold rush was now on and San Francisco was a city of tents. He served for six years in California in the hard-bitten mining communities and won their profound respect. The conception of world-wide evangelization laid hold of him, and after a visit to Canada he was in 1862 outward bound to Australia where he spent some three years in evangelistic missions. From there he came by clipper to South Africa.[4] The Wesleyan ministers welcomed him: "His unassuming manners, his scrupulous delicacy in abstaining from any interference in local church affairs, his shrewd observations, and his intense devotion, won their affection, and they honoured the gifts of God in him."[5] The beginnings at Cape Town, Port Elizabeth, and

[1] *Missionary Principles and Plans* (1869), 76–8. For the relevant official resolutions, see 85–6. The total number of London Society missionaries in all South Africa at this time was thirty-five.

[2] Beach and Fahs, *World Missionary Atlas* (1925), 54.

[3] The decision of the General Conference to begin a mission was taken before the discovery of gold early in 1848 was made known.—C. G. Moore (ed.), *William Taylor of California, An Autobiography* (1897), 58.

[4] *Ibid.*, 56–61, 78–138, 158–207.

[5] J. Whiteside, *History of the Wesleyan Methodist Church of South Africa* (1906), 265.

Uitenhage were disappointing. At Grahamstown signs of the coming revival appeared. At King William's Town the ideal interpreter was discovered—Charles Pamla of Annshaw, an African candidate for the Methodist ministry. Together the two evangelists plunged into the work, visiting among others the stations of Kamastone, Butterworth, Clarkebury, Morley, Buntingville, Shawbury, and Osborn. Their itinerary was prolonged into Natal. It was estimated that all told some 6,000 Africans were won for the faith. A fresh wind had swept over the land. The effects were not evanescent. It is acknowledged that the revival of 1866 "marks the beginning of a distinct era in the history of the Methodist Church in South Africa".[1] A literary contribution of some note was the Xhosa version of the Bible by J. W. Appleyard, Wesleyan missionary in Kaffraria, published in 1865. The version was subject to considerable criticism in which Tiyo Soga was severe and Lovedale apparently took the lead.[2] As a result a translation committee representative of various Societies was appointed, of which Appleyard was a member, which in due course produced a standard version. Nevertheless it is said that " 'Appleyard's Version' remains to this day a favourite version of many of the Xhosa-speaking people."[3]

The South African mission of the Free Church of Scotland had, in its Institution at Lovedale, initiated a notable if somewhat limited training centre. Alexander Duff, when returning from Calcutta in 1864, visited Lovedale and from this much followed. In 1867 James Stewart, who had been with Livingstone on the Zambezi for some months and had since graduated in medicine, was appointed to the Lovedale staff. But it was not quite as innocent as that, for he was the bearer of instructions from the Home Committee, some of which had to do with a change of policy for the Institution. William Govan, who was still Principal, urged the maintenance of the existing policy. In

[1] Findlay and Holdsworth, *History of the Wesleyan Methodist Missionary Society*, IV (1922), 289–91; *Wesleyan Missionary Notices*, XIV (1867), 1–31; J. Whiteside, *op. cit.*, 263–78; C. G. Moore (ed.), *op. cit.*, 208–9; W. Taylor, *Christian Adventures in South Africa* (1867), *passim*.

[2] *The Kafir Bible. Rev. J. W. Appleyard's Version. Judged by Missionaries of Various Denominations and Others* (1866); J. W. Appleyard, *An Apology for the Kafir Bible*, being a Reply to the pamphlet entitled, etc. (1867). Appleyard had already published *The Kafir Language: comprising a Sketch of its History . . . and a Grammar*, pp. xxii+390 (1850).

[3] R. H. W. Shepherd, *Lovedale, South Africa, The Story of a Century, 1841–1941* (1940), 145.

1869 the Committee, of which Duff was now Convener, asserted its choice between the conflicting alternatives: "Whether it should be the aim of the Seminary to give such an education as will attract Europeans as well as Natives, and place Native pupils on the same educational level as European pupils, while seeking to impart to the whole a Christian tone and direction, or whether it should be the aim of the Seminary directly to meet the need of general as well as Christian instruction which prevails among the Natives by making Christian truth the central subject of instruction and seeking to train up Native preachers and Native teachers? With the alternative before them the Committee decide in favour of the latter."[1] There was no doubt of the meaning of the decision and Govan resigned, handing over the reins to Stewart. It was said that most of the missionaries approved of Govan's policy, but there was no ill will, and Govan himself stated there was no one to whom he could hand over the work—work over which he had presided from the start—with such confidence as to James Stewart. With his principalship a great expansion took place—student enrolment rose in four years from 92 to 480—and Lovedale was fairly launched on its now familiar career.[2] In 1877 the educational centre of Blythswood, named after the magistrate, Captain Blyth, who transmitted the request for it, was opened in the Transkei, thanks to remarkable African generosity.[3]

The Dutch Reformed Church of South Africa[4] maintained certain mission work within Cape Colony which was known as the Inland Mission. An event that considerably increased its efficiency was the setting up in 1877 of a Training School for Missionaries at Wellington. It owed its inception to Andrew Murray, the saintly minister who was a notable accession from Scotland to the Dutch Reformed Church of the Cape. As this was originally a private undertaking, the financial support was not guaranteed, and Andrew Murray gave liberally of his personal means to maintain it.[5]

The Anglican Church in South Africa suffered some severe stresses and strains in this period, and Bishop Gray was involved in difficult litigation. The two cases of note were those of

[1] Shepherd, *op. cit.*, 160.
[2] *Ibid.*, 163–5; Du Plessis, *op. cit.*, 361.
[3] Shepherd, *op. cit.*, 179–81; J. Stewart, *Dawn in the Dark Continent* (1906), 196–201.
[4] This title applies to the Church of the Cape alone, and dates from the time before the appearance of the Orange Free State and the Transvaal. In these the above title is followed by the name of the province.
[5] Du Plessis, *op. cit.*, 290–3.

W. Long, a clergyman of his own diocese, and of Bishop Colenso of Natal, which will be noticed in connexion with that colony. The case of W. Long arose out of Gray's initiative in setting up a diocesan Synod in 1857. Both this Synod and a second called in 1861 Long declined to recognize as legal. He was thereupon suspended by the bishop. Long applied to the Supreme Court of the Cape where the case was heard in 1861. Gray made his defence in person, affirming that his suspension of Long was not tied up with the question of the legality of Synods but was the result of his refusal to acknowledge the authority of his bishop. Gray won his case. It was carried to the Privy Council, and there he lost it. The judgment was delivered on June 24, 1863. "The bishop said truly that the judgment would lead to strifes which would not end in his time, nor have they ended in ours."[1]

The self-denying devotion with which Robert Gray served his diocese and the vast region for which he was Metropolitan, together with his unflinching loyalty to the truth as he saw it, can be denied by none. He spent himself utterly in the service and died at Cape Town on September 1, 1872. There was some delay in the selection of a successor. Finally William West Jones was appointed. He was consecrated on May 17, 1874 and arrived at Cape Town on August 31. He was to give thirty-four years' service to South Africa at a critical period of the country's development, being created archbishop in 1897. When Gray had begun there was one diocese with fourteen clergy. West Jones found six dioceses, and 127 clergy serving in them.[2]

The Muslim Malays of Cape Town had been the concern of certain Anglican clergy from 1823, and the Cape Malay Mission was the result. In this Gray took much interest. But before 1870, on the initiative of a member of the Legislative Council, a religious teacher was sent from Constantinople, at the Sultan's ex-

[1] Lewis and Edwards, *Historical Records of the Church of the Province of South Africa* (1934), 157. For a summary statement of the arguments involved, see *Ibid.*, 147–57; and for Gray's own version of events, C. Gray, *Life of Robert Gray* (1876), I, 472–536; II, 577–91. A sidelight on the situation in general as a visitor saw it is provided by Lady Duff Gordon, writing in March, 1862: "The English Bishop of Capetown appoints all the English clergy, and is absolute monarch of all he surveys; and he and his clergy are carrying matters with a high hand. . . . All the physicians in a body, English as well as Dutch, have withdrawn from the Dispensary, because it was used as a means of pressure to draw the coloured people from the Dutch to the English Church. . . . The colonial bishops are despots in their own churches, and there is no escape from their tyranny but by dissent. The Admiral and his family have been anathematized for going to a fancy bazaar given by the Wesleyans for their chapel."—Fairbridge, *op. cit.*, 140–1.

[2] Lewis and Edwards, *op. cit.*, 113–16; H. Moore, *The Land of Good Hope* (1911), 176.

pense—a certain Abou Bekr—to teach the Malays more precisely the tenets of Islam. With East African developments, steamers began to ply between Cape Town and Zanzibar and this gave a fillip to pilgrimage to Mecca. The pilgrims on their return gave some stiffening to believers, Muslim schools were opened, and a new feeling of brotherhood was experienced among the Malays, with the result that conversions to Christianity practically ceased. Gray wrote of the situation in his last year: "I have nearly come to the conclusion that I shall never do much for the Malays except through a Brotherhood." West Jones had an equal concern for this mission. It was estimated that by 1875 one-fifth of the population of Cape Town was Muslim, and other centres were receiving an increasing number. West Jones was fortunate in securing J. M. Arnold who had had missionary experience in North Africa, India, and Java, and was well equipped for the work, to take charge of it. Arnold found himself working in 1876 among some 8,000 Muslims. He worked with success, and baptisms were soon on the increase.[1]

In the episcopal interregnum between Robert Gray and West Jones a new diocese appeared on the South African scene, that of St. John's, Kaffraria. The first bishop was Henry Callaway, consecrated in 1873, not only a missionary of twenty years' service but also ranking as a distinguished Zulu scholar. As early as March 1872 he had been approached: "They have been speaking to me of being bishop of a diocese that is to be created if possible for Kaffraria. But I have no idea that it would be right to leave my present work. I have taken root and should not transplant well, unless God transplants me with His Own Hand. There is a great deal to do which seems cut out for me."[2] As soon as he had reached his decision, with characteristic thoroughness he set out to survey the land and reported the size of the diocese as rather larger than Scotland, the population as some 600,000 of whom only 2,500 were Europeans, and the principal tribal units to be Pondos, Galekas, Fingoes, Griquas, and Hottentots. He settled in Pondoland about fifteen miles from the St. John's River which gave the diocese its name. The Scottish Episcopal Church had taken the new diocese under its wing.[3]

[1] Lewis and Edwards, *op. cit.*, 95–99. Lady Duff Gordon made some interesting contacts with the Muslim Malays of Cape Town.—Fairbridge, *op. cit.*, 41–43, 59–60 (cf. 52–7), 135–6, 139–40.
[2] Lewis and Edwards, *op. cit.*, 365.
[3] M. S. Benham, *Henry Callaway* (1896), 259–62, 267; Lewis and Edwards, *op. cit.*, 534.

In 1847 the Roman Catholic vicariate of the Cape of Good Hope had been divided into western and eastern vicariates. In the western vicariate the Dominican Patrick Raymond Griffith, who had been vicar apostolic of the undivided vicariate, was in 1862 succeeded by Thomas Grimley. Grimley made schools a priority and introduced the Dominican Sisters and the Marist Brothers to the vicariate. In 1869 he could report that in seven years the number of scholars had risen from 80 to 400, and that their schools had become eligible for Government grants.[1] The Protestant strength in the country he found rather a trial, and the activity of the Bishop of Cape Town in both the educational and religious spheres highly regrettable in one devoted to the propagation of heresy.[2] But there were Protestants who abjured their error; in 1865 he had received twenty during Lent.[3] Grimley judged the Protestant missionaries had made a useful contribution in a purely intellectual direction, but had not succeeded at all in moral reform. The Boers were so antagonistic that they refused hospitality to a Roman priest if recognized as such.[4] At the close of Grimley's tenure of office there were eight missionaries besides himself, five Marist Brothers, eight Dominican Sisters, twelve churches built, and a Catholic community of 7,000.[5] When he died in 1871 he was followed as vicar apostolic by John Leonard in 1872, who was to give thirty-five years to the direction of the vicariate.[6]

The central prefecture of the Cape of Good Hope, from 1873 to 1882 in the care of the Missionary Fathers of Lyons,[7] was virtually the northern section of the western vicariate. In 1873 the two pioneers, Gaudeul and Pasquereau, landed at Port Nolloth and made their way up the light railway to the copper mines of Little Namaqualand south of the Orange River. The mining town of Springbok which Grimley had visited in 1869 they found fallen on hard times for the mine had closed down. But in a population of some 250 (100 of them Europeans) there was but a handful of Catholics. However they were just in time

---

[1] *Cath. Ency.*, VI (1909), 645; *Annales de la Propagation de la Foi*, XLII (1870), 242-3.

[2] "Ses catéchistes se sont répandus de tous côtés pour attirer les habitants sous sa prétendue autorité spirituelle. L'Angleterre d'ailleurs lui fournit largement les moyens de propager l'hérésie."—*Annales*, XLII (1870), 238. Gray would scarcely recognize himself in the role assigned him.

[3] *Ibid.*, XXXVII (1865), 481.

[4] *Ibid.*, XLII (1870), 238-9, 239-40.

[5] *Ibid.*, 245.

[6] *Ibid.*, XLV (1873), 141.

[7] La Société des Missions Africaines (de Lyon).

to divert from the Protestant church a marriage from a Catholic family, and even ventured to re-baptize two children to whom the Protestant rite had been administered.[1] They made contact with neighbouring settlements where mines were working: Ookiep with 1,500 population, Concordia with 400 (a handful of Catholics here), and Spectakel with 100 people only. Farther north lay Pella on the Orange River, the one-time station of the London Mission, but now abandoned.[2] Grimley had the idea of a settlement in the neighbourhood on the lines of the Jesuit reductions in Paraguay. That particular plan did not material-ize, but the two men, having surveyed the mining villages, decided on Pella and started here the first station of the new mission. A small chapel was ready by Christmas 1874 in which the first mass was celebrated and on January 1, 1875 the image of the Virgin was put in place as they consecrated the first Roman Catholic mission on the banks of the Orange River to Our Lady of the Sacred Heart. Before long ten families had settled around them, Damara, Hottentot, and Griqua.[3] On the withdrawal of the Missionary Fathers of Lyons in 1882, part of the central prefecture became the Orange River prefecture in the care of the Oblates of St. Francis of Sales, while the rest was then incorporated in the western vicariate.[4]

The eastern vicariate, under the guidance of the Irishman Moran who became vicar apostolic in 1856, had, as well as the western, seen schools opened with sisters in charge. Moran wrote in 1865: "After some ten years' experience as vicar of this province I am convinced that to hold our own, let alone ad-vance, in this country, we are dependent above all on our schools."[5] Upon Moran's transfer to New Zealand in 1870 as the first Bishop of Dunedin, he was succeeded in 1872 by Jacques David Ricards who had already seen twenty-two years' service at the Cape. Ricards was responsible for the coming of the Trappists in 1880. He invited Francis Pfanner, Prior of the Trappist (Reformed Cistercian) Monastery in Bosnia to estab-lish a monastery in Cape Colony, with an adaptation of their rule to missionary life. The invitation was accepted and in July 1880 he landed with thirty-one companions at Port Elizabeth. The original site selected proving unsuitable, the party moved

---

[1] Obviously in ignorance of the fact that baptism with serious intent and in the Triune Name, whether by layman or heretic, though irregular, is accounted valid.
[2] See Vol. I, 228.
[3] *Annales*, XLVI (1874), 51–67; XLVII (1875), 305–8.
[4] *Cath. Ency.*, VI, 645.
[5] *Annales*, XXXVII (1865), 481.

into Natal at the request of Jolivet, then vicar apostolic of the vicariate, and settled at Mariannhill some fifteen miles from Durban.[1]

(2) East and West of the Drakensberg

It was in this area of south-eastern Africa that the greatest density of Bantu population was to be found.[2] North-east of the Kei between the Drakensberg and the sea lay a British colony, Natal, flanked by Pondoland and Tembuland to the south and Zululand to the north. Some of the Wesleyan and Anglican activity already recorded had included the still independent Tembu-Pondo territory beyond the Kei. In 1856 Natal had become a Crown Colony distinct from the Cape, with its own Legislative Council three-quarters of whom were elected. British settlers had already been arriving to the tune of some thousands (4,500 in the period 1848–51) as planters on the fertile lands of the Colony. The crops were of the semi-tropical variety—cotton, coffee and sugar, but sugar soon outstripped them all and in the historian's words became king in Natal. But plantations demanded labour and this was not forthcoming in sufficient amount from the reserves. Various proposals, the importation of convicts among them, having been turned down by the Governor, Sir George Grey, there was finally approved a scheme to introduce indentured coolie labour from India. The necessary arrangements having been completed, the first batch arrived at the end of 1860. There were various statutory provisions to secure the Indians from exploitation: among them a three-year term, with an extension to five if desired; then either "a free passage home or Crown land to the value of the passage."[3] As J. H. Hofmeyr once observed: "The ultimate end of this policy was clear from the outset. The coolie was to be welcomed as a permanent settler in the Colony, and as a contribution to its prosperity. The conception of the Indian as a stranger forcing himself upon a reluctant community had not emerged."[4] This introduced not only a new racial strand but new religious elements—Hinduism and Islam. In five years' time there were some 6,500 Indians employed in the Garden Colony. Mean-

[1] Ibid., XLIII (1871), 310–11; Cath. Ency., VI, 645; IX (1910), 661.
[2] W. Fitzgerald, Africa (2nd ed., 1936), 205 (map showing distribution of Bantu population in South Africa in 1921).
[3] Walker, op. cit., 304–5; Ency. Brit. (1947), XVI, 130–1.
[4] Jan H. Hofmeyr, Christian Principles and Race Problems (Hoernlé Memorial Lecture, 1945), 23.

while the European population of 1856, numbering 8,000, was barely doubled in a decade. Land speculators however were busy, allowing squatters rather than cultivators to take up tenancies, so that Walker sums up the situation: "Natal thus came perilously near to being, in the unkind words of John X. Merriman, 'a white forwarding agency in a native territory'."[1]

The missionaries of the American Board, the first to become established in the land, steadily maintained their work among the Zulus in the Colony though there was no spectacular advance. But results were beginning to appear, for in 1858 the Board reported: "Ten years ago there were no churches, and not more than two converts; now, eight churches contain nearly two hundred members." There were at the time twelve stations in operation with thirteen missionaries and their wives on the active list.[2] That there was a vital Christian movement among the churches was evidenced a couple of years later when quite spontaneously, Aldin Grout reported, at the annual meeting in 1859 commemorating the arrival of the first missionaries (a festival of remembrance the Zulu Christians had themselves initiated) the question was raised: How may some of our own number serve as missionaries? It turned out that the African members had already been talking the matter over for two years among themselves. The generous impulse, left fluid in this discussion, was crystallized the following year in the formation of a Home Missionary Society. The acid test, as some would say, of the reality of their intentions was demonstrated by the gift at the foundation meeting of £31 17s. od.[3]

Daniel Lindley, one of the original band that arrived in 1835, had returned from his ministry among the Boers and in June 1847 resumed missionary work among the Zulus, this time in the recently demarcated Inanda location, to the immediate north-west of Durban. Here the remainder of his missionary career was spent. After ten years at Umzinyati, the first Inanda centre, he removed in 1857 to a more fertile area, for there were now seventeen Christian families on the station and the ambitious younger men wanted better land to plough. But the cost of removal was a difficulty. Sir George Grey heard of Lindley's quandary and said: "Remove. What will it cost you?" It turned out to be £100. "Make out a statement of the case and if I find

---

[1] Walker, *op. cit.*, 306. A concise account of Natal in the 'fifties will be found in E. W. Smith, *The Life and Times of Daniel Lindley* (1949), 310–14.
[2] *The Missionary Herald* (A.B.C.F.M.), LIV (1858), 3.
[3] *Ibid.*, LVI (1860), 34; LVII (1861), 34.

I have the money I will give you that amount." Lindley was deeply gratified: "I was prepared to expect liberal things from his Excellency, but not exactly such generosity as this."[1] Alexander Duff, who as we have seen visited Lovedale on his way from India in 1864, was also a guest of the American Board in Natal. Here too his championship of the educational weapon in missionary enterprise stimulated the missionaries to put into operation schemes already contemplated. An Institution for boys, adequate to preparing Zulu teachers, was begun at Aman-zimtote, while a Girls' Seminary was started in Inanda. This was a courageous move in the mid-'sixties with the American Civil War having a constricting effect on funds from the States. Thanks to colonial generosity these two institutions were set upon their way. The Seminary at Inanda opened its doors in 1869 and nineteen Zulu girls trooped in, described affection-ately by Lindley as "black, dirty little angels". The next year there were thirty, ranging in age from eight to sixteen, some described by Lindley as "pet daughters in important families". That it set a high educational standard is indicated by what colonists said of it, as Lindley reported them: "The white people who come along express a wish that the white girls could have the privilege of attending such a school. Some say outright that it is too good for Kafirs."[2]

In 1869 the American Board called attention to its aim of planting self-supporting and self-governing churches, with a ministry springing from the Christians of the land. Nathaniel Clark, Secretary of the Board, suggested that steps should be taken to select and ordain Zulu pastors for seven churches of the mission. Lindley welcomed the proposal but not so his more conservative colleagues. Nevertheless by 1873 there had been six such ordinations. Of these men the most outstanding was James Dube who in December 1870 became minister of the Inanda church to Lindley's genuine delight. The churches planted by the missionaries were now becoming rooted in Zulu soil.[3]

The work of the Wesleyan Church in Natal had begun in ser-vice to the European community. From 1850 it made consider-able strides for a number of the British immigrants were Methodists, among them lay preachers and class leaders who

[1] E. W. Smith, *op. cit.*, 271, 314–15.
[2] *Ibid.*, 382–3, 385–6.
[3] *Ibid.*, 396–403; *The Missionary Herald*, LXXV (1879), 240. James Dube died in 1877. His son, John L. Dube, became a distinguished Zulu minister.

served the expanding Church. Thus it was that in 1855 it was possible to organize the Natal District of the Church as a self-contained unit. The work of William Taylor and Charles Pamla had extended to Natal in 1866, Pamla undertaking most of the work among African congregations. The result was an addition of 500 members to the Church. Traceable to the revival was a spontaneous movement among the African Christians named *Unzondelelo*, a term signifying zeal or desire, and designed for active evangelism among the Zulu kraals. By 1878 it had become organized as the "Wesleyan Native Home Mission". The Indian coolie community was not overlooked and Ralph Stott, with eighteen years' missionary experience and equipped with Tamil and Hindustani, was transferred to Natal to commence the Indian Mission in 1862. He laboured—and the term is justified—for eighteen years amidst his Asian community with scant result.[1]

The Anglican diocese of Natal had been set up in 1853 with J. W. Colenso as its first bishop. He had been Second Wrangler, Prizeman and the holder of a Fellowship at St. John's, Cambridge. He was a forceful personality with independent views that created problems for the Church. He early came to the conclusion that polygamists who had entered into their matrimonial engagements before knowing the Christian demand in marriage should not be asked to dissolve all of these save one, but admitted to baptism as they were. This was a view at variance with almost universal mission practice.[2] His theological views as stated in sermons and in particular in a *Commentary on the Epistle to the Romans* (1861) caused grave concern to the orthodox within the Anglican Church in South Africa, and it was primarily on these views that the charges laid against him were based.[3] In the realm of Biblical scholarship he propounded the view, original in his day, that the internal evidence of the

---

[1] Findlay and Holdsworth, *op. cit.*, IV, 294, 295–6; Whiteside, *op. cit.*, 366–7; Du Plessis, *op. cit.*, 300–2.

[2] G. W. Cox, *The Life of John William Colenso, Bishop of Natal* (1888), I, 63–7. The first authoritative Anglican ruling on the subject was given at the Lambeth Conference in 1888 when it was decided that a polygamist might be received as a catechumen but not be baptized, while the baptism of the wives of polygamists was permissive.—*World Missionary Conference, 1910*, II (The Church in the Mission Field), 321–3.

[3] Lewis and Edwards, *op. cit.*, 161–3; Cox, *op. cit.*, I, 128–70, 703–4; C. Gray, *op. cit.*, II, 21–31; A. T. Wirgman, *Life of James Green, Dean of Maritzburg* (1909), I, 36–74, 104–27. Colenso did not share the High Church view of sacramental efficacy; he wrote to Gray (7.8.61): "You have long been aware that I do not agree with those who hold what is called the sacramental system, and that I regard their views as unsound and unscriptural."—Cox, *op. cit.*, I, 703.

Pentateuch was inconsistent with Mosaic or even unity of authorship, and in other respects he adopted a critical attitude (in the technical sense of the term) towards the literature of the Old Testament. These views were expounded in his *The Pentateuch and the Book of Joshua Critically Examined* which appeared in 1862.[1] Gray, who had hoped that the English bishops might not only express disapprobation but bring to trial, was left to take action himself. The Court of the Metropolitan found all the charges proved and sentenced Colenso to be deposed from the office of bishop and prohibited from the exercise of any ministerial office within the Province. Execution was deferred, but on May 1, 1864 the Metropolitan's sentence of deposition was ordered to be read in all the churches of the Natal diocese.[2] Colenso appealed to the Privy Council whose Judicial Committee gave judgment on March 20, 1865 concluding that "the proceedings taken by the Bishop of Cape Town and the judgment or sentence pronounced by him against the Bishop of Natal are null and void in law."[3] In December 1865 Gray resorted to the extreme step of excommunication.[4] Colenso applied to the Supreme Court of Natal for control of all existing Church property, as himself the legal trustee, and his contention was upheld.[5] As in the Metropolitan's eyes Natal was now without a bishop, a successor was sought and only with difficulty secured. Finally W. K. Macrorie, the fifth to whom the see had been offered, accepted the difficult appointment and was consecrated at Cape Town in January 1869, and in February entered Natal with the style of Bishop of Maritzburg.[6] As he was legally denied the use of the existing cathedral he had to consecrate another. Meanwhile Colenso continued at his original residence at Ekukanyeni (the house of light) until his death in 1883. But there still remained those who were loyal to what he had taught them, and not until 1910 was the breach in the diocese of Natal finally healed.[7]

This rift in relations, persisting for half a century though with

[1] Lewis and Edwards, *op. cit.*, 163–4; Cox, *op. cit.*, I, 481–696. The "People's Edition" was published in 1875.

[2] Lewis and Edwards, *op. cit.*, 167–70, 319; Gray, *op. cit.*, II, 70–105, 638–40; Wirgman, *op. cit.*, I, 149–56; Cox, *op. cit.*, I, 272–327.

[3] Lewis and Edwards, 170–2; Gray, II, 191–2, 641–50; Wirgman, I, 168; Cox, I, 259–63; E. A. Walker, *Lord de Villiers and his Times* (1925), 29–30.

[4] Lewis and Edwards, 173; Gray, II, 248; Wirgman, I, 208. The sentence of excommunication was published in Maritzburg, January 7, 1866.

[5] Lewis and Edwards, 173; Cox, II, 116–22.

[6] Lewis and Edwards, 329. On the effect of these events on support from the S.P.G., see C. F. Pascoe, *Two Hundred Years of the S.P.G.* (1901), I, 331–2.

[7] Lewis and Edwards, 354.

diminishing effect, was inevitably a heavy handicap on the
Christian witness of the Anglican Church. Nevertheless there
was good missionary work done, the outstanding contribution
being made by Henry Callaway, called in 1873 to be the first
Bishop of St. John's, Kaffraria. He had for some years been a
member of the Society of Friends and on return to the Anglican
Church was appointed to Natal in 1853. He had already graduated in medicine and was now ordained. When he found fellow
missionaries rather despondent about their work, he traced their
lack of success to their ignorance of the Zulu language.[1] He at
once concentrated upon its study with excellent results. With
this essential instrument at his disposal he was able to embark
upon a scientific study of Zulu social customs, historical traditions, and religious beliefs which he did to such good effect that
his writings on these subjects are still authoritative.[2] He resisted
Colenso's conclusions regarding the baptism of polygamists,
adopting the position later endorsed by the Lambeth Conference of 1888.[3] He also translated into Zulu various Bible portions, though missionaries of the American Board had already
been active in this field.[4] He displayed an ecumenical spirit in
church relations by no means revealed in all his contemporaries.
He advised against a mission institution at Maritzburg, assign-
ing as one reason "the fact that the Wesleyans have occupied
the ground before us, and I think it very undesirable to present
rival institutions to the Kaffirs".[5] Later as bishop he declared to
his Synod in 1875: "We must allow the principle that wherever
we see the fruits of the Spirit we must refer them to the work of
the Spirit, and acknowledge, not theoretically only but practically, that from Him, and from Him alone, proceed 'all holy
desires, all good counsels, and all just works'. On this principle
we shall be able to rejoice at any good work done, though not

---

[1] Colenso was a distinguished exception here. He produced textbooks in Zulu
required for the schools and also compiled a small-scale grammar: *First Steps in
Zulu: being an Elementary Grammar of the Zulu Language* (156 pp., 2nd ed., 1871). He
was also responsible for some Biblical translation: Genesis, Exodus, Samuel, and
the whole of the New Testament.—Lewis and Edwards, *op. cit.*, 161. The Zulu-
English Dictionary, his most important work, was published in 1861.

[2] Notably *The Religious System of the Amazulu* (1870), offered in the Zulu text,
with translation and annotations; reprinted by the Folk Lore Society (1884).

[3] *Vide supra*, p. 262, *n* 2; M. S. Benham, *Henry Callaway* (1896), 134–45.

[4] The American missionaries, who were the first to provide Zulu with a written
form, had translated portions of the Old and New Testaments from 1846 to 1868.
In 1872 the revised New Testament appeared and in 1883 the whole Bible. Callaway translated Psalms (1871), the Prophets (1872), Genesis to Joshua (1871–5),
the Gospels (1877). All were printed and published locally.—E. M. North, *The
Book of a Thousand Tongues* (1938), 354.

[5] Lewis and Edwards, *op. cit.*, 358.

done by ourselves, and outside our own Church, and it may even be in ways we do not think desirable."[1] He was concerned that an African ministry should be encouraged, laying greater stress on ability to minister to the spiritual needs of their countrymen than on a high standard of western education. Before he left his Zulu people he had the joy of seeing ordained in 1871 the first two candidates, men whom he had personally prepared. It was to be 1880 before St. Alban's College appeared and still later before a theological department was provided.[2] The Anglican mission to the Indians in Natal was also a late arrival, H. F. Whittington, versed in Tamil, being the pioneer in 1878, but it was 1883 before the work was organized on a permanent basis by L. P. Booth.[3]

The Mission Board of the Church of Sweden sent its first missionary to South Africa, O. Witt, in 1876; he was at first associated with Bishop Schreuder. The original purpose to enter Zululand was foiled by the outbreak of war, so in 1878 the first station was begun in Natal, near the Zululand border by the Blood River, tributary of the Tugela, and named Oscarsberg in honour of King Oscar of Sweden. It was not until 1888 that Zululand was at last entered and the first station set up at Ekutuleni.[4]

The Roman Catholic vicariate apostolic of Natal was erected in 1850 with Allard as the first vicar apostolic. He was succeeded in 1874 by Charles Jolivet of the Oblates of Mary Immaculate, the Oblate Fathers having arrived in Natal in 1851.[5] Jolivet was an energetic director of the mission and by 1877 had in Maritzburg a convent of the Sisters of the Holy Family with boarding school, primary school, and home of refuge, with the promise of an orphanage to follow. The Catholics, he affirmed, had outstripped both the Government of Natal and Protestant Missions in their educational provision, but he only claimed one third of their enrolment as Catholic.[6]

North of the Tugela, northern boundary of Natal, lay independent Zululand. Here Cetshwayo was king, having established himself in 1856 as heir-apparent and real ruler of the nation after a sharp contest with his rival and succeeding on his father's

[1] Benham, *op. cit.*, 284–5.
[2] Lewis and Edwards, *op. cit.*, 363, 381–2.
[3] *Ibid.*, 377.
[4] Du Plessis, *op. cit.*, 385–6.
[5] Schmidlin, *Catholic Mission History*, 738; *Annales*, XLVII (1875), 149–50.
[6] *Annales*, XL (1878), 411.

death in 1872. H. P. S. Schreuder of the Norwegian Missionary Society had already been permitted to start work in the country, and the Hermannsburgers, thanks to his introduction, had also been admitted.[1] By the early 'eighties the Norwegians had opened ten stations from the Tugela to the Umfolozi: Umpumulo (1850), Empangeni (1851), Entumeni (1852), Mahlabatini (1860), Eshowe (1861), Inhlazatshe (1862), Imfule (1865), Umbonambi (1869), Hlabisa (1871), Ekombe (1880), and Ungoye (1881).[2] The first baptism on the mission took place on June 6, 1858. The following year six were baptized and early in 1860 another seven. It was an unexpected response after the dry years; missionary Oftebro said: "We are as if in a dream." Within four years there were thirty conversions.[3] In 1866 Schreuder visited Norway and was consecrated in Bergen cathedral the first missionary bishop in the Church of Norway. He now established and supervised a new mission in Madagascar, in addition to his responsibilities in Zululand. New organizational developments by the Society left Schreuder uneasy, and in June 1873 he resigned to the regret of the Society he had served so well. He decided to continue in Zululand and there was formed in Norway a "Committee for the Church of Norway Mission established by Schreuder". He retained the station of Entumeni but the others remained with the Norwegian Missionary Society as did their missionaries. He survived until 1882 but his success was small numerically, the new venture then counting but some seventy members. His earlier achievements with his service of all but forty years, together with his introduction of the Hermannsburg and Swedish Missions to the country, have won for him the title of the apostle of Zululand.[4]

Missionaries under the auspices of the S.P.G. first entered Zululand in 1860 when the station of Kwamagwaza was begun, half-way from the Tugela to the Umfolozi. Robert Robertson, introduced by Colenso, was the founder, with some converts from Natal as the nucleus of the new community. He won the respect of Mpande and Cetshwayo. When Mrs. Robertson died in 1864 under tragic circumstances, Cetshwayo expressed his

---

[1] *Vide supra*, pp. 145–6.

[2] S. Solberg, *Norsk Misjonsatlas* (1944), 21; A. Burgess, *Unkulunkulu in Zululand* (1934), 133, 136, 148, 150, 154; O. G. Myklebust, "Sør Afrika" in *Det Norske Misjonsselskaps Historie*, III (1949), 29–30, 32, 45–6, 59–60, 86.

[3] Burgess, *op. cit.*, 145, 147–8.

[4] *Ibid.*, 152, 154–5, 165, 166. The mission of the Church of Sweden, arriving on the eve of war, was first established in Natal, and only moved into Zululand in 1887. But their establishment took place under the aegis of Bishop Schreuder.— *Vide supra*, p. 265.

sympathy: "*Mfundisi*, we are very sorry; the *insika*[1] of your house has come down." S. M. Samuelson, a Norwegian, joined the mission in 1861 and four years later opened the second station some twenty-four miles from Kwamagwaza and called St. Paul's. Here was won the convert Umfezi who narrowly escaped death for the faith and had for a time to flee the country. Endhlozane (1873), St. Andrew's (1874), and The Komati (1874) were further stations begun before the Zulu War. Meanwhile in 1869 the Bishop of Maritzburg had been given episcopal care of the Zululand mission and steps had at once been taken to create a missionary bishopric for the field. T. E. Wilkinson was consecrated bishop in 1870 and for five years supervised the work. It was reported that Cetshwayo declined to receive Wilkinson as more than a rank-and-file missionary, there being already a "Bishop of Zululand" in Schreuder.[2] On Wilkinson's retirement in 1875 there was, unhappily for the mission, a lengthy interregnum before Douglas McKenzie was appointed his successor in 1880. By then the Zulu War was over and a new political situation had supervened.[3]

Zululand, as an independent state based on a military régime, could not well be expected to offer the open door to Christian missions. As in Dahomey where similar conditions prevailed, the missionaries might busy themselves with good works always provided they did not baptize converts who would then defy their chief. No *imperium in imperio* would be tolerated, and from the point of view of the king this was not unreasonable. On Cetshwayo's formal accession to power at Mpande's death in 1872 he had made this position clear in conversation with Theophilus Shepstone.[4] Five years later the Zulu chiefs complained to Shepstone's representative: "If a Zulu does anything wrong, he at once goes to a mission station, and says he wants to become a Christian; if he wants to run away with a girl, he becomes a Christian; if he wishes to be exempt from serving the king, he puts on clothes, and is a Christian; if he is an *umtagati* [evil doer], he becomes a Christian. All these people are the subjects of the king; and who will keep a cow for another to milk it? . . . The missionaries desire to set up another power in the land, and as Zululand has only one king that cannot be

---

[1] Centre pole which supports the conical roof of a hut.
[2] Colenso to Domville, 4.12.70.—Cox, *op. cit.*, II, 238.
[3] Pascoe, *op. cit.*, I, 335–9; Lewis and Edwards, *op. cit.*, 654, 656, 661–4; E. & H. W., *Soldiers of the Cross in Zululand* (1906), ix, 8–27.
[4] Reported in Pascoe, *op. cit.*, I, 339; and see below, p. 268 *n.*

allowed."[1] It seemed clear that the missionaries could not carry their point of liberty to convert, without external political interference in their interest, and this the British authorities were naturally unwilling to undertake.[2] There was undoubtedly persecution of converts, and the threat to kill was on occasion carried out, but there seems little doubt that such cases—and the evidence suggests they were few—led to exaggerated statements which, coming back to Cetshwayo, did not ease an already difficult situation.[3]

Into the somewhat intricate political situation that lay behind the Zulu War of 1878–79, it is unnecessary to enter here. Suffice it to say that in 1877 Sir Bartle Frere had arrived in South Africa to carry through a proposed confederation but Shepstone's sudden move in April 1877 in annexing the Transvaal queered the pitch. A disputed claim to the Blood River territory abutting on the eastern frontier of the Transvaal was submitted to arbitration, Cetshwayo consenting. Frere, anticipating a decision adverse to the Zulus, was prepared with troops. The award was in favour of the Zulu claims. Frere could not ignore it, but he "accompanied the promulgation of the award with an ultimatum which virtually applied to the Zulus the principles of disarmament he was already applying to the coast tribes." The time limit expired without Zulu submission, and four columns of troops invaded Zululand on January 11, 1879. In ten days' time 800 of them, not to mention African auxiliaries, were wiped out at the battle of Isandhlwana. It was a major military disaster. Cetshwayo was not taken till August 28 in the same year. He was restored to a shadow of his

[1] Quoted from Parliamentary Papers (C. 1961, p. 47) by Colenso and Durnford, *History of the Zulu War and its Origin* (2nd ed., 1881), 181–2.

[2] Shepstone's record of conversation with Cetshwayo in 1872, runs: "The result of our conversations on the subject of the missionaries was an understanding that those who were already in the country should not be interfered with, and that, if any of them committed an offence for which the offender might be considered deserving of expulsion, the case should be submitted to the Government of Natal, and its assent be received before the sentence should be carried out. It is necessary to explain that the Zulus have no idea of inflicting any punishment upon a missionary except that of expulsion from the country. I did not consider it wise to attempt to make any arrangements in favour of native converts."—Quoted from Parliamentary Papers (C. 1137, p. 19) by Colenso and Durnford, *op. cit.*, 181.

[3] On the question of authentic cases, see Colenso (ed.), *Cetshwayo's Dutchman* (1880), 178; Colenso and Durnford, *op. cit.*, 188–90. On the general question of the status of missionaries in Zululand, represented from different angles, see J. E. Carlyle, *South Africa and its Mission Fields* (1878), 250–9; Cox, *op. cit.*, II, 685–9 (Appendix E); Colenso and Durnford, *op. cit.*, 180–90.

former kingdom in 1883, but only survived a year.[1] Mission stations had disappeared in the general conflagration, but with the post-war settlement the work was gradually resumed.[2]

West of the Drakensberg lay Basutoland and the Orange Free State. In Basutoland, which the French missionaries by a quarter of a century's devoted service had made their own, shrewd Moshesh was still at the helm, needing all his wisdom to pilot his country safely through the political quicksands of south-eastern Africa. When J. H. Brand became President of the Free State in 1864 he sought the help of Philip Wodehouse, now Governor of the Cape, to settle the disputed frontier with Basutoland, for the Basuto were renewing their claims to land lost them by the Warden Line award. Wodehouse however practically confirmed the Warden Line. This left dissatisfaction which broke into war in 1865. The Free State commandos eventually gained control and by the Treaty of Thaba Bosiu of April 1866 peace was restored but at the price to the Basuto of considerable annexations. The French missionaries were thereupon expelled by the Free State Volksraad (Brand dissenting) from the conquered territory. The unrelenting terms of the Boer victors soon led to a stiffening of resistance and war broke out again, Moshesh repudiating the Treaty accepted under duress. This turn of events resulted in the direct annexation of Basutoland by Wodehouse in 1868 in response to Moshesh's own desire and to the chagrin of the Free State. By the Second Treaty of Aliwal North of February 1869 the territory in dispute was apportioned between the belligerents. In December 1869 the Imperial Government ratified the agreement.[3] "Three months later the aged Chief of the Mountain died. But he had lived long enough to save his people from being 'broke up as the Hottentots were'."[4] The rest of the story of political relations is soon told. In 1871, with new developments in South Africa, Basutoland was annexed by the Cape; though rule from Cape

[1] Walker, *A History of South Africa*, 370–1, 380, 383–4; *Lord de Villiers and his Times*, 137–8; Colenso and Durnford, *op. cit.*, 198–398; A. T. Bryant, *Olden Times in Zululand and Natal* (1929), 680–1.

[2] Pascoe, *op. cit.*, 339–40; Colenso and Durnford, *op. cit.*, 400 and *n*.

[3] Walker, *History of South Africa*, 321, 325–6, 327–9, 332.

[4] *Ibid.*, 332. Lagden's comment is equally definite: "It would be idle to deny, taking all circumstances into consideration, that the Free State at one time gained such complete ascendancy over Basutoland as almost to crush it out of existence. But for British intervention in the hour of extremity the Basuto must have been deprived of the cream of their country if not exterminated. Therefore we must regard the Convention of 1869 as a dominating factor in their life."—G. Lagden, *The Basutos* (1909), II, 457–8.

Town was not exactly the Basuto's choice, it was tolerated until unwarrantable interference, as they saw it, took place. In 1879 the Cape Government attempted to disarm the Basuto. "The chiefs petitioned the Queen to whom they had given their country, but the handing in of guns was fixed for April 1880."[1] Thus the War of Disarmament began. But the agreement reached after a year's contest left them with their guns. Again the inevitable upshot was imperial control, and on March 13, 1884 the Basuto received Protectorate status.[2]

It was in such times that the second generation of workers in Basutoland were called to fulfil their missionary vocation. The two outstanding names are those of François Coillard who reached the field in 1858 and Adolphe Mabille who, with his wife Adèle, a daughter of Casalis, arrived in 1860. By 1862 four more recruits had arrived—Paul Germond, Frédéric Ellenberger, Louis Duvoisin, and Émile Rolland—and the second generation was in harness. Four of these (all but Coillard and Rolland) were from Switzerland (Canton de Vaud) and thus for the first time a new national element appeared in the mission with a rather more pronounced Free Church background and the conception of the gathered Christian community.[3] If this preserved them from identifying the Church with the nation, it exposed them to the risk of overlooking the value of the national heritage for any rooting of the faith in the land.

The second period of the mission (1860–84), running up to the date of the British Protectorate, was dominated by the personality of Adolphe Mabille. In more senses than one he was the successor of Thomas Arbousset at Morija.[4] A main concern was the preparation of African evangelists and pastors, and for this purpose a central school was projected. Alexander Duff, during his call at South Africa in 1864, visited the Annual Conference of the Basuto mission and advocated the cause of education in the interests of evangelism.[5] Then again, some more regular assembly of representatives from the churches, to foster their unity of life and purpose, was set afoot, a foreshadowing of the synods that were to be. In the same connexion some codifica-

---

[1] Walker, *op. cit.*, 387.

[2] *Ibid.*, 348, 386–7, 390, 399–400.

[3] "Les anciens missionnaires avaient été parfois tentés de confondre un peu trop l'Église avec la nation. Ce danger n'existait pas pour les nouveaux arrivants; il ne menacera plus jamais la mission."—E. Jacottet, "Histoire de la Mission du Lessouto" in *Livre d'Or de la Mission du Lessouto* (1912), 265.

[4] An exhaustive study of his life and times is presented in E. W. Smith, *The Mabilles of Basutoland* (1939).

[5] *Ibid.*, 134.

tion of disciplinary standards was seen to be desirable, though
the ever-present risk of legalism in the African Church was
apparent here.¹ Just as the promise of these encouraging developments appeared on the horizon the heavy clouds of war
overspread the sky and quickly burst upon the mission. The
war of 1865–68 between the Free State and the Basuto had
broken out. The Boers were instructed to respect mission
life and property and this was observed, but with the cession
of the so-called Conquered Territory the missionaries were
told to leave. True, they were offered residence as farmers
only, but this they naturally declined. The Free State action
created a bad impression outside the country. Seven French
missionaries were conducted out of the territory to Aliwal North
and for two years (1866–68) were in exile from their churches.²
The prospects of the mission were bleak. Then came Wodehouse's intervention and the proclamation on March 12, 1868
of a British Protectorate. The Basuto nation was saved, and
thereby the continuance of the mission assured.³ On the political stage the turning-point had been reached. Troubles
enough still lay ahead but never again would the Boers be able
to work their will upon the nation.

Moshesh lived to see the deliverance but did not long survive
it. In his last months the missionaries found him unusually
responsive to the Christian message. One day he announced he
had become a believer and desired his old missionaries Casalis
and Arbousset to be so informed. His public baptism was
arranged but he died on March 11, 1870 before receiving the
rite. Those who were in touch with him in his last days were
convinced of the reality of his conversion. With his passing there
disappeared a dominant figure from the South African scene.
"For the Basuto", says Edwin Smith, "it was as if the sun had
been blotted from the sky."⁴

During the ensuing decade the country progressed and the
mission prospered. The number of communicants which in 1872
had reached 2,117 was doubled by 1880, while the total of
adult members rose in the same period from 3,502 to 5,984.⁵ In

¹ Jacottet, *op. cit.*, 269, 274–5, 280.
² *Ibid.*, 292–4. "L'État libre n'était plus seulement l'ennemi des noirs, il était
devenu celui de la mission chrétienne." De Kiewiet describes the Free State action
as "a sad blunder".—*British Colonial Policy and the South African Republics* (1929),
192–3.
³ Adèle Mabille wrote of the joyful excitement of that day.—E. W. Smith, *op.
cit.*, 173.
⁴ *Ibid.*, 182–5; Jacottet, *op. cit.*, 314–15.
⁵ Jacottet, *op. cit.*, 329.

1868 Mabille had founded a boys' secondary school which he hoped would provide both schoolmasters and evangelists. It was in 1880 however that the fulfilment of a cherished plan was realized in the Bible School which was to render invaluable service by training African pastors for the African Church.[1]

The provision of a Christian literature was assiduously pursued, and the printing press at Morija developed into a publishing centre of outstanding importance. In Bible translation many collaborated, and by 1878 the publication of the Scriptures in various portions in Basutoland was complete. In 1881 a revised version in one volume was produced by the British and Foreign Bible Society.[2]

Added to the political tangle of the time as an embarrassment of the mission was the entry during the 'sixties and 'seventies of competing missionary agencies seeking the suffrages of the Basuto. In 1862 Bishop Allard and Father Gérard of the Oblates of Mary Immaculate visited the country, a first station named Roma was begun, and both missionaries and Sisters of the Holy Family started work. In 1867 a second was opened at St. Michael and ten years later a third, St. Joseph, was in existence. When Jolivet visited the field in 1877 he celebrated pontifical mass and reported seventy-two adult baptisms on the occasion.[3]

The first Anglican contact was made in 1863 when Edward Twells, first Bishop of the Orange Free State (later styled the diocese of Bloemfontein), visited Moshesh and sought consent to commence a mission. An open-air service was held on the occasion attended by Moshesh and his chiefs.[4] It was not until 1876 however that permanent work began. The French missionaries were perturbed, but Bishop Webb alleged that their Christian teaching was incomplete: "The doctrine of the apostolical succession is set aside by you, and that of the sacraments is enfeebled."[5] John Widdicombe, who was responsible for initiating

---

[1] *Ibid.*, 339–40; E. W. Smith, *op. cit.*, 197, 225.

[2] The collaborators in translation were D. F. Ellenberger, J. Maitin, H. M. Dyke, A. Mabille, S. Rolland, L. J. Cochet, and L. Duvoisin. The revision was undertaken by A. Mabille, D. F. Ellenberger, and D. de Verlen.—E. M. North, *op. cit.*, 310.

[3] Schmidlin, *op. cit.*, 657 and n. 57; *Cath. Ency.*, II, 346; *Annales*, L (1878), 413, 416–17, 418; Jacottet, *op. cit.*, 282–3; E. W. Smith, *op. cit.*, 238.

[4] Lewis and Edwards, *op. cit.*, 395.

[5] *Journal des Missions Évangéliques* (1877), 374, quoted in Du Plessis, *op. cit.*, 356; J. E. Carlyle, *South Africa and its Mission Fields* (1878), 168–74; E. W. Smith, *op. cit.*, 238–9. Mabille, who was deputed to try to dissuade Webb's people from entering, referred to them as Puseyites. Robert Gray reported in 1860: "Recently I have been urged to found a Mission among Moshesh's people. I have replied that if the old chief asks me, and I can do so without interfering with the French Missionaries, I will pledge the Church of England to do so."—Gray, *op. cit.*, I, 457.

the work, made contact with M. Coillard and Father Gérard, and among the half-dozen rules to guide the mission stated that the labours of missionaries already in the country should be respected, that controversy should be avoided, and that no members of other churches under discipline should be received.[1]

In the Orange Free State lying between the Orange and the Vaal the Dutch Reformed Church of the Free State, which had formed a separate synod of its own, in 1874 set up a General Mission Committee, the object of which was stated to be the evangelization of native races. They were to begin at home in the Free State, and later to cross the Zambezi.[2]

The Wesleyan missionaries who had trekked with the Barolong in search of a new home eventually found it in territory subject to Moshesh and set up their headquarters at Thaba Nchu. This station was retained throughout the disturbing times of the 'forties and 'fifties but was not to remain a Wesleyan station only. In 1865 an Anglican mission entered, and when the old chief Moroko died in 1882 the succession was disputed between a Wesleyan and an Anglican. The Free State Government intervened, and as a result absorbed the Barolong territory. In 1851 the Wesleyans entered Bloemfontein and soon spread to other centres.[3]

The Primitive Methodist Missionary Society arrived on the scene in 1870. In response to an invitation from a Mr. Lindsay, then at Aliwal North on the Cape side of the Orange River, the first missionary, Henry Buckenham, began work in the town. He was joined in due course by John Smith who proposed an energetic policy: first, a line of stations through the Colony from Port Elizabeth to Aliwal, and then: "We should go directly to some of the numerous tribes of Eastern Africa, which, as yet, have never been visited by any missionary Society." The response was meagre, so that we find him writing three years later: "If our friends at home cared to extend mission work in Africa we could soon furnish them with a plan, but as they do not sufficiently support the present work, it is useless to write about extension." After ten years' service, with developments to

---

[1] J. Widdicombe, *Fourteen Years in Basutoland* (1891), 75–6; Lewis and Edwards *op. cit.*, 464.
[2] Beach and Fahs, *World Missionary Atlas* (1925), 55; Walker, *op. cit.*, 309–10.
[3] Findlay and Holdsworth, *op. cit.*, IV, 266–7, 331, 328; Du Plessis, *op. cit.*, 300; J. Whiteside, *History of the Wesleyan Methodist Church of South Africa*, 338–42.

report both in the Free State and the Cape, he was the moving spirit in securing a pioneer mission north of the Zambezi.[1]

With the creation of the diocese of Bloemfontein in 1863, founded as the bishopric of the Orange Free State, the Anglican Church entered on an active policy north of the Orange River under the direction of Edward Twells (1863–69) and Alan Becher Webb (1870–83), the first two bishops. It was potentially a vast diocese, extending, despite its name, without definition of boundary west of the Drakensberg and north of the Orange River. Thus Webb included both Basutoland and the Transvaal within his sphere, and Bechuanaland was not overlooked.[2]

Roman Catholic missionaries were in the Free State from 1859, the Oblates of the Immaculate Conception being the first to arrive. When Jolivet visited Bloemfontein in 1877 (his first visit was in 1875), there was a convent of the Sisters of the Holy Family in being and a flourishing boarding-school not long established.[3] When he proceeded to Kimberley in the Diamond Fields (diamonds had first been discovered ten years before) he was received by a cavalcade of 150 mounted men and thus escorted into the mushroom city of tents and huts.[4]

(3) North and South of the Limpopo

In the region between the Vaal and the Zambezi we enter a territory with not so complicated a political background as the area to the south, and with less congestion of missionary effort. Between the Vaal and the Limpopo lay the Transvaal Republic while to the west were the Bechuana tribes and to the north the Mashona and Matebele.

The Dutch Reformed Church of South Africa, Church of the Transvaal, appointed a Mission Committee in 1853, with the evangelization of native races as the declared object. The Transvaal itself naturally became the principal field. The pioneers however entered the country under the auspices of the Dutch Reformed Church of the Cape. They were Henry Gonin, a Swiss, and Alexander McKidd, a Scot, who arrived in South Africa in 1861. Both went to the Transvaal though on separate missions. McKidd went to the Zoutpansberg, an elevated

[1] H. B. Kendall, *The Origin and History of the Primitive Methodist Church* (n.d.), II, 497–8, 502; Thirty-second *Annual Report of the Primitive Methodist Missionary Society* (1875), xxviii; Thirty-fifth *Annual Report* (1878), xxvii.
[2] Lewis and Edwards, *op. cit.*, 391–434; Du Plessis, *op. cit.*, 356–8.
[3] Schmidlin, *op. cit.*, 657 and *n.* 56; *Annales*, L (1878), 421.
[4] *Annales*, L (1878), 421–2.

region in the north-east of the country. He did not live long. Stephanus Hofmeyr of Cape Town then took up his work and served for thirty years among white farmers and Se-Pedi-speaking tribes. Gonin went to the Khatlas on the Bechuana-land border. He was to give forty-five years' devoted service to a tribe that became Christian under his ministry.[1]

The Berlin Missionary Society entered the Transvaal in 1860, and this proved to be its most successful field. In that year Merensky and Grützner arrived at Lydenburg in the eastern Transvaal whence they attempted without success to effect an entry among the Swazis to the south. The Swazi chief wanted firearms, not missionaries, so back they came to Lydenburg.[2] On Boer advice they settled with the tribe of chief Maleo of the Kopas, naming their first station Gerlachshoop.[3] The next year the missionaries Endemann and Nachtigal arrived. This re-leased Merensky to move north to the Pedis among whom the second station was started. In both cases there were distressing developments. Maleo with an ally revolted in 1863 and success-fully defied the Boers, but when the following year a Swazi army fell upon them they were crushed and mangled. In 1865 Gerlaschshoop was abandoned, and the missionaries with the remnant of Kopa survivors trekked south. At the same time the Pedi enterprise came to an end. The chief Sekukuni soon turned violently against the missionaries and their converts at three stations that had been opened. They were banished from the country. They then joined forces with the Kopa survivors and settled on land they had purchased, naming the place Botschabelo (city of refuge). This became a flourishing head-quarters of the mission where a teacher-training centre and industrial departments were developed. By 1876 there were 1,057 baptized residents so that Merensky became in the eyes of the neighbouring tribes himself a chief with his own people, often enough larger than their own. Moreover it was not with any pleasure that local chiefs began to see some of their most industrious and reliable people slip away to Botschabelo on acceptance of the Christian faith.[4] Then a notable expansion of the mission took place: eleven stations were established in the

---

[1] Beach and Fahs, *op. cit.*, 55; Du Plessis, *op. cit.*, 285–6.

[2] Lydenburg had separated in 1856 from the South African Republic, but was united with it again in the year the missionaries arrived.—McCall Theal, *History of South Africa, 1854–72* (2nd ed., 1900), 38, 132.

[3] General von Gerlach, a Director of the Society, had desired work to be started in the Lydenburg district.

[4] J. Richter, *Geschichte der Berliner Missionsgesellschaft, 1824–1924* (1924), 239.

period 1865–70, and in the following decade another twelve—twenty-four head stations in this field alone. They now extended from the urban centres of the south—Pretoria, Lydenburg, Potchefstroom and Heidelburg—to the Vendas in the Zoutpansberg of the north. The Berlin Mission had become the leading mission in the Transvaal.[1]

The Hermannsburg response to Pretorius' invitation in 1857 to send a mission to Sechele's people had been accepted, and Schulenburg established himself among the Ngwatos. But with the coming of a new Superintendent, Hardeland, to the field in 1860 there were personal difficulties; and the northern missionaries were dismissed. The London Mission had meanwhile undertaken work with the tribe. The Hermannsburg mission now worked within the western Transvaal from Pretoria to the frontier. Here Bethany became the leading station among the Kwenas of the district. This field proved more successful than the Zulu. Moreover, the Berlin and Hermannsburg missionaries, working one to the east and the other to the west of Pretoria, proved good neighbours, sharing a common Lutheran tradition.[2]

The Swiss Free Church of the Canton de Vaud that had already supplied workers to the Paris Society in Basutoland now began an independent mission in the Transvaal. In May 1869 two theological students about to complete their studies—Ernest Creux and Paul Berthoud—addressed a letter to the Synod conveying their offer of missionary service. They were accepted and spent a three-year apprenticeship in Basutoland. Early in 1875 they were *en route* to the north, reaching Pretoria in May, and their objective, the Spelonken in the north-eastern Transvaal, two months later.[3] Here two unexpected difficulties awaited them. The first was one of language. They had learned Sesuto in Basutoland, but now found themselves settled among the Magwamba, one of the emigrant colonies in the Transvaal of the Thonga nation.[4] A new language had therefore to be

---

[1] J. Richter, *op. cit.*, 214–26, 233–44; J. E. Carlyle, *South Africa and its Mission Fields* (1878), 272–80.

[2] G. Haccius, *Hannoversche Missionsgeschichte*, II (1907), 330–69.

[3] *Bulletin Missionaire publié par la Commission des Missions de l'Église évangélique libre du canton de Vaud*, I (1872–5), 3–9, 276, 293; E. W. Smith, *The Mabilles of Basutoland*, 215–16.

[4] The Thongas were established around and to the north of Delagoa Bay, on both sides of the Limpopo. Magwamba was the name given to the colony of refugees in the Spelonken by their neighbours, the Vendas. An alternative name for the Thongas used by Europeans is Shangaan.—H. A. Junod, *The Life of a South African Tribe* (2nd ed., 1927), I, 15, 19.

learned. The second obstacle came from the Government. They had settled without any official authorization in writing, and when challenged had no answer officially acceptable. An awkward situation developed and the climax came with the arrest and imprisonment at Marabastad, the Zoutpansberg headquarters, of both Creux and Berthoud for more than a month.[1] Their first station was named Valdezia as reminiscent of the homeland.[2] Here they were speedily at work, including scattered European farms in their ministrations. François Coillard who visited Valdezia in 1877 was delighted with what he found. "Valdezia is for us", he wrote, "the Elim of our journey"—a prophetic forecast, for Elim was the name given to the second head station in 1882.[3] The missionaries had brought with them in 1875 several Basuto helpers; much as these were valued, there was deep satisfaction when in 1879 the first four Gwamba candidates were sent to Morija for training as teacher-catechists under Adolphe Mabille.[4] Valdezia lay just inside the tropics; malaria was therefore to be expected, and in due course they paid the usual price. Within five years the Creux family had lost two children, while Berthoud returned on furlough a widower and childless—all three children having died.[5] In 1882 the Free Churches of Geneva and Neuchâtel approached the Free Church of Vaud with a view to united support of the mission. This was happily achieved in the following year and the name appropriately changed to *Mission Romande au sud de l'Afrique*.[6] In both the Transvaal field and the following extension among the Thongas of Portuguese East Africa its missionaries have made a distinguished contribution to the growth of the Christian Church and have won laurels in linguistic and ethnological studies.[7]

An Anglican clergyman, J. H. Wills, was appointed to Pretoria in 1870 to care for the handful of Anglicans there, while in the same year the Provincial Synod recommended that a bishopric be created for the Transvaal. The annexation of the

[1] From August 2 to September 9, 1876.—*Bulletin Missionnaire*, II (1876–8), 30, 59–60, 99–100, 144. For du Plessis's comment on this official blunder, see du Plessis, *op. cit.*, 332–3.
[2] At the instance of the Committee.—*Bulletin Missionnaire*, II, 144.
[3] *Ibid.*, II, 197–9. The Elim station was originally called Waterfall and was first begun in 1879.—*Ibid.*, IV (1882–3), 6.
[4] *Ibid.*, III, 36–7.
[5] *Ibid.*, III, 149–50.
[6] *Ibid.*, IV, 7, 147–9. The Council's official name was *Conseil de la Mission des Églises libres de la Suisse Romande*.
[7] Notably: H. A. Junod, *The Life of a South African Tribe* (1913, 2nd ed., 1927), an anthropological classic.

republic by Shepstone in 1877 gave a spur to events and in 1878 Henry Brougham Bousfield was consecrated as first Bishop of Pretoria. He began with five clergy widely scattered, for Rustenberg and Lydenburg had rising churches. The retrocession of the country to the Boers in 1881 radically altered the political background, with the result that the status of the diocese changed from colonial to missionary.[1]

With the known attitude of the Boers to Roman Catholicism it was not to be expected that any missionary entry would be permitted in the days of independence. The Roman Catholics in the republic had, however, achieved full civil liberty in 1869 under Pretorius, thanks to his deal with Portugal. That country was involved in the Delagoa Bay controversy with Britain and the Transvaal's support was welcome. A commercial treaty was therefore concluded between the two countries "specially safeguarding the Mozambique trade in slaves and guns", and the new status granted Roman Catholics was an added gesture to please the Portuguese.[2] But with the British annexation in 1877 there was added religious liberty, and Jolivet for one was quick to take advantage of it. He was on the spot at once in 1877 and secured what he described as an excellent site for developments. But it was starting from zero.[3]

Leaving the Transvaal and crossing the Limpopo to the west we enter the territory of Sechele's and Sekhome's peoples, the Kwenas and the Ngwatos. The Transvaal Boers having exercised their power across the ill-defined boundary had succeeded in squeezing out the London missionaries for the time being. Later, at the instance of Pretorius, as we have seen, they had installed the Hermannsburg missionaries in 1859.[4] Owing to internal controversy in the Hermannsburg mission the northern men had later been denied support, so the story went, and Shoshong had in consequence been abandoned. In these circumstances the London Mission decided to resume their connexion with the station, and appointed John Mackenzie, after the failure of the Makololo enterprise, to go there in 1862.

[1] Lewis and Edwards, *op. cit.*, 573–4, 580, 581, 582; C. F. Pascoe, *op. cit.*, I, 354–7.

[2] Walker, *A History of South Africa*, 338 and *n.* 5.

[3] *Annales*, L (1878), 423–5. He reported: "Nous sommes donc libres dans ce beau pays; mais nous n'y avons rien, ni église, ni école, ni même un pied-à-terre. Les rares catholiques sont disséminés un peu partout."

[4] *Vide supra*, pp. 162–3.

Shoshong was an important town with a population of 30,000.[1]
Here Mackenzie was to work for seven years, completing a decade north of the Orange River without a furlough. Roger
Price was a colleague at Shoshong until 1866 when he was
transferred to Sechele's Kwenas.[2] To their surprise Schulenberg
of the Hermannsburg Society turned up soon after their arrival
to resume his work. Happily an amicable arrangement was
arrived at, despite the fact that English Independent Free
Church and German Lutheran State Church were to be in
double harness. They agreed to teach the Christian truths they
held in common, and found the area concerned sufficiently extensive to keep them fully employed. But Schulenberg was soon
recalled.[3]

Life in Shoshong in those days provided its thrilling excitements, not to say grave anxieties. The Ngwatos had succeeded
in keeping free from the Matebele yoke and were liked none
the better for it. The fact that missionaries were now resident in
Matebeleland was not yet a guarantee of peaceful intentions on
the part of Umsiligazi. In 1862 a full-scale Matebele raid
occurred that inspired a good deal of alarm. The people of
Shoshong retired to their retreat in the mountains with the men
under arms and awaited the worst. A skirmishing party of some
strength under Khama, son of Sekhome, attacked the Matebele
and gave them some punishment, but then had to beat a hasty
retreat. The Matebele warriors however remained content with
raiding cattle-posts and did not advance to do battle at the foot
of the mountains. Their retirement was a great deliverance.[4]

An internal crisis occurred in 1865, precipitated by the success of the mission. In connexion with initiation rites as practised among the Ngwatos, each chief surrounded by his sons
would pay a daily visit to the camp where the initiates were in
seclusion. "Proud is the Bechuana father", writes Mackenzie,
"who is surrounded by a number of his sons on these occasions.

[1] The London Mission connexion was a long one. Livingstone had visited the
Ngwatos in 1842 and Robert Moffat in 1855. An African agent had been stationed
there.—J. Mackenzie, *Ten Years North of the Orange River* (1871), 227–8.

[2] *Ibid.*, 423.

[3] Mackenzie says of it: "The London Society never censured us for taking this
step; but I afterwards learned with regret that our friend's conduct had been disapproved of by his superiors. I even heard it hinted by others of his Society that our
colleague was half suspected of having been inoculated during our co-operation
with some of our dangerous 'English views', and I could see that such a catastrophe
as the slightest falling away from inherited Lutheranism would be deeply deplored."
—*Op. cit.*, 250. Cf. Du Plessis, *op. cit.*, 376. Schulenburg retired within the year.—
Mackenzie, *op. cit.*, 265.

[4] Mackenzie supplies an eyewitness account.—*Op. cit.*, 269–85.

There is an honour connected with this which no distinction of rank can supply."[1] Judge then of Sekhome's feeling of humiliation to find himself proceeding alone, not one of his five eldest sons being now willing so to endorse the tribal custom. Eventually two yielded and Sekhome announced that these and these alone were now his children, and denounced the Word of God as a bad thing, seeing it incited the young to disobey their parents. This produced a lasting quarrel between Sekhome and the missionaries, while it split the tribe, Khama the son and heir in particular being greatly admired. Both Khama and Khamane, the two eldest sons, remained steadfastly loyal to what had become their Christian convictions, despite the bitter persecution to which they were now exposed. Eventually there was nothing for it but for Khama to retire to a mountain fastness and there remain under siege. After some pitiless intrigue on the part of Sekhome, the chief realized he had lost the loyalty of his people and fled to a neighbouring chieftain for refuge. Khama, who had never intrigued against his father for power, had now received it.[2] Mackenzie records the influence of these events on the Christian mission: "In the end the missionary was the only public character who succeeded in keeping his place in the midst of so many plots and counter-plots. By the blessing of God he was able to secure and to retain the confidence of the people. He came at length to be recognized as the friend of all and the enemy of none. . . . The Christian life and character were a new force in the town of the Bamangwato. . . . It was exhibited not only by the missionary, but by their own countrymen who had 'entered the Word of God'."[3]

A pioneer enterprise of the London Missionary Society at this time was a mission to Lake Ngami. The chief Lechulatebe had asked for a missionary but so malarious a region had then discouraged any attempt at settlement. In 1875 however a new mission at Lake Ngami was under consideration by the Directors in response to a request from Moremi, now chief in succession to his father Lechulatebe, and J. D. Hepburn, missionary at Shoshong, undertook the preliminary journey in 1877 with his wife and their three children, accompanied by two African evangelists. The sufferings were great, but their object was so far achieved that Hepburn was able to transmit a favourable

[1] *Ibid.*, 411.
[2] *Ibid.*, 412–22, 425–50. Khamane afterwards relapsed into paganism.
[3] *Ibid.*, 451. Sekhome showed his confidence by a secret visit to Mackenzie just before his flight: "I now had a glorious opportunity of rewarding good for evil, and took advantage of it."—*Ibid.*, 449.

report, and while awaiting the Directors' decision stationed there the two devoted African evangelists. The mission at the lake, a heroic enterprise, got well under way so that by 1880 Hepburn could report: "The reaping has overtaken the sowing."[1]

When the mission to the Makololo was projected by the London Society a second had been coupled with it: a mission to the Matebele. The missions were to be linked not only geographically but diplomatically. The Makololo would be given more confidence, it was hoped, to return to their earlier temporary and more healthy residence north of the Zambezi, if the marauding Matebele who had driven them from it were also to receive the messengers of peace. The one ground of hope in the Matebele enterprise was the strong personal friendship existing between Robert Moffat and Umsiligazi. For this reason Moffat had been asked to lead the mission and had readily consented. It was proposed that he should spend about a year with his junior colleagues—William Sykes and Thomas Morgan Thomas, together with his son John Smith Moffat as an independent worker.[2] When the Transvaal Boers got wind of the undertaking they gave notice to Moffat that nothing would be done without their consent; this applied to both Makololo and Matebele mission parties. The London Mission men were the virtual holders of the so-called "Missionaries' Road" from the South to Central Africa which it was the declared intention of the Transvaal Boers to close.[3] The missionaries denied the Boer claim to territory through which the road ran. Moffat was in no mood for parley, which he realized would be futile, so submitted the matter to Sir George Grey, Governor of the Cape, the Directors doing the same both to Grey and the Home Government. Grey immediately communicated with the President of the Republic, on the basis of the Treaty of 1852, the Secretary of State supporting him. The road remained open.[4]

[1] Eighty-second *Report of the London Missionary Society* (1876), 95; J. D. Hepburn, *Twenty Years in Khama's Country* (1895), 35–96.
[2] Sixty-fourth *Report of the Directors* (1858), 16–17.
[3] Walker, *op. cit.*, 185, 287, 289.
[4] Sixty-fifth *Report of the Directors* (1859), 11–12. Grey's letter to Moffat (19.3.59) contained a cordial appreciation of the missionaries and their work. C. W. de Kiewiet is critical of Moffat's alarm and says: "It was nothing but a storm in a tea-cup."—*British Colonial Policy and the South African Republics, 1848-1872* (1929), 252–4. John Mackenzie is as definite on the other side, saying that Grey's expostulations "saved Kuruman to the natives and the free highway into the interior to England".—J. Mackenzie, *Austral Africa* (1887), II, 238. The official Boer letter of warning to Moffat, together with the correspondence between Grey and Pretorius, will be found in J. P. R. Wallis (ed.), *The Matabele Journals of Robert Moffat, 1829-1860* (1945), II, 160–1.

The missionaries set out on their journey of some 600 miles by way of Sechele's Lithubaruba and Sekhome's Shoshong. They arrived at Umsiligazi's headquarters on October 27. Moffat recorded the misgivings he could not repress about the enterprise.[1] When the chief was desired to assign a site for the mission, he would evade the request. "He could not help manifesting kindness to me, his old friend", wrote Moffat, "but he studiously avoided, by various excuses, to comply with my requests." But Moffat was later apprised of the reason: "He told me in a private conversation that information had reached him that the Missionaries were spies, and that in every instance they had been the precursors of the marauding Boers." Moffat cleared up the difficulty, and Umsiligazi concluded: "I know well the Boers hate you because you love me."[2] After two months' delay a highly eligible site was offered and gratefully accepted at Inyati, the first station of the Matebele mission. The missionaries went to view it on December 23, 1859. They were soon at work; a week later they were preparing the ground for sowing and planting. Moffat left Inyati on June 18, 1860. He and his old friend never met again. It was the strength of their friendship that had secured the first concession to European residence within the tribe.

It proved a hard furrow to plough. In 1863 John Mackenzie visited the mission with J. S. Moffat, who was returning from leave via Shoshong, and has recorded his impressions. It was a journey of 330 miles. They found Mr. and Mrs. Sykes at Inyati, and Mr. Thomas bereaved, Mrs. Thomas having died from malaria in June 1862. "The Matebele mourned for her", says Mackenzie, "with a sorrow as deep as their admiration had been high."[3] The close-knit structure of a tribe based on military despotism was soon apparent. As Mackenzie put it: "Matebele society may be said to exist for the chief." His contact with Matebele soldiers gave him the impression that "the mental and spiritual parts of their nature had become very much dwarfed by disuse." He found that after four years' teaching a number would admit that the Word of God was "truly a good word",

---

[1] J. P. R. Wallis, *op. cit.*, II, 202–3.

[2] Sixty-sixth *Report of the Directors* (1860), 7–8. Moffat discovered that a messenger from the south had been the source of reports alleging that the Boers followed the missionaries, and that when the word of God was received it meant one man one wife. As Moffat remarks, "Think only how such a report . . . must have tingled in the ears of a despot with his more than two hundred wives, and his officers with their harems." See also J. Mackenzie, *Ten Years North of the Orange River*, 314–15.

[3] J. Mackenzie, *op. cit.*, 286–7, 303–6.

but they would only make the admission in private.[1] Yes, it was a hard and stony soil. John Smith Moffat, who served for the first seven years, wrote twenty-eight years later (January 18, 1888): "A few individuals may have been influenced for good, but there is no organic result, by which I mean that there do not seem to be three, or even two, people of the tribe who trust each other and recognize each other as Christians. In my stay with the chief I have seen no indication that the life of the tribe is in any way touched by the Gospel."[2]

(4) *From the Zambezi to the Nile*

One factor governing the earlier European interest in West than in East Africa was the question of distance. From England (say) to Zanzibar by water was more than twice as far as from England to Lagos. But in 1869 an event that was revolutionary in world travel took place: the opening on November 17 of the Suez Canal. The effect on Africa was twofold; South Africa was no longer on the sea-route from Europe to the East, and Europe's commercial interest in East Africa was stimulated by the shorter sea passage—shorter by 2,000 miles—that trade would have to travel.[3] This improvement in communications was to open wider the door for Christian missions as well as for western trade.

The transfer of the Universities' Mission under Tozer from the Shiré highlands to Zanzibar meant a radical change in milieu. True while there was slave-raiding in one there was slave-trading in the other, but where one was pagan, with the opportunity which this implied, the other was Muslim without veneer. Tozer admitted that he and his colleagues, in so far as they had been welcomed to Zanzibar, had been welcomed as Englishmen rather than as Christian missionaries, and even for this he acknowledged indebtedness to the English Consul. As for expansion: "So far as the Sultan's authority extends, we may fully expect protection for ourselves and toleration for our converts, which perhaps is all that we have any right to demand of a Mahometan prince."[4] Tozer of course had chosen Zanzibar

---

[1] *Ibid.*, 324, 331, 335.

[2] R. U. Moffat, *John Smith Moffat* (1921), 218.

[3] Coupland enlarges on the significance for East Africa of the Canal.—R. Coupland, *The Exploitation of East Africa, 1856-1890* (1939), 83–5. Walker points out, as a by-product of the change, that Anglo-Indians no longer spent their leave at the Cape.—*Op. cit.*, 394.

[4] Tozer to Committee (6.1.65).—*Report of the O.C.D.D. Mission to Central Africa for 1864* (1865), 4–5.

not as a mission field but as a base for later operations on the mainland, and in that connexion began to prepare for an African agency by starting schools—first one for boys, with one for girls soon after. The first pupils were gifts by the Navy from captured slave-dhows. By 1871 St. Andrew's College at Kiungani had appeared.[1] Two years later Tozer resigned and was followed in the episcopate by Edward Steere who had joined the mission in 1863.

In 1867 the first contact had been attempted with the mainland, when C. A. Alington set out to visit Kimweri, chief of Usambara. The following year a second visit had been paid. Kimweri declined to have missionaries at headquarters but said they might settle near the coast. Eventually Magila was selected, a village where the chief Kifungiwe (who was a minor) was a son of Kimweri, but the station was only supplied intermittently. Climate and disease were once again taking their toll and workers were few.[2] Under Steere's leadership a more vigorous policy was now pursued. Magila was staffed with new workers, while Steere in 1875 set out on a missionary journey to Nyasaland a dozen years after he had first seen it in the unhappy withdrawal of 1863. In command of the carriers from Lindi, the port from which they set out, he was fortunate to have Chuma, one of Livingstone's "faithfuls". They reached the village of Mataka, a Yao chief, some seventy miles from the Lake, which Livingstone on his last journey had found attractive as a possible mission post.[3] Steere was the first white man after Livingstone to arrive at Mwembe, Mataka's village. He was warmly welcomed, but once again the chief did not approve of a mission at headquarters; his reputed interest in the slave-trade probably made him nervous. In 1876 on a second journey Steere selected Masasi, north of the Rovuma behind Cape Delgado, as a station to be begun among the Yaos—the first resumption of work in the Lake Nyasa region.[4] The mission was now caring for liberated slaves in considerable numbers, a colony for them having been opened at Mbweni on Zanzibar island in 1874. There was development at Masasi where a new station to the south, Newala, was begun in 1878. But perhaps the most impressive event was the closing of the slave-market at Zanzibar

[1] *Ibid.*, 6; Anderson-Morshead, *The History of the Universities' Mission to Central Africa, 1859–1909* (1909), 48–50, 52.

[2] Anderson-Morshead, *op. cit.*, 54–8.

[3] *Vide supra*, p. 200.

[4] R. M. Heanley, *A Memoir of Edward Steere* (2nd ed., 1890), 137–8, 140–7, 189–95.

in 1873, thanks to the tireless efforts of the Consul, Sir John Kirk. The Treaty with the Sultan was signed one month after Livingstone's death. Part of the slave-market was at once purchased for the mission, and on Christmas Day 1873 there was here laid the foundation stone of Christ Church cathedral, while on Christmas Day 1879 the completed building was formally opened.[1]

In the early 'sixties a Roman Catholic mission was begun in Zanzibar, with an extension before long to Bagamoyo on the mainland opposite, whence the caravan route started for Ujiji on Lake Tanganyika. The initiative came from the French island of Bourbon or Réunion. The Abbé Fava, Vicar-General of St. Denis, was the active leader under encouragement from his bishop, Amand Maupoint of St. Denis. In advance of his arrival with his party there was French building activity in Zanzibar that excited British suspicion. Admiral Keppel had reported that they were erecting "a large barrack capable of holding twelve hundred men in the centre of the town of Zanzibar". London inquired of Paris, and "M. de Thouvenal explained that the barrack was to be a religious foundation comprising hospital, schools and workshops".[2] Meanwhile a French corvette had delivered at Zanzibar the Abbé Fava with two Jesuit priests, Jego and Schimpff, and six Sisters of the Daughters of Mary (a religious foundation set up in 1845 in Réunion), with a body of artificers. Colonel Rigby, the British Consul, commented: "I think there is no doubt that this mission, conveyed here by the French naval Commander-in-Chief, is an enterprise of the French Government. It has created great excitement amongst the Arabs and African population, being considered as the certain prelude to French aggression."[3] In July, in reply to an inquiry from Lord John Russell about the building Keppel had reported, Rigby wrote: "It could with ease accommodate 1,200 men, and probably as many as 2,000 . . . the most extensive range of buildings in the town. The Abbé Favat [sic], Vicar-General of La Réunion, and a Surgeon of the French Navy, who wears his uniform, are at the head of the establishment, which I have no doubt is an enterprise of the French Government, being on a scale too vast to be supported

---

[1] Anderson-Morshead, *op. cit.*, 82–7. The internal arrangements were not yet done, but when the altar was later erected it was placed where the whipping-post had stood.

[2] C. E. B. Russell, *General Rigby, Zanzibar and the Slave-Trade* (1935), 174.

[3] Rigby to Russell, 2.1.61.—*Ibid.*, 175.

by private charities."[1] The missionaries later admitted having received a capital grant of 15,000 francs from the Réunion Government.[2] M. de Thouvenal persisted from Paris that the building was for mission purposes only, but if desired he would sign a joint convention to respect the territorial integrity of the Sultan's dominions. The offer was accepted, and an Anglo-French Declaration to this effect was signed on March 10, 1862 in Paris.[3]

Whatever the original intent, Maupoint relinquished the mission in 1862 and it was then entrusted to the Fathers of the Holy Ghost, whose Superior for the mission, Antoine Horner, arrived in Zanzibar on June 16, 1863. Activities had already been set going there: a hospital for Europeans, a "cottage hospital" and out-patients' department for Africans, a pharmacy, and workshops. A beginning had been made with a school by purchasing children in the slave-market.[4] But Horner was soon across the water (August 1863) at Bagamoyo where Fava the year before had purchased an eligible site adequate to accommodate all the activities of a mission station. A soldier from the French consulate had been assigned to Horner, and he carried letters of commendation from the Sultan. A flourishing centre was established here which won praise from all who saw it. Sir Bartle Frere visited it ten years later, and wrote of it: "I would recommend it as a model to be followed in any attempt to civilise or evangelise Africa."[5] In 1869 the Sultan granted the mission at Bagamoyo a concession of first-class land for an agricultural project for training the boys from the orphanage. Both boys and girls had been transferred to Bagamoyo by 1869.[6] Three years later a major disaster overtook the mission. In April 1872 a terrific hurricane devastated Zanzibar and the nearby mainland. Two-thirds of the flourishing clove and coconut plantations of the island were wiped out; all the vessels in the harbour save one (which was powerful enough to get to sea)

---

[1] Rigby to Russell, 1.7.61.—*Ibid.*, 175.
[2] *Annales*, XXXIX (1867), 24.
[3] Russell, *op. cit.*, 175; Coupland, *op. cit.*, 33–6.
[4] *Annales*, XXXV (1863), 125, 130; XXXIX (1867), 24.
[5] Coupland, *op. cit.*, 355; *Annales*, XXXIX (1867), 25, 28–31. Incidentally Horner was critical of the Anglican Mission in Zanzibar and reported as a representative comment by Europeans: "Il n'y a ici qu'une mission, c'est la mission catholique."—*Ibid.*, 42–3. Cf. G. Warneck in *Allgemeine Missions-Zeitschrift*, XIII (1886), 305.
[6] *Annales*, XLII (1870), 49. In 1866 there were 110 orphans being educated by the missionaries in Zanzibar, all purchased in the slave-market.—*Ibid.*, XXXIX 1867), 38.

were sunk or dashed ashore. Bagamoyo did not escape. In the previous two years activities had been largely concentrated here, so that on the eve of the hurricane it boasted workshops, an agricultural project, a nursery, elementary schools, a junior college, and a novitiate for African sisters. A Christian village had grown up with some 300 young people in addition to the staff of five priests, eleven brothers, and nine sisters. There were fifty or so separate buildings. The hurricane laid practically the whole establishment level with the ground. Of the fifty buildings only four second-class affairs, freakishly spared by the storm, remained to give shelter. And this was in the period after the French disaster in Europe of 1870 when the home resources were heavily depleted. But with strong hearts and fine courage the missionaries raised up what had been cast down, and when Sir Bartle Frere was their guest a year later, he could pay the tribute we have already quoted.[1]

The Church Missionary Society still maintained a mere foothold on the mainland at Rabai, with the solitary Rebmann devoted to the service and humbly determined to be faithful to the last. On three occasions the Committee sent a colleague— in 1864, 1866, and 1867. The first died almost at once, the second was invalided before arriving, the third gave five years' service. For eight years the station was placed under the Bishop of Mauritius (1865–72). Rebmann meanwhile became totally blind, and at last, after twenty-nine years' service without a furlough, retired to Württemburg in 1875 where he died the following year. But the work was not then abandoned though it changed its form. In 1873, after his diplomatic mission to Zanzibar, Sir Bartle Frere addressed the C.M.S. Committee recommending Mombasa as a settlement for freed slaves. He further intimated that such a centre under C.M.S. auspices might expect to receive, along with the Universities' Mission in Zanzibar and the Roman Catholics at Bagamoyo, an allocation of the liberated. Action was taken and on May 7, 1875 the purchase was completed of a site near Mombasa and the new settlement appropriately named Frere Town. On September 4

---

[1] *Annales*, XLIV (1872), 416–26; Coupland, *op. cit.*, 55–7. Lieutenant V. L. Cameron also visited the mission in 1873, when setting out to relieve Livingstone, and found about 300 African children in training.—Cameron, *Across Africa* (1877), I, 13–14. An exploratory journey inland took Horner 120 miles from the coast to the Uluguru Mountains, some 8,000 ft. high, where he established the station of Mhonda. After sixteen years' unsparing service ill health compelled retirement in 1879. He died the following year at Bordeaux.—*Proceedings of the Royal Geographical Society*, N.S. II (1880), 388, 514.

the first thirty-one liberated Africans, and on September 19, another party of 271 were landed from British warships. A new epoch in the East Africa mission had begun.[1]

By this time Methodist missionary partners were established on the coast to the north of Mombasa. The Foreign Mission Committee of the United Methodist Free Churches had its attention directed to East Africa by a lay official, Charles Cheetham, who had read J. L. Krapf's book, *Travels, Researches and Missionary Labours in Eastern Africa*, and was especially impressed by his plea for the Gallas. He corresponded with Krapf who in November 1860 met the Mission Committee. Krapf recommended a party of four men, two English Methodists and two Swiss from the St. Chrischona Missionary Institution in which he was interested; and further, he generously offered to take out the party and see them established. Decision was taken on these lines. T. Wakefield and J. Woolner with Krapf and two Swiss colleagues reached Zanzibar on January 5, 1862. Krapf seems to have had some misgiving about their possible reception in Zanzibar, derived no doubt from the rebuff to the Hermannsburg party coupled with his own alleged meddling in politics.[2] However, all was well, for when the French Consul had secured right of entry for the Roman Catholic mission from Réunion, the British Consul had at once claimed equivalent rights for British missionaries; thus the political sky was clear. After visiting Rabai to meet Rebmann, Krapf proposed a division of forces: Wakefield and Woolner for Usambara to the south, and the two Chrischona men for Kauma among the northernmost Nyikas, and so a stepping-stone to the Gallas. Wakefield and Woolner went south to Pangani where the governor found their Zanzibar papers unsatisfactory. This defect having been rectified, no eligible site was then found available, so they returned north. Meanwhile the Kauma chiefs had proved agreeable but the two Swiss had discovered that they had mistaken their vocation and in April they returned to Europe. Ribe, some sixteen miles north-west of Mombasa, was now fixed upon as a mission centre and was occupied in July. In the same month Woolner went into hospital at Zanzibar and in September was invalided home. Krapf left for Europe on October 2, 1862. After ten months in the field Thomas Wakefield was now left alone. In six months' time an able colleague joined him; Charles New reached Zanzibar on April 7, 1863. In the follow-

---

[1] Stock, *History of the Church Missionary Society* (1899), II, 433; III, 77, 84–5.
[2] *Vide supra*, pp. 116–17.

ing year a further reinforcement arrived in E. Butterworth who only survived however for a few weeks.[1]

Wakefield and New still had the Gallas in mind and after one or two prospecting tours set out in October 1866 by sea for Malindi and thence inland. Relations between the Gallas and the Swahili being anything but cordial, contact with the former was not easy and much caution was required. Eventually they reached the Galla chief of Ganda, a village of some 300 people beyond the Tana, and found they would be most welcome if they would offer protection from the Masai. Indeed, they found this warrior tribe dreaded throughout the land, the lightest rumour of their approach causing consternation. They did not discover here a desirable mission centre. Moreover they began to be sceptical about the earlier estimates of Galla population —some eight millions had even been suggested. Later knowledge has shown the figure to be almost grotesque. They were at Ribe again in February 1867.[2]

In 1871 Charles New undertook a memorable journey to the Chaggas and was the first European to ascend Kilimanjaro. Setting out on July 13 he called on Rebmann who gave it as his "decided opinion that the day for mission work in the countries to which I was going had not yet arrived", and that the country was far more unsettled than on the occasion of his own journeys twenty-three years before.[3] The Chaggas were at length reached, and their reluctance to permit the climb having been overcome, at a second attempt Charles New reached the snow-clad summit with one African companion on August 28. On his safe return to camp the people were amazed and said, "The white man is a god."[4] A furlough was now due, on the eve of his departure for which he was recruited for the Livingstone Search Expedition, but this was abandoned on Stanley's arrival from Ujiji.[5] On New's return to East Africa he set out once more to visit the Chaggas on December 3, 1874 but it was his last journey. He died in February 1875. With colleagues coming and going, frustrations with the Nyika, and raids from the Masai,

---

[1] E. S. Wakefield, *Thomas Wakefield* (2nd ed., 1904), 16–35, 37; C. New, *Life, Wanderings, and Labours in Eastern Africa* (1873), 6–22, 135.

[2] C. New, *op. cit.*, 159–258. New has described the Gallas, and was the first to report the so-called Dual Organization in respect of marriage, whereby inter-marriage was permissible only between the two sections into which the tribe was divided. New pointed out how valuable a safeguard this was against inbreeding.— *Ibid.*, 273–4; cf. W. H. R. Rivers, *Social Organization* (1924), 29 and Appendix III.

[3] C. New, *op. cit.*, 293.

[4] *Ibid.*, 419–32.

[5] *Ibid.*, 511–19.

Wakefield held on until 1887. But the work at the coast never flourished. It was a quarter of a century after Wakefield's time when the more rewarding mission on the highlands of Mount Kenya was begun.

In Abyssinia the 'sixties and 'seventies were a stormy time for missions from Europe. The political background was that of the latter part of the reign of Theodore and the anarchy that followed his downfall. Theodore had conquered Gondar in 1854 and was crowned in the ancient capital the following year by the *abuna* Salama. The Englishmen Bell and Plowden, who had come as adventurers to Abyssinia in the 'forties and risen to considerable importance, now came to the court as friends and advisers of the emperor. When both lost their lives in 1860 to the deep grief of Theodore, a sinister change came over him, as if restraining hands had been removed. Wallis Budge summarizes the ensuing tyranny: "He treated the laws of the country and immemorial customs as non-existent, and made his will the law of the country. He laughed at the advice of his counsellors and the clergy, he ill-treated the Abuna Salama, he insulted the priests and the learned men of his court, and he heaped fresh taxes and burdens upon the peasants, and seized their lands."[1] He was sensitive as to his humble origin and it was on this account that the missionary Stern was imprisoned. Henry Aaron Stern, a converted German Jew, had come to Abyssinia for the London Society for Promoting Christianity among the Jews when it began work among the Falashas. In a book he published two years later he so offended Theodore on this point that he was tried and sentenced to death in November 1863, but the sentence was commuted to rigorous imprisonment.[2] In the following year Cameron, the British Consul, was clapped into prison. A proposal of Theodore to send an embassy to Great Britain had received no answer from the Queen. By a fatal error the letter was apparently overlooked. The emperor thought it had been deliberately ignored, and girded at the insult; hence Cameron's fate. The British next sent the Levantine, H. Rassam, to secure the prisoners' release, but he was himself thrown into gaol with them, and some sixty other Europeans

---

[1] E. A. Wallis Budge, *A History of Ethiopia* (1928), II, 497–8.
[2] H. A. Stern, *Wanderings among the Falashas* (1862). Stern stated that Theodore's mother sold *Koso*, or worm medicine, and that his early name *Ledjkoso*, meant son of worm medicine. "Theodore never forgave Stern for this insult."—Wallis Budge, *op. cit.*, II, 504. Stern later recorded his experiences in *The Captive Missionary* (1868).

as well.[1] The Government now bestirred itself, concerned for the effect on British prestige in the East if it were "commonly reported that England did not trouble herself to rescue her servants".[2] The British Expedition to Magdala under Sir Robert Napier was set in motion. Theodore's tyrannies had alienated chiefs and people who rendered to the Expedition help indispensable in such a country on a 400-mile march inland from the shore base. Magdala, Theodore's fortress, fell on April 13, 1868 and as the victors entered Theodore took his own life. The prisoners had already been released.[3] Napier left Abyssinia in May having no mandate for any political action, so there ensued the old struggle of chieftain against chieftain with anarchy now following on tyranny.

John IV (1868–89) was Theodore's successor, though not for four years was the anarchical confusion partially quelled. John then attempted in 1874 to check the Galla raids with indifferent success. An Egyptian army took the opportunity to invade the country but after some preliminary success was disastrously defeated.[4] Under such conditions the Roman missions could do little more than wait hopefully for better times. Of the two vicariates that of Abyssinia in the north was for practical purposes conterminous with Tigré. The number of Catholics in 1868 was estimated to be about 8,000, dispersed in nine parishes, with three European priests and one brother, and an Abyssinian clergy of fourteen priests. They had lost three vicars apostolic in a decade; the fourth, Marcell Touvier, took office in November 1869.[5]

The *abuna* Salama, imprisoned by Theodore, had died in October 1867.[6] His successor Athanasios, forty-second in the line, was appointed by the Coptic Patriarch in 1869.[7] In the following year severe persecution of the Catholics broke out; the unexpected victory of John of Tigré over Gobazie of Amhara, so the missionaries alleged, was ascribed by the *abuna* to his own effective co-operation, and as an appropriate thanks-

---

[1] Jones and Monroe, *A History of Abyssinia* (1935), 132; D. Mathew, *Ethiopia* (1947), 191–3.

[2] Mathew, *op. cit.*, 195–6.

[3] Wallis Budge, *op. cit.*, II, 501–19; Mathew, *op. cit.*, 196–205; Stern, *op. cit.*, 368–95. Krapf was with the Expedition as interpreter to Napier.—Stock, *op. cit.*, II, 135. H. M. Stanley was also with it as war correspondent.—Stanley, *Coomassie and Magdala* (1874), Part II.

[4] Wallis Budge, *op. cit.*, II, 521–22.

[5] *Annales*, XL (1868), 365, 378; XLI (1869), 472; XLII (1870), 154–5.

[6] Mathew, *op. cit.*, 195.

[7] H. M. Hyatt, *The Church of Abyssinia* (1928), 291.

giving he demanded the purging of the land from the Catholic invasion. The missionaries were put to the ban of the empire. The four mission centres and all Catholic churches were destroyed, and apostate Abyssinians vigorously recalled to their first loyalty. Touvier retired with his colleagues to Massawa which de Jacobis had used as an asylum under similar circumstances, and endeavoured to hold one or two border outposts.[1] Not till the reign of Menelik II (1889–1914) was there to be peace.

The vicariate apostolic of the Gallas, committed at first to Italian Capuchins and in 1863 transferred to the French Province, was centred in Shoa to the south. Here Massaja continued as the able leader of the mission until expelled by Menelik at the instance of John IV.[2] He reported in 1865 some 800 Catholics at four stations, but admitted five years later: "Our affairs are not much advanced in this country."[3] In 1866 he made an interesting experiment by establishing at Marseilles a seminary where an indigenous clergy should be trained together with the preparation of Franciscans for the field. In three years' time eighteen young Abyssinians were in residence, but in 1872 the enterprise was abandoned as they could not support the unaccustomed climate.[4] In 1880 ill health compelled Massaja to relinquish his command, and recognition was later given to his apostolic labours when on November 10, 1884 he was elevated to the cardinalate by Leo XIII.[5]

Missionaries of the Evangelical National Missionary Society of Sweden, founded in 1856, came to the border of Abyssinia ten years later and began work at Massawa. The indefatigable Krapf had interested them in this area, with a hope of extension to the Gallas. There was little to show in the early days.[6]

The ever-present background to work in the Sudan on the human side was the slave-trade. Names indissolubly associated with the early attempts at its suppression are those of Samuel White Baker and Charles George Gordon. Baker began as explorer: "In the year 1861", he wrote in his *Journal*, "I determined to commence an expedition to discover the sources of the

---

[1] *Annales*, XLIII (1871), 328, 331, 335–6; XLIV (1872), 340, 347–8, 349–50; XLV (1873), 441–5, 457; XLVIII (1876), 85–6, 90–1; L (1878), 231.
[2] Hyatt, *op. cit.*, 106.
[3] *Annales*, XXXVII (1865), 14–15; XLII (1870), 68.
[4] *Annales*, XXXVIII (1866), 321–2; XLI (1869), 474; XLIV (1872), 150.
[5] *Cath. Ency.*, X, 29–30.
[6] K. S. Latourette, *A History of the Expansion of Christianity*, VI, 34.

Nile, with the hope of meeting the East African Expedition under Captains Speke and Grant somewhere about the Victoria lake."[1]

Speke, convinced of the truth of his identification of Lake Victoria as the source of the Nile, had set out on his third journey of exploration in 1859 to establish it. Sir Roderick Murchison's "Speke, we must send you there again" set things moving; James Augustus Grant, also of the Indian Army, was appointed companion, and on April 27 the two set out from England. On September 30 a move was made from Bagamoyo and yet another journey, memorable in African annals, was begun. Marching along the caravan route to Tabora, they then struck north to the lake. But progress was slow and constantly hampered by avaricious chiefs claiming that heavy toll on the travellers which they regarded as their due and squeezing their victims to the limit before permitting any advance. At last these repelling regions had been traversed and they emerged into Karagwe, the hospitable kingdom of the friendly Rumanika, by November 1861. There followed the march to Uganda where the travellers were received in state by Mutesa and entertained for half a year. Mutesa then "gave the road" to the explorers and in July 1862 they took their leave. On the 28th they were at the Ripon Falls: "The expedition had now performed its functions. I saw that old father Nile without any doubt rises in the Victoria N'yanza." There followed the descent of the river until Gondokoro was reached in February 1863, and the meeting with Baker marked the end of a journey famous in geographical discovery.[2]

Meanwhile Baker had been busy in the Nile valley. In fourteen months he explored the basin of the Blue Nile and was back in Khartoum in June 1862.[3] He then wrote of it: "Without the White Nile trade Khartoum would almost cease to exist; and that trade is kidnapping and murder."[4] Then, ascending the White Nile he met Speke and Grant at Gondokoro who told him the exploration job was not yet finished and handed it on to him.[5] Pursuing it in 1863–64 he discovered the Albert Nyanza to the north-west of Lake Victoria and thus cleared up the prob-

[1] T. D. Murray and A. S. White, *Sir Samuel Baker, A Memoir* (1895), 43.
[2] J. H. Speke, *Journal of the Discovery of the Source of the Nile* (1863), *passim*; J. A. Grant, *A Walk across Africa* (1864), *passim*.
[3] S. W. Baker, *The Nile Tributaries of Abyssinia* (1867), *passim*.
[4] S. W. Baker, *The Albert N'Yanza* (1869 ed.), 11.
[5] *Ibid.*, 66.

lem of the Nile sources.[1] But he also came face to face with the terrible realities of the slave-trade: "Gondokoro was a perfect hell. . . . The camps were full of slaves, and the Bari natives assured me that there were large depots of slaves in the interior belonging to the traders that would be marched to Gondokoro for shipment to the Sudan a few hours after my departure. I was the great stumbling-block to the trade, and my presence at Gondokoro was considered as an unwarrantable intrusion upon a locality sacred to slavery and iniquity."[2] But they had not seen the last of him. In 1869 when Baker was attached to the Prince of Wales' party in Egypt, the Khedive Ismail proposed to him the command of an expedition for the suppression of the slave-trade on the White Nile and the pacification of the Sudan. The offer was accepted. In December 1869 he was *en route* for Khartoum.[3] He was away four years. To succeed in suppressing the slave-trade within that period was clearly beyond him—or any other—but at least it can be claimed that he "laid the foundation of a repressive policy which was elaborated and improved by his successor, Colonel Gordon."[4] Baker's commission expired in April 1873. In October Gordon was offered the appointment and accepted.[5] But after three years, finding that the Governor-General of the Sudan was conniving at the slave-trade and thwarting his own policy in the equatorial region, he decided to resign. However his objections were met and he reported of a visit to the Khedive, February 13, 1877: "He gave me the Sudan."[6] The next two to three years were excruciating but successful; he was able to write on July 21, 1879: "God has enabled me, or rather has used me, to do what I wished to do— that is, break down the slave-trade."[7] His resignation was now

---

[1] Baker stated the solution concisely: "The Albert N'yanza is the geat basin of the Nile: the distinction between that and the Victoria N'yanza is, that the Victoria is a reservoir receiving the eastern affluents, and it becomes a starting point or the most elevated *source* at the point where the river issues from it at the Ripon Falls: the Albert is a reservoir not only receiving the western and southern affluents direct from the Blue Mountains, but it also receives the supply from the Victoria and from the entire equatorial Nile basin. The Nile as it issues from the Albert N'yanza is the *entire* Nile; prior to its birth from the Albert lake it is *not* the entire Nile."—*Ibid.*, 439. Italics in original. Thus the White Nile solved the problem of the equatorial sources while the Blue Nile accounted for the annual inundation.

[2] *Ibid.*, 61.

[3] Murray and White, *op. cit.*, 132–3, 148–55.

[4] *Ibid.*, 201.

[5] He declined the salary of £10,000 p.a. and would take no more than £2,000, since Egyptian peasants were being mulcted for the State Treasury.—B. M. Allen, *Gordon and the Sudan* (1931), 13.

[6] *Ibid.*, 109.

[7] *Ibid.*, 152.

definite. Egyptian officials in Cairo, with no bias against the slave-trade, were gratified to see him go; the new Khedive, Tewfik, who seems at one time to have feared that Gordon would set up, in Oriental fashion, as an independent ruler, was in the end sorry to lose him.[1]

During these years and in this region the Roman Catholic missionaries were struggling to establish their work in the vicariate of Central Africa. A crisis had been reached in 1861, when the missionary operations were entrusted to the Franciscans, with J. Reinthaler from the Province of Styria as vicar apostolic. He arrived in January 1862 with thirty-four Franciscans from Austria and Venice. But hope was quickly dashed: missionaries died—Reinthaler among them within four months —they removed to Syria, they returned to Europe. At last all stations were abandoned save Khartoum where one father and one brother remained in residence. Reinthaler had no immediate successor; the direction of the mission was transferred to the Vicar Apostolic of Egypt.[2] In 1865 further steps were suggested: a division of the vicariate between the Verona Institute and the Franciscans was proposed, but this failed to materialize; also the reopening of Shellal with helpers from Casoria's African Institute at Naples was attempted but within eight months it was closed once more. In 1870 Khartoum was again the only station, with three fathers and a lay brother, and the cost had been some forty lives laid down.[3]

Meanwhile Daniel Comboni had been inspired with a new idea: to save Africa by means of Africa, the familiar plan of African agency. And the idea took shape: in 1867 he opened in Cairo two institutes for Africans, one for boys and one for girls. That for boys, dedicated to the Sacred Heart of Jesus, was under the auspices of the Verona Seminary directed by Louis de Canossa, while that for girls, dedicated to the Sacred Heart of Mary, was under the Marseilles Sisters of Saint Joseph of the Apparition. The whole was subject to Louis Cuircia, Vicar Apostolic of Egypt. There were two main ends in view: first, to give a specific Catholic training against a background of liberal education to young Africans designed for missionary service among their own people; and to prepare European missionaries for the conditions awaiting them, to enable them to learn Arabic

---

[1] *Ibid.*, 159–61. Allen has exposed Lytton Strachey's innuendoes about Gordon's personal habits in the Sudan as being entirely without foundation.—*Ibid.*, 82–101.

[2] *Annales*, XLIII (1871), 121; *Sudan Notes and Records*, XXVII (1946), 114.

[3] *Annales*, XLIII (1871), 121–3.

and to supply the knowledge of elementary medicine and certain handicrafts essential to successful settlement; second, to use the resources of the Institutes to evangelize the Negro population of Cairo, estimated in 1870 at some 25,000, almost all brought there by the slave-trade. Comboni reported that there were Catholic families, whose slaves were usually pagan or Muslim, who had no interest in their conversion since they regarded them as things, not persons, and feared if they once became Catholics and so might be free, they would immediately clear off; not to mention the masters' reluctance to lose the Muslim market, for no Muslim would buy a Christian slave.[1] The two institutes, which in view of the second aim included in each a sick ward and a school and offered catechumenate instruction, were set up in December 1867. Four years later they reported eight missionary priests, one theological student, four brothers, and twenty-one Negroes in the one; six sisters, eighteen Negro teachers, and forty-two Negro girls and women in the other.[2]

In 1871 Comboni proposed to draw on the resources of the Institutes, European and African, to establish a new mission in Kordofan, an extensive territory south-west of Khartoum hitherto untouched by Christian effort. In May 1873 he was at Khartoum with a considerable mission party, and by July had reached El-Obeid, the capital of Kordofan. The slave-trade was still actively pursued despite official decrees. El-Obeid, so missionary Losi reported to Comboni a year later, was glutted with slaves. Indeed the missionaries made their own purchases with which to begin their work of Christian instruction twice daily.[3] Comboni's personal enterprise was unrelaxing, for in October 1873 he despatched a reconnoitring party southwards to the Nuba mountains, which reached Delen where a mission was begun two years later. A temporary withdrawal came to an end in 1877 when Gordon authorized the missionaries to reoccupy Delen among the Nubas. At a nodal point on the Nile Comboni founded the base for another mission in 1874 —Berber, junction of the Atbara and the Nile, and caravan centre for traffic from Egypt and the Red Sea. Here the Camil-

---

[1] *Annales*, XLIV (1872), 21–4. Comboni says that Pius IX had himself suggested Cairo as a suitable centre for the Institutes.

[2] *Annales*, XLIV (1872), 43; Comboni also opened two missionary institutes in Verona: in 1867 one for men, and in 1872 one for sisters.—*Sudan Notes and Records*, XXVII, 117, 120.

[3] *Annales*, XLVI (1874), 43–5; XLVII (1875), 357, 360; *Sudan Notes and Records*, XXVII, 118–19.

lian Fathers were established. From this vantage ground he planned to reach Suakin on the Red Sea and even to stretch down to the Abyssinian border, but the realization of these ambitions was not yet. Nevertheless G. Martini was despatched by way of the Blue Nile to the Abyssinian frontier in 1876 to survey and report.[1] In July 1877 Comboni was raised to the episcopate and granted full authority as Vicar Apostolic of Central Africa, a status he had richly earned.[2] But there were heavy trials still to face; famine following drought in 1877, and flooding with consequent hordes of mosquitoes and ensuing malaria in 1878. Ten missionaries died in Khartoum alone. And the losses continued to mount; in the one month of September 1881 there were six deaths. Exhausted with his truly sacrificial labours Comboni died in Khartoum on October 10, 1881.[3] It was the eve of disaster for the Sudan: the Mahdi was soon to emerge from the Nuba mountains and unfurl the standard of revolt.

In Egypt the Protestant activity of note during these decades was that of the United Presbyterian Church of the United States. Paulding of their Damascus mission was the first to propose it. After a visit to Egypt in 1851–52 he reported to the General Synod of the West in 1853 that the time seemed propitious "to open a new station in Cairo". The Synod took immediate action and resolved, May 21, 1853: "That our missionaries be instructed to occupy Cairo at their earliest possible convenience." Thomas McCague and his wife, appointed by the Board, reached Cairo on November 15, 1854 and were joined by James Barnett of the Damascus mission the next month. J. R. T. Lieder of the C.M.S. and Lauria of the London Mission to the Jews welcomed them to Egypt. The Coptic authorities were not so cordial.[4] With G. Lansing's arrival in 1856 an extension to Alexandria was undertaken. Lansing had served five years in Damascus and already had command of Arabic, so was himself posted to Alexandria, entering on the work in October 1857. Two existing schools under Scottish Presbyterian auspices were soon taken over by the mission: the girls' school in 1858

---

[1] *Annales*, XLVII (1875), 362, 364; *Sudan Notes and Records*, XXVII, 119, 121.

[2] *Annales*, XLIX (1877), 459.

[3] *Sudan Notes and Records*, XXVII, 121–4.

[4] A. Watson, *The American Mission in Egypt* (1898), 61, 64, 69–70. O. F. Martin and his wife had also arrived in Cairo in December, 1854, on behalf of the American Missionary Society for work among the Copts, but they retired with no successors after four years.—*Ibid.*, 73–4.

and the boys' the following year.[1] These operations aroused the Copts who decided, in order not to be dependent on the American schools, to open twelve Coptic schools in the city, but with little result. With the opening of a girls' school in Cairo in 1860 the educational work of the mission was fairly launched.[2] Also in 1860 a presbytery of the United Presbyterian Church was organized in Egypt under authorization from the General Synod in the United States, and with this the nucleus of independent growth appeared. The McCagues retired on health grounds in 1861, as Barnett also did temporarily after seventeen years' service in the Near East.[3]

In 1860 evangelistic tours were begun on the Nile and became a regular feature, in the determination to occupy the Nile Valley. A Nile boat, the *Ibis*, was purchased and annual itinerations lasting several months were undertaken. The procedure was to go up to Aswan with as little delay as possible, and then float downstream tying up village by village for preaching and book distribution.[4] In 1865 the first station south of Cairo was begun at Asyut, the virtual capital of Upper Egypt. Here boys' and girls' schools were opened with success. In the following year a station was begun in El-Faiyum to the south-west of Cairo, and again boys' and girls' schools were started. Meanwhile in Cairo the first congregation of the United Presbyterian Church was organized when four Egyptian elders and three deacons were elected. Further, six candidates were accepted for training in Christian work—sign of a healthy, growing Church.[5]

There were encouragements and sore trials during the years. When the American Civil War cut down severely grants from home local friends were very kind, and romance even came to the rescue. The Maharajah Dhulup Singh of the Panjab, himself a Christian long domiciled in England, contracted a marriage with Bamba, the first female convert of the mission. As a thankoffering in 1864 the Maharajah made a gift to the funds of £1,000 and promised £500 annually for two additions to the

---

[1] These had been independently organized. The girls' school, conducted by a Miss Pringle, was supported by a ladies' society in Paisley. The boys' school had been started by a Scottish Society for the Conversion of the Jews in default of a Protestant College which they had hoped to establish. In 1857 the school had been transferred to the Mission Committee of the United Presbyterian Church of Scotland.—*Ibid.*, 93–5, 98, 108.

[2] *Ibid.*, 110, 117–18.

[3] *Ibid.*, 112–13, 124–5. Barnett returned in 1865 and served for ten more years.

[4] *Ibid.*, 118–19, 126–7, 140–1, 173. Lansing found that Lord and Lady Aberdeen, during a visit to Egypt, had been active in Bible distribution along the Nile valley. —*Ibid.*, 126.

[5] *Ibid.*, 156, 176, 191–2.

staff.[1] On the other side of the account must be entered the severe persecution initiated by the Coptic Patriarch in 1867. Visiting in person Asyut and other stations, where there were burnings of the Protestants' books (Scriptures were not exempt), he condemned with condign threats the work of the missionaries. But this whirling hurricane did not destroy the seed sown.[2] In the decade 1870–80 the number of missionaries had increased from eighteen to twenty-two; Egyptian ordained ministers from one to six, other workers from eight to twenty-five, organized churches from two to eleven, and members from 180 to 985. The twelve weekday schools of 1870 had become forty-four by 1880, while the books sold in the latter year exceeded 20,000. A vigorous work had been begun, destined to grow in strength and influence.[3]

In reaching Cairo, neighbour across the Libyan desert to Tripoli, Tunis and Algiers where our survey began, we have found the continent encircled with Christian missions—encircled but not yet penetrated. There are enclaves of advance, however, and further drives to reach the heart of Africa are soon afoot.

[1] *Ibid.*, 163–72.
[2] *Ibid.*, 199–211.
[3] *Ibid.*, 279, 302. In 1870 the Kaiserwerth deaconesses had opened a hospital in Cairo.—K. S. Latourette, *op. cit.*, VI, 27.

LIVINGSTONE'S LEGACY

DAVID LIVINGSTONE was laid to rest in Westminster Abbey on April 18, 1874. "Brought by faithful hands over land and sea", the body had reached England on April 15 and been identified by Sir William Fergusson as the body of Livingstone, the fracture and false joint of the left arm providing the decisive evidence.[1] The funeral was an occasion of national mourning—mourning for the passing of the ardent friend of Africa, coupled with deep thanksgiving for his life and work. The pall-bearers appropriately were all linked with his African career: H. M. Stanley and Jacob Wainwright, W. C. Oswell and W. F. Webb, Sir Thomas Steele and E. D. Young, John Kirk and Horace Waller.[2] Robert Moffat, a venerable figure with half a century's work in Africa behind him, was among the mourners.

> *Open the Abbey doors, and bear him in*
> *To sleep with king and statesman, chief, and sage,*
> *The Missionary, come of weaver-kin,*
> *But great by work that brooks no lower wage.*

> *He needs no epitaph to guard a name*
> *Which man shall prize while worthy work is known;*
> *He lived and died for good—be that his fame:*
> *Let marble crumble: this is Living-stone.*[3]

It was a poignant occasion for them all. Livingstone had lived and died for Africa. He had lifted the veil from unknown regions, yet frustration and disappointment seemed to dog his steps. The two inner-Africa missions had ended in disaster, and no official support was forthcoming for the positive policy in the

[1] The full report of Sir William Fergusson may be found in *The Lancet*, 1874, I, 565–6. The significant passage runs: "The state of the left arm was such as to convince everyone present who had examined it during life, that the limb was Livingstone's. Exactly in the region of the attachment of the deltoid to the humerus, there were the indications of an oblique fracture. On moving the arm there were the indications of the ununited fracture. A closer investigation and dissection displayed the false joint which had long been so well recognized by those who had examined the arm in former days."—*Ibid.*, 566.

[2] Jacob Wainwright had been asked by Susi and Chuma, as the only literate members of their party, to read the burial service over Livingstone at Ilala. Steele, Oswell, and Webb, African hunters, were warm friends of the early days; Kirk and Young were on the Zambezi expedition, Waller with the Universities' Mission.

[3] *Punch*, LXVI (1874), 172.

lands of the slave-raiders. Indeed the Arab slave-trade was still rampant when he died, and his own words were graven on his tomb: "All I can add in my solitude is, may heaven's rich blessing come down on every one, American, English or Turk, who will help to heal this open sore of the world."[1] Yes, he had struggled on to the end with little to encourage in those things he laid most to heart. Yet within a decade there was the promise of a new Africa coming to the birth, and doing so more as the result of his own work and influence than those of any other single man. He left a rich inheritance in opportunity, inspiration, and goodwill. Sir Bartle Frere, then President of the Royal Geographical Society, wrote prophetic words to Livingstone's daughter Agnes: "As regards the value of the work he accomplished, it might be premature to speak—not that I think it possible I can over-estimate it, but because I feel sure that every year will add fresh evidence to show how well-considered were the plans he took in hand, and how vast have been the results of the movements he set in motion."[2] For Christian missions indeed, doors were soon thrown open in such rapid succession—not without sharp vicissitudes in the attempt to enter—that Societies found themselves embarrassed. Yet money and men appeared as they were needed, and missionaries from Britain, America, and the continent of Europe began to push beyond the occupied coastal fringe in a steady advance to the interior territories. It was Livingstone's death that stabbed men to attention and, before its influence had passed, generated in many the high resolve to share in the fulfilment of his dreams.

(1) *Territory Bequeathed*

David Livingstone stands *facile princeps* among African explorers. In the story of the opening-up of Central Africa—for continuous travel in the heart of the continent, for discovery of outstanding geographical features, for patient observation and scientifically accurate recording—he has no peer.[3] Of all the territory from which he first drew the veil that of the Shiré

[1] These are the closing words of a letter he wrote on May 1, 1872 to the *New York Herald*, "trying to enlist American zeal to stop the East Coast slave-trade".—*Last Journals*, II, 181-2.

[2] Blaikie, *Life of David Livingstone* (1906 ed.), 385.

[3] In E. W. Smith's anthology of African exploration, from Mungo Park to Stanley, Livingstone claims one-third of the nineteen entries.—E. W. Smith, *Exploration in Africa* (1929), *passim*. W. A. Elliott's illuminating chronological diagram of African explorers in the nineteenth century, showing the period each notable explorer actually spent in Africa, places Livingstone at the head of the list with Stanley, placed second, having half as many years to his credit.—W. A. Elliott,

highlands and around Lake Nyasa seemed to him the best adapted for the putting into practice of the positive policy—to oust the slave-trade and begin the regeneration of Africa by commerce and Christianity. He wrote of it to Professor Sedgwick of Cambridge, May 27, 1859: "I cannot have much heart to open up a country for a parcel of Portuguese pedlars in men's bodies and souls; but I trust in Providence. . . . I would rather have gone up to make our experiment in the Makololo country at once; but it has turned out for the opening of a highland lake region, and I pray that our own Christian people may be permitted to enter and spread our blessed Redeemer's kingdom."[1] After his death the Christians of Scotland determined to raise their memorial to him in this region which was accepted as the territory he had bequeathed. "Nyassaland", writes Coupland, "with all it has meant and may mean for Africa, has been well called 'the heritage of Livingstone'. And it was on the Zambesi Expedition that Livingstone, so to speak, acquired the property and wrote his will."[2]

The initiative was taken by James Stewart who had visited the Shiré in the days of the Zambezi Expedition with a view to recommend a Scottish missionary enterprise but had on that occasion turned it down as being inopportune.[3] When he was present in Westminster Abbey on April 18, 1874 the original proposal, which he had never finally rejected, was irresistibly revived. "On my return to Scotland from the funeral", he says, "I consulted with some friends as to whether the time had not now arrived to again take up the idea of the projected mission. The subject was carefully considered through an entire summer night, and only when daylight was beginning to appear was the matter finally concluded. But the resolve was made to reopen the question of the South African Mission, and give it the name of Livingstonia."[4] At the ensuing General Assembly of the Free

---

Nyaka, The Story of David Livingstone (1908), 105. From another angle H. H. Johnston, who writes primarily of Livingstone as explorer, says: "David Livingstone may be said to have initiated the scientific exploration of Central Africa by the European race."—H. H. Johnston, *Livingstone and the Exploration of Central Africa* (1891), 7. See also Stanley's remarkable tribute in *The Congo and the Founding of its Free State* (1885), II, 385.

[1] Monk (ed.), *Dr. Livingstone's Cambridge Lectures* (2nd ed., 1860), 364.

[2] R. Coupland, *Kirk on the Zambesi* (1928), 263.

[3] *Vide supra*, p. 183. Stewart had reported that the country was too disturbed for immediate action to be taken, to Livingstone's deep disappointment.—Livingstone, *The Zambesi and its Tributaries*, 413–14; Blaikie, *op. cit.*, 271; J. P. R. Wallis (ed.), *The Zambesi Journal of James Stewart, 1862–1863* (1952), 32–4, 228–9.

[4] J. Stewart, *Livingstonia: its Origin* (1894), 45–6; quoted in J. Wells, *The Life of James Stewart* (1908), 125.

Church of Scotland in May, Stewart in a notable speech proposed as the truest memorial of Livingstone the planting of a missionary settlement, at once industrial and educational, which might become for Central Africa "a great centre of commerce, civilisation and Christianity. And this I would call Livingstonia."[1] The Foreign Missions Committee, which had been meditating a mission to Somaliland in the eastern horn of Africa, was won over to the new proposal and the Livingstonia Mission of the Free Church of Scotland was decided upon. Stewart being himself committed to Lovedale at the time (he was on furlough in 1874) could not consider the leadership but proposed Lieutenant E. D. Young, R.N., for the post. Young already knew the country; he had spent two years with Livingstone on the Zambezi Expedition, and under the auspices of the Admiralty and the Royal Geographical Society had organized and led the Livingstone Search Expedition of 1867 when the traveller's death had been reported by the deserting Johanna men.[2] Young was granted two years' leave of absence to conduct and settle the Livingstonia mission party. This consisted of E. D. Young, Robert Laws (graduate in medicine and ordained), two engineers, a seaman, a carpenter, and an agriculturist.[3] They were also equipped with a small screw-steamer for the lake, the *Ilala*, specially built in sections for convenient transport beyond the cataracts. Here was the positive policy being applied in good measure. And no time was wasted: in little more than a year after the Abbey funeral, on May 21, 1875 they left London and were outward bound.

It was a happy augury that Scottish Presbyterian Churches then separated joined in the enterprise: the Free Church, the United Presbyterian, and the Reformed Presbyterian together. Moreover in the preparatory stages Captain Wilson, R.N., with ten years' East African experience, and Horace Waller formerly of the Universities' Mission, both members of the Church of England, rendered what a later Assembly gratefully recorded as "invaluable services". This co-operation of presbyterian and episcopalian in such an enterprise, linked so to speak in ecumenical embrace, would have gladdened the heart of David Livingstone. The Church of Scotland had also been stirred to

---

[1] J. W. Jack, *Daybreak in Livingstonia* (1901), 26.

[2] *Vide supra*, p. 201.

[3] "Messrs. George Johnston (carpenter), John Macfadyan (engineer and blacksmith), Allan Simpson (second engineer), Alexander Riddell (agriculturist), and William Baker (seaman, R.N.), made up our ship's company."—E. D. Young, *Nyassa; A Journal of Adventures* (1877), 15.

begin a mission in the same area and desired fraternal relations with the Free Church in the matter. The first link was the sending of Henry Henderson, appointed to survey the land for the Established Church, in association with the Free Church party.[1]

Three phases—they are scarcely periods save the third—may be distinguished in the early years of the Livingstonia mission according to the leadership respectively of E. D. Young, James Stewart, and Robert Laws. Young was leader until his departure in November 1876. He was responsible for conducting the pioneer party, transporting the steamer to the lake, and selecting the first site for the mission. He accomplished all with the efficiency to be expected of an experienced naval officer, tempered with a genuine missionary devotion. They travelled in the *Ilala* to the foot of the falls, passing on the way the graves of Mrs. Livingstone at Shupanga, of Bishop Mackenzie at the Ruo (where Young had an iron cross to erect), of Scudamore and Dickinson at Chibisa's, and of Thornton on reaching the falls, and calling at each to salute the dead. Young found that in every case neighbouring Africans had spontaneously cared for the graves, keeping them clear of voracious tropical undergrowth.[2] At the Murchison Cataracts the problem was to transport the dismantled *Ilala* some fifty to sixty miles, as Robert Laws described it, "through bush country, over rough rocks, with a climb of over a thousand feet, and no road whatever".[3] This was safely accomplished thanks to the settlement on the Shiré of some of Livingstone's Makololo. They had established themselves at Chibisa's in the days of the Zambezi Expedition and had improved their situation to such an extent that they were now the heads of considerable communities, due to their known antagonism to the slave-trade and their reception in consequence of thousands of refugees. By this time they controlled the Shiré from Chibisa's to the Ruo, having wisely combined against parties on the prowl for slaves, coming up from Portuguese settlements, to whom they became an impenetrable barrier. They were not models of chiefly behaviour by outside standards; theirs was a tyrannical rule, and they could be cruel, but their ever-grateful memory of Livingstone was undimmed. They welcomed Young and his companions with enthusiastic delight, and he testifies: "They laid themselves out to render us

---

[1] J. W. Jack, *op. cit.*, 25, 28, 30–1, 34–5, 36. Robert Laws was the contribution of the United Presbyterians.—W. P. Livingstone, *Laws of Livingstonia* (1922), 37–8.
[2] Young, *op. cit.*, 26, 31–2, 37–8, 54.
[3] R. Laws, *Reminiscences of Livingstonia* (1934), 12.

any service that they could devise or we suggest." It would have gone ill with the expedition had they not found these devoted friends with power to help effectively. When for instance Young saw three stalwart Makololo march in with 300 men, some having come forty miles to serve and bringing their food with them, he could not but reflect on the delays and frustrations of an earlier expedition: "My comrades little knew . . . of the weary weary waitings and cajolings it used to take in the early days to get half-a-dozen men together to carry a few burdens!" This improvement was an incidental element in Livingstone's legacy. All told 800 men tramped with their loads of bulky calico or steel sheets and engine sections without a thief or a deserter. Young admits he had his anxieties: what if some vital part of the *Ilala* were lost among the boulders or thrown down in disgust as the carrier decamped? "Yes," he wrote, "let this ever stand to the African's credit, that 800 of these men worked and worked desperately for us, . . . over a road which furnished at almost every yard an excuse for an accident, or a hiding place . . . but at the end of the sixty miles, we had everything delivered up to us unmolested, untampered with and unhurt." When Stewart's party arrived in 1876 there assembled 1,000 carriers to climb the boulder-strewn bank of the Cataracts.[1]

The party had entered the Shiré on August 27 and by September 6 were at the Cataracts. Progress had been slow owing to the deep draught of the *Ilala*, thus grounding her on sandbanks in tortuous channels, but a vessel sufficiently deep and powerful was necessary to be seaworthy on a lake often swept by fierce tempests, as was abundantly proved in the event.[2] By October 9 the *Ilala* was reassembled and steamed north for the lake, and three days later proudly shot out upon the majestic expanse of waters, "the first steam-vessel that had ever entered upon an African lake".[3] The selection of a site for

[1] For the contemporary situation of the Makololo, see Young, *op. cit.*, 34–40, 46–7, 51, 53, 168, 170, 173–80, 185, 190–1. With the coming of an unscrupulous type of European adventurer they passed under a cloud, but revived with the advent of a British administration.—J. W. Jack, *op. cit.*, 49–50. For tribute to the carriers, see Young, *op. cit.*, 53, 59, 218.

[2] The *Ilala's* draught was 4 feet. A draught of 1 foot only was needed to float in the shallows.—Young, *op. cit.*, 28, 42. The plates of the hull were only three thirty-seconds of an inch thick.—Laws, *op. cit.*, 17.

[3] Young, *op. cit.*, 60, 66–7. The name *Ilala* was deliberately selected with a severely practical purpose: "We felt that possibly we should meet with natives on the Lake who were acquainted with that part of the country in which he [Livingstone] perished, and that our naming our vessel thus would be a ready means to show them that we had taken up his work where he left it, and were prepared to do all honour to his name."—*Ibid.*, 13–14.

THE PLANTING OF CHRISTIANITY IN AFRICA

the mission settlement was the first and urgent business. After a rapid preliminary survey a position on the western side of Cape Maclear was chosen at the foot of two great rock mountains. Here the first tent was set up on October 18, 1875. It was naturally an important consideration with Young to have safe anchorage for the *Ilala*, and that was afforded. There was no population on the spot, but the *Ilala* was the link with many sea-shore settlements, and sons of the Makololo chiefs were sent to the school which was now begun. In half a dozen years there was removal to a more favourable centre, but Robert Laws could write nearly sixty years later: "Looking back I feel that we were rightly led to choose that place as our first station." Young also had an eye to security, and realizing that the slavers of the lake might seek to eliminate them, had a log fort constructed along the front of the mission buildings then erected, made by laying the trunks of trees one on the other to a thickness of six feet. The population around the mission had grown to be about 500 by the time of removal.[1]

The next priority was a survey of the lake shores. After a preliminary cruise to test the brave little *Ilala*, Young and Laws with Macfadyan the engineer and Baker the seaman set out on November 18, just one month after pitching their tents, to circumnavigate the lake. They cruised northwards along the eastern shore and found abundant evidence of the slave-trade, while Arabs they met were plainly disturbed at finding a British steamer invading their preserves. One half-caste indeed clearly thought the game was up and offered to sell his dhow! The annual transport of slaves across the lake was reported as 10,000. This was significantly confirmed by Bishop Steere of the Universities' Mission who in December of this same year paid his visit to Mataka's through whose town passed one of the two slave routes to the coast. Steere estimated, from caravans he actually passed, a traffic of 5,000 annually by this route alone.[2] The Free Church Committee had served Young with strict written instructions on no account to bring about hostilities, and this injunction he faithfully observed.[3] Ruined villages fringing the shore and in some cases dwellings built on piles off-shore were sad evidence of the marauders by land. As they approached the northern end of the eastern shore they came under

[1] *Ibid.*, 76, 88, 154, 188; Laws,, *op. cit.*, 16; J. W. Jack, *op. cit.*, 92.
[2] Young, *op. cit.*, 99–100, 125–8; R. M. Heanley, *A Memoir of Edward Steere*, 148–9.
[3] Young, *op. cit.*, 71.

the shadow of a gigantic mountain range with precipitous walls
falling sheer into the black waters below, by far the loftiest
mountains at any point around the lake. They extend for 100
miles and average 10,000 feet in height. Young called them the
Livingstone Mountains, a name they still proudly bear.[1] By
December 12 the lake survey was complete and the party back
at Cape Maclear. They were the first Europeans to visit the
northern end of the lake and the first to circumnavigate it and
to discover its total length to be close on 400 miles. Their own
journey of well over 1,000 miles, despite terrific storms to which
the lake is subject, was carried through without serious mis-
hap.[2]

It had been arranged that on Young's completion of his engagement James Stewart of Lovedale should come up to relieve
him. The first mail they had received for over ten months
brought the intelligence that Stewart would shortly arrive.
Accordingly on August 12 Young took the *Ilala* to the head of
the Cataracts, and then proceeded to Matiti at the foot among
the Makololo where there was weary waiting for a couple of
months in the enervating climate of the Shiré valley. At last on
October 12 they were all aboard the *Ilala* bound for Cape
Maclear.[3] Young's period of command was now at an end. On
November 2 he took his farewell, three weeks' travel brought
him to Quelimane, and on December 14 he sailed for home. He
spoke with modesty of his own share in planting in Central
Africa the first mission to survive: "Thanks to Him who had
guarded and guided us from the first, I had been enabled by
His help to carry out that part of the work which had fallen to
my lot in this great undertaking, and Dr. Stewart was on the
spot to develop the plan on which we had at first agreed. If I
had hitherto been the adze to rough-hew the project of Livingstonia into shape, with him now lay the part of the chisel to cut
out the sharper lines."[4] He was deeply and truly Christian in
his attitude to partners in the missionary task, and said in
reference to the surviving influence of Bishop Mackenzie's brief
career: "Whatever harvest may be reaped around the Lake,
it will be a sorry day when it shall be denied that 'he that
planteth and he that watereth are one', on the edge of that
blood-stained plain to which Livingstone's spirit first led

[1] *Ibid.*, 111; A. Silva White, *The Development of Africa* (1890), 43.
[2] Young, *op. cit.*, 131–2.
[3] *Ibid.*, 157, 213–15, 222–3.
[4] *Ibid.*, 227.

men of many ways of thinking, but undivided in a common hope."[1]

With the arrival of James Stewart the second phase of the mission opened. He brought a British reinforcement of four: William Black medical graduate and ordained, together with an agriculturist, an engineer, and a weaver.[2] A party for the Church of Scotland mission came with them. In addition Stewart brought four African agents from Lovedale in response to a request from Laws. When volunteers were asked for at Lovedale thirteen students stood forward. The four selected were Shadrach Mngunana, William Koyi, Isaac Wauchope, and Mapassa Ntintili. They were representative of both the Xhosa and Fingo peoples, long in conflict but now symbolically one in Christian service. Mngunana, the first African teacher of a school at Lake Nyasa, was a consumption casualty the year after his arrival, while Wauchope contracted such severe malaria that he was invalided to the Cape. Koyi later gave notable service in reaching the warrior Ngoni.[3]

In September and October 1877 Stewart and Laws set out on a second circumnavigation of the lake, one object being to discover a more central site for the headquarters of the mission. The island of Likoma at one time appealed to the Scottish imagination as a kind of Iona, but being on the eastern, slave-trade side of the lake was therefore rejected. It was later occupied by the Universities' Mission. The general policy was to be expansion from the base by establishing stations on the lake shore, behind which centres in the hills would be set up in a chain running north to south. Half-way up the west side accordingly seemed indicated as the site for the new base station, but they were undecided as between Bandawe and Matete, both almost opposite Likoma.[4] Before James Stewart's return to Lovedale his cousin, also James Stewart, a civil engineer, had arrived on leave from India to assist the mission for a brief period. Laws met him on the Zambezi and on the

[1] *Ibid.*, 189–90. Young received a warm welcome in Scotland and proved a valuable ally in missionary advocacy.—J. W. Jack, *op. cit.*, 91.

[2] John Gunn, agriculturist; Robert S. Ross, engineer and blacksmith; Archibald C. Miller, weaver.—J. W. Jack, *op. cit.*, 84.

[3] Shepherd, *Lovedale, South Africa*, 185–6; Laws, *op. cit.*, 54–5, 61; J. Stewart, *Dawn in the Dark Continent* (1906), 237. Wauchope was later ordained, and in the first World War served as chaplain to South African Bantu in a Labour Corps, who were lost when their transport, the *Mendi*, was torpedoed.—Laws, *op. cit.*, 57.

[4] Laws, *op. cit.*, 65–6. The journey is described in a paper, "The Second Circumnavigation of Lake Nyassa", read by James Stewart to the Royal Geographical Society, 10.3.79.—*Proceedings of the R.G.S.*, I, N.S. (1879), 290–304.

way up took him ashore to see the graves, from Mrs. Living-stone's at Shupanga to Thornton's at Matiti at the foot of the Cataracts. Stewart remarked: "This is a queer country where the only things you have to show me are graves." "Yes," said Laws, "but they are the milestones of Christianity marking its advance into the interior."[1] The first graves were now being dug at Cape Maclear, for in addition to Mngunana, William Black was himself a casualty. His early and sudden passing was a heavy loss.[2]

With Stewart's return to Lovedale in December 1877 the leadership of the mission devolved on Robert Laws, and this he held till his retirement after fifty-two years in Nyasaland. This marks no longer a phase but a major period. Meanwhile James Stewart, civil engineer, had discovered that his vocation was that of a missionary in Nyasaland. He resigned from the Indian Civil Service and became an invaluable colleague in Central Africa. It was now necessary to come to a decision about the proposed change of station. To this end Laws and Stewart con-ducted an intensive survey of the western shore and uplands with Koyi as interpreter to the Ngoni, the dominating tribe of the region. Bandawe was chosen after much consideration and even experimental residence, for the future of the mission was bound up with the decision. The removal, which was a major undertaking, was begun in March 1881.[3]

This change of residence brought the mission into immediate contact with new peoples, the Tonga and the Ngoni. The Tonga on the lake shore had suffered much from Ngoni attacks and were even found building their villages on sandbanks for greater security. The Ngoni, like the Matebele south of the Zambezi, were a Zulu warrior emigration from the days of Chaka, whose chief Zungandawa crossed the Zambezi and reached Fipa on Lake Tanganyika. At his death the more powerful headmen hived off and set up as independent chiefs. Groups settled east and west of Lake Tanganyika, and others, after various disrup-tions, east and west of Lake Nyasa.[4] These Ngoni were also known as Maviti. Under this name E. D. Young had met them in the Shiré valley and won a remarkable personal ascendancy

[1] Laws, *op. cit.*, 57, 60.
[2] *Ibid.*, 60-1.
[3] *Ibid.*, 67-84; J. W. Jack, *op. cit.*, 110, 139-41. The centre at Cape Maclear was retained as an outstation. A condensation of Dr. Laws' Report of this journey is supplied in the *Proceedings of the R.G.S.*, I, N.S. (1879), 305-21.
[4] Seligman, *Races of Africa*, 193-4; W. A. Elmslie, *Among the Wild Ngoni* (1899), 22-8.

that served to protect the peoples he was with.[1] Laws was now to have his relations with Mombera the Ngoni chief whom he first met in 1879. As with Moffat and Umsiligazi, so here the chief conceived a strong friendship for the missionary that by slow and interrupted stages promoted the work of the mission, safeguarded the Tonga, and generally made possible the transition from war to peace.[2] Here William Koyi won his spurs as a fearless evangelist.[3]

On the very eve of the transfer came the public baptism of the first convert of the mission, March 27, 1881. The entry in the Mission Journal recording the event stated: "This is a red-letter day in the history of the Livingstonia Mission. . . . Last Sabbath Dr. Laws intimated that Albert Namalambe would be baptized to-day. The school was crowded, and the attention throughout the whole service was intense. . . . Dr. Laws asked Albert to address the people. This he did in a humble yet manly and true-hearted way, and with a respect for the older people which gained the attention of all. He told them the reasons why he had sought baptism and his desire to obey God's law. He had been living among them, he said, and they knew if he were speaking the truth. He pleaded earnestly with all to accept of Christ's mercy. . . . Prayer was offered, after which Namalambe was baptized in the name of the three-one God by the name of Albert."[4] There was no landslide for there were no diluted standards in order to win converts. Only nine were baptized in the first decade.[5] Meanwhile the educational service of the mission was slowly developing. The first regular school began with Stewart's arrival when Shadrach Mnugunana became the first teacher—the pioneer African schoolmaster in Central Africa. The enrolment was seventeen boys—sons of chiefs, ex-slaves, and orphan refugees. By 1881 there were two schools with ninety scholars: fifty-one boys and thirty-nine girls.[6]

With that thoroughness of application characteristic of their nation, the Scottish missionaries were not content to depend upon interpreters longer than was necessary. Nyanja was the principal language at the southern end of the lake, and it was without delay reduced to a written form, a grammar produced, and the books essential to the early stages of the work translated.

[1] Young, *op. cit.*, 177–80, 182–3, 211–12.
[2] Laws, *op. cit.*, 72, 74–5; Elmslie, *op. cit.*, 94–5, 98–103.
[3] Elmslie, *op. cit.*, 91–2.
[4] Jack, *op. cit.*, 117.
[5] Laws, *op. cit.*, xiii.
[6] Jack, *op. cit.*, 119, 121.

By 1881 a hymn-book for worship and a school primer were in being, while the Gospel of Mark, begun in 1876, was completed in MS., having already been subject to revision.[1]

Meanwhile the sister mission of the Church of Scotland had been struggling to strike root in the Shiré highlands. Henry Henderson, associated with Young's party, had been assigned the task of selecting a suitable site for the mission. Henderson was a son of the manse who had gone to Australia from a spirit of adventure. He had declined a suggestion that he should enter the ministry, doubting his motives. Thus after graduating at Edinburgh he went to Queensland and for twelve years lived the life of the Australian bush. He then returned to Scotland and was taking some classes at Edinburgh University while seeking light on the next step, when the need for a pioneer in the Lake Nyasa country came to him as his call. He offered and was appointed, travelling out with the Free Church party and spending the early days with them at Cape Maclear. He accompanied Young and Laws on their circumnavigation of Nyasa in 1875, but the lake shores yielded nothing that appealed to him as suitable. He now resolved to search the Shiré highlands which Livingstone had always commended for settlement but from which the Universities' Mission had felt compelled to retreat. So with an interpreter and four carriers he climbed up from the Shiré valley where the *Ilala* had landed him, and passed round the western slopes of Mount Zomba; then, leaving on the east Magomero where Bishop Mackenzie had settled, he proceeded south to Mount Ndirande. On a ridge running west and south from Ndirande he felt assured lay the site he was seeking. Down again to the lower Shiré valley to await his outcoming party in a village of one of Livingstone's Makololo—the usual weary wait of weeks in the absence of regular communications—and then up to the spot selected (Henderson having first reconnoitred it again to make assurance doubly sure) where, thanks to carriers provided by the Makololo, they all arrived with their possessions on October 23, 1876.[2]

The party consisted of Macklin a medical man, and five artisans of whom John Buchanan later rose to some importance in the country. He had come as an agriculturist and it was he

---

[1] *Ibid.*, 131–2. The language is sometimes referred to as Chinyanja, with the word's appropriate class-prefix as in vernacular usage.

[2] W. Robertson, *The Martyrs of Blantyre* (1892), 55–64; Young, *op. cit.*, 93, 152; A. Hetherwick, *The Romance of Blantyre* (n.d.), 18–22.

who first introduced the planting of coffee. On reaching the site selected for the mission, which was named Blantyre for obvious reasons, the missionaries found themselves at an elevation of 3,000 feet above the sea on what Livingstone called the third plateau of the Shiré highlands, some forty miles south of the Zomba range and about the same distance from Lake Shirwa. It was a splendid location and Henderson had served the mission well in selecting it.[1] The strain of the journey from the coast had told however (they had landed at Quilimane on August 6), and despite their healthy situation they were soon to suffer a good deal from malaria, evidently having caught the infection on the prolonged river passage. They were settled in and that was all; there was no working out. Under these circumstances in December 1876 Henderson appealed to the Livingstonia Mission for help and received a generous response. Stewart and Laws took turns in caring for the work, and artisans and African agents were also shared with the sister mission. Henderson, who had felt his commission discharged with the choosing of the site and the settlement of the missionary party on it, retired in April 1877. The retirement however proved temporary. In 1882 he returned as general agent of the mission and served until his death from malaria in 1891, after the tragic loss of wife and child.[2]

In July 1877 James Stewart, C.E., came over from Cape Maclear and took charge of the work at Blantyre for a year, infusing new life into the undertaking. One of his first tasks as a skilled engineer was the laying out of the mission station on an attractive plan with Indian-style bungalows as dwelling-houses. Good roads were made radiating from the station, and a mile-long channel surveyed to bring water into it. Altogether a general air of prosperity began to appear. And to crown all, Stewart even engineered a road ten feet wide and sixty miles long from the lower to the upper Shiré via Blantyre, thus relieving both missions of the problem of transport alongside the Cataracts. For long this was known as the "Stewart Road". If Henderson selected the site, it was Stewart who established the station. On July 12, 1878 he passed on the charge of it to Duff Macdonald, the first ordained missionary appointed by the

---

[1] Jack, *op. cit.*, 85; J. Buchanan, *The Shiré Highlands as Colony and Mission* (1885), 201, 202. Mackay, the boatman of the Blantyre mission, was the first loss. He travelled in a boat on the lake and was seized with a fatal illness on his return to Cape Maclear.—Laws, *op. cit.*, 60-1.

[2] Jack, *op. cit.*, 95-6; Laws, *op. cit.*, 55-6; Robertson, *op. cit.*, 66-7, 72-3; Duff Macdonald, *Africana* (1882), II, 21.

Established Church. He was accompanied by his wife, the first European woman to reside in the country.[1]

Blantyre was faced with a problem to which the mission at Cape Maclear was not exposed—that of refugee slaves seeking asylum. These were not turned away and for this there seemed good precedent from Livingstone's day. But two inevitable complications thereby arose: on the one hand, slave-owning chiefs became angered at losing what they regarded as legitimate property, and felt justified in seeking compensation by such plunder of mission goods as they could manage. And on the other hand, the reception of such refugees produced a community without a chief; was not the missionary to exercise such functions, in other words, to be responsible for civil jurisdiction? Out of this developed a crisis for the mission. Corporal punishment was administered, and on one occasion, in a joint European-African session, a murderer was condemned to death and executed. Disquieting reports began to circulate at home, in 1881 a commission of inquiry was appointed by the Assembly, and in consequence certain lay agents were discharged. Duff Macdonald resigned though not personally involved. It was at this point that Buchanan left the mission. The whole was an unhappy chapter in the history of Blantyre.[2]

Duff Macdonald had shown a keen interest in African life and in his brief tenure, from July 12, 1878 to July 1, 1881, he had been both language student and alert observer of African affairs. He selected Yao for his linguistic investigations and, in addition to school books in that language, had translated the Gospels of Matthew and Mark and historical sections of the Old Testament. His two volumes of *Africana* preserve much material of value. It was a calamity that such a man found his position untenable.[3] He was succeeded by an ordained missionary, David Clement Scott who arrived in October 1881. A clear policy had now been laid down and Scott had to apply it: no more refugee slaves to be received; and further, if the owners of those already accepted entered a claim, this should be settled by payment of ransom which the individuals concerned would then

[1] Jack, *op. cit.*, 96–7, 126; Hetherwick, *op. cit.*, 28–9; Buchanan, *op. cit.*, 202 (for plan of station).
[2] Hetherwick, *op. cit.*, 26–8, 31–2; Duff Macdonald, *op. cit.*, II, 27–31, 34–5, 41–5, 251–5, 260; J. du Plessis, *Évangelisation of Pagan Africa*, 303–4; R. Oliver, *The Missionary Factor in East Africa* (1952), 59 and *n*. The contemporary discussion is reported in *The Missionary Review* (Princeton, N.J.), IV (1881), 256–60, 310–14, 430–2; V (1882), 12–21.
[3] Duff Macdonald, *op. cit.*, II, 127–8, 141–2, 260–1.

work off as a debt.[1] Scott was successful in carrying the policy into effect. He also entered upon the educational and religious work of the mission with the powers of a skilled organizer and made an outstanding contribution with his Nyanja dictionary.[2]

Though invalided in a little over three years he returned to continue his leadership until 1898 in a steadily expanding work. Meanwhile Alexander Hetherwick had arrived at Blantyre on August 13, 1883. After fifteen years' apprenticeship he was to serve a full thirty as overseer of the flock and director of the mission. Long continuity of oversight was now to be assured.[3]

A third enterprise was the direct result of Livingstone's call for help to squeeze out the slave-trade by legitimate commerce as well as to preach the Christian message. The brothers, John William and Frederick Lewis Maitland Moir, born in Edinburgh in 1851 and 1852 respectively, were of the age at Livingstone's death to be fired with devotion to the cause for which he died. Throwing up comfortable positions they first of all served as unpaid volunteers on a road that was projected from the coast to Lake Nyasa, to by-pass the hampering restrictions of the Portuguese and other human difficulties on the Zambezi route. Sir Thomas Fowell Buxton and Sir William Mackinnon were backers of the enterprise and Kirk at Zanzibar gave invaluable support. But when the road had been engineered for twenty miles from Dar-es-Salaam the project fell through. The Moirs returned to Scotland in 1878, having been out a year. They now determined themselves to open up regular communications and trade with the lakes by the Zambezi route.[4] Coincidentally there had developed a movement, under the inspiration of Stewart of Lovedale, for an independent commercial company which should lift from the missionaries' shoulders the burden of transport and the general trading concerns inevitable in a country without a recognized currency. Through the Livingstonia Mission Committee action was taken by leading Glasgow business men among whom John Stevenson was the leading spirit, and the Livingstonia Central Africa Company Limited was formed on June 21, 1878 with a preliminary nominal capi-

[1] This was the policy in operation at Cape Maclear.—F. L. M. Moir, *After Livingstone*, 22.
[2] *A Cyclopaedic Dictionary of the Mang'anja Language* (1892).
[3] Hetherwick, *op. cit.*, 38–46; W. P. Livingstone, *A Prince of Missionaries* (n.d.) 11–22.
[4] F. L. M. Moir, *After Livingstone; An African Trade Romance* (n.d.), 1–6.

tal of £20,000. The brothers Moir were appointed joint-managers.[1]

An individual attempt to operate legitimate trade, inspired by a genuine human concern, had been earlier made by H. B. Cotterill. Son of Bishop Cotterill of Edinburgh, he had been a master at Haileybury College and Harrow School. Livingstone's reports of the slave-trade had so deeply moved him that he sought to serve in its extinction. Sir Bartle Frere suggested he might do so by writing but this he rejected and determined to throw himself directly into the fray. His old boys at Harrow subscribed £500 for a fine steel boat for Lake Nyasa, he invested in a stock of trade goods, and sailed with the 1876 contingent for Central Africa. He generously helped at Cape Maclear, though not a member of the mission staff, and did some useful exploring work in the course of which he lost all his goods in a disaster on the lake. At the end of 1877 he returned to England. Before he left he presented his steel boat, the *Herga*, to the mission. It was a noble venture, but it showed pretty conclusively that something beyond solitary individual action was required.[2]

The new company, soon to be known as the African Lakes Company, was to maintain regular communications between Quilimane and Lake Nyasa, establish depots, and engage in trade, thus cutting the slave-routes as far inland as possible. It was hoped to link up later with Lake Tanganyika, a hope that was in due course fulfilled. The whole was a formidable undertaking and owed its initial success to the leadership of the brothers Moir. Traffic in liquor was excluded and in firearms severely restricted, which at first hampered trade relations in slave-ridden country where such commodities were in principal demand. A paddle-steamer, the *Lady Nyasa* of slender proportions, was provided for service on the Zambezi and lower Shiré. The *Ilala*, serving the upper Shiré and the lake, was later transferred from the Livingstonia Mission to the Company. The headquarters were set up at Blantyre a mile from the mission, and the name Mandala soon became familiar to African patrons of the Company. So correct were the relations of the brothers Moir with Africans that disputes from far and near were before long referred to them and their decisions always accepted. The later developments of the company were extensive.[3]

[1] *Ibid.*, 7–8; Wells, *The Life of James Stewart*, 139 and *n*.

[2] Young, *op. cit.*, 215–16; Laws, *op. cit.*, 53–4, 62; Jack, *op. cit.*, 85–6, 106–7.

[3] Moir, *op. cit.*, 12, 17, 40–51, 62–3; Jack, *op. cit.*, 215–20. "Mandala" was the African name for John Moir, from the reflection of light from his spectacles. As a trade name it came to carry valuable goodwill.

Thus the heritage of Livingstone was accepted by his Scottish heirs and the transformation from pillage and destruction to prosperity and the arts of peace for which he lived and laboured grew slowly to reality. "It is to the eternal credit of the Scottish missions", runs an official statement, "that next after Livingstone's name in the roll of Nyasaland's great pioneers must be inscribed the names of Robert Laws of Livingstonia and Alexander Hetherwick of Blantyre, to whose services the country largely owes the growth of a *Pax Britannica* rather than the imposition of a *Pax Romana*."[1]

(2) *Tasks Inspired*

While many, whose purpose was inspired by Livingstone's own devotion, were thus engaged in claiming for Christianity and civilization the territory he had found so beautiful by nature yet so disfigured by man, there were also others whom he had inspired to carry on his work, whose undertakings over far-flung territories opened up regions he had never seen and set forth opportunities he had never known. Foremost among these for the extent of territory traversed and the range of opportunity disclosed, stands Henry Morton Stanley.

When Stanley bade farewell to Livingstone in March 1872 it took all his strength of will to maintain self-control: "We wrung each other's hands, and I had to tear myself away before I unmanned myself. 'Good-bye, Doctor—dear friend!' 'Good-bye!' "[2] It was two years later, when Stanley was returning from the Ashanti War in April 1874, that he first heard Livingstone was dead: "Livingstone had then fallen! He was dead! He had died by the shores of Lake Bemba, on the threshold of the dark region he had wished to explore! . . . The effect which this news had upon me, after the first shock had passed away, was to fire me with a resolution to complete his work, to be, if God willed it, the next martyr to geographical science, or, if my life was to be spared, to clear up not only the secrets of the Great River throughout its course, but also all that remained still problematic and incomplete of the discoveries of Burton and Speke, and Speke and Grant."[3] The latter object led him to Uganda, the former took him down the Congo to the Atlantic.

[1] *Annual Report on Nyasaland for the Year 1946* (1948), 53. Robert Laws had been offered the post of first Governor of Nyasaland.—P. M. Shepherd, *Molepolole: A Missionary Record* (1947), 8.

[2] H. M. Stanley, *How I Found Livingstone* (1872), 435.

[3] H. M. Stanley, *Through the Dark Continent* (1878), I, 1.

The Abbey service intensified his resolve and he left it with a keen edge to his purpose: "I laboured night and day over my book, 'Coomassie and Magdala', for I was in a fever to begin that to which I now had vowed to devote myself." The book was finished within three weeks.[1]

Sponsored by the *Daily Telegraph* and the *New York Herald* the expedition's arrangements at the European end were speedily in hand and Stanley sailed once again for East Africa on August 15, 1874. Within three months the necessary preparations at Zanzibar had been completed and on November 12 the expedition crossed to the mainland. Five days later the lengthy cavalcade filed out of Bagamoyo on the quest. With Stanley were three white companions in a total party of 356 persons; there was liberal provision of equipment and for emergency needs four-footed transport in the form of half a dozen riding asses.[2] They set out on the Ujiji route but when half-way to Tanganyika they struck north-west to the Victoria Nyanza, reaching its southern shore on February 27, 1875. Here the main body encamped while Stanley with a scouting party carefully explored the eastern shore and finally arrived in Uganda on April 5, to be favourably received by the king, Mutesa.[3]

Mutesa had succeeded his father Suna in 1857 when he was about eighteen. Suna left sixty-one sons of an age to be candidates for the throne. Mutesa was selected for the honour by palace officials and his sixty rivals liquidated to a man. It was not long before Mutesa took the reins into his own hands. According to traditions supplied to Stanley he was thirty-fifth in the line from Kintu, the legendary founder of the kingdom.[4] The first Arab to enter Uganda appears to have been Ahmed bin Ibrahim of Zanzibar, who visited Suna about 1844 and twice later. On one occasion he is said to have protested in the name of Allah against Suna's inhuman order for a sacrificial holocaust. The unheard of temerity that would rebuke the despot startled Suna into attention and he asked to know more

[1] *Ibid.*, I, 2.

[2] *Ibid.*, I, 2–4, 81–3. Stanley gives an objective yet quite appreciative account of the work of the Universities' Mission at Zanzibar and the French Catholic Mission at Bagamoyo. Three pupils of the Universities' Mission were in his party.— *Ibid.*, 75–80.

[3] *Ibid.*, I, 67, 81–3, 141–2, 145. Uganda (the root Ganda with the Swahili prefix) has become so entrenched in the literature through the usage of explorers with Swahili interpreters that it is retained in preference to the locally correct form, Buganda.—Thomas and Scott, *Uganda* (1935), vi–vii.

[4] J. M. Gray, "Mutesa of Buganda", *The Uganda Journal*, I (1934), 23; Ham Mukasa, "Some Notes on the Reign of Mutesa", *Ibid.*, I, 124–9; Stanley, *op. cit.*, I, 380.

of this religion. Ahmed is said to have set forth some of the elements of Islam but Suna was never claimed as a convert. An old and torn Muslim treatise in Arabic survived in the possession of Mutesa, who had some knowledge of the language.[1] The first Europeans to be seen in Uganda were Speke and Grant who arrived in 1862 on the memorable visit that established in broad outline the solution to the problem of the Nile sources.[2] An American on the staff of Gordon then in the service of the Khedive, Chaillé-Long, was despatched to Mutesa in 1874 with an Egyptian flag. He retired in a month.[3] Stanley arrived the following year.

Commissioned though he was to engage in geographical research, Stanley's religious convictions led him to improve the occasion of his contact with Mutesa. He has given us his own record of his early religious impressions as a workhouse boy, and has admitted that they would scarcely have survived the pressures of a journalist's city life, adding: "Religion grew deep roots in me in the solitude of Africa."[4] The share of Livingstone in that development he does not divulge. It is therefore not surprising to find him reporting on April 10: "Since the 5th April, I had enjoyed ten interviews with Mtesa, and during all I had taken occasion to introduce topics which would lead up to the subject of Christianity. Nothing occurred in my presence but I contrived to turn it towards effecting that which had become an object to me, viz. his conversion. . . . I simply drew for him the image of the Son of God humbling Himself for the good of all mankind, white and black, and told him how . . . He was crucified . . . and yet out of His great love for them, while yet suffering on the cross, He asked His great Father to forgive them."[5] An early endorsement of his teaching came from an unexpected quarter. Within a week of his own arrival there appeared an emissary from Gordon, Linant de Bellefonds. The Frenchman proved to be a member of the Reformed Church, and when appealed to by Mutesa about points of Christian teaching used terms so similar to Stanley's that king and chiefs were much impressed, for there had been no opportunity for

[1] J. M. Gray, "Ahmed bin Ibrahim—The First Arab to reach Buganda", *The Uganda Journal*, XI (1947), 82.

[2] J. H. Speke, *Journal of the Discovery of the Source of the Nile* (Everyman ed.), 232–359; J. A. Grant, *A Walk Across Africa* (1864), 219–35; *The Uganda Journal*, I, 129–32.

[3] B. M. Allen, *Gordon and the Sudan*, 30; *The Uganda Journal*, I, 30–1.

[4] Dorothy Stanley (ed.), *The Autobiography of Sir Henry Morton Stanley, G.C.B.* (1909), 23–8.

[5] Stanley, *op. cit.*, I, 202.

collusion.[1] Stanley determined to use at once the occasion presented by Linant's visit and to address a letter to the Christian public of Britain and the States, appealing for a Christian mission to be sent to Uganda without delay. He wrote of the interest Mutesa had shown in his own religious efforts: "He has caused the Ten Commandments of Moses to be written on a board for his daily perusal—for Mtesa can read Arabic—as well as the Lord's Prayer and the golden commandment of our Saviour, 'Thou shalt love thy neighbour as thyself' "; and made comment: "Though I am no missionary, I shall begin to think that I might become one if such success is feasible." He painted the opportunity in more glowing colours than the sequel warranted, but more of that anon. Meanwhile the letter dated April 14, 1875 was forwarded in two copies, to the *Daily Telegraph* and the *New York Herald* respectively, by Linant and then by Gordon to their destinations. The letter appeared in the *Daily Telegraph* on November 15, 1875 with results to be in due course recorded.[2]

Having completed his circumnavigation of the lake—the first explorer to do so—and thus settled the question of effluents and affluents in relation to the Nile sources, Stanley returned to Mutesa and continued his self-imposed missionary labours. Mutesa's interest in his copy of the Bible and Book of Common Prayer gave Stanley an idea: he produced with the help of a youth named Dallington in his party—a pupil of the Universities' Mission—an abridged Bible in Swahili, with St. Luke translated entire. When the choice between Islam and Christianity was before king and chiefs, Stanley reports Mutesa as deciding not by teaching only but by conformity in life: "The Arabs come here for ivory and slaves. . . . The white men, when offered slaves, refuse them, saying, 'Shall we make our brothers slaves? No; we are all sons of God.' I have not heard a white man tell a lie yet. Speke came here, behaved well, and went his way home with his brother Grant. They bought no slaves, and the time they were in Uganda they were very good. Stamlee came here, and he would take no slaves. Abdul Aziz Bey (M. Linant) has been here, and is gone, and he took no slaves. What

---

[1] *Ibid.*, 207.

[2] *Ibid.*, 209–10. The story of a blood-stained letter recovered from a boot of the murdered Linant was stated by Gordon himself to be a fabrication. "The letters I sent home . . . never fell into the jungle as described. Linant arrived safely, and was with me three days before his death."—*The Times*, May 17, 1876. Cf. H. H. Johnston, *The Uganda Protectorate* (1902), I, 222–3; Thomas and Scott, *op. cit.*, 15 n. 1; H. B. Thomas, "Ernest Linant de Bellefonds and Stanley's letter to the *Daily Telegraph*"—*The Uganda Journal*, II (1934–5), 7–13.

Arab would have refused slaves like these white men?" And so the die was cast for Christianity, and Mutesa professed himself a convert. But the conversion was nominal only—could it under the circumstances well have been otherwise?—and Stanley was not unaware of this, though he entertained unduly optimistic hopes about the future. To secure what he believed had at least been so far achieved he released Dallington from his service and the youth became not only Christian instructor but also court scribe to Mutesa where communications other than Arabic were concerned.[1]

Stanley had a decisive demonstration before he left that the ancestral paganism still ruled Mutesa's heart. In the course of war with rebellious Uvuma a chief was seized as prisoner of war—an old man of sixty or so—and Mutesa was about to burn him at the stake in reprisal for a peace envoy of his own having been treacherously done to death. Stanley, alarmed at the dire vengeance Mutesa proposed to exact, made an urgent appeal on the basis of his recent teaching, that as Christians we should love our enemies. But Mutesa was not yet domiciled in the New Testament; he savagely claimed blood for blood. In vain Stanley appealed to his erstwhile convert. Then he played a last card to avert the tragedy; he appealed to the ever-watchful ancestors, not only to Kintu who hated bloodshed, but also to Kamanya and Suna, his immediate predecessors: "At the mention of Suna and Kamanya in the spirit-land looking down upon him, the tears began to well in his eyes. . . ." It was the effective appeal: the old chief was reprieved.[2]

But there was much more to it than that. Was Mutesa ever directly attracted to the Christian religion? Or were its associations with white men of marked personality, representatives of a shadowy but powerful nation beyond the seas, the real reason for his apparent interest? There is good evidence to suggest that a political and not a religious motive lay behind. Recent events had led Mutesa to fear the loss of his country to an advancing Egyptian imperialism. Baker and Gordon, though never in personal contact with Mutesa, were in succession both involved on behalf of the ambitious Khedive whom they served. Their own dominating interest of course was the suppression of the

---

[1] Stanley, *op. cit.*, I, 322, 324–5, 405, 417–18. Dallington wrote to Bishop Steere, April 23, 1876 telling of his work and asking for school supplies. Steere commented: "We may claim the credit of being *the first* in Uganda, though we have no wish to hold it against the 'C.M.S.'. "—Heanley, *A Memoir of Edward Steere*, 196–7, where Dallington's letter is reproduced. Italics in original.

[2] Stanley, *op. cit.*, I, 334–7.

slave-trade, but coupled with this was the Khedive's policy of annexation of the equatorial regions; and with Egyptian interference in the affairs of Unyoro,[1] Uganda's northern neighbour, Uganda became directly concerned.[2] It is significant that the only two instances recorded of Mutesa staging scenes of frightfulness by inhuman executions in the presence of foreign visitors were before Egyptian envoys.[3] It was plainly Mutesa's policy to secure his own independence by maintaining Unyoro as a buffer state. Stanley had taken farewell of Mutesa in November 1875. On February 6, 1876 Dallington did his best to produce in English a letter from Mutesa to Gordon suggesting three possibilities with respect to Unyoro (as it would now seem) though the letter left Gordon mystified, both as to its origin and purpose.[4] Four years later a second letter reached Gordon from Mutesa, this time in plain English thanks to a missionary scribe, and it significantly began: "I am very glad that you have taken your soldiers out of Unyoro, and now I write this letter to send you my compliments and friendship."[5] It has been bluntly asserted that Stanley was duped by the calculating Mutesa who played up to him on the religious issue for the sake of getting white men who would stand for his independence against the threatened Egyptian aggression.[6] Be that as it may, the political motive was strong, and Mutesa's nervousness at Egyptian pretensions must be borne in mind for the understanding of later events.

Stanley had been engaged upon his first objective—the tracing of the extreme southern sources of the Nile—from January 17, 1875 to April 7, 1876.[7] He now turned south to Tanganyika to investigate its central and southern shores (he had explored the extreme northern section with Livingstone) before

[1] As with "Uganda", the Swahili form; "Bunyoro" in local usage.
[2] Baker annexed Unyoro in the name of the Khedive in 1872.—Murray and White, *Sir Samuel Baker*, 185, 192. Mutesa's action on the occasion of Baker's invasion was not as co-operative as it was made to appear.—Cf. *The Uganda Journal*, I, 28–9. For Gordon's activity in respect of Unyoro, see *ibid.*, I, 30–4; B. M. Allen, *op. cit.*, 67, 78; and on his brief entanglement in Uganda in 1876, *The Uganda Journal*, I, 33–4; V, 284–5.
[3] *The Uganda Journal*, I, 30, 34.
[4] The letter is reproduced in facsimile in G. B. Hill, *Colonel Gordon in Central Africa* (1885), at p. 160, and in *The Uganda Journal*, V (1937–8), at p. 68. The most convincing interpretation of the letter is that by G. H. E. Hopkins in *The Uganda Journal*, VIII (1940–1), 37–8.
[5] G. B. Hill, *op. cit.*, 160 n.
[6] J. M. Gray in *The Uganda Journal*, I, 33, 35.
[7] Stanley, *op. cit.*, I, 480–2.

turning west to the Great River. On May 27 he was at Ujiji and memories of the past crowded in upon him: "But the grand old hero, whose presence once filled Ujiji with such absorbing interest for me was gone!" In sailing south he at first traversed territory he had travelled over with Livingstone, as at Urimba, "ground which I looked upon with reverence". But these familiar scenes were soon left behind, and by July 31 he with a select party had sailed around 810 of Tanganyika's 930 miles of shore.[1] By October 27 the expedition had reached Nyangwe on the Lualaba, the "Great River"—338 miles travelled in forty-three days from Ujiji to which they had first returned, a third of the time taken by Arab caravans. Nyangwe was the farthest west of any Arab settlement, and the limit in that direction reached by Livingstone. From here began the great journey into the unknown. By contract with Hamed ibn Mohammed, better known to history as Tippu Tib, this Arab trader-adventurer was to accompany Stanley's expedition with a large armed party for a specified distance, in order to encourage Stanley's people at the outset. And so on November 5, 1876 they set out with their faces to the north to trace the Great River to the sea. Tippu Tib withdrew in much under contract time, daunted by the perils of the way, but by then Stanley and his 149 people were all afloat. He estimated, allowing a month for cataracts which the contour of the continent had led him to expect, that they might see the ocean by the end of April 1877. But it was to be mid-August.[2] The obstacles presented by man and nature would have seemed insuperable, seen together in advance. But they were met and overcome as they appeared, thanks to the stout courage and travel-wisdom of the leader and the loyalty, gradually deepened by joint experience of adversity, of his band of followers. As the African proverb has it: Step by step finishes the longest journey.

The dense equatorial forest into which they had to plunge was the first major obstacle across their path. And if nature was resistant, man was reluctant. The memory of an earlier Arab aggression in the district they first traversed led to the villagers' panic flight, so that purchase of supplies became impossible. "Man refused us and the forest rejected us," wrote Stanley. And then came sharper trials both from nature and from man. The

---

[1] *Ibid.*, I, 509; II, 21, 60.

[2] *Ibid.*, II, 107-8, 114, 117, 126, 193, 195. Tippu Tib was the son of a half-caste Arab merchant of Zanzibar and a Negro slave-woman. Tippu Tib was a nickname, variously explained. See S. L. Hinde, *The Fall of the Congo Arabs* (1897), 8 *n.* 1.

seven cataracts of Stanley Falls took three weeks to pass; and they were now immersed in cannibal country where strangers were fair game, and to pass through without a fight for their survival proved impossible. The war drums began to beat at first sight of them and the cry, "Meat! Meat!" rang out from the aggressors, armed with deadly spears and poisoned arrows, and exulting in all the assurance of a replenished larder. By February 1, 1877 Stanley had recorded "twenty-eight desperate combats", and four more were yet to come. Five days later, on February 6, he wrote in his Journal: "The greatest danger, an ever-recurring one, is that which we have to encounter each time the wild howling cannibal aborigines observe us. Indeed, the sense of security is shortlived, our pleasure evanescent; but the sense of danger is always present and pervades our minds whether in our sleeping or our waking hours." But here and there were chiefs and people prepared to respond to the cry of "Peace!" and "Friend!" and so the strain was at rare intervals relieved. On February 8 came a most welcome word from a friendly chief at the apex of the arch of the Great River, in an-swer to Stanley's question asking the name of that water: *Ikutu ya Kongo!* "There had really been no doubt in my mind", he wrote, "since we had left the Stanley Falls that the terrible river would prove eventually to be the river of Congo-land, but it was very agreeable to be told so." Just beyond this point also they found at Upoto a few old Portuguese muskets in possession of the people, further proof of through communication with the Western Ocean. The generous width of the river along the thousand miles of navigable waterway between Stanley Falls and the extensive cataracts of the Lower Congo was studded with islands, thus permitting the expedition to thread its way to some extent unobserved and so to escape arousing the inhospitable attentions of the riverine tribes, save when hunger compelled them to approach a village to barter for a meal. There was game, but to shoot would be to call the cannibals, for from Upoto onwards the tribes possessed firearms. Finally came a series of thirty-two falls, some of thunderous power, in the Lower Congo, and the now exhausted and dispirited people put their undaunted leader to the final test. At one point three miles' travel took them thirty days. In the concluding stages they were desperately short of food, but at last reached Boma below the Cataracts: "On the 9th August 1877, the 999th day from the date of our departure from Zanzibar, we prepared to greet the van of civilization." The expedition had travelled some 7,000 miles all told, and by the great Congo journey had marked the close of the period of major exploration in Central Africa, initiated by Livingstone's journey to Lake Ngami a generation before.[1]

The penetration of so vast a range of inhabited territory, with the evidence of a thousand miles of navigable water on one of the great rivers of the world, opened up a missionary opportunity in Africa hitherto unequalled in extent and scarcely to be paralleled for high adventure. Within a year the first advances from the west were under way, but these belong rather to the succeeding period. The explorer's high achievement was real enough, but by contrast to Livingstone's great record its lustre became dimmed for some by stories that were current of a resort to firearms not customary in African exploration. Kirk, asked by the British Government for a confidential report, had replied that he regarded the charges as "substantially true", and added: "His proceedings will prove one of the principal obstacles that future explorers and missionaries will have to meet when following his track."[2] Stanley's own letters to the press from Lake Victoria had occasioned the first serious misgivings and led to public protest from the Anti-slavery and Aborigines Protection Societies. Derby as Foreign Secretary had then instructed Kirk to inform Stanley "that you have no authority to make use of the British flag as giving countenance to your proceedings in the interior of Africa."[3] Stanley admits that he regarded Livingstone as far too lenient, speaking of his "excessive mildness" in his behaviour to his African followers, and presents his own treatment as having been firm but just; though this must be distinguished from the point at issue which was his conduct in defence against assault.[4] Perhaps the reply of Robert Arthington a decade later to a request for the loan of the mission steamer *Peace* was not so wide of the mark: "I have much regard for you personally, although I cannot, dare not,

---

[1] *Ibid.*, II, 254–5, 268, 277, 281, 283, 286, 295, 301, 420, 443, 461, 467. There had been 114 deaths in the expedition, of which Stanley records particulars.—*Ibid.*, II, 510–13. He took the survivors home to Zanzibar by way of the Cape

[2] Coupland, *The Exploitation of East Africa, 1856–1890* (1939), 329 and *n.* 2.

[3] *Ibid.*, 324–7.

[4] Stanley, *op. cit.*, II, 66–7, 86. Aware of circulating stories, he wrote in the Preface: "That the rule of my conduct in Africa has not been understood by all, I know to my bitter cost; but with my conscience at ease, and the simple record of my daily actions, which I now publish, to speak for me this misunderstanding on the part of a few presents itself to me only as one more harsh experience of life."—*Ibid.*, I, vii.

sanction all your acts. . . . God seems to have given you a noble soul."[1]

Three days after Stanley's letter had appeared in the *Daily Telegraph* of November 15, 1875 the Church Missionary Society received an offer of £5,000 to enable them to answer the call for missionaries for Uganda. Within five days the Committee resolved to undertake the proposed mission and within six months the special fund stood at £12,000. Also within six months a party of eight had been appointed. The leader was Lieutenant George Shergold Smith, R.N., whose father had been a midshipman on H.M.S. *Myrmidon* which released the slave-boy Adjai Crowther; Charles Thomas Wilson was the ordained clergyman, John Smith the medical man, Thomas O'Neill the civil engineer and architect; on the mechanical side were Alexander M. Mackay engineer, W. M. Robertson blacksmith, and G. J. Clark shipwright. The eighth, J. Robertson an agriculturist, had been rejected by the doctors but was allowed to go at his own risk and charges. The home authorities were not unaware of the nature of the undertaking: "They have committed themselves to a difficult, and, even in some respects, dangerous enterprise."[2]

By June 26, 1876 the whole party was at Zanzibar. An intermediate station was established the same year at Mpwapwa, some 230 miles inland from Bagamoyo on the Ujiji route, and the attempt then made to push forward to Lake Victoria. The difficulties were formidable: the proposed mission would have a supply line to the coast some 700 miles long, without intermediate stations save Mpwapwa; the temper of the intervening tribes had yet to be ascertained, and the climate to be proved. J. Robertson who had ventured at his own risk was dead within three months; the mechanics G. J. Clark and W. M. Robertson were invalided home, and Alexander Mackay was sent down the line on health grounds. But Mackay improved the time of waiting in characteristic fashion by cutting a road from the coast to Mpwapwa in conjunction with the London Mission party bound for Tanganyika. Roger Price's proposal to use ox-transport had first given the idea, but tsetse killed the hope of such an alternative to head porterage. Meanwhile half the original party was left to go forward: Wilson and O'Neill were at the southern shore of the lake by January 29, 1877; Shergold

---

[1] H. M. Stanley, *In Darkest Africa* (1890), I, 47. Stanley had written to Arthington, as the donor of the *Peace*, to request the loan of it for the Emin Pasha expedition. The whole of Arthington's letter is quoted.

[2] *Proceedings of the C.M.S.* (1876), 54–5.

Smith and the doctor not until April 1. While here Dr. John Smith succumbed to an attack of fever on May 11. They were now three by the lake. The *Daisy*, a small steam launch, had been conveyed to the lake in sections and in Mackay's absence was now put together and converted to a sailing-boat. At the end of June letters were received from Mutesa, written by Dallington, Stanley's boy from the Universities' Mission, urging the missionaries to advance quickly. Smith and Wilson now resolved to sail direct to Uganda and made a record crossing in thirty hours. On June 30, 1877 they reached Rubaga, the then capital of Uganda, and two days later were received by Mutesa. Letters from the Sultan of Zanzibar and from the Society were read to the king by Dallington and appeared to give much satisfaction.[1] Mutesa then called attention to a multi-coloured flag, and said: "I hoist the flag because I believe in Jesus Christ." Shergold Smith reports that the next day "from some cause he seemed suspicious of us, and questioned us about Gordon, and rather wanted to bully us into making powder and shot. . . . He asked after Queen Victoria, and wished to know which was greatest, she or the Khedive of Egypt." This conversation was significant but scarcely surprising, since the missionaries had found an Egyptian force in the country. Shergold Smith, writing to Kirk, reported that the Egyptians were annoyed by Mutesa's so-called Christian flag, and had ordered him to haul it down but he had refused. At the end of July Shergold Smith left Uganda to rejoin O'Neill at the south of the lake, and again wrote to Kirk: "If you would use your influence to prevent the annexation of Mutesa's dominions to Egypt, I shall be much obliged." Meanwhile Derby, the Foreign Secretary, had been memorialized by the Church Missionary Society to the same effect, and when a copy of the memorial reached C. T. Wilson he read it to the king. Towards the end of 1878 Gordon abandoned his Victoria Nyanza project.[2]

Tragic events soon followed Shergold Smith's return to O'Neill to bring up their goods. They became involved in a quarrel between an Arab trader and the chief of the island of Ukerewe by giving asylum to the trader. The chief attacked, and they were massacred almost to a man, including Shergold Smith and O'Neill. Nothing beyond this fact is known. The date has been fixed as about December 13, 1877. Wilson

[1] *Ibid.* (1877), 45–6; (1878), 54; Stock, *History of the C.M.S.*, III, 99–101.
[2] Stock, *op. cit.*, III, 101–2; J. M. Gray, "Sir John Kirk and Mutesa", *The Uganda Journal*, XV (1951), 7–8, 10–11.

received the news at the end of the month.[1] He was now alone
in the Nyanza mission. Mackay, on hearing of the tragedy,
pushed on to join Wilson, but only reached the shores of the lake
by June 1878. "He at once went over to Ukerewe", says Stock,
"unarmed, to assure Lukongeh that the followers of Jesus did
not avenge wrongs but forgave them." Wilson, after a year
alone in Uganda, went to meet Mackay and they both then
set out for Mutesa's capital, but being wrecked *en route* they did
not arrive until November 1878, when Mackay first saw the
land with which his name was to become indissolubly linked.[2]

Meanwhile a relief party of four men had left England in May
and proceeded by the Nile route. On August 9 they had reached
Khartoum, and Gordon then arranged their transport to
Uganda at his personal expense. They did not arrive until
February 1879. They had barely been welcomed when a further
complicating factor appeared in the already somewhat complex
politico-religious situation. This was the arrival of two representatives of Lavigerie's White Fathers to initiate a Roman
Catholic mission. They also arrived in February 1879. When
Lavigerie's intentions had become known, Dr. R. N. Cust, a
member of the C.M.S. Committee, had waited personally on the
archbishop at Algiers, but failed to persuade him to seek one
of the many unoccupied fields. There was of course the well-
known position that Protestants, being propagandists of error,
do not from the Roman standpoint occupy a field in the sense
that would justify their own exclusion. But more than this,
Lavigerie was not only an energetic and imaginative missionary
director; he was also a loyal son of France with a nice sense of
political possibilities and not devoid, on this level also, of an
imperial vision. Whatever the long-term policy, a mission of the
White Fathers under Léon Livinhac as Superior was despatched
to the Victoria Nyanza in 1878, reaching the lake shores at the
south-west in January 1879. Siméon Lourdel as the most pro-
ficient in Swahili with a lay brother was sent forward to negotiate an entry with Mutesa, and arrived at the court in February,
much to the chagrin of Wilson, Mackay, and their colleagues.
The French missionaries were reported to have brought for
Mutesa most acceptable presents: firearms, ammunition, and
articles of military equipment. Mackay reported after Livin-

---

[1] *Proceedings of the C.M.S.* (1878), 56. A series of coloured lithographic pictures
from original sketches by O'Neill, including one by Shergold Smith, with accompanying text, was published by the C.M.S. under the title: *Sketches of African
Scenery from Zanzibar to the Victoria Nyanza* (1878).

[2] Stock, *op. cit.*, III, 104.

hac's arrival their denouncing to Mutesa of the Protestant mission. Mutesa asked in due course if they would promise him an alliance with France, but this they naturally could not undertake. The development of this tangled triangular situation— Arab Muslim, English Protestant, French Roman Catholic— falls to be considered later. Meanwhile Mutesa proclaimed himself once more a Muslim.[1]

The news of the acceptance of the invitation from Uganda by the Church Missionary Society led in its turn to further developments. There was living in the city of Leeds a wealthy recluse, Robert Arthington. He came of Quaker stock, and on his parents' death inherited a fortune of some £200,000. With a university education and cultured interests but no business commitments, he seemed at liberty to enjoy the life of the independent gentleman. But serious concerns took hold of him, and a letter found among his papers seemed to provide the clue to a sudden change of life and habit. It was from a missionary correspondent and read: "Were I in England again, I would gladly live in one room, make the floor my bed, a box my chair, and another my table, rather than the heathen should perish for lack of the knowledge of Christ." This became literally the pattern of his life. He was no miser, for he was unaware of the full extent of his growing resources, but he became an intense student of the world missionary situation. He is said to have had less confidence in Episcopacy, Presbyterianism, and Methodism with their highly organized connexional systems than with the more mobile and adventurous agents, as he saw them, of the Baptist and London Missionary Societies.[2]

In 1875 Arthington addressed a letter to the Directors of the London Missionary Society in which he said: "You know that the Presbyterians of Scotland have taken in hand the Nyassa; and that the Church Missionary Society is likely to take in hand the Victoria Nyanza; that is, the inhabitants of their shores, for evangelisation. I propose we should take in hand Lake Tanganika. I have the joy, therefore, of offering five thousand pounds towards the purchase of a suitable steamer, and the establishment of a missionary station at some eligible place on

[1] *Ibid.*, III, 103, 105–6; *Proceedings of the C.M.S.* (1879), 42–3; *Annales de la Propagation de la Foi*, LI (1879), 368–71; LII (1880), 310. Lourdel quickly appreciated the politico-religious situation: "La religion est, à ses yeux, une affaire de politique. Aussi, nous a-t-il demandé de faire alliance avec la France; il craint l'attaque des Arabes qui sont aux portes de son royaume. Nous n'avons pu lui promettre cette alliance, ce qui a refroidi un peu son zèle."

[2] A. M. Chirgwin, *Arthington's Million: The Romance of the Arthington Trust* (n.d.), 11–25, 29.

one of the shores of that lake."[1] The offer was accepted, and after full consultation with the Presbyterian and Anglican Committees, preparations were put in hand. As one friend said for many: "Your Society is the executor of Livingstone and we rejoice to know that your directors have accepted the trust."[2]

Roger Price, the survivor of the ill-fated Makololo mission, was appointed to survey the ground. He went as far as Mpwapwa in 1876, experimenting with ox-transport with apparent success. The following year he set out with five companions to reach Ujiji: J. B. Thomson, E. S. Clarke, and A. W. Dodgshun were ordained men; E. C. Hore was a master mariner, and Hutley a builder. They reached Zanzibar in July 1877, little realizing the trials that lay ahead. Wagons and carts drawn by oxen were now employed and the road Mackay was in process of cutting through from Saadani to Mpwapwa was used, but this time the oxen were lost *en route*. Price denied that the disease from which they died was nagana caused by tsetse, but it seems probable that it was none the less.[3] Expensive head porterage had then to be used for the completion of the journey to the lake. Roger Price was now deputed to visit England to consult the Directors and did not return, while E. S. Clarke decided to retire.[4] Meanwhile Thomson, Hore, and Hutley pushed on and were at Ujiji by August 25, 1878. On September 22 Thomson died. Dodgshun now struggled on alone with the remaining stores but was frustrated, deserted by his carriers, and plundered, until at last he reached Ujiji on March 27, 1879 only to die within a week.[5] At that moment E. J. Southon a doctor and

[1] Eighty-second *Report of the Directors* (1876), 95–6.
[2] C. W. Mackintosh, *Some Pioneer Missions of Northern Rhodesia and Nyasaland* (1950), 38.
[3] *A. M. Mackay* (1891), 51, 54–8; Stock, *History of the C.M.S.*, III, 80, 99–100. "It is now known that extensive belts lie between the coast and Mpwapwa," Dr. E. W. Smith tells me, who has supplied the first detailed account in *Roger Price, His Life and Times*.
[4] Price was relieved of his appointment by the Directors and returned to his station at Molepolole on the Bechuana Mission.
[5] *Missionary Travels and Adventures in Africa: or the Life of David Livingstone, LL.D., with a brief account of the Commencement of the Mission at Ujiji* (1880), 307–18. The policy of a leap inland was not that of Roger Price. "He had consistently advocated", writes Dr. E. W. Smith, "the building of intermediate stations, but the Directors insisted on their going right through—this was the root of all the disasters." Doubtless he had learned his lesson on the ill-fated Makololo expedition. It is interesting to note that the Church Missionary Society, despite the initial leap inland to Uganda, had now adopted the policy of intermediate stations. Mpwapwa, occupied by a lay agent in 1876 but vacated when his health broke down, was selected as an intermediate station in 1878 when the Society assigned four European missionaries, one a doctor, to re-establish it, adding: "Other intermediate stations are also contemplated." These were opened in due course.—*Proceedings of the C.M.S.* (1878), 56–7.

W. Griffith an artisan, under the leadership of Joseph Mullens the Foreign Secretary, were preparing to sail. They were at Zanzibar in May and left on June 13 for the lake. Mullens was buried at Mpwapwa on July 12; his companions reached Ujiji by September 23. The baleful list of losses was for the time being at an end. Southon now settled in Urambo east of the lake, at the invitation of the powerful chief Mirambo; Griffith began work in Uguha west of the lake; Hore prospected by journeys on the lake itself and was the first to make an accurate survey of it. In the event, the territory to the south-west of the lake— the region of Livingstone's last journeys—proved to be the Society's Central African field.[1]

Once the London Mission enterprise was fairly launched in 1877, Robert Arthington acted again, this time on the west. On May 14, 1877 he wrote to the Baptist Missionary Society, proposing a mission to the Congo, and offering £1,000 towards it. At this date Stanley was at Nzabi in the course of his difficult transit of the Cataract region, so that the world was not yet informed that the Lualaba and the Congo were one. But Arthington had apparently divined it, for he wrote: "I hope we shall soon have a steamer on the Congo . . . and carry the Gospel eastwards . . . as the way may open as far as Nyangwe."[2] Two months later the Society decided to commence a mission in the Congo basin and commissioned George Grenfell and Thomas Comber, missionaries already seasoned by service in the Cameroons, to begin the venture. They received their instructions on January 6, 1878 in Cameroons, and in less than a month were sailing on the waters of the Lower Congo.[3] However they were not to be the first to settle, for the Livingstone Inland Mission had set its hand to the work in 1877 and had its first missionaries on the field by February 1878.[4]

(3) Goodwill Secured

The most elusive and yet not the least significant of Livingstone's bequests to posterity was the store of goodwill he had won for himself and for those who were acclaimed as his "brothers". It was his greatest glory to have opened a path in personal relationships between white and black in remote

---

[1] R. Lovett, *The History of the London Missionary Society* (1899), I, 654–6; E. C. Hore, *Tanganyika: Eleven Years in Central Africa* (1892), 52–6, 91–4, 98–100.

[2] Chirgwin, *op. cit.*, 46.

[3] G. Hawker, *The Life of George Grenfell* (1909), 95–100.

[4] F. E. Guinness, *The New World of Central Africa* (1890), 180, 183.

regions as well as a path upon the map. He left behind among Africans the memory of a white man who respected them and cared for them. He took the trouble of trying to understand them and, in doing so, discovered a real respect which is the indispensable basis of cordial relations.

Thus to take but two examples, he understood their views of land, and he appreciated the positive achievements of their doctors. He knew that land for the African is not a commercial commodity, but the indispensable basis of life, like water and air, that should be available for all. It is sacrilege to sell it outright, but an occupation right can be assigned, when the tenant scarcely even paying a token "peppercorn" type of rent but rather making occasional presents, has usufructory benefits but no proprietary rights. On the journey to Loanda this knowledge stood him in good stead in resisting the payment of tribute demanded for passing through the country where slave-traders had disturbed African customary practice. Thus he reports of one such occasion: "They said they wanted the customary tribute. . . . I asked what right they had to demand payment for leave to tread on the ground of God, our common Father? If we trod on their gardens we would pay, but not for marching on land which was still God's and not theirs. They did not attempt to controvert this, because it is in accordance with their own ideas." And again, remarking that payment for guides is recognized but not for traversing a country: "The aborigines all acknowledge that the untilled land, not needed for pasturage, belongs to God alone, and that no harm is done by people passing through it."[1]

His attitude to African medical practice was enlightened, and based on a real respect for an African doctor as a fellow practitioner. This may surprise those who have thought of the medicine-man as nothing but a charlatan, consciously imposing upon gullible patients. But even granting honesty in the profession, there is still required some skill in diagnosis for suitable treatment to be given. It has sometimes been rather easily assumed that all African treatment is based upon a mistaken diagnosis and so is best swept away. Livingstone knew better. He was prepared to recognize the tribal doctor as a fellow professional and was rewarded by being so treated himself. He observed medical etiquette in his relations with them and this was reciprocated. A couple of significant passages bear this out: "Those doctors who have inherited their profession as an heir-

[1] Livingstone, *Missionary Travels and Researches in South Africa*, 341, 351-2.

loom from their fathers and grandfathers generally possess some valuable knowledge, the result of long and close observation; but if a man cannot say that the medical art is in his family, he may be considered a quack. With the regular practitioners I always remained on the best terms, by refraining from appearing to doubt their skill in the presence of their patients. Any explanation in private was thankfully received by them, and wrong treatment changed into something more reasonable with cordial good will, if no one but the doctor and myself were present at the conversation." And further: "I refrained from going to any one unless his own doctor wished it, or had given up the case. This led to my having a selection of the severer cases only, and prevented the doctors being offended at my taking their practice out of their hands. When attacked by fever myself, and wishing to ascertain what their practices were, I could safely intrust myself in their hands on account of their well-known friendly feelings." It was this knowledge and experience that led to his including in his instructions to Dr. Kirk on the Zambezi Expedition, a paragraph on the subject: "They possess medical men among themselves who are generally the most observant people to be met with. It is desirable to be at all times on good terms with them. In order to this, slight complaints, except among the very poor, ought to be referred to their care, and severe cases before being undertaken should be enquired into of the doctor himself and no disparaging remark ever made on the previous treatment in the presence of the patient. This line of conduct will lead to the more urgent cases only being referred to you; time and medicine will both be saved while your influence will be extended."[1] Livingstone's

---

[1] *Ibid.*, 130, 188; cf. 194–5 for African treatment of malaria; Coupland, *Kirk on the Zambesi*, 105. One or two references that support Livingstone's view of African doctors may be of interest. Inoculation for smallpox was known and practised among the Shonas and Ngwatos.—Mackenzie, *Ten Years North of the Orange River*, 252; Blennerhassett and Sleeman, *Adventures in Mashonaland* (1893), 249–50. A quite remarkable instance of tracheotomy which saved the life of a European child is reported from personal experience in South Africa in the 'seventies.—Marina King, *Sunrise to Evening Star* (1935), 123–4. W. C. W. Eakin, who was the first to identify sleeping sickness in Nigeria, found that African doctors distinguished two stages in the disease, and would operate in the first when gland enlargement had occurred, by excising the glands and thus curing the patient.—*Annals of Tropical Medicine and Parasitology* (Liverpool School of Tropical Medicine), VIII (1914), 414–15; cf. Plate XX for instruments used and scarification after successful operation. Henry S. Wellcome, at the opening of the Wellcome Historical Medical Museum in 1913, shared the same respectful attitude: "In the course of my long researches into the history of medicine, I have come to the conclusion that we can gain a great deal of useful information from primitive peoples in the art of healing, and particularly in surgery. In my own personal experiences amongst primitive

own acuteness of observation and shrewd anticipations of medical scientific discovery add weight to his considered regard for
African doctors.[1]

These particular instances reflect the fundamental attitude of
the man and show how remarkably free he was from that subtle
spirit of condescension and patronage which casts such a blight
on inter-racial relations, missionary circles not excepted. As he
once expressed it to a correspondent: "I, who have been
intimate with Africans who have never been defiled by the
slave-trade, believe them to be capable of holding an honourable rank in the family of man."[2] In short, if Christian love is
fundamentally, as has been asserted, a fulness of respect for
another's personality, then Livingstone's attitude was simply
the truly Christian one.

And this leads to the recording of the fact, not always remembered, that he remained throughout the Christian missionary—
not in the sense of being the appointed representative of a duly
constituted Society, but as a witnessing and practising Christian,
speaking for his Master both by word and deed. And he realized
that the two were inseparable for effective witness in Africa. He
wrote of Africans within a year of the end: "Nothing brings
them to place thorough confidence in Europeans but a long
course of well-doing. . . . Goodness or unselfishness impresses
their minds more than any kind of skill or power. . . . The
prayer to Jesus for a new heart and right spirit at once com-
mends itself as appropriate."[3] The truth of this remark and at
the same time the effective and lasting influence of Livingstone
on Africans who had lived with him are demonstrated in the
case of Wikatani. Wikatani was a slave-boy, liberated by Living-

---

races, I have sometimes found traces of the origin of what are usually regarded as
entirely modern discoveries."—*African Society Souvenir Programme, Wellcome Historical
Medical Museum* (1928), 51. Livingstone found surgery "rather at a low ebb".—
Op. cit., 130. The best African monograph on the subject is that on the Mano tribe
of Liberia, where in surgery the doctors are reported as "extremely conservative".
—G. W. Harley, *Native African Medicine* (1941), *passim*. Dr. E. W. Smith tells me
that he has had personal experience of the efficacy of African medicines, having
been successfully treated by an African doctor for dysentery and when a snake spat
in his eye.

[1] Sir R. Havelock Charles has called attention to comments by Livingstone on
the relation of insects to disease, almost prophetic, which are often overlooked, e.g.
Mosquitoes "appear so commonly at malarious spots that their presence may be
taken as a hint to man to be off to more healthy localities"; and that the tsetse
was responsible for poison in the blood "the germ of which enters when the pro-
boscis is inserted to draw blood".—*The Church Missionary Review*, LXIII (1912),
503.

[2] Blaikie, *op. cit.*, 298.

[3] *The Last Journals of David Livingstone*, II, 201.

stone and Mackenzie, who had been sold by his father. After two years with the mission he went with Livingstone to Bombay where he was with Dr. Wilson until Livingstone's return from England, when he joined him for the last journey. But when passing Lake Nyasa he found a brother and sister still alive and desired to stay with them. Livingstone at once released him from his service with a parting gift. This was in September 1866. In October 1875 Wikatani introduced himself to Lieutenant Young, leader of the Free Church of Scotland mission, who found him unusually helpful. Wondering what had survived after ten years' isolation, Young asked what he remembered, and was told: "This is what Dr. Livingstone taught me:

> *This night I lay me down to sleep,*
> *I give my soul to Christ to keep.*
> *If I should die before I wake,*
> *I pray to God my soul to take. Amen."*

This, and a few questions and answers of Dr. Wilson's, had not been forgotten.[1]

Those who have followed in Livingstone's steps have found a striking unanimity of testimony to his influence. Chauncey Maples of the Universities' Mission, to become later the Bishop of Likoma, was in the Rovuma valley in November 1877, more than a decade after Livingstone had passed that way. One who said he had known a white man in old days asked to see him; he entered, carrying an old coat on his shoulder, and began to tell of a white man with whom he had travelled to Mataka's ten years before: "A white man, he said, whom to have once seen and talked with was to remember for ever—a white man who treated black men as his brothers, and whose memory would be cherished all along that Rovuma valley after we were all dead and gone. Then he described him—a short man with a bushy moustache and a keen, piercing eye, whose words were always gentle and whose manners were always kind, whom as a leader it was a privilege to follow, and who knew the way to the hearts of all men. . . . Then he showed me the coat; it was ragged now, he knew, but he had kept it those ten years in memory of the giver, from whom it had been a legacy when they parted at Mataka's. To no one but an Englishman would he part with it; but he let me have it as one of Livingstone's brothers (he said),

---

[1] *Last Journals*, I, 108–8; Young, *op. cit.*, 63, 147, 184.

and it now lies in the museum at Charterhouse School."[1] Seven
years later, in September 1884, François Coillard of the Paris
Mission found himself in Barotseland in country Livingstone
had visited thirty years earlier, and wrote that he had become
a legendary character. At the conclusion of the various memories
he recorded, he added: "This much is certain, that Livingstone
preached by the purity of his life and his uncalculating self-
devotion more than by any spoken word. The old men who
have known him and have journeyed with him speak of him
with enthusiasm and always end by saying, 'The doctor! Ah!
he was not a man like any other, he was a god!' "[2] Again, forty
years further on, Miss Mabel Shaw has described her meeting
with an old man who had seen Livingstone on the Luapula:
" 'He had clothing on his feet,' the old man said excitedly. 'I
was a boy, I went near, I touched, but the head man pulled
me back. "You'll be bewitched by his medicine," they said.'
Then he sat long in silence, and at last he said, as if to himself:
'And he laughed, there was love in his eyes, he was not fierce.'
Again the silence I dare not disturb. 'He made a path through
our land, and you his followers have come, God's Light-
bringers; and more come to-day.' "[3] These memories among
Africans of a white man they trusted were of immeasurable
value in the days of high-power European invasion so soon to
follow, for— "To this day the path he took is marked by a greater respect for the white man than other routes."[4]

No less precious on the European side of the account was the
ideal Livingstone left white men of the obligation that lay upon
them for honourable dealing with Africans when the overwhelming weight of the European invasion came crashing in
upon their fragile, simple societies. He had inherited the moral
purpose that inspired Granville Sharp and William Wilberforce
and Thomas Fowell Buxton in their anti-slavery crusade, and
with this same purpose he inspired his countrymen to such a
degree that, as Lord Elton says: "His supreme achievement was
that on the eve of the new imperialism . . . he taught his own
fellow-countrymen that the true mission of Europe was to promote the welfare of Africa. . . . It was the tradition of Living-

---

[1] *Chauncey Maples, Bishop of Likoma* (1897), 16–17. The coat has now been deposited at the Blantyre Memorial.—Macnair, *op. cit.*, 303 *n*.
[2] Edouard Favre, *François Coillard*, III (1913), 96–8; cf. F. Coillard, *On the
Threshold of Central Africa* (1897), 60.
[3] Miss Shaw's Journal Letter, June, 1928, quoted in Campbell, *Livingstone*,
348–9.
[4] *Ibid.*, 22. Cf. Commander Cameron's testimony, *Across Africa* (1877), I, 356.

stone, living on in Kirk and Lugard, which ensured that even in its least worthy moments the British Government never altogether forgot that its first obligation in Africa was to promote the welfare of Africans."[1] That he should have caught the imagination of the British people on the eve of the scramble for Africa was indeed a crowning mercy.

Rich as is the legacy of Livingstone, let a simple testimony conclude it. A biographer who was anything but sympathetic with his religious views but who knew at first hand the country and people where he travelled has given his considered verdict:[2] "Livingstone was a really great and good man, and it is impossible to belittle him by recounting the truth, the whole truth, and nothing but the truth."

[1] Lord Elton, *Imperial Commonwealth* (1945), 382–3.
[2] H. H. Johnston, *Livingstone and the Exploration of Central Africa* (1891), vi.

INDEX

337